Dante's
PURGATORY

Portrait of Dante Alighieri

Dante's
PURGATORY

TRANSLATED

with Notes and Commentary by

MARK MUSA

Illustrated by Richard M. Powers

INDIANA UNIVERSITY PRESS

Bloomington

ACKNOWLEDGMENTS

I would like to thank John C. McGalliard and especially Thomas Bergin for reading and commenting on this version of the Purgatory. *Their suggestions, though not always heeded, were always most helpful. Many thanks also to Lisa Davis for lending a beautifully keen eye to the final version of this book. And I must thank so many of my students who listened, commented on, and discussed this translation as well as the notes and commentary with me in and out of the classroom. My wholehearted thanks to all of you!*

Library of Congress Cataloging in Publication Data
Dante Alighieri, 1265–1321.
Dante's Purgatory.
Translation of Purgatorio from the author's
Divina commedia.
Includes bibliographical references.
1.Musa, Mark. II.Title. III.Title:
Purgatory.
PQ4315.3.M8   851'.1   80–8098
ISBN 0–253–17926–2   1 2 3 4 5 85 84 83 82 81

FOR *ISABELLA*

again — nine years later — with love

CONTENTS

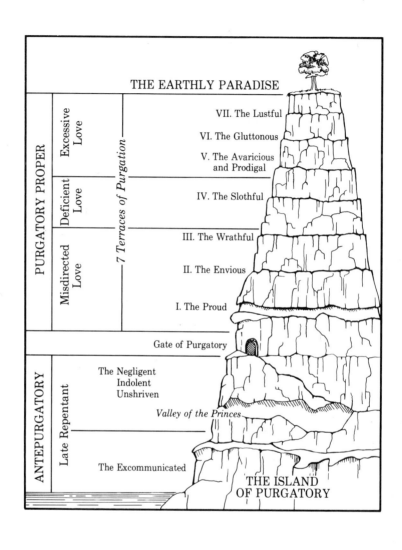

THE EARTHLY PARADISE

PURGATORY PROPER

Excessive Love

VII. The Lustful

VI. The Gluttonous

V. The Avaricious and Prodigal

Deficient Love

IV. The Slothful

Misdirected Love

III. The Wrathful

II. The Envious

I. The Proud

7 Terraces of Purgation

Gate of Purgatory

ANTEPURGATORY

Late Repentant

The Negligent Indolent Unshriven

Valley of the Princes

The Excommunicated

THE ISLAND OF PURGATORY

lust - intense sexual desire

. glutton - one who eats to excess

greed - avarice, recklessly extravagen tor
wasteful

slothful - laziness

Wrathful - voilent anger

Envy - resentful awareness of
another's advantage

proud - showing or feeling
superiority toward others.

Dante's

PURGATORY

Purgatory -
Intermediate state after
death for purification by
expiating sins
place or state of temporary
suffering.

ABBREVIATIONS

a. articulus
Aen. *Aeneid* (Virgil)
Ars amat. *Ars amatoria* (Ovid)
Conf. *Confessiones* (Augustine)
Consol. philos. *Consolatio philosophiae* (Boethius)
Conv. *Convivio* (Dante Alighieri)
Decam. *Il Decameron* (Giovanni Boccaccio)
De civ. Dei *Ad Marcellinum De civitate Dei contra paganos* (Augustine)
De doct. Chris. *De doctrina Christiana* (Augustine)
De mon. *De monarchia* (Dante Alighieri)
De vulg. eloqu. *De vulgari eloquentia* (Dante Alighieri)
Eclog. *Eclogues* (Virgil)
Epist. *Epistolae* (Dante Alighieri)
Eth. Nicom. *Ethica Nicomachea* (Aristotle)
Hist. *Historiarum adversum paganos libri septem* (Orosius)
Inf. *Inferno* (Dante Alighieri)
lect. lectio
Metam. *Metamorphoses* (Ovid)
Metaphys. *Metaphysica* (Aristotle)
Moral. *Moralium libri, sive Expositio in librum b. Iob* (Gregory I)
Nat. hist. *Naturalis historia* (Pliny)
obj. objectio
Par. *Paradiso* (Dante Alighieri)
Phars. *Pharsalia* (Lucan)
Purg. *Purgatorio* (Dante Alighieri)
q. quaestio
resp. respondeo
Summa theol. *Summa theologica* (Thomas Aquinas)
suppl. supplementum
Theb. *Thebaid* (Statius)

CANTO I

HAVING LEFT THE Inferno behind, Dante announces his
intention to sing of the second kingdom, Purgatory, and calls
upon the Muses, in particular Calliope, to accompany his song.
As the dawn approaches, he feels a sense of renewal, and, looking up into the heavens, he sees four stars. Turning his gaze
earthward again, he discovers standing near him a dignified old
man: Cato of Utica. Cato thinks Dante and Virgil are refugees
from Hell, and he questions them as to how they managed to
escape. Virgil explains that Dante is still a living man, and that,
at the command of a lady from Heaven, he, Virgil, has been
sent to guide this man on a journey for the purpose of his
salvation. Already this journey has taken them through Hell,
and now it is their intention to see the souls of Purgatory. Cato
assents to their passage. He then instructs Virgil to bind a reed
around the Pilgrim's waist and to be sure to cleanse him of
every trace of stain from the infernal regions. The two poets
descend to the shore, where they proceed to carry out Cato's
instructions. The purgation is marked by a miracle: when Virgil
pulls a reed from the ground, another springs up immediately
to take its place.

For better waters, now, the little bark
   of my poetic powers hoists its sails,
   and leaves behind that cruelest of the seas.   *3*

And I shall sing about that second realm
   where man's soul goes to purify itself
   and become worthy to ascend to Heaven.   *6*

Here let death's poetry arise to life,
   O Muses sacrosanct whose liege I am!
   And let Calliope rise up and play   *9*

her sweet accompaniment in the same strain
   that pierced the wretched magpies with the truth
   of unforgivable presumptuousness.   *12*

The tender tint of orient sapphire,
   suffusing the still reaches of the sky,
   as far as the horizon deeply clear,   *15*

renewed my eyes' delight, now that I found
  myself free of the deathly atmosphere
  that had weighed heavy on my eyes and heart.   *18*

The lovely planet kindling love in man
  made all the eastern sky smile with her light,
  veiling the Fish that shimmered in her train.   *21*

Then to my right I turned to contemplate
  the other pole, and there saw those four stars
  the first man saw, and no man after him.   *24*

The heavens seemed to revel in their flames.
  O widowed Northern Hemisphere, deprived
  forever of the vision of their light!   *27*

And when I looked away from those four stars,
  turning a little toward the other pole,
  where no sign of the Wain was visible,   *30*

I saw near me an ancient man, alone,
  whose face commanded all the reverence
  that any son could offer to his sire.   *33*

Long-flowing was his beard and streaked with white,
  as was his hair, which in two tresses fell
  to rest upon his chest on either side.   *36*

The rays of light from those four sacred stars
  struck with such radiance upon his face,
  it was as if the sun were shining there.   *39*

"Who are you two who challenged the blind stream
  and have escaped from the eternal prison?"
  he said, moving his venerable locks.   *42*

"Who guided you? What served you as a lamp
  to light your way out of the heavy night
  that keeps the pit of Hell forever black?   *45*

Are all the laws of God's Abyss destroyed?
  Have new decisions now been made in Heaven
  so that, though damned, you come up to my cliff?"   *48*

My leader quickly seized me by the arm;
  his words, his touch, the way he looked at me,
  compelled my knees and brow to reverence.   *51*

Then he addressed him: "Not on my behalf
   have I come here; a lady sent from Heaven
   asked me to guide this man along his way.   54

But since it is your will that we reveal
   the circumstances of our presence here,
   how can my will deny yours what it asks?   57

This man has not yet seen his final hour,
   although so close to it his folly brought him
   that little time was left to change his ways.   60

So I was sent to help him, as I said;
   there was no other way to save his soul
   than by my guiding him along this road.   63

Already I have shown him all the Damned;
   I want to show him now the souls of those
   who purge themselves of guilt in your domain.   66

How we came here would take too long to tell;
   from Heaven comes the power that has served
   to lead him here to see and hear you now.   69

May it please you to welcome him—he goes
   in search of freedom, and how dear that is,
   the man who gives up life for it well knows.   72

You know, you found death sweet in Utica
   for freedom's sake; there you put off that robe
   which will be radiant on the Great Day.   75

We have not broken Heaven's timeless laws.
   This man still lives; Minòs does not bind *me;*
   I come from that same Round where the chaste eyes   78

of your dear Marcia still plead with your soul,
   O blessed heart, to hold her as your own;
   for love of her, then, bend your will to ours,   81

allow us to go through your seven realms,
   and I shall tell her how you have been kind—
   if you will let me speak your name below."   84

"Marcia was so enchanting to my eyes,"
   he answered then, "that while I was alive,
   there was no wish of hers I would not grant.   87

She dwells beyond the evil river now,
    and can no longer move me by that law
    decreed upon the day I issued forth.   90

But if a heavenly lady, as you say,
    moves and directs you, why your flattery?
    Ask in her name, there is no need for more.   93

Go with this man, see that you gird his waist
    with a smooth reed; take care to bathe his face
    till every trace of filth has disappeared,   96

for it would not be fitting that he go
    with vision clouded by the mists of Hell,
    to face the first of Heaven's ministers.   99

Around this little island at its base,
    down there, just where the waves break on the shore,
    you will find rushes growing in soft sand.   102

No other plant producing leaves or stalk
    that hardens could survive in such a place —
    only the reeds that yield to buffeting.   105

When you are ready to begin to scale
    the mountainside, do not come back this way;
    the rising sun will show you where to climb."   108

With that he vanished. From my knees I rose,
    and silent, drawing closer to my guide,
    I looked into his eyes. He said to me: 111

"Follow my footsteps; now we must turn back,
    for over there the plain begins to slope,
    descending gently to the shore below."   114

The dawn was gaining ground, putting to flight
    the last hour of the night; I recognized,
    far off, the rippling waters of the sea.   117

We made our way along that lonely plain
    like men who seek the right path they have lost,
    counting each step a loss till it is found.   120

When we had reached a place where the cool shade
    allowed the dew to linger on the slope,
    resisting a while longer the sun's rays,   123

my master placed both of his widespread hands
   gently upon the tender grass, and I,
   who understood what his intention was,   126

offered my tear-stained face to him, and he
   made my face clean, restoring its true color,
   once buried underneath the dirt of Hell.   129

At last we touched upon the lonely shore
   that never yet has seen its waters sailed
   by one who then returned to tell the tale.   132

There, as another willed, he girded me.
   Oh, miracle! When he pulled out the reed,
   immediately a second humble plant   135

sprang up from where the first one had been picked.

.

NOTES

1–6. *For better waters:* The first tercet introduces the theme
of the sea voyage, a metaphor both for the journey undertaken
by Dante the Pilgrim and for the process of composition in
which the genius of Dante the Poet is involved. The same
image with the same twofold implication is found in the
Paradise at the beginning of Canto II, and here the "little bark"
has become a mighty ship, the metaphor being considerably
developed to include Dante's readers in their boats. The presence of this image already in the *Inferno* would seem to be
guaranteed in lines 1 and 3 of this canto: the words *For better
waters, now . . . , and leave behind that cruelest of the seas* are
surely reminders of the Pilgrim's earlier travels through Hell.
Yet no reference to "Dante's ship" is to be found in the first
canticle. For an explanation of this inconsistency, see notes to
Purg. I, 7–12 and 115–36.

7–12

The Invocation to the Muses points both backward to the
beginning of the *Inferno* and forward to the beginning of the
Paradise. The Invocation in the *Inferno* is contained in one tercet; actually, it consists of one line: "O Muses, O lofty intellect,
help me now"; in the other two lines of the tercet Dante calls
upon his own memory to record faithfully what he has seen
(*Inf.* II, 7–9).

In our passage the Invocation, expanded to two tercets, singles out Calliope, leader of the Muses. The appeal is made more elaborate by the allusion to the arrogant daughters of King Pierus: the Poet asks of Calliope that she do him the favor of accompanying his poetry with the same strain, the same exalted music that had served to bring low the presumptuous princesses. By contrasting himself with the "magpies," the Poet stresses his modesty: unlike them, he has not challenged; he simply seeks for help. (The need for humility is constantly stressed in the *Purgatory;* there will be other allusions to it in this canto.) At the same time, however, it seems clear that Dante the Poet has been cautiously gaining confidence in his own poetic powers.

And the difference between the Invocation here and that of the *Inferno* may explain the absence, there, of the image of the Poet's ship. At the beginning of his poem, when he must humbly beg the Muses, simply: "Help me now," how could he posit the "ship of his talent"?

7. *Here let death's poetry arise to life:* The *morta poesia,* "dead poetry," of the original must refer to the poetry of the *Inferno,* "dead" in that it treated of souls dead to God and to His grace. But note also the suggestion of resurrection contained in this line.

9. *Calliope:* The greatest of the Muses, who, in Greek mythology, presides over heroic or epic poetry.

11–12. *that pierced the wretched magpies:* Pierus, king of Emathia in Macedonia, had nine daughters, to whom he unwisely gave the names of the nine Muses. In their presumption they challenged the Muses to a contest in song, in which they sang the praises of the Titans who waged war against Jupiter (cf. *Inf.* XXXI). Defeated by Calliope, who was chosen to represent all the Muses, they were punished by being transformed into magpies (cf. Ovid, *Metam.* V, 294–678).

13–30

These six tercets are devoted to a description of the sky: the passage is important if only because it invites us to imagine the experience of the Pilgrim, who, having emerged from the darkness of Hell, is allowed for the first time to see the heavens above him. And this description of the heavens with which the

Purgatory begins is, in fact, the beginning of the end of the *Divine Comedy,* for the *Paradise* concludes with the Beatific Vision of God in the Empyrean. From this moment on we will never be able to forget the heavens above the Pilgrim, the heavens toward which he will be climbing throughout his journey in Purgatory and into which he will enter, still continuing to ascend, at the beginning of the *Paradise.*

As for the graphic details of the description, it is indeed a clear and delicate glow of color that strikes our eyes after the grim reds and dead blacks of the skyless Hell. The atmosphere of *Purgatory* contrasts strongly with that of the *Inferno,* sensuously as well as spiritually. A new vocabulary is in evidence: the gentle glow (13), the spreading color (15), the smiling eastern sky (20), the heavens lit with joy (25) (there is a similar delicate treatment of the details of the landscape at the end of the canto). And opposed to the heavy, sullen despair and excruciating torment of Hell, Purgatory holds out the prospect of new hope. Though there will be much stress in this canticle on the arduous, painful purgation of the soul, we are constantly made aware of the increasing capacity of the soul for love, knowledge and self-perfection: the note of hope was already sounded within the first two tercets treating of the "sea voyage": *For better waters, now . . .*

Already the Invocation to the Muses had contained the suggestion of the resurrection motif in line 7; now, in the description of the heavens, we learn that the time is just before dawn, the hour of rebirth and new beginnings. Moreover, because of the position of the stars that are described here, it has been determined by scholars that the date is supposed to be April 10, 1300, Easter Sunday. The Pilgrim descended into Hell on Good Friday, and now he rises from the "dead atmosphere." The main events in Dante's poem—the descent of the Pilgrim into Hell, his emergence into Purgatory, and his final ascent into Paradise—are an imitation of the central events of divine history: the death, resurrection, and ascension of Christ.

The eastern origin of the sapphire directs our gaze to that point on the horizon where the sun, symbol for Christ, is just about to rise. At this same point the planet of love, Venus, has risen with the constellation of Pisces, which it outshines, lighting up the whole eastern sky. Pisces is the last of the twelve signs of the Zodiac. The sun, when it rises, will be in the first sign, Aries, or the Ram.

23. *those four stars:* No living man since the time of Adam and Eve has seen the four stars that the Pilgrim now sees. These stars would have been visible to Adam and Eve because the Garden of Eden, in which they were placed after their creation, was located at the top of the mountain of Purgatory (the Pilgrim is now at the bottom of this same mountain). After the Fall, Adam and Eve were driven from the garden, and they and their offspring—the whole human race—were consigned to inhabit the lands opposite the Earthly Paradise, that is, according to Dante's geography, the Northern Hemisphere. Hence, the stars of the southern sky would be invisible in the inhabited northern part of the globe.

Allegorically, the four stars represent the four cardinal virtues: Prudence, Temperance, Justice, and Fortitude. A problem arises when, in lines 26 and 27, Dante laments the fact that the inhabited world is widowed, deprived forever of the sight of these stars (or virtues). But it is not likely that the poet is saying that after the Fall the world was deprived and will continue to be deprived of the virtues of Prudence, Temperance, Justice, and Fortitude! Surely Virgil and the other noble shades of antiquity now in Limbo possess these four virtues; in fact, it was the pagan philosophers who were the first to describe them. And every Christian, if he is prepared to receive sanctifying grace, will be endowed with these virtues (as well as with the three theological virtues). In the case of the Christian, the four virtues in question are referred to as the "infused" cardinal virtues; the pagans may possess only the "acquired" cardinal virtues.

But, though these virtues can be possessed in individual cases by pagans and Christians alike, they no longer form an inevitable part of human nature as they did before the Fall. When God endowed Adam with a combination of these virtues and an immortal body, He created a perfect man. This perfection was to pass to Adam's progeny, but when Adam sinned and lost Eden, mankind lost Eden and human nature was defiled. This Edenic state of existence was never to be recovered. Even with the Redemption, when Christ opened up the way for man to Salvation, we were not restored to the perfect Edenic existence of our first parents, with the natural infusion of virtue and the immortality of the body.

Thus, the first reference to the four stars leads to a lament, actually, over the loss of Eden; and this lament anticipates the great joy the Pilgrim will experience when, at the end of Canto XXVII, he is led by Virgil to the entrance of the preternaturally beautiful Earthly Paradise and encouraged to "let pleasure be your guide."

See Singleton (1958), pp. 159–83, for the allegorical significance of the four stars as it is revealed in the course of the journey up the mountain of Purgatory.

30. *no sign of the Wain:* The constellation of the Wain (or Big Bear, *Ursa Major*), since it is near the North Pole, is not visible in the Southern Hemisphere.

31–75

Here we are introduced to Cato of Utica, the guardian of the Antepurgatory. Cato (Marcus Porsius Cato Uticensis, 95–46 B.C.) was a devout Stoic who became famous for his stern moral principles. Although he opposed the ambitions of both Caesar and Pompey, when the civil war broke out in 49 B.C., he sided with the latter against Caesar. After Caesar's victory at Pharsalia, Cato continued his resistance in Northern Africa, where he joined forces with Metellus Scipio, but they were defeated at the battle of Thapsus, and all of Africa, with the exception of Utica, fell into Caesar's hands. Rather than submit to Caesar, Cato resolved to take his own life. He reportedly spent the night before his suicide reading Plato's *Phaedo,* which deals with the immortality of the soul.

Dante's profound admiration for the character of Cato is expressed in earlier writings. In *Monarchy* (II, v, 15) he calls Cato "that most severe author of true liberty," and in the *Convivio* (IV, xxviii, 121–213) he makes the startling analogy: "And what earthly man is more worthy to represent God himself than Cato? Certainly none." Dante's appreciation of Cato belongs to a tradition that our poet inherited from antiquity: in particular, he must have known Lucan (*Phars.* II, 380–90), who praises Cato's integrity, and Cicero, who in the *De Officiis* justifies and idealizes Cato's suicide.

How can one justify the appropriateness of Cato's presence on the shores of Purgatory and of his role as guardian of the repentant souls newly arrived to begin, in time, the process of purgation? As for the fact of Cato's suicide, it will become clear from Virgil's words to him later (73–75) that Dante, like Cicero, viewed this idealistically, not as an act meriting punishment but as a supreme reaffirmation of the great Stoic's love of freedom. Not only was Dante ready to judge the pagans in terms of their own moral code; perhaps he even looked upon Cato's death as reflecting the sacrificial death of the Savior. (In early illustrations of the *Comedy* Cato is sometimes shown with a radiating nimbus.) At any rate, it could be argued that since the labors of the souls in Purgatory are devoted to the pursuit of ultimate spiritual freedom, and Cato had died for the sake of political freedom, he could most fittingly be conceived as their guardian—if we remember that throughout the *Purgatory* we are offered as ideal, a blend of civil and moral liberty. The role of "guardian" was perhaps suggested to Dante by the allusion to Cato in *Aen.* VIII, 670, where he is represented as lawgiver of the virtuous souls in the Elysium.

Now, in itself, there is nothing incongruous about the idea of a virtuous pagan occupying a position of authority over Christian souls, whom he encourages upward toward Heaven in their struggle to achieve salvation (*Purg.* II), once we accept the contributory role of Virgil himself in the Pilgrim's search for salvation. In fact, a parallel between the two pagans is suggested by a comparison between Cato's sudden appearance from nowhere in *Purg.* I, 31, and that of Virgil in *Inf.* I, 62 (and Cato, like Virgil, belongs, as we shall learn, to Limbo). Yet most critics believe that Cato has been saved. The only possible evidence to this effect is to be found in verses 73–75, in which Virgil, praising Cato for his suicide, mentions the fate of his body on the Judgment Day: " . . . Utica . . . there you put off that robe which will be radiant on the Great Day." And this prophecy of Cato's radiant body has been for most scholars a prophecy of his entrance into Heaven—delayed until the Judgment Day.

Of the few who find verse 75 inconclusive, some seek for new evidence of Cato's salvation outside our canto (cf. Chimenz, p. 326, who refers us to *Par.* XX, with its discussion of *fides implicita*). Others abandoning the possibility of Cato's ascent to Heaven, imagine a different explanation for this ambiguous line: Ciardi (p. 38) is content to speak vaguely of a "special triumph" for Cato on the Judgment Day; Carroll (p. 7) suggests that on that day Cato will return to Limbo as lawgiver, in line with the role assigned him in the *Aeneid* (see note to I, 89). Carroll's would seem to be the more likely interpretation: the evidence of verse 75 in favor of Cato's salvation is surely weak (and to seek the explanation of *Purg.* I in *Par.* XX is unwarranted). Still, I must confess that I do not completely understand the implications of verse 75.

31. *I saw near me an ancient man, alone:* The description of the heavens gives way to a description of Cato's face, but in his face the stars will be seen again.

34. *streaked with white:* Cato's beard with its mixture of colors is a fitting emblem of Purgatory—which place is not completely shrouded in darkness, as is the Inferno, nor totally imbued with light, as is Paradise: in Purgatory we will see the regular alternation of day and night. In addition, the souls in Purgatory, although they have been saved, are still not entirely cleansed from the stain of sin until they are released.

37–39. *The rays of light:* If we think in terms of Cato as lawgiver, it is tempting to see in this description a parallel with Moses the lawgiver: Cato, standing at the foot of a mountain with his face brightly lit, could remind us of the moment (Gen. 35:29) when Moses came down from the mountain with the Tables of the Law in his hands, "and the skin of his face shone because he had been talking with God." Furthermore, Cato's present position in Purgatory might recall the fate of Moses, who came in sight of the Promised Land but could not enter it.

40. *the blind stream:* This is the "little stream" that comes from Lethe and flows into Cocytus. The Pilgrim and his guide had followed the course of this stream out of Hell, through the earth, to the lower slope of the mountain of Purgatory (cf. *Inf.* XXXIV, 127–34).

73–75. *You* know: The inevitable separation of the body from the soul at death, as well as the place and the circumstances of this event, is a recurrent theme in the opening cantos of the *Purgatory.*

73. *Utica:* Second most important city in ancient North Africa (after Carthage), located on the coast approximately thirty miles northwest of Carthage. Utica was the scene of the last stand of Pompey against Caesar, as well as the place where Cato subsequently took his life.

79. *your dear Marcia:* In 56 B.C. Cato gave his second wife, Marcia, to his friend Hortentius. When Hortentius died, Marcia asked Cato to take her back. The episode, recorded in Lu-

can's *Pharsalia* (II, 326 ff.), was seen by Dante in the *Convivio* as an allegory of the soul's tardy return to God at the onset of old age. Marcia is mentioned among the souls of the virtuous pagans in Limbo (*Inf.* IV, 128).

89. *by that law:* This reference to a law that was proclaimed the day Cato left Limbo behind is not too clear. To most scholars it represents the absolute distinction between the Damned and the Blessed, made forever on that day of the Harrowing of Hell, when the elect souls were rescued from Limbo; Cato's allusion to it here would explain his estrangement from Marcia. But to the few who believe that Cato is not saved, that his rescue from Limbo along with the Patriarchs differed from theirs in far more than the mere postponement of his ascent to Heaven, the law in question would apply only to Cato's unique situation: it would represent the divine decision to rescue Cato from Limbo that he might serve in Purgatory for a finite period of time, only to return to Limbo. In favor of this "private" interpretation is Cato's reference in verse 90 to "the day I issued forth." But would such a special dispensation be called a "law"? In any case, this interpretation would not explain Cato's estrangement from Marcia, as would the generally accepted one.

92. *why your flattery?:* Cato accedes to Virgil's request for the Pilgrim's admission because of the intervention of the "heavenly lady" in his behalf—not because of Virgil's flattery. The choice of the word (*lusinghe*) is interesting: it does invite a more critical re-reading of Virgil's deferential words to Cato.

After summarizing their journey up to this point, Virgil pleads movingly with Cato to look with pleasure upon the Pilgrim's arrival, because of the purity of his goal—which Virgil likens to that of Cato: "He goes in search of freedom," Virgil tells Cato. "How dear that is . . . *you* know." And he bolsters his request by a reference to Cato's glorious fate "on that Great Day." The factual statement that follows (that the Pilgrim is still alive, that Virgil is from Limbo) leads immediately to praise of Cato's wife and to an attempt to exploit the tenderness Virgil assumes to exist in their relationship. Cato's rebuff is unmistakable. Is it, perhaps, deserved?

95. *a smooth reed:* The reed will now replace the cord that the Pilgrim wore fastened round his waist while going through the Inferno. The Pilgrim tells us (*Inf.* XVI, 100–108) that with this

cord he had once foolishly hoped to ensnare the leopard (which he encountered in the opening canto of the *Inferno*), a confession of his excessive self-confidence. At Virgil's request, however, he discarded the cord, which was then made to serve Virgil's mysterious purpose (*Inf.* XVI, 112–14). Now, in order to ascend the Mount of Purgatory, he must be girded with a reed, clearly symbolizing humility, the opposite of his former self-confidence.

107. *the mountainside:* the mountain referred to by Cato is, of course, Mount Purgatory, which dominates the small island on which the two travellers have recently found themselves. It is mentioned belatedly and is never presented to view as a part of the topography; it is the mountain of Salvation, and its presence is to be taken for granted.

Virgil and the Pilgrim, following the dark passage leading up out of Hell, had evidently emerged from an opening in the slope of the mountain, so close to the bottom that the descent to its foot and to the shore around it, which Cato now enjoins upon them, will amount simply to a token act suggestive of humility. When the Pilgrim came out upon the slope his first act, as we know, was to look up at the sky. Then he let his eyes rest on Cato's face: up to this point he has seen nothing of the landscape.

115–36

Now at last, after a final glance at the sky, the Pilgrim is able to gaze on the terrain itself and the waters surrounding the shore. Our discussion of the elaborate description of the sky (13–30, beginning "The tender tint of orient sapphire") mentioned the "new vocabulary" of the *Purgatory* to be found in the sensuous descriptions. Here, too, the Poet chooses from a new lexicon that could have no place in the *Inferno:* rippling waters (117), cool shade (121), dew (122); note, too, the word "gently" (125), used of a human gesture, which perfectly captures the mood of the lines describing natural phenomena.

And as the Pilgrim makes his way down the slope, the reader is reminded of his entrance into the Dark Wood; there, too, a deserted shore (*piaggia diserta: Inf.* I, 29); there, too, a mountain of Hope, but one that appears suddenly, mysteriously, only to prove inaccessible. Whereas he felt he had lost forever the right path he had wandered from, now he and Virgil go confidently in search of it (119–20). Thus, the Pilgrim who reaches the shore (130) to participate in the ritual that will prepare him for the ascent is very different from the figure who appears in the first canto of the *Divine Comedy*.

But as he reaches this shore where the reeds of humility grow, a contrasting figure comes to mind: the mention of the lonely shore that never saw a man sail on its waters and return (130–32) is a clear evocation of the great ill-fated voyage of Ulysses, who, according to the story invented by Dante (*Inf.* XXVI), dared to pass through the forbidden Pillars of Hercules into the unknown waters of the South Atlantic, where, finally, a storm sank his ship, not far from a dark mountain-island. This must have been, according to Dante's geography, the same mountain of Purgatory, at whose foot the Pilgrim now finds himself, cleansed of the fumes of Hell and ready to ascend once he has been girded with the reed of humility. It was precisely Ulysses' lack of humility that cut short his voyage just off the shores of Purgatory.

That the voyage of Ulysses is meant to be seen as a foil to the progress of the Pilgrim is also shown by a verbal link between the passage that closes *Purg.* I and the final lines of *Inf.* XXVI: *com' altrui piacque.* The Pilgrim girds himself "as pleased Another" (133); when Ulysses' ship goes down, the waters close over it "as pleased Another" (*Inf.* XXVI, 147). "Altrui," of course, is God, the God who condemned Ulysses' "mad flight" (*folle volo, Inf.* XXVI, 125) but now approves of the Pilgrim's preparations (in spite of his past *follia,* mentioned by Virgil to Cato here in line 59).

Though it is only at the end of this canto that we find a clear allusion to the voyage of Ulysses (one recognized by most scholars), there is, perhaps, a suggestion of it at the very beginning: in the opening lines when the poet applies to himself the metaphor of a sea voyage in the "little bark of my poetic powers." Here, Dante is looking forward both to the success of his Pilgrim's journey and to the successful accomplishment of his own poetic endeavor: to the proper use of his talent. But Ulysses, too, had been blessed by a God-given talent—which, misdirected by his *follia,* led him to his destruction.

That the Pilgrim's encounter with Ulysses in Hell had made him keenly aware of the dangers inherent in the possession of extraordinary gifts is powerfully suggested in the well-known passage of the *Inferno* when the poet speaks of the necessity he feels, whenever he remembers the events of that canto, to curb his talent lest it speed where virtue does not guide (XXVI, 19–24). And in these words, perhaps ("lest talent speed where virtue does not guide"), we have in embryonic form that image of the "bark of my poetic powers," missing from the beginning of the *Inferno* and appearing full-fledged only in the opening lines of *Purg.* I—an image suggested by the experience of Ulysses.

Now the absence of the image at the beginning of the *Divine Comedy* has already been attributed to the poet's modesty at this point. But to explain its absence there is not to explain its presence here; perhaps this image of a successful sea voyage would never have taken shape without the challenge of Ulysses' failure.

127. *my tear-stained face:* Surely the tears this line refers to are not the Pilgrim's recent tears of humility but those he shed upon witnessing certain scenes of punishment in Hell. As such, they would form part of the "trace of filth" (96) that Cato urged be wiped away. For, according to Carroll (p. 12), the Pilgrim's past tears had made him less fit to climb the mountain.

134–36. *When he pulled out the reed:* The springing back of the reed is modeled on an episode in the sixth book of the *Aeneid* (135–44): the Sibyl tells Aeneas that, in preparation for his descent into the underworld, he must pluck a golden bough to carry with him as a kind of a passport—and no sooner is the bough pulled out than another springs up to take its place. Similarly, here, the reed (of humility) is the Pilgrim's necessary passport to the mountain of Purgatory.

This reminiscence of Aeneas at the end of the first canto of the *Purgatory* must remind the reader of the moving line in *Inf.* II when the Pilgrim cries out to Virgil: "But I am not Aeneas, I am not Paul." By the end of *Inf.* I Virgil had explained that he had been chosen by heavenly powers to guide the Pilgrim through Hell and Purgatory toward Paradise. The Pilgrim at first accepts the challenge of such a journey; later, his humility—or, as Virgil will call it, his cowardice—makes him recoil from the venture. At the very beginning, Virgil has presented himself to the Pilgrim as the creator of the *pius Aeneas;* now, in *Inf.* II, the Pilgrim, become fearful, reminds him of the preeminence, the sublimity, of that figure predestined to be the founder of the Roman Empire; Aeneas, he said, could well be permitted to visit the Kingdom of the Dead—but, he adds, "I am not Aeneas."

And surely, with the echo here of *Aen.* VI, the repetition of the miracle of the "plucked plant reborn," Dante intends to assure the reader of the success of his Pilgrim, to elevate him to the rank of that Aeneas he had earlier praised so highly. Thus it is with a reminder of the successful voyage of Aeneas, preceded by a reminder of the tragic doom of Ulysses, that the first canto of Dante's *Purgatory* ends.

CANTO II

As the sun rises, Dante and Virgil are still standing at the water's edge and wondering which road to take in order to ascend the mountain of Purgatory, when the Pilgrim sees a reddish glow moving across the water. The light approaches at an incredible speed, and eventually they are able to discern the wings of an angel. The angel is the miraculous pilot of a ship containing souls of the Redeemed, who are singing the psalm *In exitu Israël de Aegypto*. At a sign from the angel boatsman, these souls disembark, only to roam about on the shore. Apparently, they are strangers, and, mistaking Virgil and Dante for familiars of the place, they ask them which road leads up the mountainside. Virgil answers that they, too, are pilgrims, only recently arrived. At this point some of the souls realize that the Pilgrim is still alive, and they stare at him in fascination. Recognizing a face that he knows in this crowd of souls, Dante tries three times in vain to embrace the shade of his old friend Casella, a musician; then he asks Casella for a song and, as he sings, all the souls are held spellbound. Suddenly the Just Old Man, Cato, appears to disperse the rapt crowd, sternly rebuking them for their negligence and exhorting them to run to the mountain to begin their ascent.

The sun was touching the horizon now,
    the highest point of whose meridian arc
    was just above Jerusalem; and Night,   3

revolving always opposite to him,
    rose from the Ganges with the Scales that fall
    out of her hand when she outweighs the day.   6

Thus, where we were, Aurora's lovely face
    with a vermilion flush on her white cheeks
    was aging in a glow of golden light.   9

We were still standing at the water's edge,
    wondering about the road ahead, like men
    whose thoughts go forward while their bodies stay,   12

when, suddenly, I saw, low in the west
    (like the red glow of Mars that burns at dawn
    through the thick haze that hovers on the sea),   15

a light—I hope to see it come again!—
　　moving across the waters at a speed
　　faster than any earthly flight could be.　　　　*18*

I turned in wonder to my guide, and then,
　　when I looked back at it again, the light
　　was larger and more brilliant than before,　　　*21*

and there appeared, on both sides of this light,
　　a whiteness indefinable, and then,
　　another whiteness grew beneath the shape.　　　*24*

My guide was silent all the while, but when
　　the first two whitenesses turned into wings,
　　and he saw who the steersman was, he cried:　　*27*

"Fall to your knees, fall to your knees! Behold
　　the angel of the Lord! And fold your hands.
　　Expect to see more ministers like him.　　　　*30*

See how he scorns to use man's instruments;
　　he needs no oars, no sails, only his wings
　　to navigate between such distant shores.　　　*33*

See how he has them pointing up to Heaven:
　　he fans the air with these immortal plumes
　　that do not moult as mortal feathers do."　　　*36*

Closer and closer to our shore he came,
　　brighter and brighter shone the bird of God,
　　until I could no longer bear the light,　　　　*39*

and bowed my head. He steered straight to the shore,
　　his boat so swift and light upon the wave,
　　it left no sign of truly sailing there;　　　　*42*

and the celestial pilot stood astern
　　with blessedness inscribed upon his face.
　　More than a hundred souls were in his ship:　　*45*

In exitu Israël de Aegypto,
　　they all were singing with a single voice,
　　chanting it verse by verse until the end.　　　*48*

The angel signed them with the holy cross,
　　and they rushed from the ship onto the shore;
　　he disappeared, swiftly, as he had come.　　　*51*

The souls left there seemed strangers to this place:
    they roamed about, while looking all around,
    endeavoring to understand new things.   54

The sun, which with its shafts of light had chased
    the Goat out of the heavens' highest field,
    was shooting rays of day throughout the sky,   57

when those new souls looked up to where we were,
    and called to us: "If you should know the road
    that leads up to the mountainside, show us."   60

And Virgil answered them: "You seem to think
    that we are souls familiar with this place,
    but we, like all of you, are pilgrims here;   63

we just arrived, not much ahead of you,
    but by a road which was so rough and hard—
    to climb this mountain now will be like play."   66

Those souls who noticed that my body breathed,
    and realized that I was still alive,
    in their amazement turned a deathly pale.   69

Just as a crowd, greedy for news, surrounds
    the messenger who bears the olive branch,
    and none too shy to elbow-in his way,   72

so all the happy souls of these Redeemed
    stared at my face, forgetting, as it were,
    the way to go to make their beauty whole.   75

One of these souls pushed forward, arms outstretched,
    and he appeared so eager to embrace me
    that his affection moved me to show mine.   78

O empty shades, whose human forms seem real!
    Three times I clasped my hands around his form,
    as many times they came back to my breast.   81

I must have been the picture of surprise,
    for he was smiling as he drew away,
    and I plunged forward still in search of him.   84

Then, gently, he suggested I not try,
    and by his voice I knew who this shade was;
    I begged him stay and speak to me awhile.   87

"As once I loved you in my mortal flesh,
without it now I love you still," he said.
"Of course I'll stay. But tell me why you're here." 90

"I make this journey now, O my Casella,
hoping one day to come back here again,"
I said. "But how did you lose so much time?" 93

He answered: "I cannot complain if he
who, as he pleases, picks his passengers,
often refused to take me in his boat, 96

for that Just Will is always guiding his.
But for the last three months, indulgently,
he has been taking all who wish to cross; 99

so, when I went to seek the shore again,
where Tiber's waters turn to salty sea,
benignly, he accepted me aboard. 102

Now, back again he flies to Tiber's mouth,
which is the meeting place of all the dead,
except for those who sink to Acheron's shore." 105

"If no new law prevents remembering
or practicing those love songs that once brought
peace to my restless longings in the world," 108

I said, "pray sing, and give a little rest
to my poor soul which, burdened by my flesh,
has climbed this far and is exhausted now." 111

Amor che ne la mente mi ragiona,
began the words of his sweet melody—
their sweetness still is sounding in my soul. 114

My master and myself and all those souls
that came with him were deeply lost in joy,
as if that sound were all that did exist. 117

And while we stood enraptured by the sound
of those sweet notes—a sudden cry: "What's this,
you lazy souls?" It was the Just Old Man. 120

"What negligence to stand around like this!
Run to the mountain, shed that slough which still
does not let God be manifest to you!" 123

souls. (Later, when the sun has risen higher, it will be the ability of the Pilgrim's body to cast a shadow that serves as a key motif in the Antepurgatory.) Though they do nothing but stare, motionless, their curiosity is compared to that of an eager crowd surrounding the bearer of news, pushing and shoving. Heedless of everything but this newly discovered marvel, the souls forget the purpose of their journey, which should remain always uppermost in their minds (74–75: " . . . forgetting . . . / the way to go to make their beauty whole"). They should be thinking only of purifying their souls.

71. *the messenger:* In Dante's time messengers of either peace or victory customarily carried an olive branch as a token of the good news they bore. This was a practice inherited from Roman antiquity.

91. *O my Casella:* From the scanty information available, most of which seems to derive from this canto, we know that Casella, a musician and singer, was a friend of Dante's and very likely set to music Dante's canzone "Amor che ne la mente mi ragiona," if not others as well. Documents mentioning his name indicate that he was a Florentine, though the commentary of the Anonimo fiorentino (fourteenth century) refers to him as "Casella da Pistoja." The manuscript of a thirteenth-century ballad by Lemmo da Pistoia (Vatican MS. 3214) includes the annotation "Casella diede il suono" ("Casella wrote the music"); a document dated July 13, 1282, and preserved in Siena records that Casella received a fine for loitering in the streets at night! Since Casella was a singer, it is appropriate that Dante recognize him by his voice (86).

98. *But for the last three months:* The change in attitude on the part of the angel-pilot, mentioned by Casella, is generally understood in light of the fact that in 1300, during the great Jubilee Year, Pope Boniface VIII granted a plenary indulgence to those participating in a pilgrimage to Rome. This papal bull makes no mention of any special indulgence for the souls of the dead, but Dante here seems to be following a common belief that it did.

If the pilot's new attitude has been in effect for three months, and Casella was already at the Tiber waiting before this change took place, why did not Casella take advantage of the change immediately instead of waiting three months? This is never explained. See Porena, p. 27.

101. *where Tiber's waters turn to salty sea:* Ostia, where the Tiber River enters the sea, is the place where souls departing for Purgatory gather to await transport. Actually, all souls that have not been damned gather there, according to Casella; this can only mean that the souls destined for Heaven must first climb the mountain of Purgatory. Ostia was the seaport of Rome, and Rome was a natural point of departure for the souls of the Blessed since it was the center of the church.

107–108. *that once brought / peace to my restless longings:* Surely as Dante the Poet wrote these words he was aware of the vanity of his younger self's easy satisfaction. According to the teachings of St. Augustine, the human heart can find rest only in God (*Conf.* I, i: . . . *et inquietum est cor nostrum, donec requiescat in te, "* . . . our hearts are restless till they rest in Thee"). Consequently, it must remain restless until united with Him after death in the Beatific Vision. Aesthetic pleasure may seem to set the heart at rest, but such pleasure is fallacious and is to be avoided as a distraction from the journey to God.

112. *Amor che ne la mente mi ragiona* ("Love that speaks to me in my mind"): The first verse of the second canzone, which Dante comments on in the third book of his *Convivio*. In the *Paradise* (VIII, 37) Dante has Charles Martel quote the first verse of the first canzone of the *Convivio*. In the *Purgatory* (XXIV, 51) Bonagiunta da Lucca will cite the opening verse of Dante's most important canzone in the *Vita nuova: Donne ch'avete intelletto d'amore.* For a discussion of Casella's song, see Freccero.

115. *My master and myself and all those souls:* Again the souls are distracted from their journey, and this time the Pilgrim, together with Virgil, shares their mood of utter absorption. But this scene is described by the poet rather sympathetically: he emphasizes the beauty of the music; he seems to treat respectfully the sensitive receptivity of the audience—which contained perhaps a few souls destined for Heaven, as well as Virgil and the Pilgrim, both exemplary figures—a distinguished group committing a "distinguished sin." In itself, the enjoyment of music and poetry is legitimate, even recommendable, under appropriate circumstances. What these souls, newly arrived

from earth, had failed to see was that, from this time on, there would never again exist for them circumstances favorable to even the most refined of earthly pleasures.

Perhaps Dante, who loved the arts, allowed himself to be lenient here in his treatment of this mass reaction of self-indulgence—knowing that Cato would come two lines later to utterly condemn these souls.

120. *It was the Just Old Man:* Cato unexpectedly materializes out of nowhere (again!) to sternly rebuke the laggard souls for having surrendered to the perverse sweetness of Casella's song, thus completely neglecting their journey to God.

Cato's anger at the souls who have momentarily forgotten God may remind one of the anger of Moses, who, coming down from the mountain with the tablets of the Law, found the Jews worshipping a golden calf. (For another parallel between Cato and Moses, see note to *Purg.* I, 89.)

Of course, the two instances of defection are not of the same degree of gravity; indeed, the reader may feel that Cato's angry words to the newly arrived, confused, leaderless group are unduly severe. In fact, there can be no doubt that his advice to them, "Run to the Mountain, shed that slough . . ." (122) is of no practical worth whatsoever: they cannot begin their purgation until God wills it, and Cato's impatience is unrealistic. But Dante evidently found it fitting that the newly arrived souls hear words that would shake them to their depths, and he chose Cato to deliver them—this pagan soul of harshly uncompromising, impatient idealism, who took his own life rather than compromise. If Dante once wrote that Cato was perhaps worthy to represent God Himself (see note to I, 31–75), he may have been thinking of the Old Testamentary Jehovah, given to wrath.

That the poet assigns to Cato the task of rebuking the self-indulgent souls makes still more difficult the solution of what would have been a difficult problem anyway: since the poem sung by Casella for the delight of the group was written by the younger Dante, one may wonder if criticism of the souls' behavior is not also intended as criticism of the type of poetry that Dante used to write. But, even granted we were sure just how to classify *Amor che ne la mente mi ragiona* (cited in verse 112 of this canto), why should Dante's earlier poetry concern Cato? He was interested now in the correct behavior of the newly arrived souls, not in the Pilgrim, and surely not in the subtleties of his verse—of which he may not have heard a word. For further discussion of Cato's rebuke, see Hollander.

122. *shed that slough:* The slough is the old skin that a serpent sheds. The image here is one of abandoning the old ways and adopting the new. It is an image of rebirth that works well with the resurrection and dawn motifs that run through the first two cantos.

CANTO III

As THE CROWD of souls breaks up, Virgil seems ashamed
of having permitted the Pilgrim's self-indulgence. But they resume their journey and Dante raises his eyes to take in the
enormous height of the mountain that stretches up toward
Heaven. Then, looking down, he sees his own shadow on the
ground in front of him and becomes alarmed when he fails to
see the shadow of his guide, thinking, for one brief second, that
he has been deserted. This leads to an explanation by Virgil of
the diaphanous bodies of the dead: though a shade casts no
shadow, it is yet sensitive to pain and heat and cold; such is the
mysterious will of the Creator, which cannot be understood by
human reason. In the meantime, they have reached the foot of
the mountain but find the slope impossible to scale because it is
too steep. They then see a band of souls moving toward them
with unbelievable slowness, and they set out to meet them in
order to ask directions. The souls are amazed to see the Pilgrim's shadow; their spokesman, Manfred, explains that, despite his excommunication by the church, he has been saved
through everlasting love by repenting at the very end of his
life. Because of this delay, however, he is required to wait in
the Antepurgatory thirty times as long as he waited on earth to
repent—though this period can be shortened by the good
prayers of the faithful in the world.

In sudden flight those souls were scattering,
   rushing across the plain and toward the hill
   where Reason spurs the probing of the soul,   3

but I drew closer to my faithful friend.
   And where could I have run without his help?
   Who else but he could take me up the mount?   6

He looked as if he suffered from remorse—
   O dignity of conscience, noble, chaste,
   how one slight fault can sting you into shame!   9

Now when he had resumed his normal stride,
   free of the haste that mars man's dignity,
   my mind, confined till then to what took place,   12

broke free, and now was eager to explore:
  I raised my eyes to marvel at the mount
  that grew out of the sea toward Heaven's height.   15

The sun behind us blazing red with light
  outlined my human form upon the ground
  before me, as my body blocked its rays.   18

I quickly turned around, seized by the fear
  that I had been abandoned, for I saw
  the ground was dark only in front of me;   21

and then my Comfort turned to me and said:
  "Why are you so uneasy—do you think
  that I am not here with you, guiding you?   24

Evening has fallen on the tomb where lies
  my body that could cast a shadow once;
  from Brindisi to Naples it was moved.   27

If now I cast no shadow on the ground,
  you should not be surprised. Think of the spheres:
  not one of them obstructs the others' light.   30

Yet bodies such as ours are sensitive
  to pain and cold and heat—willed by that Power
  which wills its secret not to be revealed;   33

madness it is to hope that human minds
  can ever understand the Infinite
  that comprehends Three Persons in One Being.   36

Be satisfied with *quia* unexplained,
  O human race! If you knew everything,
  no need for Mary to have borne a son.   39

You saw the hopeless longing of those souls
  whose thirst, were this not so, would have been quenched,
  but which, instead, endures as endless pain: 42

I speak of Plato and of Aristotle,
  and many others." Then he bent his head,
  remaining silent with his anguished thoughts.   45

By now we had come to the mountain's foot,
  and there we found a rocky slope so steep
  the nimblest legs would not have served you there.   48

The craggiest, the cruelest precipice
  between Turbia and Lerici would seem,
  compared with this, inviting stairs to climb.   51

"How can we tell," my guide said, stopping short,
  "just where this mountain face might slope enough
  to let someone who has no wings ascend?"   54

While he was standing there, his head bent low,
  searching his mind to find some helpful way,
  and I was looking up at all that rock—   57

along the cliffside to my left, a crowd
  of souls was coming toward us, moving slow,
  so slowly that they did not seem to move.   60

"Master," I said, "look over there! You'll see
  some people coming who should know the way—
  if you have not yet found it by yourself."   63

He looked up then, and said with great relief:
  "Let us go meet them, for they move so slow;
  and you, dear son, be steadfast in your hopes."   66

We were as yet as far from that long crowd
  (even after we had gone a thousand steps),
  as a good slingsman's hand could throw a stone,   69

when they all pressed together suddenly
  and huddled up against the towering rock;
  too stunned to move, they stared in disbelief.   72

"O you elect who ended well your lives,"
  Virgil began, "I ask you, in the name
  of that same peace I know awaits you all,   75

to tell us where the mountain slopes enough
  for us to start our climb: the more one learns,
  the more one comes to hate the waste of time."   78

As sheep will often start to leave the fold,
  first one, then two, then three—then, hesitantly,
  the rest will move, with muzzles to the ground,   81

and what the first sheep does, the others do:
  if it should stop, they all push up against it,
  resigned to huddle quiet in ignorance—   84

just so I saw the leaders of that flock
  of chosen souls take their first steps toward us,
  their faces meek, their movements dignified.   87

But when the souls in front saw the sun's light
  was broken on the ground to my right side,
  my shadow stretching to the rising cliff,   90

they stopped, and started slowly shrinking back;
  all of the rest that followed on their heels
  did as they did, not knowing why they did.   93

"Before you ask me I will answer you:
  this form you see breaking the sunlight here
  upon the ground is a man's body. But,   96

this should not startle you; you can be sure
  that not without the power coming from Heaven
  does he come here seeking to scale this wall."   99

Thus spoke my master. And that worthy group,
  with gesturing hands that urged us to turn round,
  replied: "Go lead the way ahead of us."   102

Then one soul cried: "Whoever you may be,
  look back as you walk on and ask yourself
  if you have ever seen me down on earth."   105

I turned to him and looked hard at his face:
  a handsomely patrician blond he was,
  although a sword wound cut through one eyebrow.   108

When I, in all humility, confessed
  I did not recognize him, he said: "Look,"
  as he revealed a gash above his breast.   111

Then with a smile he said, "Manfred I am,
  grandson of Empress Constance, and I beg you,
  when you are with the living once again,   114

go to my lovely child, mother of kings
  who honor Sicily and Aragon;
  whatever may be rumored, tell her this: 117

As I lay there, my body torn by these
  two mortal wounds, weeping, I gave my soul
  to Him Who grants forgiveness willingly.   120

Horrible was the nature of my sins,
    but boundless mercy stretches out its arms
    to any man who comes in search of it,   123

and if the Pastor of Cosenza, sent
    by Clement in his rage to hunt me out,
    had understood those words in God's own book,   126

my body's bones would still be where they were:
    by the bridgehead near Benevento trenched
    under the guard of a heavy mound of stones.   129

Now they are swept by wind and drenched by rain
    outside my kingdom, by the Verde's banks,
    where they were brought by him with tapers quenched.   132

The church's curse is not the final word,
    for Everlasting Love may still return,
    if hope reveals the slightest hint of green.   135

True, he who dies scorning the Holy Church,
    although he turns repentant at life's end,
    must stay outside, a wanderer on this bank,   138

for thirty times as long as he has lived
    in his presumptuousness—although good prayers
    may shorten the duration of his term.   141

You see how you can make me happy now
    by telling my good Constance I am here;
    explain to her this law that holds me back,   144

for those down there can help us much up here.

NOTES

5. *And where could I have run without his help?:* These lines,
which express so warmly the Pilgrim's recognition of his de-
pendence on Virgil, render more poignant his despair a moment later, when, seeing only his own shadow on the ground
and not that of his guide, he fears he has been abandoned
(19–21).

7. *He looked as if:* Virgil's reactions to the consciousness of
his sin here are exemplary: any offense, no matter how slight,

should inspire in the noble soul feelings of shame and remorse.

14. *I raised my eyes to marvel at the mount:* As the Pilgrim looks up, we are reminded once again (cf. *Purg.* I, 115-36) that he finds himself now in the same situation that he was in at the beginning of the *Inferno:* at the foot of a mountain he wished to climb (cf. *Inf.* I, 16-17: "I raised my head and saw the hilltop shawled / in morning rays of light").

16. *The sun behind us:* The two poets have begun their journey on the eastern side of the island; the recently risen sun lies behind them as they turn to face the mountain. The theme of Dante's shadow begins in these lines, with his first experience since emerging from Hell of seeing before him the shadow his body has cast, and continues in the next line with his momentary alarm at failing to see Virgil's shadow. From now on the Pilgrim's shadow will distinguish him from the other souls in Purgatory, as his breathing did in the dim light of *Purg.* II (67-69). The shadow seems to represent all the earthly vanities to which living men are attached.

25-27. *the tomb where lies / my body that could cast:* By order of Augustus, Virgil's body was taken from Brindisi, where he died in 19 B.C., to be buried in Naples. Dante's lines recall the familiar epitaph for Virgil quoted in Suetonius's *Vita Virgili,* XXXVI: *Mantua me genuit; Calabri rapuere; tenet nunc Parthenope; cecini pascua, rura, duces* ("Mantua bore me; in Calabria [Brindisi] I died; Parthenope [Naples] now holds my bones; I sang of shepherds, fields and heroes").

This mention of the transfer of Virgil's body is a preparation for Manfred, whose body, he will tell us (127-32), was disinterred and taken outside of the kingdom of Naples. The separation of body and soul (26) is a recurrent theme in the Antepurgatory. Anticipation of the Last Day, when soul and (glorified) body will be reunited, has appeared in connection with Cato (*Purg.* I, 75).

28. *If now I cast no shadow:* Virgil's explanation of the absence of his shadow briefly touches on the various aspects of the "diaphanous body" of the shades; a fuller explanation of these phenomena will be given by the poet Statius in Canto XXV.

37–45. *Be satisfied with* quia *unexplained:* In his speech, Virgil addresses all of mankind, both directly in his apostrophe, "O human race," and by addressing himself to the protagonist, who represents Everyman.

As for Virgil's terminology, Carroll (p. 39) explains, "In scholastic phraseology, the *quia* is equivalent to the *fact,* the thing that can be demonstrated by means of the *effect.* It is opposed to the *quid,* the thing which is demonstrated by its final *cause.* Dante's meaning is that human reason, being powerless to penetrate to the essence or *quiddity,* must remain contented with the *quia,* the fact as seen in its effects."

The ancient philosophers were not content with the *quia,* and yet, living outside the Christian dispensation, they were unable to see beyond it, since the light of reason alone could not penetrate the mystery of God (cf. *Inf.* IV, 34–42). Had they been able to know Christ, they would have been taken by Him into Heaven, where, among the elect, their every intellectual desire would finally have been satisfied in the contemplation of the Beatific Vision. Virgil's anguished meditation is brought on by the realization that he too, along with Aristotle and Plato, is one of these souls eternally condemned to hopeless longing (cf. in particular *Inf.* IV, 39). In the course of the *Purgatory,* Virgil will become an increasingly pathetic figure.

50. *Turbia and Lerici:* Both towns are located on the Italian Riviera. Lerici lies south of Genova near La Spezia; Turbia between Monaco and Nice. Between these two towns along the coast, the mountains descend abruptly—indeed, perpendicularly—into the sea, making passage all but impossible.

55. *While he was standing there:* Virgil looks down and within himself in search of the right way. The Pilgrim looks up and about, outside of himself. Thus he sees a potential source of aid coming down the road, which Virgil, scrutinizing only his own rational faculties, fails to find. The journey up the mountain of Purgatory will demand a certain openness, as well as faith and trust.

60. *so slowly that they did not seem to move:* The abnormal, nightmarish slowness with which the Excommunicated move is most puzzling. Those who see in it a reflection of the fact that these souls were "slow" to repent have jumped to too easy a conclusion: not only is postponement of an act quite different

from the slow performance of an act but there is no indication that this group waited longer than any other to repent (Manfred, their spokesman, died relatively young). Moreover, this group does move, does go forward, while the group next to be seen cannot manage to get on their feet.

70–72. *when they all pressed together suddenly:* It seems only natural that the group of souls should be startled at the sight of Virgil and the Pilgrim: two souls, apparently attached to no group, coming from the opposite direction. What is puzzling is the slowness with which they show their reaction: the two travellers, surely in sight of them, had covered one thousand paces walking toward them before they stop to huddle and to stare.

79. *As sheep will often start to leave the fold:* The Excommunicated souls are presented as sheep, and the comparison has a double force. In the first place, since they chose to live their lives without the spiritual guidance of the church, they now have no leader, no shepherd, but blindly follow the sheep in front without knowing why. In the second place, this slow forward movement without knowing the way is in fact the virtue of faith as defined by St. Thomas Aquinas. Thus, these souls carry out Virgil's earlier admonition (37) to be content with the *quia,* without knowing the why or how.

88. *But when the souls in front saw the sun's light:* That the souls are amazed when they see that the Pilgrim's body casts a shadow is to be expected. This phenomenon could not occur in Hell; nevertheless, we are made aware that the Pilgrim still has his mortal body in the *Inferno* by the fact that his weight makes a boat settle in the water, his foot dislodges a stone, and he accidentally kicks one of the Damned in the head.

101. *with gesturing hands:* The gesture is the typical Italian one of pushing the back of one's hand toward a person. According to Castelvetro, the backs of these souls' hands are facing the Pilgrim and his guide because "when we call a person to us we indicate this to him with the palm of our hand, and when we would have him depart from us we gesture with the back of our hand."

108. *although a sword wound cut through one eyebrow:* There is nothing in the account of the nature of diaphanous bodies (*Purg.* XXV, 34–108) to explain how or why Manfred bears his mortal wounds in the afterlife.

112. *Manfred I am:* Manfred (1232–66) was the natural son of Frederick II, who legitimized him and stipulated that he should be regent during the reign of his half-brother, Conrad IV. At Conrad's death, Manfred once more assumed regency, as Conrad's son, Conradin, was an infant. Upon a rumor of Conradin's death, Manfred was made king of Sicily. He was a Ghibelline and an excommunicate (in fact, he had been excommunicated twice, by Alexander IV and Urban IV), and Urban could not bear to see him occupy the throne. Urban offered the crown to Louis IX of France and, upon his refusal, to his brother, Charles of Anjou. Charles decided immediately to take possession of his kingdom and waged a fierce attack against Manfred. Betrayed by his followers and outnumbered by the French, Manfred was killed at the battle of Benevento in 1266.

After the battle, Charles refused Manfred's body honorable burial in consecrated ground because he had been excommunicated. Instead, he had him buried near the bridge at Benevento, where his army filed past, each dropping a stone upon the grave so that a huge cairn was formed. Later, however, Pope Clement IV insisted that Manfred's body be disinterred and moved outside the limits of the kingdom of Naples (and thus outside church territory). The body was then thrown on the banks of the river Verde and left unburied.

One may compare the ignominious transportation of Manfred's body with the glorious and respectful removal of Virgil's body by imperial order from Brindisi to Naples (III, 25–27). Ironically, however, despite the earthly glory accorded him, Virgil is numbered among the Damned, while Manfred is among the Blessed.

113. *Empress Constance:* Constance (1154–98), wife of Henry VI, was the mother of Frederick II of Sicily. Since Manfred is the natural son of Frederick, he identifies himself with reference to his paternal grandmother.

115–16. *my lovely child, mother of kings:* Manfred's daughter and grandmother had the same name, Constance. His daughter's two sons became respectively the King of Aragon and the King of Sicily.

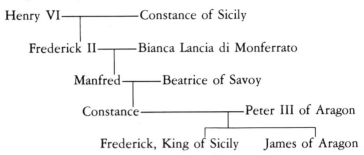

121. *Horrible was the nature of my sins:* Manfred was said by his enemies to have murdered his father, his brother Conrad, and two of his nephews, and to have attempted to murder his young nephew, Conradin.

124. *the Pastor of Cosenza:* This particular Archbishop of Cosenza has been identified as either Bartolomeo Pignatelli or his successor, Tommaso d'Agni. In any case, the archbishop referred to here had Manfred's body disinterred on the order of Pope Clement IV and cast outside church territory (see note to III, 112).

126. *had understood those words in God's own book:* The words in question may well be verse 37 in John 6: "Him that cometh unto me I will in no wise cast out."

131. *outside my kingdom:* Again the theme of exile is introduced. It will be repeated with Jacopo del Cassero, Buonconte, and Pia in Canto V.

132. *with tapers quenched:* When the bodies of the Excommunicated were taken to their grave, the mortuary candles were first extinguished, then carried upside down.

135. *if hope reveals the slightest hint of green:* Green is the color of hope. Manfred's hope and faith at the end of his life have brought him to Purgatory and allow him to smile as he tells the gruesome story of his death and the vindictiveness of the pope. There is even a glimmer of hopefulness in the ignominious disposition of Manfred's body on the banks of the

Verde, which is Italian for "green." (During his life, according to contemporary accounts, Manfred always dressed in green.)

139. *for thirty times as long as he has lived:* The poet's choice of the number thirty was possibly inspired by a provision in Canon Law that calls for a thirty-day period of grace before the ban of excommunication goes into effect.

140. *good prayers:* Here begins the theme of "intercession." Throughout the Antepurgatory, there is an emphasis on the value of intercessory prayer, offered by the faithful on earth in behalf of the souls who are purifying themselves in Purgatory. This doctrine will be repeated and refined in the cantos that follow.

143. *Constance:* Manfred's daughter, who died in 1302, at Barcelona. Her mother was Beatrice of Savoy. In 1262 she married Peter III of Aragon, who thereupon claimed the sovereignty of Sicily.

CANTO IV

AFTER LISTENING TO Manfred for some time (the Pilgrim being deeply absorbed), the two poets are shown a gap in the rock through which they may begin their ascent. The climb is arduous, and they must use both hands and feet in making their way. When they finally reach a ledge, the Pilgrim is exhausted and they stop to rest. He is puzzled by the fact that the sun is on their left, and Virgil explains that this phenomenon is due to the geographical location of the mountain of Purgatory. Furthermore, he adds, the mountain is such that it is most difficult to climb at the beginning but becomes easier and easier, until at last it requires no effort. Their conversation, however, has been overheard and is interrupted by a sarcastic remark from behind a massive rock. The speaker is Belacqua, an old friend of the Poet's, who, together with the other souls on this level, belongs to the second class of the Late Repentant: the Indolent. They must wait outside the gates of Purgatory proper for as many years as they put off repentance on earth. Belacqua repeats the doctrine that prayer can shorten their period of waiting, adding the qualification that it must be prayer from a heart in the state of grace.

When any of our senses is aroused
    to intensity of pleasure or of pain,
    the soul gives itself up to that one sense,   *3*

oblivious to all its other powers.
    This fact serves to refute the false belief
    that in our bodies more than one soul burns.   *6*

And so it is that when we see or hear
    something which wholly captivates the soul,
    we easily can lose all sense of time.   *9*

The sense aware of time is different
    from that which dominates all of the soul:
    the first is free to roam, the other, bound.   *12*

And I was now experiencing this truth,
    listening to that soul and marvelling.
    The sun had climbed a good fifty degrees,   *15*

and I had not been conscious of the fact,
    when at some point along the way, those souls
    cried out in one voice: "Here is what you seek."   *18*

A peasant, at the time the grapes grow ripe,
    with one small forkful of his thorns could seal
    an opening within his hedge more wide   *21*

than was the gap through which my guide and I
    were forced to climb, the two of us alone,
    once we had parted company with that flock.   *24*

Up to San Leo, down to Noli, climb,
    climb to the top of Mount Bismantova
    on your two feet, but here a man must fly: *27*

yes, fly—that is to say, with the swift wings
    of strong desire, and following that guide
    who gave me hope, spreading his light before me.   *30*

Squeezed in between the tight walls of the pass,
    we struggled upward through that broken rock,
    using our hands and feet to climb the ground.   *33*

Once we were through that narrow passageway
    up the high cliff and on an open slope,
    "Master," I said, "where must we go from here?"   *36*

And he replied: "Now, do not change your course,
    keep climbing up the mountain, close to me,
    until we find a more experienced guide."   *39*

The peak rose higher than my sight could reach,
    the slope soared upright, steeper than a line
    drawn from mid-quadrant to the center's point.   *42*

I felt my strength drain from me, and I cried:
    "O my sweet father, turn and look at me;
    unless you slow your pace, you'll lose me here."   *45*

"My son," he said, "keep climbing, just to there,"
    and pointed to a ledge, not far above,
    that made its way around the mountain slope.   *48*

His words were like a goad, and I strained on
    behind him, climbing with my hands and knees
    until I felt the ledge beneath my feet.   *51*

And here we both sat down to face the east,
to rest, as we surveyed all we had climbed —
a backward glance can often lift the heart. 54

I looked down at the shoreline far below,
and then looked up: the sun, amazingly,
was shining to the left of us. The Poet 57

was well aware that I was stupefied
as I observed the chariot of light
making its course between us and the north. 60

"Now, were Castor and Pollux," he began,
"to take that mirror in their company,
whose light is shed below and heavenward, 63

you would perceive the flaming Zodiac
revolving even closer to the Bears —
unless the sun strayed from its ancient path. 66

If you would understand how this may be,
try to imagine Zion and this Mount
located on the earth in such a way 69

that while each lies in different hemispheres,
the two of them share one horizon; then,
the lofty path, which Phaëton's chariot 72

could not hold fast to, had to pass this height
on one side here, but on the other there —
as you must see, if you think carefully." 75

"Oh, master, you are right!" I answered him;
"Now, finally, I clearly understand
this point that always baffled me before: 78

of Heaven's moving circles, the mid-one
(called the Equator by astronomers),
which always lies between winter and sun, 81

is, for the very reason you set forth,
as far north from this place where we now stand
as once the Hebrews saw it to the south. 84

But would you kindly tell me, if you please,
how much more climbing we must do: this peak
soars higher than my eyes can see." And he: 87

"This Mount is not like others: at the start
    it is most difficult to climb, but then,
    the more one climbs the easier it becomes;   90

and when the slope feels gentle to the point
    that climbing up would be as effortless
    as floating down a river in a boat—   93

well then, you have arrived at the road's end,
    and there you can expect, at last, to rest.
    I say no more, and what I said is true."   96

Hardly had he stopped speaking when we heard
    a voice not far away: "But, probably,
    you'll feel like sitting down before you do!"   99

Both of us turned to where the voice had come
    and to our left we saw a massive rock
    that neither one of us had noticed there.   102

We went up to the boulder and, behind,
    there were some people hidden in its shade:
    so many sprawling shapes of indolence.   105

There was one there who, you could tell, was tired,
    for he sat with his arms hugging his knees,
    letting his head droop down between his legs.   108

"O my dear master, look at him!" I said,
    "See that man? Lazier he could not look,
    not even if 'Lazy' were his middle name."   111

That shape then turned to look at us, and said,
    raising his face no higher than his thigh:
    "If you're so energetic, run on up."   114

And then I knew who this soul had to be!
    Exhausted, out of breath, nevertheless,
    I struggled toward him. Finally, when I   117

stood by his side, he raised his head a bit
    and said: "Is it quite clear to you by now
    just why the sun drives past you on the left?"   120

His lazy ways and his sarcastic words
    made me half smile, and I replied to him:
    "Belacqua! I'll not have to worry now   123

about your fate! But tell me why are you
   just sitting like this? Waiting for a guide?
   Or simply being your old self again?"   *126*

"Brother, what good will climbing do?" he said.
   "God's angel sitting at the gate will not
   let me begin my penitence inside.   *129*

Before I start, the heavens must revolve
   as many times as while I was alive,
   for I put off repenting till the end.   *132*

Prayers could, of course, make my time shorter here:
   prayers from a heart that lives in grace—the rest
   are worthless, for they go unheard in Heaven!"   *135*

The Poet had by now begun to climb;
   he said, "Come now, see how the sun has touched
   Heaven's highest point, while on the western shore   *138*

Night sets her foot upon Morocco's sands."

NOTES

1–12. *When any of our senses is aroused:* Dante here refutes
the idea that man possesses more than one soul. The idea of
multiple souls was set forth by Aristotle, who maintained that
man had three souls existing in a kind of hierarchical arrangement: the vegetative soul, through which growth was exhibited,
the sentient soul, which governed sensation and movement,
and the rational soul, which gave rise to man's capacity for reason. These souls were differentiated from one another by their
degrees of heat, the vegetative soul having the lowest heat and
the rational the highest heat.
   Thomas Aquinas consolidated Aristotle's idea with Christian
doctrine by maintaining that the soul is a unity endowed with
three faculties, which he called "virtues" or "powers": the vegetative, the sensitive, and the intellective (*Summa Theol.* I, 76,
3; I–II, 37, a. I, and *Summa Contra Gentiles* II, 58). If the soul
becomes completely or strongly drawn toward one of these
powers, it must of necessity neglect the others.
   This passage serves to recapitulate the theme of distraction,
which plays an important part in the previous cantos, and it

provides a philosophical explanation of the Pilgrim's experiences with Casella and Manfred. In each instance he becomes so completely absorbed in his interlocutor that he completely forgets the purpose of his journey and its overriding importance.

13. *And I was now experiencing this truth:* He has experienced the truth just demonstrated, which is that he has one soul with a set of faculties, and that the preoccupation of one faculty with a given situation or issue necessitates that the other two faculties be ignored. In this particular instance, Dante has become so absorbed in conversation with Manfred that he has not noticed the passing of time (see note to IV, 15).

14. *listening to that soul and marvelling:* The word "marvelling" (*ammirando*) has strong Augustinian connotations and in particular recalls a famous passage in the *Confessions* (X, VIII) where the vanity of admiring the natural world at the expense of one's salvation is deplored: *Et eunt homines mirari alta montium . . . et relinquunt se ipsos* ("And men go up to marvel at the heights of the mountains, and they forget about themselves").

15. *fifty degrees:* one degree of the sun's arc is equal to four minutes; therefore, fifteen degrees equal one hour. If the sun has risen fifty degrees, then three hours and twenty minutes have passed since sunrise.

18. *"Here is what you seek":* That is, here is the upward passage that you have been looking for. The "question" answered here was asked by Virgil in III, 76–77, and the unexpectedness with which the reply finally comes, nearly seventy lines later and in a different canto, serves to remind us in a rather abrupt way that Manfred's lengthy account, as well as the philosophical explanation that begins this canto, has been an element of digression delaying the forward movement of the narrative, i.e., of the journey—which is immediately resumed in the next lines, with an introductory simile that blots out the figures of Manfred's group. Somehow we are reminded of the effect of Cato's words at the end of Canto II.

25–26. *San Leo . . . Noli . . . Bismantova:* These are names of towns that are accessible only with great difficulty. San Leo is located on an extremely steep and rugged hill in the mountainous district of Montefeltro, near San Marino. Noli is a town in

Liguria on the Gulf of Genova, which can be reached by land only through a steep descent from the mountains behind it. Bismantova was a small town on a steep, flat-topped mountain of the same name, about twenty miles south of Reggio. In the Middle Ages it was strongly fortified and could be reached only by a single tortuous path; now only the bare mountain remains.

The levels and precipices of Purgatory are also accessible only with difficulty, but the difficulty is of a different sort, which Dante explains in the following lines.

27. *a man must fly:* The conception of the Pilgrim's journey to God in terms of "flight" is one of the important metaphors of the *Comedy*. Although he is still weighed down by the gravity of sin and unable to fly at this point, the Pilgrim begins to feel the need and the desire to do so. Finally, after being cleansed of his sins in the Earthly Paradise, he, in the company of Beatrice, will ascend, swiftly and effortlessly, from sphere to heavenly sphere.

37. *do not change your course:* The original *nessun tuo passo caggia* is untranslatable ("let not one step fall"?). There are three possible guesses: "do not slow down," or "do not turn back," or "do not turn left or right." I choose the last because it is the only one that answers the Pilgrim's question to his guide in the preceding line.

42. *mid-quadrant to the center's point:* That is, the mountain slopes at an angle even steeper than forty-five degrees.

43–45. *I felt my strength:* The utter exhaustion of the Pilgrim during his first climb, understandable in itself (unlike Virgil he is burdened by the weight of his body), serves, perhaps, to prepare the way for the description of the Indolent, whom the Pilgrim will encounter shortly, when he has reached the next level of the Antepurgatory.

61–75

The Pilgrim's surprise is occasioned by his seeing the sun rising to the north. Accustomed to the celestial phenomena of the Northern Hemisphere, he would naturally expect to find the sun to the south. Virgil pedantically explains that, since it is now March, the sun is in Aries. However, if it were June, when the sun is in Castor and Pollux, the Pilgrim could expect to see the sun even farther to the north, near the Big and Little Bears.

In order to facilitate the Pilgrim's comprehension, Virgil then asks him to imagine the globe with Jerusalem and Purgatory in their respective hemispheres. Since they are located directly opposite one another, they would share the same horizon, the line along which the sun travels; hence, if from Jerusalem in the Northern Hemisphere the sun appears to move from left to right, then from the mountain of Purgatory in the Southern Hemisphere it must of necessity appear to move from right to left.

Just as the Pilgrim's eyes move from "the shoreline far below" (55) to the sun, so our attention is directed from the earth heavenward, toward the sun and the stars. And the mention of Zion (68 ff.) or Jerusalem is another reminder of the goal of the Pilgrim's journey: the heavenly Jerusalem.

61. *Castor and Pollux:* The constellation of Gemini. The two were twin brothers hatched from the same egg after Leda was visited by the god Jupiter in the form of a swan. When the twins died Jupiter placed them in the heavens, among the stars.

72. *Phaëton's chariot:* The sun. Having gained permission from his father, Apollo, to guide the chariot of the sun, Phaëton lost control of the horses. To prevent a catastrophe Jupiter struck down Phaëton with a thunderbolt. Dante refers to the story again in *Inf.* XVII, 107; *Purg.* XXIX, 118–20; and *Par.* XXXI, 125.

In this reference to Phaëton, as in the reference earlier to the Gemini, we have illustrations of Dante's didactic use of mythical figures. The apotheosis of Castor and Pollux, as well as the privileged position that they enjoy "in the company of that great mirror" (62), i.e., near the sun, serves to remind us of the goal of the Pilgrim's journey and his potential success. On the other hand, the allusion to the failure of Phaëton functions as a dire reminder of the catastrophic end that awaits those who fail to keep to that "lofty path" (72).

94–96. *you have arrived at the road's end:* Only at the journey's end will the Christian heart find rest.

98–99. *But, probably:* The sardonic, lazy Belacqua with just a few words seeks to counteract the effect of Virgil's optimistic, encouraging words to the Pilgrim; there is also humor in the contrast between Virgil's long-winded and painstaking "scientific" explanations (and the Pilgrim's equally erudite response) and the appallingly indolent, *terre-à-terre* speech of Belacqua.

119–120. *Is it quite clear to you by now:* Belacqua is openly mocking Virgil's erudite discourse.

123. *Belacqua:* A Florentine lute-maker and friend of Dante's, famous for his indolence; indeed, not only his posture here, not only the sentiments he expresses, but also his laconic speech accord well with the laziness for which he was well known.

It is interesting to note that of the first two friends whom the Pilgrim meets in Purgatory, Casella is a musician and Belacqua a maker of musical instruments.

133–35. *Prayers could:* Again, the theme of intercession (cf. III, 140–41); this time, however, the doctrine is made more specific, as Belacqua states that only prayers from a heart in the state of grace can be effective in helping the souls in Purgatory.

138–39. *Heaven's highest point:* Since the beginning of the canto, the sun has reached the meridian of Purgatory, which would make the time there noon. Morocco, for Dante part of the westernmost area of human habitation, would be experiencing dusk (6:00 P.M.), so that night would just be setting foot there (see note to II, 1–6).

CANTO V

THE PILGRIM LEAVES behind the souls of the Indolent and is following in his guide's footsteps when, suddenly, he turns to look back: one of the group has discovered the Pilgrim's shadow and is calling it to the attention of the others. Virgil upbraids him for lagging behind and warns him against losing sight of his true goal. As they continue upward, they encounter a group of souls chanting the *Miserere*. They are the third class of the Late Repentant: those who died a violent death but managed to repent in their final moments. The first soul to come forward and speak is Jacopo del Cassero of Fano, who tells how he was ambushed and left to bleed to death in a swamp. Next comes Buonconte of Montefeltro. At his death there ensued a struggle between the powers of good and evil for his soul; since he had uttered the name of Mary with his dying breath and shed a tear of true repentance, the heavenly faction prevailed and bore his soul off to Paradise. But a demon took possession of his corpse and played havoc with it: he conjured up a storm and sent the mortal remains plummeting down the raging and swollen river channels. Finally La Pia steps forth and gently asks Dante to remember her.

I had already parted from those shades,
   following in the footsteps of my guide,
   when one of them back there, pointed and called: *3*

"That soul climbing behind the other one!
   Look! To his left no light is shining through!
   He seems to walk as if he were alive!"   *6*

Hearing these words, I turned around and saw
   souls staring in amazement at my form,
   at me alone—and at the broken light.   *9*

"What is it that has caught your interest so
   and makes you lag behind?" my master asked.
   "What do you care, if they are whispering?   *12*

Keep up with me and let the people talk!
   Be like a solid tower whose brave height
   remains unmoved by all the winds that blow;   *15*

the man who lets his thoughts be turned aside
    by one thing or another, will lose sight
    of his true goal, his mind sapped of its strength."   18

What could I say except: "I'm coming now"?
    I said it, and my face took on the color
    that makes a man deserve to be excused.   21

Meanwhile, across the slope ahead of us,
    people were passing, chanting *Miserere,*
    singing the psalm in alternating parts.   24

But when they noticed that the rays of light
    did not shine through my human form, they changed
    their chanting to a drawn-out, breathless "Ohhh!"   27

Then two of them, dispatched as messengers,
    came running up and started to implore:
    "We pray you, please tell us about yourselves."   30

My master answered them: "You may return,
    bearing the news to those who sent you here
    that this man's body is true flesh and blood;   33

if they were stunned, as I suppose they were,
    because he casts a shadow—now they know,
    and it could profit them to honor him."   36

I never saw a meteor at night
    cut through the tranquil air, or bolts of light
    flash through the cloudy August sky at dusk,   39

as quickly as they rushed back to their group;
    then all together they wheeled round and rushed
    toward us like a full-charging cavalry.   42

"Oh look at all those souls pressing toward us,"
    the Poet said; "each one will have his plea;
    listen to them, but move on as you do."   45

"O soul," they cried, "you there, moving toward bliss
    clothed in the body you were born with, stop,
    just for a moment, look at us and see   48

if you know anyone among us here,
    so as to bring back news of him to earth.
    Oh, wait! Where are you going? Oh, please stop!   51

We are all souls who met a violent death,
    and we were sinners to our final hour;
    but then the light of Heaven lit our minds,   54

and penitent and pardoning, we left
    that life at peace with God, Who left our hearts
    with longing for the holy sight of Him."   57

I said: "I see your faces, but cannot
    recognize one. But, O souls, born for bliss,
    if there is some way I can please you now,   60

tell me, and I will do so—by that peace
    which I go searching for while following
    from world to world so great a guide as this."   63

One soul replied: "We need no oath from you;
    all of us here know you will keep your word,
    unless some lack of power thwarts your will.   66

Now, speaking for myself, I will plead first:
    if ever you should travel to the land
    between Romagna and the realm of Charles,   69

I beg you, be so gracious as to ask
    the souls in Fano to say prayers for me,
    that I may soon begin to purge my guilt.   72

I came from Fano, but the deep-cut wounds
    from which I saw my life's blood spilling out,
    were dealt me in the Antenori's land—   75

the land where I believed I was most safe.
    Azzo of Este had me killed (his hatred
    for me reached far beyond all reason's bounds).   78

If only I had fled toward Mira when
    at Oriaco they took me by surprise,
    I still would be with men who live and breathe;   81

instead, I ran into the swampy mire:
    the reeds entangled me; I fell, and there
    I watched a pool of blood fill from my veins."   84

Another soul said: "Oh, may the desire
    that draws you up the mountain be fulfilled;
    and you, please help me satisfy my own.   87

I am Buonconte, once from Montefeltro;
   no one, not even Giovanna, cares for me,
   and so, I walk ashamed among these souls."   90

I said: "What violence—or was it chance?—
   swept you so far away from Campaldin
   that no one ever found your burial place?"   93

He said: "Below the Casentino flows
   the river Archiano, which arises
   above the convent in the Apennines.   96

Beyond, it takes another name, and there
   I made my way, my throat an open wound,
   fleeing on foot, and bloodying the plain.   99

There I went blind. I could no longer speak,
   but as I died, I murmured Mary's name,
   and there I fell and left my empty flesh.   102

Now hear the truth. Tell it to living men:
   God's angel took me up, and Hell's fiend cried:
   'O you from Heaven, why steal what is mine?   105

You may be getting his immortal part—
   and won it for a measly tear, at that,
   but for his body I have other plans!'   108

You know how vapor gathers in the air,
   then turns to water when it has returned
   to where the cold condenses it as rain.   111

To that ill will, intent on evilness,
   he joined intelligence and, by that power
   within his nature, stirred up mist and wind,   114

until the valley, by the end of day,
   from Pratomagno to the mountain chain,
   was fogbound. With dense clouds he charged the sky: 117

the saturated air turned into rain;
   water poured down, and what the sodden ground
   rejected filled and overflowed the deepest   120

gullies, whose spilling waters came to join
   and form great torrents rushing violently,
   relentlessly, to reach the royal stream.   123

Close to its mouth the raging Archiano
    discovered my cold body—sweeping it
    into the Arno, loosening the cross   126

I'd made upon my breast in final pain;
    it dragged me to its banks, along its bed,
    then swathed me in the shroud of all its spoils."   129

"Oh, please, when you are in the world again,
    and are quite rested from your journey here,"
    a third soul, following on the second, said,   132

"Oh, please remember me! I am called Pia.
    Siena gave me life, Maremma death,
    as he knows who began it when he put   135

his gem upon my finger, pledging faith."

NOTES

1. *those shades:* The souls of the Indolent surrounding Belacqua.

3. *when one of them back there, pointed and called:* The reader may well wonder how the Pilgrim, having just turned his back on the souls of the Indolent, could have noticed the gesture here indicated. Evidently, Dante the Pilgrim, on hearing their words of amazement, turns around to face them and sees a finger pointing at him; Dante the Narrator takes advantage of his omniscience to predicate the gesture at the appropriate moment in the narrative flow.

9–21. *at me alone—and at the broken light:* The souls left behind, having realized that the Pilgrim must be a living man because of the shadow cast by his body, focus their attention upon him. The Pilgrim, too easily impressed by the interest shown in him, allows himself once more to forget the importance of moving ahead in his journey—until the reproachful platitudes of Virgil bring a blush to his face.

23–24. *Miserere:* The opening word of Psalm 50, a prayer that asks God for forgiveness of sins and the purification of the soul of the sinner. Each group of souls in Antepurgatory and Purgatory proper will have its own particular prayer, with the exception of the Excommunicated and the Indolent.

29. *came running:* In contrast to the appropriately sluggish movement of Canto IV, which treated of the souls of the Indolent, this canto is fast and busy. The speed that will be everywhere apparent reflects, somehow, the violent deaths and hurried last repentances of the souls in this circle. The three speakers in the canto follow each other in rapid succession, with little or no intervention on the part of the narrator between their speeches.

37–42. *I never saw a meteor:* Note the images of speed and violence: meteors, lightning, and a cavalry charge! This passage also serves as preparation for the violent storm that is to sweep off Buonconte's body later on in this canto (106–29).

45. *but move on as you do:* Virgil, if not the Pilgrim, has learned Cato's lesson: do not waste time (see II, 120–23).

51. *Oh, wait! Where are you going? Oh, please stop!:* The language of the original Italian, "deh, perchè vai? deh, perchè non t'arresti?" communicates something of the relentless rhythm of a moving train. Actually, it is the Pilgrim and his guide who are relentless in their forward movement.

64. *One soul replied:* The speaker, who is not named in the canto, is Jacopo del Cassero. In 1296, as podestà of Bologna, he opposed the designs of the powerful and ruthless Azzo VIII of Este. In 1298, while en route to Milan to assume the office of podestà there, Jacopo was set upon and brutally murdered by Azzo's henchmen at Oriago, a town on the river Brenta between Venice and Padova. He is the first of the three speakers in this canto who died a violent death.

68–69. *to the land:* Jacopo's birthplace, Fano, was located in the March of Ancona, south of Romagna and north of the Kingdom of Naples, which was ruled by Charles of Anjou.

70–72. *I beg you, be so gracious:* Once again we are reminded of the power of intercessory prayer to help the souls in Purgatory (cf. III, 141; IV, 133–35).

75–76. *the Antenori's land:* Padova, where Jacopo thought he would be safe. The Padovans, according to legend, were descendants of Antenor, the son of Priam, who betrayed Troy to the Greeks and who, it was believed, later founded the city of

Padova. Dante names an entire division of Cocytus in Hell after him for his act of heinous treachery (*Inf.* XXXII, 88).

77. *Azzo of Este:* Azzo VIII of Este, Marquis of Este, and Lord of Ferrara, Modena, and Reggio, who died in 1308. It was believed that he murdered his own father, Obizzo, suffocating him with a pillow. Dante mentions him in an invective against degenerate princes in *De vulg.* I, xii, 38, and probably is referring to him in *Inf.* XII, 111 and XVIII, 56.

79. *Mira:* A small town between Oriago and Padova, located on a canal fed by the Brenta.

88. *I am Buonconte, once from Montefeltro:* The son of Guido of Montefeltro (*Inf.* XXVII). In 1289 he led the forces of the Ghibellines of Arezzo against the Florentine Guelphs in the battle of Campaldino. Guido's side suffered defeat and he was slain. His body was never found.

89. *no one, not even Giovanna:* The widow of Buonconte was named Giovanna, and "no one" probably refers to the daughter and brother who survived him.

95. *Archiano:* A tributary of the Arno.

104-108. *God's angel took me up, and Hell's fiend cried:* There is a similar struggle between the powers of good and evil for the soul of Guido of Montefeltro, Buonconte's father (*Inf.* XXVII). It is impossible to overlook the didactic comparison that Dante draws by juxtaposing these two figures: Guido in his later years took what he thought to be the necessary steps to assure his salvation but unfortunately overlooked the one thing that was truly necessary—sincere repentance. Buonconte, on the other hand, though he waited until the last possible moment to repent, was saved because he shed tears of true contrition. The son's salvation mocks the vain efforts of the father.

116. *Pratomagno:* A locale near Arezzo on the Arno, now called Pratovecchio.

130-36

Oh, please, when you are in the world again: The speaker is probably Pia de' Tolomei of Siena, wife of Nello della Pietra de' Pannocchieschi (see Lisini). Though Pia, unlike the first two speakers, does not give us any details, early commentators hint that her jealous husband suspected her of adultery and had her thrown from a window to her death.

Pia's brief speech shows her to be well bred, gentle, and considerate, as she asks the Pilgrim to remember her only after he has rested from his long journey. Her nobility and her elegance of speech, manifest in these few lines, recall the figure of Francesca of Rimini (*Inf.* V), if for no other reason than the fact that she is the first and only other woman allowed to speak to the Pilgrim thus far in the *Divine Comedy*. While Pia's speech is extremely short—her whole life summed up in a single decasyllable! (134)—Francesca is given to verbosity. Take, for example, Pia's simple, unpretentious assertion, "Siena gave me life." When Francesca (*Inf.* V, 97–99) informs the Pilgrim of her birthplace, it is in almost epic strains:

> The place where I was born lies on the shore
> where the river Po with its attendant streams
> descends to seek its final resting place.

It is precisely Francesca's constant self-assertion, her hunger for attention and appreciation, that stands out so strikingly against the tender self-effacement of La Pia. The contrast in the dispositions of these two women is further underlined and given a moral dimension by their positions in Hell and Purgatory, respectively. For a more detailed analysis of the character of Francesca da Rimini see Musa (1974), pp. 19–35.

134. *Siena . . . Maremma:* As with the other speeches of this canto, even the brief words of Pia contain references to geographical areas. The frequent and often detailed references to earthly geography throughout this canto underline the attachment still felt by the dwellers in the Antepurgatory to the scenes of their life on earth.

CANTO VI

THE SOULS OF those who have died by violence continue to press eagerly upon the Pilgrim. Among them Dante recognizes Benincasa of Laterina; Guccio Tarlati of Pietramala; Federigo Novello; Farinata, son of Marzucco degli Scornigiani; Count Orso of Mangona; and Pierre de la Brosse of Turenne. As he frees himself from this encumbering crowd of shades, the Pilgrim asks Virgil about the power of prayer to affect the will of Heaven. Virgil gives a partial explanation and tells the Pilgrim that he will have to wait until Beatrice gives him a more comprehensive elucidation of the matter. Noting a figure seated in silence not far away, Virgil and the Pilgrim go up to him to ask directions; upon learning that Virgil is a Mantuan by birth, the stranger embraces him. It is the shade of Sordello. At this point there is a break in the action of the poem, and Dante inveighs at length against the evil and corruption of Italy.

The loser, when a game of dice breaks up,
   despondent, often lingers there as he,
   learning the hard way, replays all his throws.   3

The crowd leaves with the winner: some in front,
   some tugging at him from behind, the rest
   close to his side beg to be recognized.   6

He keeps on going, listening to them all;
   the ones who get a handout will not push,
   and this is his protection from the crowd.   9

I was that man caught in a begging throng,
   turning my face toward one and then the next,
   buying my way out with my promises.   12

I saw the Aretine who met his death
   at the revengeful hand of Ghin di Tacco;
   I saw that soul who drowned giving pursuit.   15

I saw with hands outstretched, imploring me,
   Federigo Novello, and the Pisan, too,
   whose death inspired good Marzucco's strength.   18

I saw Count Orso, and I saw that soul
    torn from its body, so he said, by hate
    and envy—not for any wrong he did: 21

Pierre de la Brosse, I mean. And while still here
    on earth, the Lady of Brabant might well
    take care lest she end up in fouler flock.   24

Once I had freed myself from all those shades
    who prayed only that others pray for them
    and thus quicken their way to bliss, I said: 27

"It seems to me that somewhere in your verse,
    you, O my Light, deny explicitly
    the power of prayer to bend the laws of Heaven;   30

yet these souls ask precisely for such prayers.
    Does this, then, mean their hopes are all in vain?
    Or have I failed to understand your words?"   33

And he: "What I once wrote means what it says;
    yet, if you think about it carefully,
    you must see that their hopes are not deceived.   36

High justice would in no way be debased
    if ardent love should cancel instantly
    the debt these penitents must satisfy.   39

The words of mine you cite apply alone
    to those whose sins could not be purged by prayer,
    because their prayers had no access to God.   42

Do not try to resolve so deep a doubt;
    wait until she shall make it clearer—she,
    the light between truth and intelligence.   45

You understand me: I mean Beatrice,
    she will appear upon this mountain top;
    you will behold her smiling in her bliss."   48

I said: "My lord, let us make greater haste:
    I'm not as tired as I was before;
    and look! The mountain casts a shadow now."   51

"As long as daylight lasts we shall move on,
    climbing as far as possible," he said,
    "but things are not the way you think they are.   54

Before you reach the top you'll see the sun
  come out from where the slope is hiding him,
  preventing you from casting any shade.   57

But see that spirit stationed over there,
  all by himself, the one who looks at us;
  he will show us the quickest way to go."   60

We made our way toward him. (O Lombard soul,
  how stately and disdainful you appeared,
  what majesty was in your steady gaze!)   63

He did not say a word to us, but let
  us keep on moving up toward him, while he
  was watching like a couchant lion on guard.   66

But Virgil went straight up to him and asked
  directions for the best way to ascend.
  The shade ignored the question put to him,   69

asking of us, instead, where we were born
  and who we were. My gentle guide began:
  "Mantua . . ." And the other, until then   72

all self-absorbed, sprang to his feet and came
  toward him: "O Mantuan, I am Sordello
  of your own town"—and the two shades embraced.   75

(Ah, slavish Italy, the home of grief,
  ship without pilot caught in a raging storm,
  no queen of provinces—whorehouse of shame!   78

How quick that noble soul was to respond
  to the mere sound of his sweet city's name,
  by welcoming his fellow citizen—   81

while, now, no one within your bounds knows rest
  from war, and those enclosed by the same wall
  and moat, even they are at each other's throats!   84

O wretched Italy, search all your coasts,
  probe to your very center: can you find
  within you any part that is at peace?   87

What matter if Justinian repaired
  the bridle—if the saddle's empty now!
  The shame would have been less if he had not.   90

CANTO VI / 59

You priests who should pursue your holiness,
  remembering what God prescribes for you,
  let Caesar take the saddle as he should—   93

see how this beast has grown viciously wild,
  without the rider's spurs to set her straight,
  since you dared take the reins into your hands!   96

O German Albert, you abandon her,
  allowing her, ungoverned, to run wild.
  You should have been astride her saddle-bow!   99

Let a just judgment fall down from the stars
  upon your house: one unmistakable
  and strange enough to terrify your heir!   102

You and your sire, whom greed for greater wealth
  holds back up there, have let this come to pass:
  the garden of the Empire is laid waste.   105

Come see the Cappelletti, callous heart,
  see the Monaldi, the Montecchi ruined,
  the Filippeschi fearful of their fate.   108

Come, heartless one, come see your noblemen
  who suffer; help them heal their wounds; come see
  how safe it is to dwell in Santafior.   111

Come see your city, Rome, in mourning now,
  widowed, alone, lamenting night and day:
  "My Caesar, why have you abandoned me?"   114

Come see how people love each other now!
  If you cannot be moved to pity us,
  then come and feel the shame your name has earned!   117

O Jove Supreme, crucified here on earth
  for all mankind, have I the right to ask
  if Your just eyes no longer look on us?   120

Or is this part of a great plan conceived
  in Your deep intellect, to some good end
  that we are powerless to understand?   123

For all the towns of Italy are filled
  with tyrants: any dolt who plays the role
  of partisan can pass for a Marcellus.   126

Florence, my Florence! How happy you must be
    with this digression, for you're not involved—
    thank your resourceful citizens for that!   *129*

Some men have justice in their hearts; they *think*
    before they shoot their judgments from the bow—
    your people merely shoot off words about it!   *132*

Some men think twice when offered public post;
    your citizens accept before they're asked,
    shouting, "I'll gladly sacrifice myself!"   *135*

Rejoice, I say to you, you have good cause,
    rich as you are, so wise, knowing such peace!
    The facts bear out the truth of what I say.   *138*

Athens and Lacedaemon, still well known
    for ancient laws and civil discipline,
    showed but the faintest signs of order then   *141*

compared to you, who plan so cleverly
    that by the time November is half done
    the laws spun in October are in shreds.   *144*

How often within memory have you changed
    coinage and customs, laws and offices,
    and members of your body politic!   *147*

Think back, and if you see the truth, you'll see
    that you are like a woman, very sick,
    who finds no rest on her soft, sumptuous bed,   *150*

but turns and tosses to escape her pain.)

NOTES

1–9. *The loser, when a game of dice breaks up:* As Dante the
Pilgrim walks away from Jacopo, Buonconte, and La Pia, he is
surrounded by souls, each of whom wishes to detain him and
gain that moment of recognition that would enable this living
man who travels through their realm to request prayer among
the living for him. Dante compares this scene to the aftermath
of a dice game, which finds the winner elbowing his way
through a crowd of newly acquired friends, whom he satisfies
with a coin here and a coin there, thus clearing a path for himself through the crowd. And as he makes his way, he seems to

be dealing out promises as the winner might share his takings until he can break free from the crowd.

Dante has obviously chosen the metaphor of a game of dice only in order to exploit the comparison between the winner and the Pilgrim; the loser in this assumed game has no role to play in the subsequent scene with the crowd outside. Why, then, does Dante not only mention the loser first (in itself quite understandable as a means to get him out of the way) but dwell upon his reactions, and so sympathetically that the reader feels almost invited to remain behind with him?

13. *the Aretine:* Benincasa da Laterina was a jurist from Arezzo. Ghin di Tacco (14), motivated by a desire to vindicate the death sentence given to a close relative, perhaps his father or brother, entered Benincasa's courtroom in disguise, murdered him, and escaped, carrying with him the judge's head. Ghin di Tacco is mentioned by Boccaccio in the *Decameron* (X, 2) as an infamous thief and highwayman.

15. *that soul who drowned:* Guccio Tarlati da Pietramala died by drowning in the Arno following the battle of either Campaldino or Montaperti. There is some confusion among historians and commentators as to whether the Ghibelline Guccio was pursuing his enemy or being pursued at the time of his death.

17. *Federigo Novello, and the Pisan, too:* Son of Count Guido Novello, Federigo was killed in 1291 by one of the Guelphs, Bostoli d'Arezzo, in a battle that took place in the Casentino. The Pisan is Farinata, a doctor of law and son of Messer Marzucco degli Scornigiani of Pisa.

18. *good Marzucco's strength:* This is supposedly a reference to the fortitude of a Francescan Friar Minor (Marzucco) who demonstrated his "strength" by forgiving the murderer of his son, Farinata, "the Pisan" mentioned in the preceding verse (17). There are, however, no reliable records supporting the event that Dante seems to be alluding to here.

19. *Count Orso:* The son of Napoleone dell'Acerbaia, Orso was viciously murdered by his cousin Alberto di Mangona. Alberto's father, Alessandro, and Napoleone were brothers who killed each other. Both are punished among the traitors in Caina (*Inf.* XXXII, 55–58).

22–24. *Pierre de la Brosse:* Surgeon and chancellor to Philip III of France, Pierre was falsely accused of treachery by Philip's second wife, Mary of Brabant (23), and was hanged in 1278.

According to a popular account, Pierre was charged with having tried (unsuccessfully) to seduce the queen. It is more likely that he was accused of corresponding with Alfonso X, who was engaged in war with Philip at the time, and that the incriminating letters were forged on the queen's instructions. In any event, it is clear from verses 23–24 that Dante considers the queen as responsible for Pierre's death, and therefore in danger of ending up "in fouler flock" than Pierre—that is, in Hell.

24–48

Dante has already alluded several times to the power of intercessory prayer to help the souls in Purgatory (III, 141; IV, 133–35; V, 70–72). Here the Pilgrim raises the question of whether prayer actually has the power to bend the divine laws. His confusion stems from a passage in Virgil's *Aeneid* (VI, 373–76): Aeneas on his journey to Hades encounters the shade of his drowned steersman, Palinurus; he wishes to be conveyed across the river Styx, but passage is forbidden him since his body remains unburied. To his imprecations the Sibyl responds:

unde haec o Palinure tibi tam dira cupido?
tu Stygias inhumatus aquas amnemque severum
Eumenidium aspicies ripamve iniussus adibis?
desine fata deum flecti sperare precando.

Whence, Palinurus, this wild longing of yours?
Shall you, unburied, view the Stygian waters and
The Furies' stern river, and unbidden, draw near the bank?
Stop dreaming that heaven's decrees may be turned aside by prayer.

In an attempt to assuage the Pilgrim's doubts, Virgil explains that prayer disunited from God—i.e., the prayers of the damned, of pagans, of souls not in the state of grace—are inefficacious. However, "ardent love," prayer offered from a heart in the state of grace, can satisfy in a single moment, without changing divine justice, the debt of penance owed by the souls in the Antepurgatory.

One may wonder why the Pilgrim should have been disturbed by the ideas expressed in the *Aeneid:* why should he expect the pagan Virgil to have a true understanding of the efficacy of Christian prayers? Perhaps the Pilgrim remembers Virgil's words in the *Inferno* describing the deep impression made upon him by the Harrowing of Hell, which he had been able to witness soon after his arrival in Limbo. It is this Virgil, not the author of the *Aeneid,* who might now understand the difference between pagan and Christian prayers, and the Pilgrim would have been tactfully inviting Virgil to elaborate upon the development that had taken place in his understanding.

45. *the light between truth and intelligence:* Beatrice, standing, as it were, "between" Truth (the meaning of prayer) and Intellect (the Pilgrim's mind), will be able to illuminate fully for him the true meaning of prayer. The matter involves grace, which goes beyond Virgil's understanding.

49. *let us make greater haste:* The name of Beatrice has served as a whip to speed the Pilgrim on.

51–57. *and look! The mountain casts a shadow now:* Though it is only midafternoon, the Pilgrim's body cannot intercept the sun's rays; he and his guide are climbing the eastern slope of the mountain, which is lost in shadow. Thus, when the two come upon Sordello a moment later, the Pilgrim will be lacking the distinguishing mark of a living man that made him the center of attraction for the three previous groups of souls. And Sordello will all but ignore his presence.

58. *that spirit:* This is the spirit of Sordello of Goito. An adventurer and a poet, Sordello was born in the town of Goito, near Mantua, about 1200. Although relatively little is known about his life, it is likely that the wrath he incurred as a result of several episodes with women necessitated his leaving Italy. While staying with the Strasso family at Ceneda (some fifteen miles from Treviso), he secretly married Otta, a lady of the family, and fled with her to Treviso in 1227. There, he placed himself under the protection of Ezzelino III da Romano, whose sister, Cunizza, he had previously helped to abduct for political reasons. However, he soon formed a liaison with Cunizza; when Ezzelino discovered the affair in 1229, Sordello was forced to flee Treviso. After travelling to Spain and Portugal, he went to Provence and entered the service of Charles of Anjou. With Charles, he went to Italy in 1265 as part of the expedition to take possession of the kingdom of Sicily from

Manfred. Sordello shared in the distribution of Apulian fiefs made by Charles after his hold on the kingdom had become solidified. Nothing is known of Sordello's death, although his fiefs were reassigned in August 1269. For the life and works of Sordello, see Boni.

Dante's conception of Sordello as a political analyst probably derives from Sordello's political and moral poetry (all, incidentally, written in Provençal), particularly the *planh* or lament over the death of Blacatz, in which the shortcomings and vices of eight contemporary rulers are condemned with fierce indignation. It is surely this *planh* which accounts for the presence of Sordello in the *Divine Comedy,* and the role assigned to him in Canto VII of presenting the Princes in the Valley. For the text of the *planh* with English translation and commentary, see Bowra.

59. *all by himself:* Sordello is the first solitary soul that we encounter in the Antepurgatory. His "aloneness" is stressed in the original (*sola, soletta*), and his physical solitude is reinforced in the next tercet by the suggestion of inner alienation.

A number of commentators seem disinclined to respect this solitude of Sordello. Some wish to attach him to the group we have just seen of those who died a violent death; others, looking ahead, align him with the group of the Princes in the Valley of Canto VII. But what would it mean, in Sordello's case, to "belong" to this group or that? According to the story here told, according to the staging, we have been made to feel that, before catching sight of the figure of Sordello, the Pilgrim and his guide have left behind the last member of the vociferous and cohesive group gathered about Jacopo, Buonconte, and Pia. The mere existence, in the absence of any information about the historical Sordello after the year 1269, of a tradition that he died a violent death, the mere possibility that he may have come to belong to the *category* of those-who-died-a-violent-death, should not blur the clear onstage impression of splendid isolation that Dante the Poet has achieved.

As for the second group—that of the Princes in the Valley—the reader, impressed by the sight of Sordello's solitary figure in line 59, does not even know of their existence yet. To what extent this impression of his aloneness will give way to one of fusion will become evident when the princes appear (with whom, obviously, Sordello, who was no ruler, can have no "categorical" link).

While Virgil and the Pilgrim make their way toward Sordello, Dante the Poet, inspired by his memories, apostrophizes Sordello briefly. This discrete intervention prepares us for the poet's voice to be heard in the explosive, lengthy auctorial interruption that will occur a few lines later (85–151), when Dante inveighs against his native Italy.

62. *how stately and disdainful:* The description of Sordello in these terms may remind us of Farinata (*Inf.* X, 22–51), another "stately and disdainful" character associated with political strife. But the line that follows, together with this one, would rather remind us of the noble spirits of Limbo (*Inf.* IV, 112–14); of the two associations this is probably the more important, in view of the greeting that is about to take place.

66. *a couchant lion:* In Gen. 49:9 we find the phrase "requiescens accubuisti ut leo" ("He couches and couches as a lion"), which describes Judah, who will hold the sceptre until it comes to the one to whom it rightfully belongs—that is, to David. Both Judah and David are, in this context, figures of Christ, who will come to rule the world. To associate Sordello with Judah by means of the lion is another way of announcing the coming of Christ—which is going to take place allegorically in the poem in the Valley of the Princes.

Ignoring Virgil's request for directions, Sordello asks the two travellers where they are from and who they are. At the sound of the name "Mantua," Sordello, who had been so aloof, so self-absorbed, leaps to his feet and embraces Virgil warmly; the memory of this gesture so moves Dante the Poet that, as the two characters are locked in their embrace, he begins the famous invective: "Ah, slavish Italy . . . !"—and narrative time stands still as we listen to his voice for the rest of the canto. In lines 72–73 of the narrative, Sordello had interrupted Virgil; in line 76 Dante the Poet interrupts the narrative itself. Now, whenever the Poet speaks in his own voice, there must be a suspension of the narrative; we have just seen a minor example of this (61–63), but here we have the most dramatic instance of this device to be found in the *Divine Comedy:* not only the length and intensity of the apostrophe but the shock of "the two shades embraced," followed by "Ah, slavish Italy . . . !" This is the only case where narrative time is forced to give way to auctorial time by the interruption of a brief, clear-cut action already in progress.

Dante has obviously invented the gesture of Sordello in order to exploit it the next moment to dramatic effect; in other words, it is there solely for the sake of his apostrophe. He needed to insert his description precisely at this point: it should precede Sordello's presentation of the Princes in the Valley (Canto VII), and it should be delivered in the "presence" of Sordello (i.e., with Sordello onstage), whom he had chosen because of his concern for political issues. Let it, then, be inspired by a movement on the part of Sordello, a movement of affection reminding Dante, by way of contrast, of the situation in strife-torn Italy.

But why should Sordello's simple, spontaneous gesture, showing a sentimental attachment to his hometown and his fellow citizens, inspire Dante's apostrophe—how could this "provincial" reaction inspire such a broad, complex description of Italy seen from the perspective of the shamefully disorganized empire? Is not the result disproportionate to the cause—has Dante not been more clever than judicious in his exploitation of the invented embrace? Not if we remember simply that Sordello's gesture is a sign of love. A gesture of no great import (if pure in its spontaneity), the expression of a feeling probably short-lived, but a sign nevertheless of the greatest force in the cosmos. It is as if for the moment, while he contrasts Sordello's action with the state of Italy, there exists for Dante only that force, Love, and the hideous lack of it. For Dante's use of narrative technique in this canto, see Musa (1974), pp. 85–109.

71–72. *My gentle guide began: / "Mantua . . . ":* What was Virgil about to say concerning Mantua? To Sayers (p. 115) Virgil is "doubtless about to quote the inscription on his tomb in Naples . . . which begins: *Mantua me genuit*—Mantua gave me birth." But can one really imagine that Virgil, in answer to a request for factual information, would recite the Latin words of his epitaph (if he knew them): "Mantua me genuit, Calabri rapuerere, tenet nunc Parthenope; cecini pascua rura duces"?

84. *are at each other's throats:* This is clearly meant to contrast with "they embraced each other" (75).

88. *Justinian:* Author of the celebrated sixth-century code of Roman law, the *Corpus iuris civilis,* the "bridle" of line 89. Justinian was emperor of Constantinople from 527 to 565 (cf. *Par.* VI, 12).

97. *German Albert:* Albert of Hapsburg was elected Emperor of the Romans in 1298. Because his coronation in Milan was delayed by affairs in Germany, Albert never came to Italy to bring unity and order. In 1308 he was assassinated by his nephew and was succeeded by Henry VII.

106–107. *the Cappelletti . . . the Monaldi, the Montecchi . . . the Filippeschi:* The Cappelletti, the anti-imperial (Guelph) party in Cremona, opposed the Montecchi (or Monticoli) faction, which had influence throughout Lombardy. By the end of the thirteenth century both parties had declined.

The Monaldi (Guelph) and the Filippeschi (Ghibelline) were two opposing families of Orvieto. The Filippeschi were expelled from the city in 1312.

111. *Santafior:* From the ninth century to 1300 Santafiora, located in the Sienese Maremma, belonged to the powerful Ghibelline Aldobrandeschi family, who were also known as the Counts of Santafiora. By Dante's time the Guelphs of Siena had managed to erode their power considerably.

118. *Jove Supreme:* Since the poet makes it a practice never to use explicitly the name of Christ except in the *Paradise,* here he uses the pagan approximation of the Christian concept he wishes to express.

126. *Marcellus:* Of the three Roman consuls by this name, the reference here is probably to Marcus Claudius Marcellus, a partisan of Pompey who loudly opposed Caesar and the empire. Cicero's *Pro Marcello* deals with the pardoning of Marcellus by Julius Caesar at the intercession of the senate. Marcellus was later murdered by one of his own attendants while in Greece.

139. *Athens and Lacedaemon:* Two Greek cities, Athens and Sparta, where, according to Justinian's *Institutiones,* civil law originated. The allusion is to the laws of Solon (Athens) and Lycurgus (Sparta).

CANTO VII

THE ACTION IS renewed as Virgil and Sordello conclude
their elaborate embrace. Upon learning that he has embraced
not merely a fellow Mantuan but Virgil, the very glory of the
Latin race, Sordello does him further homage. Virgil explains
to Sordello the nature and scope of his journey with the Pilgrim and asks to be shown the quickest way up the mountain.
Sordello volunteers his services as guide but remarks that it is
almost nightfall and that it is the law of Purgatory that no one
may ascend the mountain at night: the darkness of the shadows
afflicts the will with impotence. However, Sordello knows of a
good place to rest and suggests that they might spend the night
there. He leads the two poets to a ledge above the Valley of the
Princes, where they see the so-called Negligent Rulers, who
are singing the *Salve Regina.* From this vantage above the valley,
Sordello points out a number of the souls below: Rudolf of
Hapsburg; Henry VII of Luxembourg; Ottokar II, king of
Bohemia; Philip III of France; Henry the Fat of Navarre; Peter
III of Aragon; his son, Charles of Anjou; Henry III of England;
and William VII (Longsword).

When this glad, ceremonious embrace
    had been repeated several times, Sordello,
    stepping back, said, "Tell me, who are you two?"   *3*

"Before those souls worthy to climb to God
    were taken to this mountain by His grace,
    my bones were buried by Octavian.   *6*

I am Virgil. The reason I lost Heaven
    was through no other fault than lack of faith."
    This was the answer my guide gave that shade.   *9*

As one who suddenly beholds a thing
    incredible will first believe and then
    misdoubt and say: "It is—it cannot be!"   *12*

so seemed Sordello. Then he bent his head
    and, this time, reverently, turned to embrace
    my master as a vassal does his lord.   *15*

"O glory of the Latin race," he said,
  "you who did prove the power of our tongue,
  O deathless excellence of my own land,   *18*

what merit or what grace grants me this sight?
  Tell me, if I am worthy of your words,
  are you from Hell and, if so, from what ward?"   *21*

"Through all the circles of the realm of grief
  have I come here," he said. "A heavenly power
  showed me this road, and with its aid I come.   *24*

Not what I did, but what I did not do
  cost me the sight of that high Sun you seek
  whose meaning was revealed to me too late.   *27*

There is a place down there made sorrowful
  by darkness of its untormented grief:
  no shrieks of pain are heard, but hopeless sighs.   *30*

I dwell with infant souls of innocence
  bit off from life by death before the sin
  that they were born with could be washed away;   *33*

I dwell with those who could not clothe themselves
  in the three holy virtues but, unstained,
  knew all the rest, and practiced all of them.   *36*

But if you know, and are allowed to tell,
  how can we find the quickest way to reach
  the place where Purgatory truly starts?"   *39*

"Since we are not restricted to one spot,
  being free to roam around and up," he said,
  "I'll be your guide as far as I may climb.   *42*

But, see, the day is coming to an end;
  at night it is forbidden to ascend,
  so we should think of some good place to rest.   *45*

Off to the right here is a group of souls;
  if you allow me, I shall take you there;
  I think you will take pleasure meeting them."   *48*

"What do you mean?" my guide said, "If a soul
  started to climb at night, would he be stopped,
  or would he simply find he could not move?"   *51*

Sordello drew his finger along the ground
   answering, "Look! After the sun has set
   you could not go a step beyond this line.   54

There's nothing that prevents our going up
   except the darkness of the shadows: this,
   alone, afflicts the will with impotence.   57

We can, indeed, go *down* the slope and roam
   as far around the mountain as we wish,
   as long as the horizon locks out day."   60

My lord, amazed by what he heard, replied:
   "In that case, take us to the place you said,
   where we would find a pleasurable rest."   63

We started on our way, and soon I saw
   a hollow in the mountain slope, just like
   the hollow that a valley makes on earth.   66

"Now we will go," the shade announced to us,
   "to where the mountain folds into a lap;
   there we will wait until the new day comes."   69

A winding path that was not very steep
   led to a point upon the hollow's rim
   where the side sloped to less than half its height.   72

Think of fine silver, gold, cochineal, white lead,
   Indian wood, glowing and deeply clear,
   fresh emerald the instant it is split—   75

the brilliant colors of the grass and flowers
   within that dale would outshine all of these,
   as nature naturally surpasses art.   78

But nature had not only painted there:
   the sweetness of a thousand odors fused
   in one unknown, unrecognizable.   81

I heard *Salve Regina;* sitting there
   upon the grass and flowers I saw souls
   hidden till then below the valley's rim.   84

"Please do not ask me," said our Mantuan guide,
   "to lead you down to where you see those souls,
   until the sinking sun has found its nest;   87

from here it is much easier to see
    the faces and the movements of them all
    than if you were among them there below.   *90*

The one who sits the highest and who looks
    as if he left undone what was to do,
    and does not join the others in their song,   *93*

was Rudolf, Emperor, who could have cured
    the wounds that were the death of Italy—
    it will be long before she lives again!   *96*

The one who seems to comfort him once ruled
    over that land whose waters flow into
    the Moldau to the Elbe to the sea: *99*

Ottokar—more respected as a babe
    than Wenceslaus, his bearded son, is now,
    feasting on lechery and idleness.   *102*

That snub-nosed figure in close conference
    with the kind-looking person at his side,
    dishonoring the lily, died in flight.   *105*

Look at him there, see how he beats his breast;
    look at the other soul, cradling his cheek
    within his palm, sighing. Father-in-law   *108*

and father of the Plague of France they are;
    they know about his dissolute, foul life,
    and that is why they feel such piercing grief.   *111*

That sturdy-looking soul seated beside
    the big-nosed one, singing in tune with him,
    was girded with the cord of every good.   *114*

If only that young man behind him there
    had lived to rule a longer time, indeed,
    true merit would have flowed from cup to cup— *117*

as did not happen with the other heirs.
    Now James and Frederick possess his realms,
    but neither got the better heritage.   *120*

Not often does the sap of virtue rise
    to all the branches. This is His own gift,
    and we can only beg that He bestow it.   *123*

My words apply to him with the big nose
    as well as Peter there, who sings with him
    on whose account Provence and Puglia grieve.   *126*

As much as this seed's plant is less than he,
    just so much more than Margaret and Beatrix
    can Constance boast her husband's excellence.   *129*

And see Henry of England sitting there
    all by himself, king of the simple life
    whose branches bear him better fruit by far.   *132*

The one who sits below them on the ground
    and who looks up at them is Marquis William,
    whose war with Alessandria has made   *135*

all Montferrat and Canavese weep.

NOTES

2. *repeated several times:* The Italian says literally, "three and four times." The reader must wait until the end of the invective against Italy to learn of the extraordinarily effusive nature of Sordello's embrace—which inspired the invective.

3. *you two:* Sordello initially addresses himself to both the Pilgrim and his guide, but after discovering the identity of Virgil, he will tend to forget about Dante's presence (see note to VI, 51–57).

4–9

Virgil answers for himself only, offering no information about his ward. He gives the time of his death and burial with reference to an important event in the history of salvation: the Harrowing of Hell. Up to the time of Christ's death, the souls of those who believed in the Messiah to come, unable to enter Heaven, were constrained to wait in Limbo. After He died, Christ descended into Hell and freed these souls, taking them with Him into Heaven. Virgil was not among this select group, and here he gives his lack of faith as the one and only reason for his loss of Heaven.

6. *Octavian:* The Emperor Augustus, the first of the Roman emperors (63 B.C.–A.D. 14).

12. *"It is — it cannot be":* This exclamation sets a tone of ambivalence, which will come to characterize the valley.

13–21

Sordello's greeting, his awe and reverence for Virgil, suggest that for him there are no higher values than those of art and earthly fame and glory. He does not respond to or even appear to hear the important information that Virgil offers regarding his loss of salvation!

16. *Latin race:* (*Latini,* "Latins.") General term for ancient and modern Italians who considered Latin their language.

21. *are you from Hell and, if so, from what ward?:* Sordello does not realize that Virgil had already anticipated and, as it were, answered both his questions (in verses 7–8). Evidently, when Sordello heard the electrifying words "I am Virgil," he must have stopped listening to the important words that followed.

As a result, Virgil's explicit answer in verses 28–36 comprises three tercets devoted to a second description of Limbo, which was already vividly described in *Inf.* IV. But here the picture is presented from the point of view of Virgil himself; it is the note of exile that Virgil sounds, anticipating the mood of the first evening hymn (see note to VII, 82), in which is concentrated the nostalgia of all the souls of the Antepurgatory. And, in fact, the Antepurgatory itself is a Limbo — though, thanks to the grace of God, a temporary one.

25–36. *Not what I did:* Whereas the inhabitants of all the other circles in Hell are punished for what they did, those of Limbo are punished for what they failed to do: acquire the three theological virtues of Faith, Hope, and Charity. Virgil proclaims the inefficacy of good works without grace: even innocent infants who have not been cleansed of the stain of Original Sin through baptism, and who therefore do not share in Christ's grace, must abide in Limbo. Thus, it is fitting that the suffering of the souls in Limbo is described in negative terms: not a torment but darkness, not shrieks but sighs.

40–45

Here we learn the general law of movement in Antepurgatory, where the souls have no assigned place (cf. *Aen.* VI,

672–75): during the day they may wander up and around, but darkness will limit all upward movement. Without the sun, the light of God's grace, there can be no movement in the direction of Paradise. (Cf. line 26, "that high Sun you seek," which serves to reinforce, in this canto, the identification of the sun with God.)

42. *I'll be your guide:* Though offering himself as guide, Sordello continues to address Virgil alone, as the original shows: "a guida mi t'accosto" (cf. also verse 47: "io ti merrò"). Sordello's indifference to the Pilgrim reflects, perhaps, his snobbishness, his interest in status.

49. *What do you mean:* Here Virgil, questioning Sordello, is cast in the role the Pilgrim ordinarily assumes with him—that of disciple. Virgil's question is also interesting in that it suggests his lack of attention to Sordello's immediately preceding statement, his suggestion that they proceed to join the group of souls nearby. Sordello had finished with the theme "limitations on the movements of the souls in Antepurgatory," but Virgil not only wishes to pursue it; he seems to dismiss Sordello's final words. "What do you mean?" refers only to the limitations on movement.
Virgil's refusal to keep up with the course of thoughts expressed by his interlocutor offers a parallel to Sordello's lack of attention to Virgil's words in verses 7–8 (see note to VII, 21).

52–53. *drew his finger along the ground:* This could easily remind the reader of the passage from the Gospel of John (8:6–8): "But Jesus, stooping down, began to write with his finger on the ground . . . and again, stooping down, he began to write on the ground." However, it is not too easy to understand what connection could exist between Sordello's explanatory gesture of tracing a line of geographical demarcation on the ground (beyond which the souls may not pass, except when it is light) and Christ's mysterious act of writing on the ground in the scene with the woman taken in adultery and her accusers. Singleton (1973, p. 144) quotes the same biblical passage but offers no explanation.
It is, perhaps, not impossible that we are expected to look ahead in John 8, after the scene with the adulteress has been concluded, when Christ says to the Pharisees in the Temple: "I

am the light of the world. He who follows me does not walk in darkness, but will have the light of life."

66. *the hollow that a valley makes on earth:* These words underline again the similarity between the Antepurgatory and our world—even to its geography.

73–81

Among all the descriptions in classical or medieval literature of the *locus amoenus,* this one is unique. The beautiful colors of the grass and flowers are praised, but in such a way that what we see is not grass and flowers but precious stones, metals, dyes and pigments, the sheen of exotic wood: products or raw materials of industry and the mechanic arts. And the natural fragrances of the various flowers can no longer be distinguished, having been already concentrated into a perfume. Thanks to the list of metaphors, we are offered artificial opulent beauty, not the pure beauty of nature: note that the brook is missing, and the breeze and leafy trees and singing birds; these images will be found in the description of the Earthly Paradise, at the summit of the mountain of Purgatory (Canto XXVIII).

74. *Indian wood, glowing and deeply clear:* For different interpretations of this verse ("indaco legno lucido e sereno") see Cook (p. 356) and Austin. The latter takes the word "legno" to mean *lychnis* (*lignus* in medieval Latin), a bright purple jewel mentioned by several authors, among whom is Pliny (*Nat. hist.* XXXVII, xxix, 103).

82. *Salve Regina:* This reference to a hymn being sung adds an acoustic impression to those of sight and smell—as well as an indication of the presence of the valley's inhabitants.

These inhabitants have been slow in making their appearance, and the first glimpse of them is brief and colorless. In verse 46, Sordello had announced the presence of a group of souls "Off to the right here"; in verse 64 he and his guests start on their way to meet the group; in verse 71 they reach a high point from which they may look down into the valley. First the sculptured beauty of the natural scene is depicted; then the words of the hymn are heard; then, after a second reference to the grass and flowers, the Pilgrim sees souls sitting on the grass as they sing. No graphic detail is offered; we are not invited to visualize them.

But the reader is, perhaps, invited to meditate on the words and the function of the familiar song they are singing. The Marian antiphon *Salve Regina* was one of the hymns intended for the service after vespers, so that, as we hear the anonymous souls singing it in the dusk of the valley, we are made to think in terms of the daily habits of a Christian community on earth. Moreover, since it is a prayer concerned with exile and pilgrimage, it establishes a liturgical bond between believers in this world, praying for salvation after death, and the souls in the valley, already dead, already saved, but longing for entrance into Heaven. The words that apply particularly well to both groups are: " . . . to thee we cry, poor banished children of Eve, to thee we send up our sighs, mourning and weeping in this *valley of tears* . . . and after this our exile, *show unto us the blessed fruit of they womb, Jesus*" (italics mine). Cf. note to *Purg.* VIII, 37.

88. *from here:* The slope from which the pilgrims survey the souls is reminiscent of the hillock in Elysium (*Aen.* VI, 674). There Anchises points out to Aeneas the figures in the dell below them: the illustrious men who will perform great deeds in the future, serving to establish and expand the Roman Empire. It is ironic that this scene from the *Aeneid* should serve as an inspiration for Sordello's picture, in which many of the figures have failed as rulers and have even contributed to the decay of the Holy Roman Empire.

91–136

Here Sordello begins his presentation of the Princes in the Valley. It is rather clear from certain references in his speech that the hymn *Salve Regina* continues to be sung while he describes and comments upon the worldly princes. But now, as Sordello beings to speak, the brief glimpse that had been afforded the reader of the mass of singers, the "Christian community," gives way to a series of close-ups of individuals, vividly presented and sharply distinguished. (In Canto VIII [7–24] they will once more melt into anonymity as the singing of their second hymn takes the foreground.)

Sordello's presentation of the princes is not the only instance in which a group of individuals are presented by name to the reader: one thinks immediately of the roll call of the great shades in Limbo (*Inf.* IV); one may also remember Canto V of the *Inferno* when the souls of the Lustful appear and Virgil identifies "more than a thousand" of the "knights and ladies of ancient times." If one compares the three cases in the order *Inf.* V, *Inf.* IV (where it is Virgil, the pagan, who introduces the damned souls), and *Purg.* VII (where Sordello, the Christian, presents the late-repentant Princes), one will note an increase in vividness of presentation. In *Inf.* V we are offered nothing more than a listing of names accompanied (perhaps) by comments; the reader does not feel that he actually "sees" Semiramis or Helen as the flock of the Lustful fly by in the dim air above. In Limbo, some visualization is allowed: against a great blaze of light the Pilgrim makes out four figures walking toward him, and sees Homer "with sword in hand / leading the three as if he were their master." He sees on the lustrous green "the Latian King, / with Lavinia, his daughter, by his side." He sees Caesar, "falcon-eyed and fully armed." But in Sordello's picture every one of the thirteen figures is somehow made to stand out: as he calls the name of each individual, and comments, Sordello points out some physical feature, or facial expression, or posture, or, at least, the place he occupies among his fellows.

94. *Rudolf:* Rudolf of Hapsburg (1218–91), first emperor of the House of Austria, gave priority to the internal affairs of Germany and neglected Italy, allowing it to remain outside the unifying influence of the empire. It is evidently his awareness of this neglect that is revealed in his expression as described by Sordello (92–93): ". . . who looks / as if he left undone what was to do." His son, Albert of Hapsburg (the "German Albert," still alive and already excoriated by Dante the Poet in *Purg.* VI, 97–117), would be guilty of the same neglect.

The son of Albert IV, Count of Hapsburg, Rudolf I was elected emperor in 1273. However, Ottokar, the king of Bohemia, feeling that he himself should have been elected, opposed him. Rudolf, with the help of his allies, was able to defeat Ottokar and force him to surrender Austria, Styria, Carinthia, and Carniola. Later, however, Ottokar again rebelled, to be defeated and killed in 1278 near Vienna.

100. *Ottokar:* In a spirit of reconciliation, Ottokar II, king of

Bohemia from 1253 to 1278, a valiant warrior, comforts Rudolf of Hapsburg, formerly his bitterest enemy.

101. *Wenceslaus:* Wenceslaus IV (1270–1305) succeeded his father, Ottokar II, as king of Bohemia in 1278. Dante will refer to him again in the *Paradise* (XIX, 125).

103. *that snub-nosed figure:* Philip III the Bold, king of France (1245–85), called *le Camus* because of his nose, was defeated by Peter of Aragon in 1285 during the massacre of the French in Sicily. Philip was the son of Louis IX, whom he succeeded, and the nephew of Charles of Anjou. In 1262 he married Isabella, the daughter of James I of Aragon. From this marriage was born his son, Philip, who succeeded him as Philip IV, the Fair, whom Dante dubs "the Plague of France" (109).

104. *the kind-looking person:* Henry the Fat of Navarre, contrary to his kindly appearance, was reputed to have a harsh temperament. He died in 1274, suffocated by his fat. Henry was king of Navarre from 1270 to 1274, succeeding Thibaut II, his brother. His daughter Jeanne married Philip the Fair.

105. *the lily:* The lily (*fleur de lis*) was the emblem of the kings of France.

109. *the Plague of France:* Philip IV the Fair, son of Philip III the Bold and son-in-law of Henry the Fat. His reign was characterized by tyranny, corruption, and viciousness. Though never mentioned by name, he is the frequent object of Dante's scorn in the *Comedy (Purg.* XX, 85–96; XXXII, 148–60; XXXIII, 34–45; *Par.* XIX, 118). Philip died in 1314.

Philip opposed the Papacy and even went so far as to hold Boniface VIII prisoner at Agnani. He persecuted the Order of the Templars with the aim of acquiring their wealth and had their leader burned at the stake in Paris in his presence.

112. *That sturdy-looking soul:* Peter III of Aragon (1236–85), the husband of Manfred's daughter, Constance, became King of Sicily in 1282, succeeding Charles of Anjou, after the massacre of the Sicilian Vespers.

113. *the big-nosed one:* Charles I of Anjou (1226–85), champion of the Guelphs in Italy. He defeated Manfred at Bene-

vento in 1266 to become king of Sicily and Naples, later losing the throne to Peter III. Though these two were bitter rivals, here they are presented as singing in harmony. Charles married Beatrix, daughter of Count Raymond Berenger IV of Provence, in 1246, thus becoming count of Provence. After Beatrix's death in 1267, he married Margaret of Burgundy in 1268.

115. *that young man:* The reference is most likely to Alfonso III of Aragon, who was Peter III's eldest son and who reigned less than six years (1285–91).

119. *James and Frederick:* James II of Aragon and Frederick II of Sicily, the second and third sons of Peter III of Aragon, were involved in a lengthy dispute over a claim to the kingdom of Sicily.

120. *but neither got the better heritage:* Neither James nor Frederick inherited the virtue or goodness of their father.

124–26. *My words apply:* Having said in 119–20 that James and Frederick, unlike their brother mentioned in the preceding tercet, possessed none of the virtues of their father, Peter III, Dante in 124–26 points (again) to Charles I, the figure sitting beside Peter, who shares the same fate with him: his own son, Charles II, was inferior to him—hence the laments of the inhabitants of Provence and Apulia, who passed under the rule of Charles II on his father's death in 1285.

127. *this seed's plant is less than he:* This seed, the father, is Charles I; his plant, the son, is Charles II. Here we have a recapitulation of what had been hinted at in the lines immediately preceding: Charles I, like Peter III, was unfortunate in his progeny.

128–29. *just so much more than Margaret and Beatrix:* Margaret of Burgundy and Beatrix of Provence were both wives of Charles I of Anjou; Constance, daughter of Manfred, was the wife of Peter III of Aragon. Thus, Dante is really saying in verses 127–29 that Charles II is as much inferior to Charles I as Charles I is to Peter III. For thirteen lines Dante has been concerned with the frequent failure of a father to produce a son who is worthy of him. Sayers (p. 124), after working her way through verses 124–29, comments parenthetically, "Not, perhaps, one of Dante's best efforts." But she seems to be merely annoyed by the far-fetched terms of the conclusion which Dante has been supposedly leading up to: she does not admit that the conclusion itself, however simply it might have been expressed, has not been prepared for.

130–31. *Henry of England sitting there / all by himself:* Henry III (1216–72), whose son, Edward I, is credited with an enduring reform of English law, is reproached in Sordello's lament for Blacatz (see note to VI, 74) for his sloth and cowardice. His contemporaries frequently referred to his piety.

As for the reason why Henry is sitting alone, some believe it is due to his modesty, others to the fact that his lands formed no part of the Holy Roman Empire. The opinion has also been expressed that his isolation reflects the contrast his life offers to that of all the other figures in the valley; whereas the others were too preoccupied by affairs of state to think of their spiritual welfare, he was too preoccupied by his piety to think of his kingly responsibilities. But this would make of the others models of conscientious rulers, which they hardly were.

134. *Marquis William:* William VII, surnamed "Longsword," was Marquis of Montferrat from 1254 to 1292. Failing in his attempt to quell a revolt in the city of Alessandria in Piedmont, William was locked in an iron cage by his enemies and put on display until his death in 1292.

CANTO VIII

As THE PILGRIM looks on, one of the souls in the valley below rises and begins singing the *Te lucis ante.* The rest of the inhabitants of the valley join in and sing the hymn through to the end, keeping their eyes fixed on the sky. As they continue to stare upward, two angels are seen to descend from Heaven. These angels take up positions on either side of the group of souls, and Sordello explains that they have come to guard the valley against the serpent who will appear at any moment; he then announces that it is time to go down among the great shades of the valley. Having descended only a few steps, Dante recognizes the shade of Nino Visconti. Nino, righteously indignant, discusses with Dante the infidelity of widows who remarry. Virgil is explaining certain stellar phenomena of the Southern Hemisphere, when suddenly Sordello announces the coming of the serpent. No sooner does the beast appear, however, than it is put to flight by the two angel guardians. The Pilgrim then speaks to Conrad Malaspina, lavishly praising the reputation of the Malaspina family, and Conrad prophesies that Dante will one day have cause from his own experience to praise this family.

It was the hour when a sailor's thoughts,
　　the first day out, turn homeward, and his heart
　　yearns for the loved ones he has left behind,　　　3

the hour when the novice pilgrim aches
　　with love: the far-off tolling of a bell
　　now seems to him to mourn the dying day—　　　6

I was no longer listening to words
　　but looking at a soul who had stood up,
　　requesting, with a gesture, to be heard.　　　9

He raised his hands, joining his palms in prayer,
　　his gaze fixed toward the east, as if to say:
　　"I have no other thought but Thee, dear Lord."　　　12

Te lucis ante, with such reverence,
　　and so melodiously, came from his lips,
　　that I was lost to any sense of self;　　　15

the rest then, reverently, in harmony,
joined in to sing the hymn through to the end,
keeping their eyes fixed on the heavenly spheres.   18

Sharpen your sight, Reader: the truth, this time,
is covered by a thinner veil, and so,
the meaning should be easy to perceive.   21

I saw that noble host of souls, who now
in silence kept their eyes raised to the heavens,
as if expectant, faces pale and meek,   24

and then I saw descending from on high
two angels with two flaming swords, and these
were broken short and blunted at the end.   27

Their garments, green as tender new-born leaves
unfurling, billowed out behind each one,
fanned by the greenness of their streaming wings.   30

One took his stand above us on our side,
and one alighted on the other bank;
thus, all the souls were held between the two.   33

My eyes could see with ease their golden hair,
but could not bear the radiance of their faces:
light that makes visible can also blind.   36

"From Mary's bosom both of them descend
to guard us from the serpent in the vale,"
Sordello said. "He'll be here soon, you'll see."   39

Not knowing from what point he would appear,
I turned around and, frozen by my fear,
I pressed close to those shoulders I could trust.   42

Sordello spoke again: "Now it is time
for us to join the noble shades below
and speak with them—I know they will be pleased."   45

I only had to take three steps, I think,
before I reached the bottom. I saw a shade
peering at me, trying to know my face.   48

By now, the air had started turning dark,
but not so dark that we could not see clear
(so close we were) what was concealed before.   51

He made his way toward me, and I toward him—
    Noble Judge Nino, how I did rejoice
    to see that you were not among the Damned!   54

No loving words of welcome did we spare;
    then he: "How long since you have come across
    the boundless waters to the mountain's base?"   57

"Oh," I replied, "I left the realm of grief
    this morning; I am still in my first life,
    but hope to gain the other by this road."   60

When Nino and Sordello heard my words,
    both of them backed away from me, amazed,
    unable to believe what they had heard.   63

One turned to Virgil, and the other one
    turned to a soul nearby. "Corrado, rise!"
    he cried: "Come here! See what God's grace has willed!" 66

He turned to me: "I beg you in the name
    of that grace shown to you by Him who hides
    His primal cause too deep for man to delve—   69

when you have crossed the enormous gulf once more,
    tell my Giovanna she should plead for me,
    for prayers from guiltless hearts are listened to. 72

I think her mother has stopped loving me,
    for she has put aside those bands of white
    which she, poor soul, will soon be longing for. 75

From her it is not difficult to learn
    how long love's flame burns in a woman's heart,
    if sight and touch do not rekindle it.   78

The snake that leads the Milanese to war
    will not provide an emblem for her tomb
    as splendid as Gallura's cock would be."   81

These were his words, and his whole countenance
    displayed the signs of righteous zeal, the kind
    which flares up when it should within the heart. 84

My eyes kept looking at the sky just where
    the stars move slowest—as, within a wheel,
    the axle moves more slowly than the rest.   87

My guide said: "Son, what are you staring at?"
    I answered him: "At those three brilliant torches
    lighting up all the polar region here."   90

And he to me: "Those four bright stars you saw
    this morning, now are underneath the mount,
    and these have risen here to take their place."   93

But then Sordello clutched his arm and said:
    "Behold our adversary over there!" —
    he pointed to the place where we should look.   96

Along the little valley's open side
    a serpent moved — the very one, perhaps,
    that offered Eve the bitter fruit to eat.   99

Through grass and flowers slid the vicious streak,
    stopping from time to time to turn its head
    and lick its back to make its body sleek.   102

I did not see, so I cannot describe,
    how the two holy falcons took to flight,
    but I saw clearly both of them fly down.   105

Hearing those green wings cutting through the air,
    the serpent fled, the angels wheeled around,
    flying in perfect time back to their posts.   108

The shade who had drawn close to Nino's side,
    when called by him, did not at any time
    during the skirmish take his eyes from me.   111

"So may the lamp that lights your upward path
    find in your will enough sustaining fuel
    to take you to the enamelled mountaintop,"   114

he then began, "if you have recent news
    of Val di Magra or parts thereabout,
    tell me, for in that land I once was great.   117

Corrado Malaspina was my name —
    but not the elder, though I sprang from him;
    and here I cleanse the love I bore my own."   120

"Oh," I replied, "I've never visited
    the lands you ruled; the whole of Europe, though,
    has heard about your glorious domain.   123

The fame that honors your great family
    proclaims resoundingly its lords and lands,
    even to those who never travelled there.   *126*

And, as I hope to reach the top, I swear
    that your great lineage maintains intact
    the glorious honor of the purse and sword.   *129*

Habit and virtue have so shaped your race
    that while the Wicked Head perverts the world,
    they shun the path of evil, they alone."   *132*

He said: "Know that the sun will not repose
    a seventh time on the large bed the Ram
    spreads over and bestrides with all four feet,   *135*

before the kind opinion you just gave
    shall be nailed hard into your brain with nails
    truer than words you may have heard of us—   *138*

unless God's course of justice be cut short!"

NOTES

1. *It was the hour:* The time periphrasis that opens this canto
is expressed not in astronomical terms but in terms of sentiment. As the hour of compline approaches, sailors and pilgrims
experience nostalgia for the home they left behind, instead of
yearning to reach the goal of their journey. Could this be
meant to represent the mood of the princes, who have just
finished singing the *Salve Regina* with its yearning for Heaven?
If so, we must understand that the nostalgia of these souls is a
blend of longing for this world and longing for Heaven.

7-24

This passage is narrated from the point of view of the Pilgrim as he observes the group below him in the valley. Canto
VII ended with him still listening to the words of Sordello; we
learn in line 7 that his attention has been attracted away from
those words by a movement on the part of the leader of the
group below—his sense of hearing giving way to his sense of
sight. And that he is deeply absorbed in what he sees is
suggested by the sharply etched outline of the figure, who has
risen and stands with clasped hands raised toward Heaven in

prayer. Then, as the hymn *Te lucis ante* begins, the Pilgrim becomes "lost to any sense of self" (15), absorbed in both listening and watching. Finally, after the song has come to an end (and after the Poet's "invitation" to the Reader), the Pilgrim's sense of sight takes over again ("I saw": 22) as he gazes intently upon the expectant faces below him raised toward the sky, then to shift his gaze away to follow the movements of the approaching angels.

But it is not only the sensorium of the Pilgrim that is involved, nor is he the only one who is completely absorbed: the group in the valley, too, is spellbound, concentrated upon their desire, which they would communicate to God ("I have no other thought but Thee, dear Lord": 12). How heavily the air is charged with tension before the angels come and before the Pilgrim's mood is dispelled by Sordello's words of explanation!

13. *Te lucis ante:* It is clear from line 17 that Dante expected his reader to have the entire hymn in mind:

Te lucis ante terminum,	Before the ending of the day,
Rerum creator, poscimus,	Creator of the world, we beg of You
Ut tua pro clementia	
Sis praesul et custodia.	That You with Your mercy
	Be our Guardian and Protector.
Procul recedant somnia	
Et noctium phantasmata,	May dreams be kept away
Hostemque nostrum	And the spectors of night;
comprime,	And our enemy repress
Ne polluantur corpora.	Lest our bodies be polluted.
	Help us, Father all-powerful,
Praesta, pater omnipotens,	Through our Lord Jesus Christ,
Per Jesum Christum dominum,	Who together with the Holy
Qui tecum in perpetuum	Spirit
Regnat cum sancto spiritu.	Reigns perpetually with you.

Particularly relevant to the subsequent dramatic action of the poem is the line "And our enemy repress," which is a foreshadowing of the putting to flight of the serpent by the angels.

The *Te lucis ante,* even more than the first hymn, *Salve Regina,* would seem to reflect the daily life of Christians on earth: also sung at compline, it is a prayer for protection from temptation, especially in the form of evil dreams. Of course, the princes, like all the other inhabitants of the Antepurgatory, are not subject to temptation, nor do they dream (or sleep). It is as if in their interim period in the valley, before they are allowed to begin the all-important process of purgation, which alone will give meaning to their stay in Purgatory, their only role is the vicarious one of "imitating" the attitudes of a living Christian community. Something in the way of a suggestion of a dumbshow is present here.

15. *I was lost to any sense of self:* This picture of the Pilgrim caught up in ecstasy as he listens to the sweet strains of *Te lucis ante* may remind us of his mood of rapt attention as he listened to Casella's song (*Purg.* II, 112–17). Now his mood is appropriate; then it was not.

19. *Sharpen your sight, Reader:* Here Dante the Poet, addressing the reader, asks him to interpret the literal sense of the narrative in a figurative way. The only other such invitation to the reader, among the dozens of so-called Addresses to the Reader, is to be found in *Inf.* IX, 61–63 (note that both passages come in the same canto of their respective canticles: since *Inf.* I serves as Introduction to the whole *Comedy, Inf.* IX is the eighth canto of the *Inferno* proper):

> O all of you whose intellects are sound,
>   look now and see the meaning that is hidden
>   beneath the veil that covers my strange verses.

That Dante wishes the reader to remember this passage when he comes to *Purg.* VIII, 19–21, is indicated by the comparison in our passage: "the truth, this time, / is covered by a thinner veil."

In my note to *Inf.* IX, 61–63, after comparing the two auctorial invitations, I suggest, for both cases, the allegorical interpretation of the events narrated. *Inf.* IX, which concerns the coming of the angel to open the gates of Dis, represents the Harrowing of Hell, the culmination of the First Advent of Christ. Our canto, with the two angels coming as protection against the serpent, points to the Second Advent of Christ, according to the medieval conception of the *Triplex Adventus:* the intermediary Advent, after Christ's birth and life on earth and Resurrection, and before His final Coming to judge mankind—the daily coming of Christ into the hearts of individuals in order to protect them from temptation and insure their salvation. It is generally recognized that the Third Advent is enacted in Canto XXX when Beatrice comes to judge her lover at the top of the mountain of Purgatory. More on the Second Advent in connection with the Valley of the Princes can be found in Musa (1969), pp. 85–93; see also Heilbronn (1972).

24. *as if expectant, faces pale and meek:* It is surely not necessary to assume, as is often done, that the pallor in question is caused by the community's fear (of the serpent yet to come); it can be fully explained by the high degree of their expectancy as they await the longed-for coming of the angels. They seem spellbound.

This picture of the group looking heavenward with a rapt expression on their faces (which we see through the eyes of the Pilgrim before he looks away from them to the approaching angels) is the last we shall have of the princes as a body after the angels come. Sordello will continue his role as guide, and the Pilgrim will meet Judge Nino and Corrado Malaspina, but the group, the Christian community, has completely dissolved.

26. *flaming swords:* The flaming swords of the angels recall the *flammeum gladium* of the Cherubim placed at the entrance to Eden as guardians after the Fall (Gen. 3:24).

27. *broken short:* Of the many attempts to explain the "broken-off swords," the most frequent interpretation—that they symbolize God's Mercy tempering Justice—is hardly convincing: mercy toward the serpent? See note to 109–11.

28. *green as tender new-born leaves:* The green color of the angels is, of course, the symbol of hope.

37. *From Mary's bosom both of them descend:* I use the word "bosom" for the *grembo* of the original ("ambo vengon del grembo di Maria"). The primary meaning of this word is "lap," hence, "womb." In the latter sense this would offer a suggestion of the birth of Christ. The reader may remember the line from the first of the two hymns sung in the valley: " . . . show unto us the blessed fruit of thy womb, Jesus" (cf. note to VII, 82).

39. *He'll be here soon, you'll see:* Here we have clear evidence of the regular repetition (to which the inhabitants of the valley have become accustomed) of St. Bernard's contest between the angels and the serpent: the "daily coming" of Christ into the hearts of men (" . . . quotidie ad salvandas animas singulorum in

spiritu venit": Migne, CLXXXIII, 40). See Musa (1969), pp. 89–90.

41. *frozen by my fear:* Only Dante the Pilgrim is afraid. He is afraid because he does not know from which direction the serpent will come; he is reacting "symbolically" as the Christian in this life who knows he must be ever on his guard against temptation—as the Princes in the Valley need not be.

53. *Noble Judge Nino:* Nino Visconti (died 1296) was the son of Giovanni Visconti and (on his mother's side) the grandson of Count Ugolino della Gherardesca (see *Inf.* XXXIII). Between the years 1285 and 1288 he shared the office of podestà in Pisa with Count Ugolino. Considerable friction, however, existed between the two, and Nino was eventually betrayed and forced to flee the city, joining the Guelph forces that were warring against the Ghibelline order that was then established at Pisa. In 1293 he was made captain of the Guelph league and later became a citizen of Genova. There is an indirect reference to Nino in *Inf.* XXII, 81–87 (the *bolgia* of the Grafters), where the story of Nino's deputy, Fra Gomita, is told.

61–63. *When Nino . . . what they had heard:* In the fading light of the day, Dante casts no shadow (cf. *Purg.* VI, 57), and neither Sordello nor the other souls had recognized him as a living man.

71. *My Giovanna:* Giovanna, born around 1291, was Nino's daughter by Beatrice d'Este. When she was still five years old, Boniface VIII gave her the guardianship of the town of Volterra as a gesture of thanks to her father, a Guelph who favored the church. However, the Ghibellines subsequently deprived her of all her property. After living with her mother at Ferrara and Milan, she married Rizzardo da Camino, Lord of Treviso, but after his death in 1312 she was reduced to poverty. Finally she received a stipend in Florence in 1323 in consideration of her father's services. The date of her death is unknown.

73. *her mother:* Beatrice d'Este, daughter of Obizzo II d'Este and sister of Azzo VIII. She was first married to Nino Visconti, by whom she had a daughter, Giovanna. But in June 1300, not long after Nino's death, she removed her widow's white bands to marry Galeazzo Visconti, with whom she lived in Milan. Just two years later, however, the Visconti were expelled from that

city—as Nino here darkly prophesies (75). Galeazzo died in poverty in 1328 and Beatrice returned to Milan as soon as her son, Azzo, regained the lordship there. She died in 1334. Nino's reference to Beatrice as "her mother" and not as "my wife" sets the tone for his reproach that is to follow.

76. *From her it is not difficult:* On a symbolic level, Beatrice's action can be interpreted in several ways. In classical biblical typology a woman frequently represents the church. Beatrice's infidelity then could be seen as the failure of the church to adhere to her spouse, i.e., Christ. In addition, Nino's widow could symbolize the human soul, as does Cato's widow in *Conv.* IV, 28, 13 (cf. note to *Purg.* I, 31–75).

79. *The snake:* The snake is the coat of arms of the Milanese branch of the Visconti family. In this context, we cannot overlook its inevitable associations with the serpent, who will appear shortly in the valley.

81. *Gallura's cock:* The cock was the emblem of the Visconti of Pisa, whom Nino's widow abandoned. In addition, the cock is a traditional symbol of Christ and the Resurrection: announcing the dawn, he puts to flight the phantoms of the night. Dante's use of the antithetical "snake" and "cock" serves to reinforce the symbolic interpretation of Beatrice's infidelity.

89. *those three brilliant torches:* The theological virtues, Faith, Hope, and Charity. These virtues supersede the cardinal virtues symbolized by the four stars, in the sense that they are necessary to direct human actions toward God, and they are given to men through Christ. Here, near the gates of Purgatory proper, the appearance of the three stars announces a new orientation: the Pilgrim is about to leave the earthbound region of Antepurgatory and begin his ascent of the mountain of God.

94. *But then Sordello clutched his arm:* Note the concern of Sordello that Virgil know exactly where to look. According to Singleton (1973, p. 170), Sordello's gesture is "expressive of his apprehension on seeing the serpent." But would the experienced Sordello turn for aid or comfort to the inexperienced Virgil? (Cf. note to 109–11.)

95. *Behold our adversary:* The biblical adversary (cf. I Pet. 5:8), the enemy of all mankind.

99. *that offered Eve the bitter fruit to eat:* The serpent brings with it a recollection of Eve in the garden of Eden, while the angels recall Mary, the counterpart of Eve (VIII, 37).

100–108. *Through grass and flowers . . . back to their posts:* The serpent appears in the artificial setting of the valley, and we are reminded of the beauty representing all the sensual pleasures of this world. This is the locus of temptation—our world. The motion of the serpent is slow, idle, and ineffectual. The angels, on the other hand, are pure movement and energy—the image of grace in action. The confrontation of the angels and the serpent resumes, in concrete, dramatic action, the dualism of light and darkness in the cantos of the valley.

109–11. *The shade . . . did not . . . take his eyes from me:* The serpent has been defeated, the drama has come to an end, and no reaction on the part of the spectators is recorded. In fact, we cannot be certain that there were any spectators (apart from the Pilgrim) at this final stage: Corrado's eyes have remained fixed on the Pilgrim during the interval between the serpent's appearance and flight, and there is no clear evidence that any of the other princes bothered to watch the battle.

It would seem that Dante has taken pains to present as absolute the princes' indifference to the spectacular events taking place before them. The only one to comment on the appearance of the angels and of the serpent is Sordello, and, both times, his reaction merely reflects awareness of his duties as host or guide. In 37–39 he explains to Virgil the heavenly origin of the green-winged creatures and the purpose of their coming, which involves a reference to the serpent: "He'll be here soon, you'll see," he says casually. He continues by suggesting politely that it is time they go to make the acquaintance of "the noble shades below," who will be delighted to see them (43–45). Later (94–96) he briefly announces the arrival of the serpent, taking care to point out to Virgil exactly where to look (and giving no indication whatever of excitement or fear: see note to 94–96).

As for the first case, it could be said that the two pilgrims are still at the rim of the valley, and, listening to Sordello's words, they are distracted from taking in the effect produced below by the angels' arrival. But when Judge Nino comes toward the Pilgrim a few moments later, he gives no signs of having recently been shaken by some event.

The reasons for this "indifference" have already been suggested. On the superficial, the literal, plane, it is natural that the princes' long familiarity with the regularly enacted victory of the angels over the serpent would lead to lack of interest or even to ennui on their part, and, on the allegorical plane, this drama has no direct connection with their fate: they are already saved and need no protection against temptation, against the serpent. (Furthermore, the actors in the drama do not hesitate to reveal—and even play up—their own unconvincingness: the angels with their blunted swords, the serpent stopping to lick itself as a kitten might.) The drama enacted could have relevancy only for the living, whose souls are constantly in danger—just as the prayers (or, rather, the second prayer) of the princes had relevancy only for the living. But precisely because the indifference of the princes can be so easily justified (repetition of the irrelevant recognized as such), one must wonder why the poet was inspired to invent the spectacle in question.

Some commentators believe that the serpent is sent to frighten the princes, as a reminder of what had almost happened; others, that the drama was intended as food for spiritual thought: these souls had done too little thinking about spiritual matters in their lifetime. In either case, the indifference of the princes can only mean that the spectacle failed of its purpose, and that, perhaps, is the reason that no critic that I have read points out this indifference—which, after the coming of the angels, is absolute.

Surely the solution is to be found in the contrast between "before" and "after." The group in the valley is first seen, briefly, as they sing *Salve Regina,* waiting for the arrival of the angels; then, attention is focused on them as they begin their second hymn, and we are made keenly aware of their mood of concentrated attention. The picture of the group in lines 22–24 (the last time they are seen), their faces raised toward Heaven, pale with expectancy (after having sung their prayer so fervently and melodiously that the Pilgrim was spellbound) is unforgettable. For them only one thing mattered: that important moment of the day when the angels would come as they had come before and would come again—a never-failing sign of God's grace, which means for them a reassuring reminder of their salvation and, here, in the Antepurgatory, they cannot be reminded of it by the suffering of purgation. The coming of the angels was the sign.

And if they alone are granted this sign, it is surely because of their exemplary status: they represent all the souls in Antepurgatory.

112. *So may the lamp that lights your upward path:* At last Corrado, invited by Nino in verse 66 to come meet the Pilgrim, addresses him. Evidently his delay, his hesitation (as well as his steady gaze), is to be explained by his awe at the miracle of the Pilgrim's presence among the dead. In my comment on this incident (Musa, 1974, pp. 157–58), I add:

> And his delay is the last in a small series of postponements that have been introduced into the narrative. Twice Sordello is slow in performing an act which had been prepared for by the context: having proposed in lines 46–48 of Canto VII to lead the two travellers to join the souls in the valley, he delays this meeting in order to first present the Princes from a distance; the meeting actually takes place in Canto VIII, 46–48 — that is, after an interval of exactly (what might be called) one canto's length. Earlier, Sordello, asked by Virgil in Canto VI, 67–68, for directions to climb the Mountain, ignores the request in his eagerness to learn more about the two strange travellers; it is only when Virgil repeats his request in the next canto (37–39) that Sordello accedes to it by offering himself as guide. There are two other postponements, and on another plane, where it is the author himself who chooses to hold back from us information that might have come much sooner. The less conspicuous involves the slow-motion presentation to view of the souls in the valley singing *Salve Regina* — the effect being prolonged by Sordello's delayed descent into the valley where they are. And of course, there is the dramatic device of "interruption" by which the poet postpones the conclusion of the embrace between Virgil and Sordello. In every case the motivation, psychological or aesthetic, of the postponement is clear.
>
> But, though none of the cases is puzzling in itself, there is a need to explain the frequent recurrence of the same device. I suggest that it is intended as a leit-motif reminder of the reason for the presence of the Princes in the Antepurgatory — which is, of course, the reason for the presence there of all the rest. Nowhere in the scenes just described is any statement made about the all-important fact that these souls, like the rest, have been excluded from Purgatory proper because of their postponement of repentance (which, in turn entails the postponement of their expiation). And so, Sordello and Conrad are made to "imitate" the action that brought them to the Antepurgatory. Dante the Poet, too, on another plane, has reflected the same tempo of delay. And as for the fact that for each single

case it is possible to find a convincing explanation, this is simply the sign of great artistry.

114. *enamelled mountaintop:* A reference to the Earthly Paradise. The word "enamelled" (*smalto*) is also used in *Inf.* IV, 118 (*il verde smalto*) to describe the beautiful green grass on which the philosophers are seated.

118. *Corrado Malaspina:* Corrado II was the son of Federigo I, Marquis of Villafranca, and the grandson of Corrado I, "the elder" (119). He was a Ghibelline, according to Boccaccio, who mentions him and his daughter, Spina, in *The Decameron* (II, 6). Corrado died around 1294.

122-32

The house of Malaspina is honored throughout Europe. They practice the virtues of justice, generosity, and chivalry in the midst of the corrupt Europe that was apostrophized in Canto VI and that is represented by the living rulers enumerated in Canto VII.

130. *Habit and virtue have so shaped your race:* The habitual good actions of the Malaspina family, which make them an example of human rectitude, are the result of the combination of a natural good disposition given them by God and the constant and long practice of virtue. (Cf. *Conv.* I, ix, 7, where Dante says that habitual virtue cannot be had of a sudden, but must be acquired by long practice.)

131. *the Wicked Head:* This has been variously identified with Satan, with Rome or the corrupt papacy in general, or specifically with Boniface VIII, the present pope. According to the Anonimo fiorentino, it refers to the bad example given by both the pope and the emperor.

133. *Know that the sun will not repose:* This is a prophecy of Dante's exile. The sun will not return to the constellation of Aries (the Ram) seven times—that is, seven years will not pass before Dante experiences personally the merits of the Malaspina family, which he now knows only by hearsay. And, indeed, in 1306 Dante, in exile, was the guest of the Malaspina at Lunigiana.

Incidentally, this brief mention of the ram bestriding the bed anticipates the sexual imagery with which the next canto will open, and the erotic dream that the Pilgrim is about to have.

CANTO IX

THE PILGRIM FALLS asleep and, near dawn, dreams that he is being snatched up into the sphere of fire by an eagle. The imaginary heat of his dream wakes him, and he is dazed and terrified until he discovers that Virgil is sitting close by. Virgil explains that they have now come to the gates of Purgatory proper and that while the Pilgrim slept, a lady named Lucia came and bore him up there in her arms. As they draw near the gates, the Pilgrim discerns three steps of different colors leading up to them. The first is white as marble; the second is darker than purple-black, and rough and crumbling; the third is red as flaming porphyry. On the threshold of the gate, above this last step, sits a guardian angel with a naked sword, clothed in garments the color of ashes. With the tip of the sword, he traces seven *P*'s on the Pilgrim's forehead and instructs him to be sure to "wash away" these wounds during his stay in the place of purgation. The guardian then takes two keys—one gold and one silver—with which he was entrusted by St. Peter, and unlocks the gateway to Purgatory. He warns the Pilgrim that, once inside, he is not to look back again, or he will be expelled; then, the hinges of the heavy, sacred doors make a strange sound as they swing open. As the Pilgrim passes through, he hears the faint and distant strains of what seems to be the *Te Deum laudamus*.

Now, pale upon the eastern balcony,
    appeared the concubine of old Tithonus,
    arisen now from her sweet lover's arms;   *3*

her brow was glittering with precious stones
    set in the shape of that cold-blooded beast
    that strikes and poisons people with its tail;   *6*

and of the hour-steps that Night ascends,
    already, where we were, two had been climbed,
    and now the third was folding down its wings,   *9*

when I, who carried with me Adam's weight,
    conquered by sleep, stretched out upon the grass
    on which all five of us were sitting then.   *12*

At the hour when the swallow, close to dawn,
  begins to sing her melancholy lays,
  perhaps remembering her ancient woes,   15

and when our mind, far straying from the flesh,
  less tangled in the network of its thoughts,
  becomes somehow prophetic in its dreams,   18

dreaming, I seemed to see hovering above,
  a golden-feathered eagle in the sky,
  with wings outspread, and ready to swoop down;   21

I seemed to find myself in that same place
  where Ganymede was forced to leave his friends,
  caught up to serve the conclave of the gods.   24

I wondered: "Could this be the only place
  the eagle strikes? Perhaps he does not deign
  to snatch his prey from anywhere but here."   27

Dreaming, I saw him circle for a while,
  then terrible as lightning, he struck down,
  swooping me up, up to the sphere of fire.   30

And there it seemed the bird and I both burned;
  the heat of that imaginary blaze
  was so intense it woke me from my sleep.   33

Just as Achilles woke up in a daze,
  glancing around himself with startled eyes,
  not knowing where he was or whence he came,   36

when he, asleep, was taken by his mother,
  borne in her arms, from Chiron's care to Skyros
  from where the Greeks would lure him finally —   39

so I was dazed, when sleep had fled my face;
  I turned the deathly color of a man
  feeling the freezing grip of fright on him.   42

Beside me was my Comfort, all alone.
  Now it was day, the sun two hours high,
  and what I saw before me was the sea.   45

"You must not be afraid," my leader said,
  "take heart, for we are well along our way;
  do not hold back, push on with all your strength,   48

you have arrived at Purgatory now.
    You see the rampart that surrounds it all
    and, where you see the cleft, that is the gate.   *51*

Before the break of day, while your soul slept
    within your body, still at rest below
    upon the flowers of that painted glen,   *54*

a lady came. She said 'I am Lucia.
    Come, let me take this man who lies asleep;
    I wish to speed him on his journey up.'   *57*

Sordello and the other shades remained.
    She took you in her arms at break of day
    and brought you here. I followed after her.   *60*

Before she set you down, her lovely eyes
    showed me the open entrance; then she left,
    and as she went, she took away your sleep."   *63*

As one who, first perplexed, is reassured,
    and feels his fear replaced by confidence,
    once what is true has been revealed to him—   *66*

such was the change in me. And when he saw
    me free of care, my leader made his way
    up and along the bank with me behind.   *69*

Reader, you see how lofty is my theme!
    You should not be surprised if now I try
    to match its grandeur with more subtle art.   *72*

Close to the top, we reached a point from where
    I saw a gate (it first appeared to be
    merely a gap, a break within the wall)   *75*

and, leading up to it, there were three steps,
    each one a different color; and I saw
    the silent figure of someone on guard.   *78*

I slowly raised my eyes: I saw that he
    was sitting on the highest step, his face
    too splendid for my eyes—I looked away!   *81*

And in his hand he held a naked sword;
    so dazzling were the rays reflected thence,
    each time I tried to look I could not see.   *84*

He said to us: "Speak up from where you are.
　　What is it that you want? Where is your guide?
　　Beware, you may regret your coming here."　　　87

"A while ago, a lady sent from Heaven
　　acquainted with such matters," said my guide,
　　"told me: 'Behold the gate. You must go there.'"　　　90

"May she continue guiding you to good,"
　　the courteous keeper of the gate replied,
　　"and so, come forward now up to our stairs."　　　93

We reached the steps. White marble was the first,
　　and polished to the glaze of a looking glass:
　　I saw myself reflected as I was.　　　96

The second one was deeper dark than perse,
　　of rough and crumbling, fire-corroded stone,
　　with cracks across its surface—length and breadth.　　　99

The third one, lying heavy at the top,
　　appeared to be of flaming porphyry,
　　red as the blood that spurts out from a vein;　　　102

upon this step the angel of the Lord
　　rested his feet; he sat upon the sill
　　which seemed to be of adamantine rock.　　　105

Up the three steps my master guided me
　　benevolently, saying: "Ask him now,
　　in all humility, to turn the key."　　　108

Falling devoutly at his holy feet,
　　in mercy's name I begged to be let in;
　　but, first of all, three times I smote my breast.　　　111

Then with his sword he traced upon my brow
　　the scars of seven P's. "Once entered here,
　　be sure you cleanse away these wounds," he said.　　　114

Ashes, or earth when it is dug up dry—
　　this was the color of the robes he wore;
　　he reached beneath them and drew out two keys.　　　117

One key was silver and the other gold;
　　first he applied the white one, then the yellow—
　　with that the gate responded to my wish.　　　120

"Whenever either one of these two keys
    fails to turn properly inside the lock,"
    the angel said, "the road ahead stays closed.   *123*

One is more precious, but the other needs
    wisdom and skill before it will unlock,
    for it is that one which unties the knot.   *126*

I hold these keys from Peter, who advised:
    'Admit too many, rather than too few,
    if they but cast themselves before your feet.'"   *129*

Then, pushing back the portal's holy door,
    "Enter," he said to us, "but first be warned:
    to look back means to go back out again."   *132*

And then the pivots of that sacred gate,
    fashioned of heavy metal, resonant,
    turned slow inside their sockets. The rolling roar   *135*

was louder and more stubborn than Tarpeia's,
    when it was robbed of vigilant Metellus—
    its treasury made lean from that time on.   *138*

And as the grating pivots rolled, I turned,
    for I heard chanting: *Te Deum laudamus*—
    accompanied by the sweet notes of that door.   *141*

This harmony of sounds made me recall
    just how it seems in church when we attend
    to people singing as the organ plays: *144*

sometimes the words are heard, and sometimes lost.

NOTES

1–9

   These three tercets, which offer an elaborately wrought
description of the heavens in order to indicate the hour at
which the Pilgrim fell asleep, have been variously interpreted.
Four theories (one of them based on a variant reading of verse
1: *Titanus* instead of *Tithonus*) have been offered, which involve, however, only two sidereal phenomena: the solar dawn
and the lunar dawn. Those critics who accept the terms *con-*

cubine and *lover* in our passage as equivalent to 'wife' and 'husband' respectively, see in lines 1–6 a reference to Aurora, goddess of the (solar) dawn, wife of Tithonus. But only a very few of them believe that the Pilgrim waited till dawn to fall asleep; most of them take the description of 1–6 to refer to what was visible not in Purgatory but farther toward the east ("the eastern balcony"): we would have been offered a description of dawn in Italy, where the poet was writing; then, in verse 8 would come a shift to Purgatory ("already where we were"). According to this view, it would still be night in Purgatory when the Pilgrim fell asleep. And, obviously, this is also the opinion of those who (whether reading *Tithonus* or *Titanus*) believe that the rising of the moon is involved.

Just why scholars should envision a lunar phenomenon here depends on much more than Dante's reference to the goddess in line 1 as *concubine* instead of *wife;* for the readers who may be interested in the many factors involved, I suggest that they read Moore (1903) for a detailed analysis of the "lunar approach(es)" and Porena and Sapegno for the counterarguments; also, Orr, pp. 252–54. There are strong arguments for and against each of the two main interpretations.

2. *Tithonus:* Aurora, daughter of the sun, goddess of the dawn, became enamored of Tithonus, brother of Priam, and married him. She obtained for him from the gods the gift of immortality but neglected to ask for that of eternal youth. As a result he grew increasingly decrepit and shrivelled until Aurora mercifully changed him into a cicada. In classical mythology no mention is made of Tithonus's concubine, or, so far as I know, of any "goddess of the lunar dawn." Those critics who posit such a figure and such a relationship are assuming that Dante has invented an extension of the classical myth of Tithonus.

5. *that cold-blooded beast:* Given the details of the description of the "beast" in question, this phrase is most probably a reference to the constellation Scorpio, rather than to Pisces, as a number of scholars believe. As for the difficulty of associating Scorpio in the west with Aurora in the east, see the attempts of Torraca and Porena to explain this.

7. *the hour-steps that Night ascends:* By my translation "hour-steps" for the original *passi,* "steps," I indicate the choice I have made of the three possible interpretations of *passi:* not

the signs of the Zodiac, not the "watches" of the night, but the twelve hours that intervene between sunset and dawn. Thus, two hours having passed since sunset, and the third being well on its way toward completion, it must have been between 8:30 and 9:00 at night when the Pilgrim fell asleep. This seems to be the generally accepted opinion of scholars today—except for the few who believe in the first of the four theories mentioned: that the Pilgrim fell asleep when it was dawn in Purgatory.

9. *wings:* the "wings" of the third hour anticipate the morning swallow (13) and the eagle that will appear in the Pilgrim's dream.

12. *all five of us:* The five are the Pilgrim, Virgil, Sordello, Nino, and Corrado.

13–18

With no transition, the narrative passes from evening to the hour just before dawn. This is the second time-periphrasis in the canto and, like the first (1–6), it is coupled with a pagan mythological tale with strong sensual overtones. In this case, it is the legend of Philomela and Procne, the main source for which is Ovid's *Metamorphoses* (VI, 423–674). King Tereus of Thrace had married Procne, whose sister, Philomela, he subsequently raped, cutting out her tongue afterwards lest she betray him. However, Philomela managed to communicate the entire story to her sister by weaving it into a tapestry. In revenge, Procne killed her infant son and, with the help of Philomela, served up the cooked flesh of the boy to his father. Learning that he had fed upon his son, Tereus pursued the two sisters with an ax, but before he could slay them, the gods changed all three into birds. Ovid tells us that Tereus became a hoopoe, but does not specify further the fate of the two sisters. According to the generally accepted version, Philomela becomes a nightingale, and Procne a swallow; Dante, however, presents Philomela here as a swallow (later, he will refer to Procne as a nightingale: XVII, 19–21). For a discussion of the sensual overtones to this and other images in this canto and their connection to the Pilgrim's first dream, see Musa (1981).

13. *At the hour:* According to ancient and medieval popular tradition, the dreams that occur in the early morning hours, just before daybreak, are likely to be prophetic (cf. *Inf.* XXVI,

7). As we shall see, this is certainly the case with the Pilgrim's dream here.

19–33

The dream at the end of the first night in Purgatory at once brings to an end the Pilgrim's stay in the Antepurgatory, represents the transmutation of an event that he is actually experiencing while dreaming, and anticipates experiences that await him on his journey up the mountain.

The Pilgrim's mind has absorbed all the sensuousness and aimlessness of the Antepurgatory—consequently he translates his ascent to the gates of Purgatory in St. Lucy's arms (52–57), an act of which he himself was incapable, into the pagan tale of the beautiful, young boy whom Jove, disguised as an eagle, and burning with desire, snatched up from the top of Mount Ida. Lucy's gesture, a redeeming act of illuminating grace, is perceived by the naïve and earthbound Pilgrim as an act of sexual violence. It is through this unconscious perception of his that the Pilgrim is shown to be still at a most inadequate and imperfect stage in his spiritual development, still much in need of purification.

The sensual, pagan nature of the Pilgrim's dream is prepared for by the two time-periphrases which opened this canto, involving the stories of Tithonus and Philomela: in both, the voice of the poet hints at the dark, ugly side of the violent indulgence of the senses. (Incidentally, the *Te lucis ante,* the prayer recited in the last canto, asks specifically for defense against just such dreams!)

And certainly the Pilgrim is in no condition to understand or interpret the dream that his own childish unconscious has produced. Not until Virgil explains what has happened does he begin to grasp the dream's significance.

The fire that seems to consume the Pilgrim, and so wakes him, anticipates the purifying sufferings that he will see everywhere in Purgatory, and more particularly, the wall of fire through which he, like every other penitent soul, must pass to reach the Earthly Paradise. When he confronts the actual fire (Canto XXVII) he will react in fear, just as he does now in the dream and in his first few waking moments.

23. *Ganymede:* Son of Tros, the mythical founder of Troy, Ganymede was reported to be the most beautiful of all mortals.

While hunting on Mount Ida, he was snatched up by Jove disguised as an eagle, to become the cup-bearer to the gods.

According to the Homeric hymn to Eos (Aurora), the goddess of the dawn, smitten with love for Tithonus, abducted him before marrying him. This would offer a parallel to the story of Ganymede: in both cases there is the sudden translation of a mortal to heavenly regions, as the result of a violent erotic impulse.

24. *conclave:* the term used by Dante (*consistoro*) is ecclesiastical and serves to associate Jove with the Christian God.

34–39. *Just as Achilles:* In this simile the bewilderment of the boy Achilles upon waking up in a place different from the one in which he went to sleep is compared to the Pilgrim's own confusion on waking from his dream not in the lush, enamelled Valley of the Princes, where he fell asleep, but at the distant gates of Purgatory. In the first book of the *Achilleid,* Statius tells how Thetis, to keep her young son out of the Trojan War, carried him, still asleep, from (the charge of his tutor, Chiron, in) Thessaly to the island of Skyros. There, dressed as a girl, Achilles grew up among the women in the palace of King Lycomedes, until Ulysses and Diomede, anxious to recruit him for the war, tricked him into revealing his sex. According to Virgil, this is one of the three crimes for which the two Greeks are burning in Hell (*Inf.* XXVI, 61–63).

In this, the fourth reference in our canto to pagan mythology, no element of violence or sensuality is present; rather the childishness of the Pilgrim is given prominence; in comparing the bewilderment of the newly awakened Pilgrim to the bewilderment of the newly awakened Achilles, Dante is also reminding the reader of what has preceded in each case: that is, the Pilgrim is compared not to the heroic Achilles about to go into battle but to a boy being carried, asleep in his mother's arms, to safety.

55. *Lucia:* According to legend, St. Lucy of Syracuse plucked out her beautiful eyes when they were admired by an importunate suitor. For this incomparable act of chastity she was rewarded with even more beautiful eyes and became the patroness of those suffering from impaired vision. Note that it is precisely with her eyes that St. Lucy "talks to" Virgil in verse 61.

70–72. *Reader, you see how lofty is my theme:* In this Address to the Reader, the poet attempts to prepare his reader for the symbolism of the three steps he is about to climb. Or perhaps he wishes to point even further ahead to the elaborate terrace and ritual structure of Purgatory proper. Spitzer distinguishes between the different types of Addresses to the Reader in the *Comedy,* which, according to him, come to a total of nineteen. See also Auerbach.

78–84. *the silent figure of someone on guard:* The guardian holds a naked sword, the symbol of divine authority. The sword brilliantly reflects the rays of the sun, which is the symbol of God. The guardian angel may recall the cherubim with their flaming sword who were set to guard the entrance to the Garden of Eden after the Fall and expulsion of Adam and Eve. And, indeed, it might be said that this angel, too, is set at the entrance to Eden, for the Earthly Paradise is located inside the gate of Purgatory at the top of the mountain.

86. *Where is your guide?:* Some scholars deduce from the angel's question that all of the Late Repentant, when their sentence in Antepurgatory is completed, must be accompanied by an angel to the gate. It must be admitted that this question echoes Cato's words to the pilgrim pair in *Purg.* I, 43: "Who guided you?"; and we know, of course, that all the souls who arrive on the shores of Purgatory (all the Saved) must have a guide: the angel pilot who has brought them from the Tiber. But we know this (we come to learn it) as a fact; it is not a deduction. And I should hesitate to deduce, on this unprecedented occasion, anything about the conditions obtaining in Antepurgatory from the angel's question here.

94–102. *We reached the steps:* The three steps are generally taken to represent the three stages of repentance: the first step, which is white and mirrorlike, stands for self-examination; the second, black, rough step stands for sorrow for sin, or contrition; the third, flaming-red step signifies satisfaction of the sinner's debt, or penance. The color also suggests ardent love and the shedding of Christ's blood, which provided satisfaction for the sins of the world. But see also Grandgent (p. 389) and Carroll (pp. 141–44).

103–105. *upon this step the angel of the Lord:* This guardian angel represents ecclesiastical authority and is seated on adamantine rock to indicate the firm foundation upon which that authority rests: "Thou art Peter and upon this rock I shall build my church" (Matt. 16:18). And that the angel here is associated with St. Peter is clear from verse 127, where he reveals that it is from Peter that he received the keys to the gate: "And I will give thee the keys to the kingdom of Heaven; and whatever thou shalt bind on earth shall be bound in Heaven and whatever thou shalt loose on earth shall be loosed in Heaven" (Matt. 16:19).

111. *three times I smote my breast:* The traditional gesture of repentance and sorrow for one's sins. It is accompanied by the well-known words "mea culpa, mea culpa, mea maxima culpa."

113. *the scars of seven P's:* The letter *P* stands for the Latin *peccatum*, "sin." The seven *P*'s carved on the Pilgrim's forehead represent the stains of the seven Capital Sins that the Penitents must purge by their suffering on the mountain of Purgatory before their souls are ready to enter the Kingdom of Heaven. That each of the penitent souls entering the gate must go through the same symbolical ceremony is not necessary to assume.

115–17. *Ashes:* The angel, ecclesiastical authority, is here presented in his role as confessor. He wears the ashen-grey garments of penitence, and his keys symbolize the divinely delegated power of the confessor to grant and withold absolution.

124–26. *One is more precious:* On the two keys that represent the power of the confessor, Porena comments: "The gold key symbolizes the authority to absolve, which comes from God, and is therefore, by nature, superior but inherent, so to speak, in the sacerdotal quality in the abstract. The silver key symbolizes the concrete act of absolution (it disentangles, that is, unties the knot of sin); and it requires great psychological capacity [wisdom and skill] on the part of the priest, in understanding whether the sinner has really repented and merits absolution."

132. *to look back:* The "looking back" topos is common in both biblical and classical literature. We recall that God saved Lot and his family from the destruction of Sodom and Gomorrah on the condition that they not turn and look back as they fled the city. Lot's wife, ignoring this injunction, was turned

into a pillar of salt. And in classical legend, there is Orpheus, who was given permission to lead Eurydice out of Hell only if he refrained from looking behind him as they escaped. They started off, with Orpheus in the lead; then he turned around to see how Eurydice was faring, and she vanished. In the context of Purgatory, as in that of the Old Testament story, "looking back" would demonstrate a lack of resolve and an imperfect desire to attain the ultimate good.

135–38. *The rolling roar:* Metellus the tribune attempted in vain to prevent Julius Caesar, after the crossing of the Rubicon in 49 B.C., from entering the temple of Saturn at the foot of the Tarpeian rock, where the treasury was located. Lucan describes the loud grating sound that echoed in the rock when the doors to the vault were opened (*Phars.* III, 153–57, 167–68).

140. *Te Deum laudamus:* "We praise Thee, O God." This famous Ambrosian hymn of gratitude to God here appears to be sung somewhat mysteriously, on the occasion of the gates' opening to admit the Pilgrim into Purgatory. Especially appropriate in this context would be the words: *Tu, devicto mortis aculeo, aperuisti credentibus regna caelorum* ("When Thou hadst overcome the sting of death, Thou didst open to believers the Kingdom of Heaven").

141. *accompanied by the sweet notes of that door:* The harsh sound of the door turning on its hinges as it opens is sweet to the Pilgrim because of the invitation it offers, and in the verses that follow the sound is compared to the deep notes of an organ accompanying (and from time to time drowning out) the words of a hymn being sung.

I must admit that in the original, verse 141 contains no reference to the door: . . . *in voce mista al dolce suono,* "the words blending with the sweet sound"; and there are some scholars who insist that *dolce suono* could not possibly refer to the door: a sound first presented as strident and grating could not be referred to later as "sweet." I consider this reasoning naïve, and the variant that attempts to identify the "sweet sound" (cf. Chimenz) unconvincing.

CANTO X

VIRGIL AND THE Pilgrim pass through the gate, and it shuts resoundingly behind them as they make their way along a narrow path through a rocky cleft. They finally emerge from this "needle's eye" to find themselves on a deserted ledge. The wall of the cliff that rises to one side of the ledge is adorned with carvings in white marble, all of them offering examples of the virtue of humility. The first example is the scene of the Annunciation. The second carving represents David, who has put aside his kingly splendor to dance in humility before the Lord. The third shows the Emperor Trajan halting his mighty array of warriors on horseback to listen to a poor widow's plea for justice. As the Pilgrim stands marvelling at these august humilities, Virgil directs his attention to a group of souls that is moving toward them. These are the Proud, who, beating their breasts, make their way around the ledge under the crushing weight of tremendous slabs of stone that they carry on their backs.

When we had passed the threshold of the gate
    forever closed to souls whose loves are bad
    and make the crooked road seem like the straight,   *3*

I heard it close again, resoundingly;
    if I had turned to look back at the gate,
    how could I have explained this fault of mine?   *6*

Then we were climbing through a narrow cleft
    along a path that zigzagged through the rock
    the way a wave swells up and then pulls back.   *9*

"Now, we are at the point," my guide began,
    "where we must use our wits: when the path bends,
    we keep close to the far side of the curve."   *12*

This forced us into taking smaller steps,
    so that the waning moon had made its way
    to rest already in its bed, before   *15*

we finally squeezed through that needle's eye.
    When we were free, once more out on the mount,
    where this recedes enough to form a ledge,   *18*

we stopped there on the level space that stretched
    lonelier than a desert path—I, tired,
    and both of us uncertain of the way.   21

From the plain's edge, verging on empty space,
    to where the cliff-face soars again, was room
    for three men's bodies laid out end to end;   24

as far as I could take in with my eyes,
    measuring carefully from left to right,
    this terrace did not vary in its width.   27

And standing there, before we took a step,
    I realized that all the inner cliff,
    which, rising sheer, offered no means to climb,   30

was pure white marble; on its flawless face
    were carvings that would surely put to shame
    not only Polyclete but Nature too.   33

The angel who came down to announce on earth
    the peace longed for by weeping centuries,
    which broke the ancient ban and opened Heaven,   36

appeared before our eyes: a shape alive,
    carved in an attitude of marble grace,
    an effigy that could have spoken words.   39

One would have sworn that he was saying "Ave!"
    for she who turned the key, opening for us
    the Highest Love, was also figured there;   42

the outlines of her image carved the words
    Ecce ancilla Dei, as clearly cut
    as is the imprint of a seal on wax.   45

"Why don't you look at other parts as well?"
    my gentle master said, the while I stood
    close by his side, the side that holds the heart.   48

And so I turned my eyes and looked ahead
    past Mary's figure to that point where he
    who prompted me now stood, and there I saw   51

another story cut into the stone;
    crossing in front of Virgil, I drew near,
    so that my eyes could take in all of it.   54

CANTO X / 109

Carved in the spread of marble there, I saw
　　the cart and oxen with the holy Ark:
　　a warning not to exceed one's competence.　　　　57

Ahead of it moved seven separate choirs
　　testing my senses: one of these said, "No,"
　　the other one said, "Yes, they truly sing!"　　　　60

With equal art, the smoke which censers poured
　　was traced so faithfully that eyes and nose
　　could not decide between a "yes" or "no."　　　　63

Ahead, and far beyond the sacred Ark,
　　his robes girt up, the humble Psalmist danced,
　　showing himself both more and less than king.　　　　66

Depicted on the other side was Michal,
　　as from a palace window she looked on,
　　her face revealed her sadness and her scorn.　　　　69

I moved away from that place to observe
　　at closer range another story told
　　in whiteness just beyond the face of Michal.　　　　72

Here was retold the magnanimity
　　of that great Prince of Rome whose excellence
　　moved Gregory to win his greatest fight:　　　　75

there rode the noble Trajan, Emperor,
　　and clinging to his bridle as she wept
　　a wretched widow, carved in lines of grief.　　　　78

The trampled space surrounding him was packed
　　with knights on horseback—eagles, flying high,
　　threaded in gold of banners in the wind.　　　　81

That poor widow amid the mass of shapes
　　seemed to be saying: "Lord, avenge my son
　　who has been killed; my heart is cut with grief.　　　　84

He seemed to answer: "You will have to wait
　　for my return." And she, like one impelled
　　by frantic grief: "But, oh, my lord, if you　　　　87

should not return?" And he: "Who takes my place
　　will do it for me." She: "How can you let
　　another's virtue take the place of yours?"　　　　90

Then he: "Take comfort, for I see I must
    perform my duty, now, before I leave:
    Justice so wills, and pity holds me here."   93

That One for Whom no new thing can exist
    fashioned this art of visible speech—so strange
    to us who do not know it here on earth.   96

As I stood there delighting in the sight
    of these august humilities displayed,
    dear to behold for their own Craftsman's sake,   99

"See, over there, how slowly they approach,
    that crowd of souls," the Poet whispered to me,
    "they will direct us to the lofty stairs."   102

My eyes, intent on their admiring,
    were, nonetheless, not slow to turn toward him,
    for they are always eager for new sights.   105

But, Reader, when I tell you how God wills
    His penitents should pay their debts, do not
    abandon your intention to repent.   108

You must not think about the punishment,
    think but of what will come of it—at worst
    it cannot last beyond the Final Day.   111

"Master, what I see moving toward us there,"
    I said, "do not seem to be shades at all;
    I don't know what they are, my sight's confused."   114

"The grievous nature of their punishment,"
    he answered, "bends their bodies toward the ground;
    my own eyes were not sure of what they saw.   117

Try hard to disentangle all the parts
    of what you see moving beneath those stones.
    Can you see now how each one beats his breast?"   120

O haughty Christians, wretched, sluggish souls,
    all you whose inner vision is diseased,
    putting your trust in things that pull you back,   123

do you not understand that we are worms,
    each born to form the angelic butterfly,
    that flies defenseless to the Final Judge?   126

Why do your souls' pretensions rise so high,
    since you are but defective insects still,
    worms as yet imperfectly evolved?   *129*

Sometimes one sees a corbel, holding the weight
    of roof or ceiling, carved in human shape
    with chest pressed tightly down against its knees,   *132*

so that this unreality gives real
    anguish to one who sees it—this is how
    these souls appeared, and how they made me feel.   *135*

True, some of them were more compressed, some less,
    as more or less weight pressed on each one's back,
    but even the most patient of them all   *138*

seemed through his tears to say: "I can't go on!"

NOTES

    The mountain of Purgatory is surrounded by seven concentric ledges, each separated from the other by a steep cliff. On each ledge, or terrace, one of the seven Capital Sins is purged: Pride, Envy, Wrath, Sloth, Avarice (and Prodigality), Gluttony, Lust. The set-up of the First Terrace (Cantos X–XII), where souls are being punished for the sin of Pride, is paradigmatic and establishes the pattern of purgation that is followed throughout Purgatory proper.

    Each group of souls on its particular terrace is assigned a prayer. When a soul has finished purging his sin on one level, he climbs to the next, via a stairway and an angel-sentry who performs a final cleansing gesture. A beatitude appropriate to the sin that has been cleansed is assigned to each ledge. In addition, on each terrace of Purgatory proper, we will encounter representations of the sin being purged on that terrace, as well as examples of the virtue that is opposed to that sin. The representation of the sin is intended to incite disdain for the sin, while the representation of the virtue is designed to inspire souls to the emulation of virtuous behavior. These representations take on various forms—on the First Terrace they appear as carvings in the stone of the mountain. The examples that comprise the "disdain for the sin" and the "inspiration for virtuous behavior" are drawn both from Christian and pagan lore.

But the first example of every virtue is always taken from the life of the Blessed Virgin Mary.

2. *whose loves are bad:* Love, in Dante's view, is the force behind all human action. Just as good works are an extension of love rightly directed, so sin is an extension of love disordered, of love perverted for the sake of evil. The belief that love is the central ordering principle of the universe goes back to Aristotle; he posited that the force of love, which manifested itself in each object's search for its "right" or natural position, was what kept the planets in regular motion and motivated temporal and seasonal progressions. Hence love would be synonymous with physical order, and, by extension, with what is "right" or natural spiritually, or what is good. The belief that love was the supreme ordering force in the universe continued and developed into the Middle Ages. A prayer ascribed to St. Francis of Assisi reads, "Set love in order, Thou that lovest me." What the souls in Purgatory must do is redirect their love and, through purgation, set it in order with divine love. (See Virgil's discourse, *Purg.* XVII, 103 ff.)

5. *if I had turned:* The pilgrim seems to be learning his lesson: not to look back and to concentrate on his forward progress.

7–16

The general critical consensus is that the path "that pitched from side to side" is, quite simply, a zigzag path. However, as far back as Pietro di Dante and Benvenuto da Imola, commentators have admitted the possibility that the path itself is actually pitching from side to side. This latter interpretation is not as patently absurd as it would first appear to be. On a symbolic level, it would certainly reinforce the idea that the beginning of the journey of purgation that leads to God is indeed difficult, laborious, and tortuous. And furthermore, Sayers (p. 341) observes that "The negotiation of a moving barrier or 'pass perilous' of a similar sort is a commonplace of Other-World Journeys, both in Classical and romantic folk-lore, the most famous instances being the Clashing Rocks through which the Argonauts have to steer, and the falling portcullis past which Owain has to leap both in the Celtic and French versions of the story."

7. *a narrow cleft:* The narrow passageway through which the Pilgrim and Virgil must pass suggests the difficult road to Heaven: "How narrow the gate and close the way that leads to life! And few there are who find it" (Matt. 7:14). The gate of Purgatory' and this narrow path stand out in marked contrast to the entrance to the Inferno, where the gate is very wide.

16. *needle's eye:* Cf. Matt. 19:24: "It is easier for a camel to pass through the eye of a needle than for a rich man to enter the kingdom of heaven."

20. *lonelier than a desert path:* The loneliness, the desertlike quality, of the ledge along which the Proud must slowly move will be referred to again in the following canto (XI, 15).

31–32. *on its flawless face / were carvings:* The carvings here illustrate examples of the virtue of Humility; they will be followed two cantos later by "carved examples" of the vice of Pride. Thus, on the first cornice, Dante has chosen to represent the relevant pair of contrasts on the visual plane, imagining illustrative scenes carved with consummate art. For some possible visual sources of Dante's literary pictorialism here on the Terrace of Pride, see Fiero.

33. *Polyclete:* Polycletus was a celebrated Greek sculptor (ca. 452–412 B.C.) and a contemporary of Phidias. Just as Phidias was thought to be unsurpassed in carving images of the gods, so Polycletus was thought to execute perfect carvings of men. One of his works, a carving of a bodyguard of the king of Persia, came to be called, because of its perfection, "the rule." He is acclaimed by Aristotle, Cicero, Pliny, Quintilian, and others.

34–45

As will always be the case, the first example of the virtue illustrated is taken from the life of the Virgin Mary; here, the scene of the Annunciation is chosen to represent humility on Mary's part. When the angel Gabriel appeared to Mary and explained to her that she, though still a virgin, would bear the son of God, she acquiesced completely to God's will, replying, "Behold the handmaid of the Lord [*Ecce ancilla Dei*], let it be done unto me according to Thy will" (Luke 1:38).

36. *which broke the ancient ban and opened Heaven:* From the time of Original Sin until the death of Christ, Heaven had been

closed to mankind (the "weeping centuries" of verse 35), and all the souls destined for Heaven during this period went to Limbo (see *Inf.* IV, 52–63). With the coming of the Redeemer (the Annunciation alluded to in verse 34), the "ancient ban" was lifted and Heaven was opened to mankind.

41. *for she who turned the key:* The Virgin Mary in conceiving Christ "unlocked" for mankind the love of God.

48. *the side that holds the heart:* The Pilgrim is now standing to the left of Virgil.

55–69

The second exemplum of the virtue opposed to the vice of Pride is a carving depicting King David dancing in humility before the Ark of the Covenant as it is being brought to Jerusalem. After his victory over the Philistines, David reassembled his troops and prepared to bring the Ark to Jerusalem from the house of Abinadab. Uzzah and Ahio, sons of Abinadab, led the cart bearing the Ark as they travelled. When the oxen pulling the cart stumbled, Uzzah reached out to steady the Ark and touched it, whereupon God struck him dead for his presumption. David, frightened and displeased, decided to leave the Ark at the house of the Hittite Obededom. While it was there, Obededom prospered, and David decided once again to bring the Ark to Jerusalem. As the Ark entered the city, David could be seen dancing before it in worship and humility (II Sam. 6:1–17). By dancing, David humbled himself before God and his people, thus showing himself to be "both more and less than king." The carving depicts only this incident from the second stage of the Ark's journey, but Dante reminds the reader beforehand (57) of Uzzah's sacrilegious act.

57. *a warning not to exceed one's competence:* This is a reference to the presumptuous act of Uzzah, who accompanied the Ark during the first stage of its journey (see note to 55–69).

In a letter to the Italian cardinals (*Epist.* XI, 9, 12) Dante denies a comparison made between himself and Uzzah for his allegedly unwarranted interference in church affairs: while Uzzah touched the sacred Ark, Dante says, he only wishes to guide the oxen who have strayed from the right path.

59–60. *one of these said, "No":* This is his sense of hearing, which says, "No," while his sense of sight tells him, "Yes, they truly sing." In the next tercet (61–63) it is the senses of sight and smell ("eyes and nose" [62]) that cannot agree.

66. *both more and less than king:* By dancing reverently before the Ark, David humbles himself before God, thus showing himself to be both "more and less than king"—more than a king in the eyes of God and less than a king in the eyes of his fellow man.

67. *Michal:* David's first wife, Michal, daughter of King Saul, who observed with disdain and reproach her husband's humble dance of joy. For her arrogant attitude she was punished with sterility (cf. II Kings 6:23).

73–93

The third example is taken from the life of Trajan, Roman emperor from A.D. 98 to 117. In the carving, he is seen pausing on the way to battle to listen to the grievances of a poor widow who clings to his bridle. He displays humility by recognizing his obligation to the widow and halting his army to put himself at her service. This story was extremely popular in the Middle Ages and is recounted in the *Fiore di filosofi,* as well as in John the Deacon's ninth-century life of St. Gregory (*Sancti Gregorii Magni Vita,* II, 44).

75. *moved Gregory to win his greatest fight:* St. Gregory I, "the Great," born at Rome ca.540; pope from 590 to 604. In the Middle Ages it was widely believed that through the intercession of Gregory, the soul of the emperor Trajan was called back from Hell and allowed to return to life that he might repent and secure salvation. Dante will place the soul of Trajan in Paradise (*Par.* XX, 44–45).

94. *That One:* God is the artist (cf. *Inf.* XV, 11). Dante's presentation of God as artist prepares the reader for the appearance of Cimabue and Giotto in the next canto.

95. *this art of visible speech:* God is the One for whom no new thing can exist. Dante likens His carvings to "visible speech" because their vividness and presence are such that the figures represented in them seem to speak, to enact the scenes in which they are depicted. In the scene of David dancing be-

fore the people, the Pilgrim hears the people singing (and smells the incense); in that between the Archangel and Mary he is able to make out a few words ("Ave"; "Ecce ancilla Dei"); as for the last scene between Trajan and the widow, the Pilgrim, inspired by the dramatic sculpture, is able to reconstruct the entire dialogue. These carvings that seemingly speak to him as he watches are unlike anything that he has seen on earth. See Baldassaro, p. 273.

103–105. *My eyes:* Dante's eyes were more than content to marvel at the works of art, but not for idle pleasure. Quickly, eagerly, he turns away upon being summoned by Virgil.

121–29

Dante the Poet addresses all those "haughty Christians" clinging to the world, who ignore and abuse their capacity for being transformed into perfected souls. The image of the changing of caterpillar into angelic butterfly, one of transformation and flight, is central to the action of the *Purgatory*. Perfection, the requisite for ascent into Paradise, is symbolically represented by weightlessness, which may become wingèdness. Since on earth the Proud go stiff-necked, with head held high, they are weighted down in Purgatory by huge stones pressing them into the ground. When the penance for Pride is completed, the soul is freed of its weight and is brought closer to the weightlessness of perfection needed to ascend into Paradise. Also, as the soul exchanges pride for humility, its love is changed from disorder to order, and a transformation takes place in the soul as it begins to assume the purity that is its "right" or natural state.

125–26: *each born to form the angelic butterfly:* This reference to the ultimate destiny of man has at times been treated in too sentimental a fashion. It is a grim reminder that man was born to die; while he is alive his body is only a grub, intended to release his soul at death; when he dies his soul, "the angelic butterfly," is immediately destined to face his Maker naked ("defenseless") and to receive God's justice. I do not believe that we are invited to think here in terms of upward, wingèd flight, of the purified soul mounting toward God to receive the reward of Heaven, as is clearly the case in the sad lines 95–96 of Canto XII: "O race of man born to fly heavenward, / how can a breath of wind make you fall back?"

CANTO XI

THE CANTO OPENS with the prayer of the Proud—an expanded version of the Lord's Prayer. Virgil then asks the penitents to tell him the quickest way up the mountain, and one of
the souls replies that he will show them an opening through
which they may ascend. This is the soul of Omberto Aldobrandesco, who acknowledges that the sin of pride in family has
ruined not only himself but his entire house. The Pilgrim is
then recognized by another soul, Oderisi of Gubbio, who proclaims against the empty glory of human talent. And Oderisi
points to still another of the souls of the Proud—Provenzan
Salvani, the presumptuous dictator of Siena.

"Our Father Who in Heaven dost abide,
   not there constrained but dwelling there because
   Thou lovest more Thy lofty first effects,   *3*

hallowed be Thy name, hallowed Thy Power,
   by Thy creatures as it behooves us all
   to render thanks for Thy sweet effluence.   *6*

Thy kingdom come to us with all its peace;
   if it come not, we of ourselves cannot
   attain to it, no matter how we strive.   *9*

And as Thine angels offer up their wills
   to Thee in sacrifice, singing Hosannah,
   let all men offer up to Thee their own.   *12*

Give us this day our daily manna, Lord:
   without it, those most eager to advance
   go backwards through this wild wasteland of ours.   *15*

As we forgive our trespassers, do Thou,
   forgive our trespasses, merciful Lord,
   look not upon our undeserving worth.   *18*

Our strength is only weakness, lead us not
   into temptation by our ancient foe:
   deliver us from him who urges evil.   *21*

This last request, beloved Lord, we make
    not for ourselves, who know we have no need,
    but for those souls who still remain behind."   24

Thus, praying for their welfare and for ours,
    those souls moved slowly bent beneath their weights—
    the slowness that oppresses us in dreams—   27

unequally tormented by their loads,
    making their tired way on the First Round,
    purging away the filth of worldliness.   30

If they, up there, pray always for our good,
    think of what we down here can do for them,
    when praying hearts are rooted in good will!   33

We ought, indeed, to help them wash away
    the stains they bring from earth, that they may rise,
    weightless and pure, into the wheeling stars.   36

"Ah, so may justice joined with pity free
    you from your load, that you may spread your wings
    and fly up to the goal of your desire,   39

show us how we may find the shortest way
    to reach the stairs; if there are many paths,
    direct us to the one least steep to climb: 42

this man who comes here with me bears a weight;
    he is invested still with Adam's flesh,
    and so, against his will, is slow to climb."   45

Some words then came in answer to the ones
    that had been spoken by my leader, but
    it was not clear to me from whom they came;   48

someone, however, said: "Follow this bank
    along the right with us, and you will find
    the road a living man can surely climb.   51

If I were not prevented by this stone
    that curbs the movement of my haughty neck,
    and makes me keep my face bent to the ground,   54

I would look up to see if I might know
    this unnamed living man, and hope to move
    him to compassion for my burdened back.   57

I was Italian, born of a great Tuscan:
  Guglielmo Aldobrandesco was my sire.
  Perhaps you never heard the name before.   60

My ancient lineage, the gallant deeds
  of my forebears had made me arrogant:
  forgetful of our common Mother Earth,   63

I held all men in such superb disdain,
  I died for it, as all Siena knows
  and every child in Compagnatico.   66

I am Omberto. And the sin of Pride
  has ruined not only me but all my house,
  dragging them with it to calamity.   69

This weight which I refused while I still lived,
  I now am forced to bear among the dead,
  until the day that God is satisfied."   72

I had my head bent low, to hear his words,
  and someone—not the one who spoke just now—
  twisted around beneath his punishment,   75

and saw my face, and knew me, and called out,
  straining to keep his eyes on me, as I
  moved with those souls, keeping my body bent.   78

"Oh!" I said, "*you* must be that Oderisi,
  honor of Gubbio, honor of the art
  which men in Paris call 'Illuminating.'"   81

"The pages Franco Bolognese paints,"
  he said, "my brother, smile more radiantly;
  his is the honor now—mine is far less.   84

Less courteous would I have been to him,
  I must admit, while I was still alive
  and my desire was only to excel.   87

For pride like that the price is paid up here;
  I would not even be here, were it not
  that, while I still could sin, I turned to God.   90

Oh, empty glory of all human power!
  How soon the green fades from the topmost bough,
  unless the following season shows no growth!   93

Once Cimabue thought to hold the field
  as painter; Giotto now is all the rage,
  dimming the lustre of the other's fame.   96

So, one Guido takes from the other one
  poetic glory; and, already born,
  perhaps, is he who'll drive both from fame's nest.   99

Your earthly fame is but a gust of wind
  that blows about, shifting this way and that,
  and as it changes quarter, changes name.   102

Were you to reach the ripe old age of death,
  instead of dying prattling in your crib,
  would you have more fame in a thousand years?   105

What are ten centuries to eternity?
  Less than the blinking of an eye compared
  to the turning of the slowest of the spheres.   108

You see that soul ahead crawling along?
  All Tuscany resounded with his name;
  now hardly is it whispered in Siena,   111

where once he ruled, and managed to destroy
  the mad attack of Florence—once, so proud
  but, now, become as venal as a whore.   114

Your earthly fame is like the green in grass:
  it comes and goes, and He who makes it grow
  green from the earth will make it fade again."   117

And I to him: "Your words of truth have humbled
  my heart; they have reduced my swollen pride.
  But who is he you spoke about just now?"   120

"That's Provenzan Salvani," he replied,
  "and he is here because presumptuously
  he sought to gain control of all Siena.   123

So he crawls on, and has crawled since he died,
  knowing no rest. And such coin is paid here
  by those who were presumptuous down there."   126

And I: "If it is true that any soul
  who has delayed repentance till the last
  must wait down there before he can ascend,   129

the same amount of time he lived on earth
(unless he's helped by efficacious prayer)—
then how has he arrived so fast up here?"   132

He said: "While at the apex of his glory,
in Siena's marketplace, of his free will,
putting aside all shame, he took his stand,   135

and there, to ransom from his suffering
a friend who was immured in Charles's jail,
he brought himself to do what chilled his veins!   138

(I say no more. My words, I know, are vague,
but your own neighbors not too long from now
will help you to interpret what I've said.)   141

It was this deed of his that sped him here."

NOTES

1–21

The first seven tercets of the canto constitute an expanded paraphrase of the Lord's Prayer, recited by the souls on the terrace of the Proud. The parts that have been added to the original text of the prayer consistently and fittingly emphasize humility (as Momigliano [pp. 341–43] shows.) They display a consciousness of human weakness and an attitude of supplication before the Almighty.

4–5. *hallowed be Thy name . . . / by Thy creatures:* The phrase added to the original "hallowed be Thy name" is reminiscent of the *Laudes creatururum* of Saint Francis, who was perhaps the greatest example of humility in the Middle Ages (see Contini [1960], pp. 33–34).

13–15. *Give us this day our daily manna:* The replacement of the original "daily bread" by a "daily manna," as well as the reference to the desert, recalls the Exodus theme of the Antepurgatory (in particular see *Purg.* II, 45). And, indeed, the Exodus figure applies as well to Purgatory proper: here, too, the souls are waiting and wandering on their desert path (X, 21).

24. *those souls who still remain behind:* That is, those still living on earth, who need protection from temptation. The reference could hardly include those "remaining behind" in the Antepurgatory, for the Late Repentant are as secure from temptation as are those within the gate. And the pronoun *ours* in the following line ("Thus, praying for their welfare and for ours") makes this clear: Dante's use of the first person plural here could only refer to Dante and his kind, that is, living men.

28. *unequally tormented by their loads:* each soul is tormented according to the gravity and extent of his own sin.

38. *that you may spread your wings:* Once again, we are reminded of the theme of flight, the central metaphor for purgatorial ascent.

44. *Adam's flesh:* Dante, too, like the souls of the Proud (28), is "burdened."

49–72

An anonymous voice speaks, which will eventually identify itself as that of Omberto Aldobrandesco (67). The entire speech is dominated by the pronoun "I" (and the possessive "my"), showing a lingering tendency toward pride and self-centeredness. The haughty Omberto defines himself in terms of family and lineage, and in terms of his reputation among others (64–66), but, at the same time, he demonstrates a clear consciousness of his own arrogance and the destruction that it wrought upon him and his entire family (67–79).

59. *Guglielmo Aldobrandesco:* This name, which occupies almost the entire verse, seems to echo the grandiose qualities of Omberto's father, the mighty Tuscan.

60. *Perhaps you never heard the name before:* No irony is intended here. Omberto is being sincere, and this line is an index of the spiritual progress toward humility that he has made thus far in Purgatory.

67. *Omberto:* Second son of Guglielmo Aldobrandesco (59), Count of Santafiora, whose hatred of the Sienese led him to abandon the Ghibelline cause and ally himself with the Guelphs of Florence and Tuscany. Omberto was the lord of a fortified castle at Compagnatico.

Two versions of Omberto's death are extant. In the more widely accepted, he was killed in May 1259 during a battle with the Sienese. His castle was besieged, and, although he was greatly outnumbered, he defended himself stoutly, finally charging into the thick of the enemy and causing a number of deaths before he was cut down. His defense against a much larger force and his final charge indicate supreme disdain for those who attacked him.

In the other, less popular, version Omberto was strangled or suffocated in his bed by hired killers of the Sienese. Verses 64–66 would seem to indicate that in this canto Omberto refers to the former version of his death.

73–78

The Pilgrim here, head bent low, body stooped, is sharing the purgation of the Proud. On each terrace of the Purgatory he will "participate" to some extent in the suffering and purgation of the sin. The participation here is particularly marked since Dante admits (*Purg.* XIII, 136–38) that his own besetting sin is Pride.

77. *straining to keep his eyes on me:* Evidently this soul's punishment is less grave than Omberto's, for he is able to lift his head, although with difficulty, and see the Pilgrim.

79. *you must be that Oderisi:* Oderisi of Gubbio does not identify himself (as did Omberto), but Dante greets him with intense enthusiasm. Oderisi (ca. 1240–99?) was an illuminator of manuscripts. In his *Life* of Giotto, Vasari states (pp. 384–85) that Oderisi was employed by Boniface VIII to illuminate some manuscripts in the papal library, and that he was a lesser artist than Franco Bolognese (see verses 82–83). Benvenuto comments that Oderisi was vain, and that he boasted that he had no equal in painting. He suggests an intended irony in Dante's calling him "the honor of Gubbio."

82. *The pages Franco Bolognese paints:* Oderisi replies to Dante with self-effacement. Though his tone differs significantly from the pompous and solemn pronouncements of Omberto, Oderisi is not yet totally devoid of pride, for he implies that his pages too, smile; and, although he concedes first place to Franco Bolognese, the old habit of pride still lays claim to some (even though a lesser) glory (84).

We have no information regarding Franco Bolognese, and (as is the case with Oderisi) no extant works can be attributed to him with any certainty.

91–93. *Oh, empty glory:* Human fame and glory are transitory; they are easily and quickly superseded. Only if a productive age is followed by a decadent and nonproductive one can the fame of that age endure, since nothing (no new glory) has come along to replace the old.

94. *Cimabue:* Cenni de Pepo, known as Giovanni Cimabue (1240?–1302?), was considered in the Florence of his day a great master. He broke from the Byzantine tradition of art to develop a more natural style.

95. *Giotto:* Giotto of Bondone (1266 or 1267–1337) was a pupil of Cimabue's who went on to surpass his master. Giotto appears to have been a personal friend of Dante's (one or two years his junior), and is most likely responsible for the famous portrait of Dante in the Bargello at Florence.

97–99. *one Guido takes from the other one:* The first is Guido Cavalcanti (1259–1300), whom Dante in the *Vita Nuova* calls his "first friend" and to whom that work is dedicated, and the other is Guido Guinizelli (ca. 1230–ca. 1276), a Bolognese poet whom Dante refers to as his "father" and the father of "all those who wrote poetry of love in a sweet and graceful style" (*Purg.* XXVI, 97–99). Both Guidos were exponents of the so-called *dolce stil nuovo*. But the poetic glory of Guinizelli, Dante lets Oderisi say, has now been obscured by that of Cavalcanti, and, perhaps, he continues, someone has already been born who will supersede them both.

Does Oderisi have Dante in mind as the one destined to drive both Guidos from the nest? If so, this praise would amount to self-praise on the part of Dante; that is, it would be a sign of his vanity, his pride. And some commentators point ahead to Canto XIII, where the Pilgrim indicates that Pride is his besetting sin. But granted that Dante the Poet would here be boasting through Oderisi of his future triumph over the two Guidos, the overall context would make this boast appear ridiculously empty: for he has also put into Oderisi's mouth words that affirm most vehemently the transitory nature of all fame and, hence, its meaninglessness. It is, of course, not impossible that Dante, while prompting Oderisi to speak so contemptuously of fame as a passing phenomenon, might be thinking that his own case would prove to be an exception to the general law.

105. *would you have more fame in a thousand years?:* Here, Oderisi's scorn of earthly fame reaches an extreme that is surely unrealistic—as if it were impossible to speak in terms of lasting fame. To take his own field of competency: was not the reputation of Polycletus still a living memory after more than a thousand years?

109. *that soul ahead crawling along:* In verse 121 he is identified as Provenzan Salvani (ca. 1220–69), Ghibelline chief of Siena. At the council of Empoli following the battle of Montaperti in 1260 (112–13) he advocated the total destruction of Florence, a plan that was successfully countered by Farinata (*Inf.* X, 91–93). He died in 1269, beheaded by a certain Cavolino de Tolomei after the defeat of the Sienese by the Florentines at Colle di Val d'Elsa. Provenzan's sins are an example of pride in temporal power.

127. *If it is true:* Here the Pilgrim asks the question that reveals his deduction based on Belacqua's words (*Purg.* IV, 130–34) about his term of waiting: all the Late Repentant must wait in the Antepurgatory (at least) the length of time of their life on earth. Thus the Pilgrim is puzzled: it has been only thirty-one years since Provenzan died, and he died at forty-nine.

137. *Charles:* Probably Charles of Anjou. Charles declared that if he did not receive ten thousand gold florins within a month's time, he would put a friend of Provenzan's, his prisoner, to death. To raise the money, Provenzan, despite his lofty station, begged alms in the Piazza del Campo in Siena and managed to buy his friend's release within the allotted time.

138. *he brought himself to do what chilled his veins:* This is a most indirect way of saying "he forced himself to beg in the public square."

139. *My words, I know, are vague:* Here, Oderisi is admitting the obscurity of the words about Provenzan just uttered in verse 138 (see previous note). But he goes on to offer a prophecy about Dante that not only is obscure but also in-

volves a logical inconsistency: granted that Dante's neighbors, the Florentines, will, by exiling him, make him understand (if *chiosar* can mean "understand") the humiliation of "begging," how can they make him understand the precise reference of verse 138?

142. *It was this deed of his that sped him here:* By my translation I suggest that Provenzan was allowed to come to Purgatory proper immediately, not simply that his waiting period was shortened somewhat. This should be the meaning of the original: *Quest' opera li tolse quei confini* ("this deed relieved him of those confinements").

CANTO XII

As THEY LEAVE the souls of the Proud, Virgil calls the Pilgrim's attention to a series of carvings in the bed of rock beneath their feet. These are the examples of the vice of Pride, of the haughty who have been brought low. Depicted in the carvings are Satan, the giant Briareus, Nimrod, Niobe, Saul, Arachne, Rehoboam, the slaying of Eriphyle by her son Alcmeon, Sennacherib's murder by his sons, the slaughter of Cyrus by Tomyris, the destruction of Holofernes and the rout of the Assyrians, and finally the fall of Troy. As they continue circling the ledge, Virgil admonishes the Pilgrim to lift his head in anticipation of the angel of Humility. With a brush of his wings, the angel removes the first *P* from the Pilgrim's forehead, and, as the two poets make their way through the pass to the next terrace, they hear a sweetly resounding song—the beatitude "Blessed are the Poor in Spirit." The Pilgrim now feels himself to be lighter, since one of the *P*'s has been removed, and is able to climb with considerably less effort.

Like oxen keeping step beneath their yoke,
   we moved along, that burdened soul and I,
   as long as my kind teacher would allow;   *3*

but when he said: "Now leave him and move on,
   for each one here must drive his boat ahead
   with sail and oar, and all the might he has,"   *6*

I stood up straight to walk the way man should,
   but, though my body was erect, my thoughts
   were bowed and shrunken to humility.   *9*

Now I was moving, happily following
   the footsteps of my master, both of us
   showing how light of foot we had become,   *12*

when, "Now look down," he said. "You will be pleased,
   and it will make your journey easier,
   to see this bed of stone beneath your feet."   *15*

As tombs set in a church floor often bear
   carved indications of the dead man's life,
   in preservation of his memory   *18*

(pierced by such recollection of the dead,
    a man is very often brought to tears—
    though only those with piety are moved):   21

just so, I saw—but far more true to life,
    being divinely wrought—stone carvings there
    covering the path that juts out from the mount.   24

I saw, on one side, him who was supposed
    to be the noblest creature of creation,
    plunge swift as lightning from the height of Heaven.   27

I saw Briareus on the other side,
    pierced through by the celestial thunderbolt,
    heavy upon the ground, frozen in death.   30

I saw Thymbraeus, saw Pallas and Mars
    still armed, close to their father, looking down
    at severed, scattered members of the giants.   33

I saw the mighty Nimrod by his tower,
    standing there stunned and gazing at the men
    who shared at Shinar his bold fantasy.   36

O Niobe, I saw your grieving eyes:
    they wept from your carved image on the road,
    between your seven and seven children slain.   39

O Saul, transfixed by your own sword, how dead
    you seemed to lie on Mount Gilboa's plain—
    which since that time has known no rain or dew.   42

O mad Arachne, I could see you there,
    half-turned to spider, sad above the shreds
    of your own work of art that sentenced you.   45

O Rehoboam, the image of you here
    no longer threatens: in a chariot,
    it flees fear-stricken, though no man pursues.   48

Depicted, too, in that hard pavement stone
    was Alcmeon, who made his mother pay
    so dearly for the accursèd ornament.   51

Depicted were Sennacherib's own sons
    assaulting him at prayer within the temple,
    and their departure, as he lay there dead.   54

Depicted was Tomyris with the ruin
and slaughter that she wrought, her words to Cyrus:
"Blood you have thirsted for—now, drink your own!" 57

Depicted was the rout of the Assyrians
who fled at Holofernes' death—it showed
the remnants of his mutilated corpse. 60

I saw Troy gaping from its ashes there:
O Ilium, how you were fallen low,
depicted on the sculptured road of stone. 63

What master artist with his brush or pen
could reproduce these shapes and shadings here?
Such art must overwhelm the subtlest mind! 66

The dead seemed dead, the living seemed alive;
no witness to the scene itself saw better
than I who trod upon it, head bent low. 69

Be proud, then! Onward, haughty heads held high,
you sons of Eve! Yes, never bow your head
to see how evil is the road you tread! 72

We had, by now, gone farther round the moun�,
and much more of the sun's course had been traced,
than I, preoccupied, could have conceived— 75

when he who always kept a watchful eye
as he moved on said: "Raise your head up now,
you have spent time enough lost in your thoughts. 78

Look over there, and see. The angel comes!
And, see—the sixth handmaiden has returned
already from her service to the day. 81

Show reverence in your face and attitude,
so that he will be glad to help us up;
think that this day will never dawn again!" 84

I was well used to his admonishments
not to waste time, so, anything he said
to that effect could never be obscure. 87

Still closer to us, clothed in white, he came,
the radiantly fair creature, and his face
was shining like a trembling star at dawn. 90

He spread his arms out wide, and then his wings.
He said: "Come, now, the steps are very close;
henceforth, the climbing will be easier." 93

To such an invitation few respond:
O race of men, born to fly heavenward,
how can a breath of wind make you fall back? 96

He led us straight to where the rock was cleft.
Once there, he brushed his wings against my brow,
then he assured me of a safe ascent. 99

As, on the way up to the mountaintop
crowned by the church, beyond the Rubaconte,
set high, above that so well-governed town, 102

the steepness of the bold ascent is cut
on the right hand by steps carved in the rock
in times when one could trust ledgers and staves— 105

so here, the bank that from the second round
falls steep has been made easier with steps
though, on both sides, the high rock presses close. 108

While we were walking toward those steps, the song
Beati pauperes spiritu! rang out
more sweetly than could ever be described. 111

How different are these passageways from those
of Hell! One enters here to music—there,
below, to sounds of violent laments. 114

As we were climbing up the sacred steps,
I seemed to feel myself much lighter now
than I had been before on level ground. 117

"Master," I said, "tell me, what heavy thing
has been removed from me? I feel as if
to keep on climbing would be effortless." 120

He answered: "When the *P*'s that still remain
(though they have almost faded) on your brow
shall be erased completely like the first, 123

then will your feet be light with good desire;
they will no longer feel the heavy road
but will rejoice as they are urged to climb." 126

Then I did something anyone might do,
    made conscious by the way men looked at him
    that he must have some strange thing on his head: *129*

his hand will try hard to investigate,
    feeling around to find, fulfilling thus
    the duty that the eyes cannot perform;   *132*

so, my right hand with fingers spread found just
    six of the seven letters that were carved
    upon my brow by him who keeps the keys.   *135*

Observing this, my master smiled at me.

NOTES

2. *that burdened soul:* Oderisi.

3. *kind teacher:* In the original the word for "teacher" is
pedagogo, or a preceptor for small boys. The humility likewise
comes through in the metaphor of the oxen and the yoke (1),
which suggests patient submission.

5. *for each one here must drive his boat ahead:* Dante's journey
is once again seen as a "voyage" (cf. *Purg.* I, 1). Furthermore,
the ship imagery recalls Ulysses (*Inf.* XXVI) and his voyage,
undertaken in pride and presumption and consequently
doomed to failure and destruction. In contrast, Dante's voyage,
for which humility is an absolute essential, will be successful.

13–24

It is significant that the examples illustrating the vice of
Pride are cut into the floor: they are to be viewed with head
bent low, in humility. And from a practical point of view, we
must remember that many of the souls on this terrace, like
Omberto, crushed beneath the weight of the stones, are incapable of raising their heads and eyes.

16. *As tombs set in a church floor:* In the three tercets (16–24)
in which the carvings on a tomb are compared to the carvings
the Pilgrim is about to see (and which are much more carefully
wrought) the only point to be deduced about the second group
of carvings is that, like the first, they were intended to preserve
the memory of the figures delineated. The tercet 19–21 has

been placed within parentheses since its relevance within the simile is doubtful.

17. *carved indications of the dead man's life:* This could refer to a family coat of arms or, perhaps, the manner in which the figure is clothed (which might reveal his profession or station in life). Or the verse might simply mean "how the dead man looked [physical features] when he was alive."

25–63

The reliefs cut into the floor present thirteen examples of the sin of Pride and the disastrous consequences that it entails. The first twelve tercets (in Italian) begin respectively with the letters *UUUU, OOOO, MMMM,* forming an acrostic, which is resumed in the three lines of the thirteenth tercet: *uom* (the Italian word for "man"). Dante's obvious message here is that Pride is a sin so common and so basic as to be practically synonymous with man. The thirteen examples, beginning with Lucifer's fall, cover a wide range of material taken (almost) alternately from a biblical and a classical source. The final climactic example, the fall of Troy, represents the destruction of not merely a powerful individual but a powerful state, a civilization.

28. *Briareus:* One of the giants (*Inf.* XXXI, 98), who challenged Jupiter; he was slain by a thunderbolt and buried beneath Mt. Etna.

31. *Thymbraeus:* Another name for Apollo. The term is derived from Thymbra, the location of a temple dedicated to Apollo. Dante would be familiar with the derivative "Thymbraeus" from its use by Statius in the *Thebaid* (I, 643, 699; III, 513, 638; IV, 515) and from Virgil (*Georg.* IV, 323; *Aen.* III, 85).

33. *the giants:* Armed with boulders and tree trunks, the giants presumed to attack Mt. Olympus, home of the gods, only to be destroyed.

34. *Nimrod:* The giant who built the Tower of Babel on the plain of Shinar (Gen. 10:10). (Cf. *Inf.* XXXI, 77–78; *Par.* XXVI, 126.)

37. *Niobe:* The daughter of Tantalus and Dione, and the wife of Amphion, King of Thebes. Proud of her seven sons and

seven daughters, Niobe boasted her superiority over Latona, who had but two, Apollo and Diana. Apollo then killed the seven sons with his bow. Diana killed the seven daughters, and Niobe was turned to stone, though tears continued to fall from her marble cheeks. Dante's version of the story comes from Ovid (*Metam.* VI, 182–312).

40. *Saul:* Son of Kish of the tribe of Benjamin and first king of Israel. He was deposed by Samuel for having disobeyed God's command by sparing a life and allowing booty to be taken (I Sam. 15:3–11). Defeated by the Philistines on Mount Gilboa, Saul killed himself with his own sword to avoid capture (I Sam. 31:4–5).

43. *Arachne:* The daughter of Idmon of Colophon, who challenged Minerva to a weaving contest. She produced a beautiful cloth on which the love-adventures of the gods were woven, and Minerva, unable to find fault with it, ripped it to shreds. Arachne hanged herself, but Minerva loosened the rope, turning it into a web and Arachne herself into a spider (Ovid, *Metam.* VI, 1–145).

46. *Rehoboam:* The son of Solomon, who succeeded his father as king of Israel. He refused to lighten the taxes imposed on his people and sent Adoram to collect them. Ten of the tribes revolted, Adoram was stoned to death, and Rehoboam fled to Jerusalem (I Kings 12:18).

50. *Alcmeon:* The son of Amphiaraus the Soothsayer and Eriphyle. Foreseeing that he would die during the expedition against Thebes, Amphiaraus concealed himself. But Polynices bribed Eriphyle with the golden necklace of Harmonia to reveal her husband's hiding place, and Amphiaraus was constrained to go to war, where he met his fate. Before he went, however, he asked his son for revenge, and Alcmeon accordingly slew his mother for her betrayal (for Amphiaraus see *Inf.* XX, 34).

52. *Sennacherib:* King of Assyria from 705 to 681 B.C., Sennacherib arrogantly made war upon King Hezekiah of Judah and the Israelites. Although outnumbered, the Israelites, with the intervention of an angel of the Lord, annihilated the Assyrian host. Sennacherib escaped the debacle but was later mur-

dered by his two sons while praying to his false gods. (See II Kings 19:36–37 and Isa. 37:37–38.)

55–56. *Tomyris . . . Cyrus:* Tomyris (or Thamyris), the queen of the Massagetae (a Scythian people), sought revenge for the treacherous murder of her son at the hands of Cyrus (560–529 B.C.), emperor of the Persians. She defeated his army and Cyrus was killed in battle. Not satisfied, however, she decapitated him and threw his head into a vessel of human blood, urging him to drink his fill!

59. *Holofernes:* The general of the armies of Nebuchadnezzar, king of the Assyrians. He attacked Bethulia, a city of the Israelites, and proudly mocked their God. Judith, a beautiful widow, delivered the Israelites by going to Holofernes' tent at night under the pretense of sleeping with him. Instead, with grim resolve, she cut off his head. The Assyrians, seeing the head of their general mounted on the wall in the morning, fled in terror.

70–72. *Be proud then:* The Poet speaks sarcastically to mankind, the sons of Eve (the "common mother" of *Purg.* XI, 63). The tone and the subject matter here take up once more the polemic of *Purg.* X, 121–29.

75. *I, preoccupied:* Absorbed in the contemplation of the floor carvings, the Pilgrim does not notice the passage of time. (On such results of the absorption of the mind see *Purg.* IV, 1–12.)

77–84

The Pilgrim, completely absorbed by the admiration he feels for the artistry of the carvings he has just seen, is brought back to reality by the voice of Virgil, who wishes to prepare him for the coming of the angel. Twice he admonishes him ("Look over there . . ."; "Show reverence"), and each time he follows his admonition with a reminder of the passage of time: "the sixth handmaiden has returned . . ."; "think that this day will never dawn again." Virgil's constant concern with the passage of time, and with the need to employ well every moment, is well known to the Pilgrim—as the following tercet reveals.

80. *the sixth handmaiden:* The sixth handmaiden is the sixth hour of the day, or noon. Note here that even the passage of

time is seen in terms of "service," that is, of submission, of humility. And "handmaiden" (*ancilla*) was precisely the word used to designate Mary, the first and foremost example of humility in *Purg.* X, 44.

93. *henceforth, the climbing will be easier:* Once the Pilgrim has been purged of the first and heaviest of the Seven Capital Sins, the root of all evil, which is Pride, the ascent will, of course, become easier. In fact, when the *P* of Pride is removed from the Pilgrim's brow, the remaining six *P*'s become dimmer (see 121–23).

95. *O race of men:* Once again the Poet rebukes mankind, but without the harshness and the sarcasm that pervade *Purg.* X, 121–29 and XII, 70–72. His tone has mellowed to that of deep regret; he is filled with sadness that so many of those born to fly heavenward fall back before a breath of wind.

I am taking it for granted, as the punctuation shows, that in the tercet 94–96 we are meant to hear the voice of Dante the Poet; the tercet does not represent a continuation of the angel's words, as some scholars believe. For a treatment of the various arguments presented, see Poletta, pp. 286–87.

98. *brushed his wings:* With this gesture the angel removes the first *P*, which stands for the sin of Pride, from the Pilgrim's forehead.

102. *that so well-governed town:* A reference to Florence, and of course, a bitterly ironic one in view of the incidents alluded to in verse 105. The church on the mountaintop is San Miniato al Monte, located on the Monte alle Croci, overlooking Florence, the river Arno, and the bridge which crosses it, the Rubaconte (today Ponte alle Grazie).

105. *in times when one could trust ledgers and staves:* This line refers to two relatively contemporary scandals in Dante's Florence: the first incident, that of the ledger, involved a Florentine Guelph, Niccola Acciaiuoli, who, along with Baldo d'Aguglione, a Ghibelline judge (*Par.* XVI, 56), destroyed a sheet of the city's public records to cover up a fraudulent transaction. The sheet contained a written confession by the former corrupt podestà, Messer Monfiorito della Marca Trivigiana, who admitted to a false and prejudicial judgment for not having condemned Acciaiuoli. The second incident, that of the stave, in-

volved Durante de' Chiaramontesi, who was overseer of the salt custom's office at Florence. In his distribution of the salt he would keep a stave of every bushel for himself. His cheating was discovered, and he was beheaded. His descendants, from an ancient and honored family, were disgraced (cf. *Par.* XVI, 105).

110. *Beati pauperes spiritu:* "Blessed are the poor in spirit." Before leaving each of the seven terraces, Virgil and the Pilgrim will hear an angel utter a beatitude. This one, the first of those of the Sermon on the Mount (Matt. 5:3), praises the virtue of Humility, which is essential to the overcoming of Pride.

118. *"Master," I said, "tell me, what heavy thing":* The Pilgrim, not knowing that the angel has erased a *P* from his forehead, must learn of it from his teacher. With his addressing Virgil as his "master," we are reminded of the beginning of the canto, where Virgil was referred to as a child's preceptor (3). Once again, with his question and in what follows (121–35), the Pilgrim is presented as the humble, bewildered child.

130–32. *his hand will try:* This image of a man who cannot see, putting his hand up to feel, prepares us for Canto XIII, concerned with the Envious, whose penance involves blindness.

CANTO XIII

THE PILGRIM AND Virgil reach the second cornice, which is the livid color of stone. Since there are no souls in sight of whom to ask directions, Virgil turns to the sun for guidance. When he and Dante have walked about a mile along the ledge, they hear a disembodied voice crying out the examples of Generosity, the virtue opposed to the vice of Envy. The first of the virtuous examples that it cites is the Virgin Mary's solicitude at the wedding feast of Cana when she tells her son, "They have no wine." The second is the attempt of Pylades to save the life of his friend by claiming, "I am Orestes," and the third is the commandment from the gospels "Love your enemy." Virgil explains that on this terrace, the sin of Envy is punished, and he indicates the souls of the Envious sitting huddled together against the face of the cliff. They can be heard reciting the Litany of the Saints, and as the Pilgrim approaches them he remarks their piteous condition. They are dressed in the coarsest of haircloth, and their eyelids have been stitched shut with iron thread. The Pilgrim has a long conversation with Sapìa of Siena, who confesses that she rejoiced in the defeat of her own townsmen at the battle of Colle.

Now we are standing on the highest step,
  where, for a second time, we saw a ledge
  cut in the mount that heals all those who climb.   3

This terrace stretches all around the hill,
  exactly like the one below, although
  the arc of this one makes a sharper curve.   6

No sign of any souls or carvings here.
  The cliff face is all bare, the roadway bare—
  save for the livid color of the stone.   9

"If we wait here until somebody comes
  to give directions," said the Poet, "our choice,
  I am afraid, will be too long delayed."   12

Then, looking up, and staring at the sun,
  he made of his right side a pivot point,
  bringing the left side of his body round.   15

"O cherished light in whom I place my trust,
  please guide us on this unfamiliar road,"
  he said, "for in this place guidance we need.   18

You warm the world; you shed your light on it;
  unless there be some reason that opposes,
  your radiant light should always show the way."   21

We had already gone along that ledge
  as far as what is called a mile on earth—
  and quickly, too, because of our good will—   24

when spirits, who could not be seen, were heard,
  as they came flying towards us, speaking words
  of courteous invitation to love's board.   27

The first voice that came flying past us sang
  out loud and clear the words *Vinum non habent;*
  then we could hear them echoing behind.   30

Before the notes had faded quietly
  into distance, another voice cried out:
  "I am Orestes!" And that voice too swept by.   33

"Oh," I said, "Father, what voices are these?"
  And just as I was asking this, a third
  said, passing by: "Love those who do you harm!"   36

Then my good master said: "The Envious
  this circle scourges—that is why the whip
  used here is fashioned from the cords of love.   39

The curb must sound the opposite of love;
  you will most likely hear it, I should think,
  before the pass of pardon has been reached.   42

Now look in front of you, look carefully
  and you will see some people over there,
  all of them with their backs against the cliff."   45

I looked ahead of me, straining my eyes:
  I saw a mass of spirits wrapped in cloaks
  the color of the stone they leaned against.   48

And then as we came closer to these souls,
  I heard the cry: "O Mary, pray for us";
  then "Michael, Peter, and All Saints," they cried.   51

I do not think there is a man on earth
    with heart so hard that it would not be pierced
    with pity if he saw what I saw then: 54

when I had come up close enough to see
    the nature of the penance they endured,
    the sight squeezed bitter tears out of my eyes.   57

Their cloaks seemed to be made of coarsest cloth,
    and one's head on another's shoulder lay,
    the inner cliff supporting all of them.   60

They brought to mind blind beggars at church doors
    during Indulgences begging their bread:
    the one leaning his head upon the next   63

to stir up pity in their fellow man,
    not only by the sound of begging cries,
    but by the looks that plead no less than words.   66

Just as the blind cannot enjoy the sun,
    so, to the shades I saw before me here,
    the light of Heaven denies its radiance: 69

the eyelids of these shades had been sewn shut
    with iron threads, like falcons newly caught,
    whose eyes we stitch to tame their restlessness.   72

I felt that I was doing something wrong,
    walking along, staring at people who
    could not stare back. I turned to my wise guide,   75

who knew quite well what his mute ward would ask,
    and waiting not for me to speak, said, "Yes,
    but let your words be brief and to the point."   78

Virgil was walking on one side of me,
    along the terrace edge where one could fall
    (for there was no protective parapet),   81

while on the other side of me were massed
    those supplicating souls whose cheeks were wet
    with tears that seeped out through the horrid seams.   84

I turned to them and said: "O souls assured
    that someday you will see the light of Heaven
    which is the only goal that you desire,   87

so may God's grace soon wash away the film
    clouding your consciousness, and thus allow
    the stream of memory to flow through pure,   90

please let me know—I would be very grateful—
    is someone here, perhaps, Italian?
    I could be very helpful if he were."   93

"My brother, all of us are citizens
    of one true city. You mean is there a soul
    who was a pilgrim once in Italy?"   96

This answer to my question seemed to come
    from somewhere up ahead, so I moved on
    to where those souls could clearly hear my words.   99

Among them I discerned one shade that looked
    expectant. How could I tell? The chin was raised—
    that searching gesture of the blind. I said: 102

"O soul, learning to dominate yourself
    for the ascent—if it was you who spoke—
    tell me your name, or where you lived." She said: 105

"I was a Sienese; here with the rest
    I mend my evil life with tears and beg
    of Him that He reveal Himself to us.   108

Though named Sapìa, sapient I was not:
    I always reveled in another's grief,
    enjoying that more than my own welfare.   111

If you do not believe me, listen now
    and you will see how far my folly went.
    In the declining arc of my long years,   114

it happened that my townsmen were engaged
    in battle just outside of Colle; I
    prayed God for what already He had willed.   117

Our men were scattered on the plain and forced
    to take the bitter course of flight. I watched
    the chase, seized with a surge of joy so fierce   120

I raised my shameless face to God and cried
    "I have lost all my fear of Thee!" I was
    the blackbird when the sun comes out awhile.   123

I did not seek my peace with God, not till
  my final hour came—and even then,
  penance would not yet have reduced my debt   *126*

had it not been for one Pier Pettinaio,
  who, moved by charity to grieve for me,
  remembered me in all his holy prayers.   *129*

But who are you, so eager to inquire
  about us here—you with your eyes unsewn,
  so I would guess, and breathing out your words?"   *132*

"My sight one day shall be sewn up," I said,
  "but not for long; my eyes have seldom sinned
  in casting envious looks on other folk.   *135*

It is a greater fear that shakes my soul:
  that of the penance done below—already
  I feel on me the weight those souls must bear."   *138*

And she: "Then who has led you here to us,
  if you count on returning down below?"
  And I: "This man with me who does not speak.   *141*

I am alive. And if you want me to,
  O chosen soul, I would be glad to move
  my mortal feet on earth on your behalf."   *144*

"Oh, what a miracle this is!" she said.
  "What evidence of God's great love for you!
  Yes, help me with a prayer from time to time.   *147*

By what you hold most dear, I beg of you,
  if ever you set foot on Tuscan soil,
  restore my name among my kinsfolk there.   *150*

They live with those who dream of Talamone,
  whose foolish hopes will make them lose much more
  than they lost looking for Diana's bed—   *153*

but, still, the admirals will lose the most."

NOTES

6. *the arc of this one makes a sharper curve:* This circle, being
further up the mountain, is smaller.

8. *bare . . . bare:* The reader is invited to note that there are no reliefs carved into the stone here, as there were on the terrace below.

11. *our choice:* The "choice" Virgil refers to is one of direction: whether he and the Pilgrim should turn left or right in proceeding along this new terrace.

14. *he made of his right side a pivot point:* An elaborate periphrasis of a turn to the right. In view of what follows (Virgil addresses the Light of Natural Reason), such a mechanical-rational analysis of a simple movement to the right might have some aesthetic justification.

16–21. *O cherished light in whom I place my trust:* Virgil addresses the sun. He and the Pilgrim will for a time be guided directly by the sun since so far they have found no one to show them the way. We must in this instance be careful not to construe the sun as an emblem of God or of the assistance of divine grace. That this interpretation would be erroneous is made clear in verse 20: if the sun were God, then it would be utterly impossible for reasons to exist that might oppose its guidance. Rather, we should see the sun as an emblem of Natural Reason, which should always guide us, unless some higher power (God's grace) takes precedence.

25. *spirits:* We have already seen in verse 8 that the walls here are bare of any carvings illustrating the virtue of Charity; instead, the exempla here are rendered audibly, by means of disembodied voices.

29. *Vinum non habent:* "They have no wine." This is the first example of charitable concern for others, and, being the first, it is taken from the life of the Virgin Mary. The incident here alluded to is the wedding feast at Cana (John 2:1–10), where Mary, acting out of concern for the happiness of others, lovingly solicits her son's first miracle: the changing of water into wine.

33. *"I am Orestes":* The second example of the virtue opposed to Envy is from antiquity; it is an illustration of generosity and friendship. Orestes was condemned to death for having avenged the murder of his father, Agamemnon; Pylades pretended to be Orestes in order to save his friend's life. Orestes,

who would not allow his friend to make such a sacrifice, then came forward asserting his identity. There followed an argument, in which each, out of concern for the safety of the other, declared, "I am Orestes." Dante may have learned of the incident from Cicero's *De Amicitia,* VII, 24.

36. *said, passing by: "Love those who do you harm!":* The third voice expresses an evangelical precept taken from the Sermon on the Mount (Matt. 5:44). Whereas the words of the first two exempla were uttered in loud, ringing voices, here the simple verb *say* is used. Perhaps the tone is quieter, more reverent, because the words are those of Christ.

38. *—that is why the whip:* Here, on the Terrace of the Envious, the images of the whip and the curb (40) appear for the first and only time, in reference to the exempla, respectively, of the virtue to be emulated and the vice to be avoided. The first exempla, which have just been presented, should serve as a "whip" to incite the souls guilty of Envy to emulate the virtue of Charity; hence the whip is "fashioned from the cords of love." The second exempla, which will be presented only in *Purg.* XIV, 130–41, should serve as a rein, a "curb" on the vice, and thus "must sound the opposite of love": they should arouse hatred of the vice of Envy.

The reader may wonder whether with my translations *scourges* and *whip* (both in verse 38) I have not falsely given to understand that a whip here serves two different functions: the punishment of the Envious and the (nonpunitive) stimulation of their souls to emulate the examples of Charity. Actually, mine is a faithful reproduction of the original: the verb that I translate as "scourge" is *sferzare;* the noun "whip" is *ferza.* It would have been better if Dante, when speaking of this circle, this terrace as a whole, had used a more general term to convey the idea of "punishment" instead of suggesting prematurely the image of a whip—which can only be punitive. Surely the specific exempla of Charity that he next alludes to could not "punish." Dante is saying: "the sin that is being purged here is that of Envy; that is why the 'whip' to emulation of the opposed virtue must serve as an incentive to Charity."

42. *the pass of pardon:* This pass is at the entrance to the next terrace, at which point the angel will remove the second *P* of

Envy from the Pilgrim's brow and admit him to the Third Terrace.

50–51. *"O Mary, pray for us"; / then "Michael":* The souls are reciting the Litany of the Saints.

53. *with heart so hard that it would not be pierced:* Just how apposite the word *pierced* (Ital. *punto*) is, at this point, the reader will see in verses 70–72.

57. *the sight squeezed bitter tears out of my eyes:* Not until verse 70 will the reader be allowed to see this "sight."

62. *during Indulgences begging their bread:* On certain days of the year special Pardons or Indulgences were given to the Faithful; these ceremonies were attended in large numbers.

63. *the one leaning his head upon the next:* The penitent Envious, who once wished the worst for their neighbors, are now, like so many blind beggars, sustaining and supporting each other.

70. *the eyelids of these shades had been sewn shut:* This image is taken from falconry: the eyes of these birds, which were captured when they were no longer fledglings, were sewn shut (with waxed silk thread, however, not with iron wire) to facilitate domestication and training.

Now at last the hideous spectacle of the *contrapasso* suffered by the Envious is revealed: since their eyes could not bear to look upon the good fortune of others, they have here been sewn shut. At first we had a description only of the cloaks in which they were bundled, drab of color (48), made of haircloth (58); then their helpless, but mutually sustaining posture (59); then their resemblance to beggars (61: to blind beggars!); then the nature of their "blindness." And now it is clear why the exempla of Charity were not represented on the visual plane. See notes to *Purg.* XIII, 8 and 25.

84. *with tears that seeped out through the horrid seams:* This description of the tears seeping out through seams recalls Dante's own reaction upon first seeing the punishment of the Envious: "the sight squeezed bitter tears out of my eyes" (57); it could be taken as an instance of the Pilgrim's "participation" in the punishment of the Envious.

94–95. *citizens / of one true city:* The Pilgrim learns a lesson, that the earthly orientation of the Antepurgatory (cf. note to V, 134) no longer prevails: there is no Malaspina here, eager to learn news "of Valdimagra or parts thereabout" (*Purg.* VIII, 116). Here all are citizens of the one true city, the Heavenly Jerusalem, and are little concerned about earthly attachments.

101. *The chin was raised:* We have already noted (70) the slowness with which the poet proceeds to the description of the faces of these souls on the Terrace of Envy. Part of the delay was dictated by realistic reasons: when first aware of the presence of the Envious, the Pilgrim could make out only a huddled mass of figures, the color of their garments blending with the color of the rock against which they were leaning. Only when he is closer to them could he see their faces; even so, he does not allow us to share the sight that "squeezed bitter tears out of my eyes" (57) but makes us wait twelve lines more (70–72). Then, however, he lets us look into their faces three times. First, the punishment of their eyes, then the cheeks wet with the tears seeping out slowly through the seams (83–84), and finally the upraised chin of verse 101: the head thrown back as if the eyes were straining blindly into space. With these three descriptions we are made aware not only of the souls' blindness but also of the Pilgrim's acute vision, a vision capable of taking in every detail.

That the Pilgrim himself was aware of the contrast between the blindness of the souls about him and his own power of sight is indeed indicated by the Pilgrim's confession of guilt in verses 73–75: "I felt that I was doing something wrong. . . ." This immediately follows the reference to the eyelids sewn together.

106. *I was a Sienese:* The speaker, we shall learn, is a woman. In the *Inferno,* only one of the Damned who speak is a woman, Francesca da Rimini (Canto V); in the *Purgatory,* two of the Penitents who speak are women: la Pia (Canto V), and now Sapìa.

109. *Sapìa:* Sapìa of Siena was the paternal aunt of Provenzan Salvani (*Purg.* XI) and the wife of Ghinibaldo Saracini. She hated her fellow Sienese and resented her nephew's rise to power. It is entirely possible that she witnessed the battle in which Salvani and the Sienese were defeated by the Florentines at Colle in the Val d'Elsa in 1269 (there was a family castle at

Castiglioncello near the plain on which the battle took place). The dates of her birth and death are not known, though according to documentation she was alive in 1274—and she must have died before 1289, the year of Pier Pettinaio's death (see Sanesi).

116. *Colle:* The present Colle di Val d'Elsa in Tuscany, where, in 1269, the Sienese Ghibellines, under Provenzan Salvani and Count Guido Novello, were defeated in battle by the Florentine Guelphs, aided by the French troops of Charles D'Anjou.

120. *seized with a surge of joy so fierce:* This verse, together with 110–11 ("I always reveled . . .") indicates that Envy may involve not only resentment of the good fortune of others but positive enjoyment of their misfortunes.

123. *the blackbird:* The early commentator Buti notes that in Italy, the blackbird is reputed to be terrified of cold, bad weather, and thus goes into hiding when winter comes. But upon the first signs of fair weather, at the least provocation from the sun, the blackbird reemerges and makes fun of all the other birds—even goes so far as proclaiming "I do not fear you, Lord, for winter's over."

127. *Pier Pettinaio:* "Peter the Combseller." He was, supposedly, a member of the Franciscan order who dwelt close to Siena, where he was in the comb business. He was known for his piety, the miracles he performed, and his honesty (he refused to sell a defective comb). He died in December 1289, and documents suggest that he was 109 years old. In 1328 the Sienese senate decreed an annual festival in his honor.

138. *I feel on me the weight those souls must bear:* Here Dante is confessing that his besetting sin is that of Pride, which is purged on the terrace below. He expects to spend very little time on this terrace with his eyes sewn up like Sapìa's (133–35).

147. *Yes, help me with a prayer:* In the Antepurgatory a number of souls had asked of the Pilgrim that when he returned to earth he solicit prayers for them from their loved ones. This is probably what Dante had in mind when he offered to "move his mortal feet" on Sapìa's behalf. But she, impressed

by the signs of extraordinary grace that the Pilgrim was enjoying, asks for prayers from the Pilgrim himself. This was probably also the hope of la Pia in the Antepurgatory (*Purg.* V, 133), who asks that the Pilgrim, when he has returned to earth (and after he has rested from his journey) remember her. The critics seem to believe that la Pia had left behind no one on whom she could depend for prayers; could the same be true of Sapìa?

Two more souls in Purgatory (Marco Lombardo in *Purg.* XVI and Guido Guinizelli in *Purg.* XXVI) will ask the Pilgrim for his personal prayers.

151. *Talamone:* In 1303 the Sienese purchased from the abbot of San Salvatore for 8,000 gold florins the small seaport of Talamone, located on a promontory at the southwestern end of the Sienese Maremma; they hoped to build a harbor equal to that of Genova or Pisa, which could accommodate a sizeable fleet. The expensive venture failed completely because the port filled up with silt as fast as it was dredged, and because the marshy surroundings were infested with malaria.

153. *Diana's bed:* Siena often had problems with the water supply, and hence the Sienese invested large sums of money and considerable time and effort in the search for an alleged underground river—christened the Diana. Later, they were to succeed, but at the time of Dante, this project, too, had resulted in failure.

154. *the admirals will lose the most:* This line must refer to the first project of the Sienese, the construction of an adequate harbor. Though some early commentators take the word *ammiragli* to refer to the contractors or supervisors engaged in the construction, it is quite possible that it is used in the sense of 'admirals' or at least 'sea captains.' In this case the verse would invoke ambitious people hoping to be admirals of a fleet that will never exist. This image is preferable because more ironical—if we sense in Sapìa's words a continuing tendency to gloat over the misfortunes of her neighbors.

Whatever underlying significance is to be sought in Sapìa's words, it must refer to her attitude at the moment and hers alone, and it should not be interpreted as merely a typical Florentine gibe at the overambitious Sienese, which Dante the Poet has put into the mouth of this sinner.

CANTO XIV

THE CANTO OPENS with the gossip of two blind souls excited by their awareness of the unprecedented presence before them of a man who is still alive; they finally ask the Pilgrim who he is and where he is from. Dante's reference to his place of origin—the valley of the Arno—touches off a lengthy outburst of anti-Tuscan sentiment from one of his interlocutors. The Pilgrim then asks their names; the speaker identifies himself as Guido del Duca and his fellow shade as Rinier da Calboli—and immediately launches into another invective, this time against the recent degeneracy of Romagna. As the Pilgrim and Virgil are leaving the souls of the Envious, they hear the sharp crack of voices—screaming out exempla of Envy. The first voice is that of Cain, and the second, that of the Athenian princess Aglauros, who was turned to stone because she envied her sister, who was loved by the god Mercury.

"Who is this roaming round our mountainside
    before his soul is given wings by Death—
    opening his eyes and closing them at will?"   3

"Who knows? All I know is he's not alone.
    Why don't you ask him, you are nearer him;
    speak nicely to him so he'll answer you."   6

There to my right, I overheard two souls
    talking about me, huddled head to head;
    they raised their faces then, as if to speak.   9

And one said: "O soul, living prisoner
    within the flesh, but moving up to Heaven,
    console us in the name of love: please tell   12

where you are from and who you are. The grace
    that God has given you fills us with awe,
    for this is something never seen before."   15

And I said: "Through the heart of Tuscany
    a little river, born in Falterona,
    winds in its course more than a hundred miles,   18

and from its banks I bring this body here;
  there is no point in telling you my name,
  for I have not as yet won fame on earth."

"If I have clearly understood the gist
  of what you have just said," replied the shade,
  "it is the Arno you are speaking of."

The other said to him: "Why would he want
  to keep the real name of that river hid,
  as if it were too horrible to say?"

The shade who had been questioned answered back:
  "I don't know why, but it could only be
  a blessing for that valley's name to die.

For from its source, where the steep mountain chain
  from which Pelorus is cut off is rich
  with waters that no other place can claim,

down to the very point where it restores
  that which the sky has taken from the sea,
  thereby supplying rivers with their flow—

virtue is loathed. Men run away from it
  as from a snake! Either the place is cursed,
  or else it's old corruption guiding them.

The dwellers in that miserable vale
  have let their nature be transformed—it is
  as if they lived on food from Circe's sty.

Past hoggish brutes who should be eating acorns
  rather than food prepared for human use,
  this river first directs its puny course;

it keeps on dropping down, to run among
  packs of small curs who snarl more than they bite;
  disdainfully, it turns away its snout.

Still farther down it falls; the more this damned
  and God-forsaken sewer-ditch expands
  the more the dogs give way to wolves; and then,

through many deep-cut gorges it descends
  to run among those foxes steeped in fraud,
  who fear no trap contrived by human skill.

I will not stop, though this man hears my words;
  in fact, it would be good for him to know
  what inspiration has revealed to me: 57

I see your grandson now leading the chase,
  hunting down wolves, the ones that pack the banks
  of that wild stream—they live in terror there.   60

He sells their flesh while they are still alive,
  and then, like worn-out cattle, slaughters them.
  Himself he robs of honor, them of life.   63

He comes forth bloody from the wretched woods,
  which even in a thousand years from now
  could not re-wood itself as once it was."   66

As at the news of some impending doom
  the face that listens shows the shock received,
  no matter from what side the danger looms—   69

just so that shade, intent on listening,
  revealed his consternation and his grief,
  as he took in the meaning of those words.   72

The words of one of them, the other's face,
  made me so curious to know the pair,
  I asked them, begged them, to reveal their names.   75

At this the shade who spoke to me at first
  replied: "And you want me to bring myself
  to do what you refused to do for me?   78

But since God wills His grace to shine in you
  so generously, stingy I shall not be:
  Guido del Duca used to be my name.   81

Envy was quick to fire up my blood:
  whenever I would see someone rejoice,
  you'd see me turning livid at his joy.   84

I sowed this envy, now I reap this straw!
  O human race, why do you place your hopes
  where partnership must always be denied?   87

This is Rinier; this is the pride and joy
  of Calboli—a house without an heir
  who might inherit any of his worth.   90

From Po to mountains, Reno to the sea,
    their house is not the only one stripped bare
    of all that's good in life and chivalry;   *93*

for all the land within these boundaries
    is choked by poisonous weeds which would resist
    all efforts to prepare the soil for seeds.   *96*

Where is Mainardi? Where is the good Lizio?
    Pier Traversaro? Guido di Carpigna?
    O Romagnols, bastard descendents, false!   *99*

When in Bologna will there grow again
    a Fabbro? When, a Fosco in Faenza,
    that noble scion of a lowly plant?   *102*

O Tuscan, I must weep when I recall
    Ugolin d'Azzo, Guido da Prata, too,
    who lived among us once. And what about   *105*

Federigo di Tignoso and his friends,
    the Traversaro clan, the Anastagi,
    both families without an heir? And those   *108*

ladies and knights, those feats, that courtly play
    which love and courtesy did once inspire
    in that domain where all hearts now grow vile? *111*

O, Bretinoro, why don't you disappear!
    Your noble families and others, too,
    have fled from the corruption in your midst! *114*

Bagnacaval does well to have no sons;
    and Castrocaro's wrong, and Conio more,
    in bothering to breed such counts as theirs.   *117*

When the Pagani's demon finally
    drops dead, they will be better off—although
    the record of their evil deeds remains.   *120*

O Ugolin de' Fantolin, your name
    is safe—since there's no chance it will be stained
    by the degeneracy of future heirs.   *123*

But now, go, Tuscan, I would rather weep,
    much rather weep, than say another word—
    our discourse has so wrung my sorrowing mind." *126*

We knew those good souls heard us move away;
    thus, by their silence we could be assured
    of having taken the right path to climb.   129

As we were walking on our lonely road
    there came, like lightning ripping through the air,
    a voice, shot out at us from up ahead: 132

"I shall be slain by all who find me!"—Then
    it rolled past us like thunder dying down
    after the sudden bursting of a cloud.   135

Our ears had just begun recovering,
    when came the rumbling of a second voice—
    one clap of thunder thundering on the other: 138

"I am Aglauros, who was turned to stone!"
    With that, instead of going on, I moved
    a little closer to my Poet. By now   141

the air around us was serene once more.
    Then Virgil said: "That was the iron curb
    devised to keep a man within due bounds.   144

But you men take the bait, swallow the hook,
    and let the Adversary reel you in—
    and neither rein nor spur avails for you.   147

The heavens wheeling round you call to you,
    revealing their eternal beauties—yet,
    you keep your eyes fixed on the ground alone,   150

and He, the All-Discerning, strikes you down."

NOTES

1. *Who is this:* This dramatic opening is a dialogue between
two unknown speakers concerning a person standing before
them whom they cannot see. Their voices break upon us, unexpectedly, without any kind of introduction. The first 126
verses of this canto are devoted to conversation, except for a
minimal amount of narrative necessary to set up the conversation, and the canto opens without even this minimal amount.
The two speakers will remain unidentified until the second half
of the canto. The first speaker will give his name in verse 81 as

Guido del Duca and that of his companion in verse 88 as Rinieri da Calboli.

8. *talking about me, huddled head to head:* Note the reference to the "huddled" position of the two souls, recalling the description of the group in Canto XIII. In the next line they will raise their faces, as Sapìa did in the same canto. But these two bits of descriptive detail are offered only after the dialogue has ended; the words come to the reader from two shades whom he cannot see (and who themselves, as he knows, cannot see).

17. *a little river:* Not infrequently Dante refers to a river in order to indicate the territory through which it runs, and several times before such a reference has served to indicate the speaker's birthplace. But there are two striking details to be noted in verses 17–19. First, the total length of the river's course is suggested: more than a hundred miles beyond the point where it arises as a rivulet; second, the river is left nameless!

21. *for I have not as yet won fame on earth:* The reason the Pilgrim gives for maintaining his anonymity is, at best, a half-hearted attempt at humility: "not *as yet* won fame."

25–26. *"Why would he want / to keep the real name":* It has already been pointed out (note to 17) that the Pilgrim, in his vague indication of his birthplace, failed to give the name of the river near which he was born. Whatever may have been the Pilgrim's reason (connected perhaps with his "modest" withholding of his own name), his omission serves a most dramatic effect: it makes possible Rinieri's puzzled question and Guido's highly emotional reaction to it, which in turn leads to the overwhelming description of the Arno's journey southward through Tuscany.

31. *For from its source:* The river Arno has its source on Monte Falterona (17) in the Apennines ("the steep mountain chain") and empties into the sea just below Pisa. Pelorus (32) is a mountain at the northeastern extreme of Sicily, believed to have once belonged to the range of the Apennines, before the waters came to form the Strait of Messina and thereby "cut off" the mountain from the range. And with verse 31 begins a six-line description of the course of the river Arno from its source to its termination, offering a somewhat more elaborate treat-

ment of the Pilgrim's reference to the length of its course ("more than a hundred miles": 18).

32–33. *is rich / with waters:* It is with this phrase that I have translated the *pregno* ("pregnant") of the original. Two other interpretations of this word have been offered: "high" (hardly convincing semantically) and "massy" (so many single mountains closely joined together). Only the last interpretation is justified by geographical facts, but many critics believe that as regards the first two interpretations, Dante may have overevaluated this important mountain range.

37. *virtue is loathed:* Immediately after the two tercets (31–36) that give the limits of the Arno's course comes a warning that all the territory through which this river passes is inhabited by vicious brutes. Then, in verse 43, the river will actually begin its journey downward, flowing between various types of animals.

42. *Circe:* Daughter of Helios, god of the sun, Circe was an enchantress who had the power of turning men into beasts.

43. *Past hoggish brutes:* As Guido traces the course of the Arno through Tuscany, he points with disgust and contempt to the inhabitants of its miserable valley, designating them as various species of contemptible animals: the "hoggish brutes" (43) are the inhabitants of Casentino; the "small curs" (47) are those of Arezzo; the "wolves" (51) are the Florentines; and finally the Pisans are represented as foxes (53). So fierce is Guido's contempt for the bestial Tuscans who live along the Arno that he is led to characterize the river itself as bestial: "it turns away its *snout*" (48).

55. *though this man hears my words:* When the speaker here, Guido del Duca (whose name is withheld until verse 81), says the words "this man," he is referring to the other penitent soul sitting beside him, who is Rinieri da Calboli (whose name is not revealed until verses 89–90).

57. *what inspiration has revealed to me:* It is well known that the souls in the Afterlife have foreknowledge of events to come; thus, we are not surprised that Guido is able to prophesy the future evil activities of Rinieri's grandson. But why should not Rinieri be possessed of the same powers of divination?

Perhaps we are meant to assume, as has been suggested by some, that prophetic visions come in snatches, now to one soul, now to another.

58. *your grandson:* Rinieri's grandson, Fulcieri da Calboli, infamously cruel and a perpetrator of atrocities against the White Guelphs (Dante's party) as well as the Ghibellines, was podestà of Florence in 1303.

60. *that wild stream:* The "little river" born in Falterona became a fierce stream in the course of its downward flow because of the many tributaries pouring their waters into it. But perhaps the epithet "wild" is intended also to reflect the nature of the various beasts of the territory through which it flowed.

68. *the face that listens:* Here, again, we are invited to look straight into the face of one of the shades on the Terrace of the Envious. But we are reminded neither of the blinded eyes nor of the typical gesture of the uplifted head. It is simply the human face we see, its features revealing consternation and grief.

81. *Guido del Duca:* Of him little is known. Possibly he was the son of Giovanni del Duca of the Onesti family of Ravenna, who settled in Bertinoro. His name appears in a document dated May 4, 1199, which states that he was a judge to the podestà of Rimini. In 1218 he, along with Pier Traversaro (98), was driven from Bertinoro and forced to flee to Ravenna. He witnessed a deed at Ravenna in 1229; this signature is the last record we have of his name.

87. *where partnership must always be denied:* In the next canto Dante asks for an explanation of these words (*Purg.* XV, 44–45), and a good part of the canto centers on Virgil's explanation of the difference between earthly and heavenly possessions. Earthly goods cannot be shared without being diminished, but divine love, which is a heavenly possession and different in nature, only increases the more it is shared.

88. *Rinier:* Rinieri de' Paolucci da Calboli, a Guelph from the city of Forlì, was podestà of Faenza (1247), Parma (1252), and Ravenna (1265). He was defeated by Guido da Montefeltro in 1276 and died at Forlì in 1296.

91. *From Po . . .* : The region here included is Romagna, bounded by the Po to the north, the Apennines to the south, the Adriatic Sea to the east, and the River Reno to the west. Both Guido and Rinieri are Romagnols.

97–111

There follows a long list of good and honorable men of Romagna, to contrast with the previous list of despicable and wicked ones along the Arno. Unfortunately all these good men are dead, and this glance backwards is filled with regret. Here is an example of the *Ubi sunt* topos, well known in medieval literature. For details about the lives of these virtuous Romagnols, see Toynbee (1968).

97. *Mainardi . . . good Lizio:* Little is known about Mainardi, other than that he was a contemporary of Guido del Duca and Pier Traversaro and was taken prisoner with the latter by the Faentines in 1170. He was reputed to be a virtuous man with knightly qualities.

Lizio da Valbona was born in the first half of the thirteenth century, a nobleman of Romagna and a contemporary of Rinieri. Boccaccio mentions him in *Decam.* V, 4.

98. *Pier Traversaro? Guido di Carpigna?:* Pier (ca. 1145–1225) belonged to the powerful Traversaro family of Ravenna. He was a staunch supporter of the Ghibellines and a close friend of the Emperor Frederick II. Several times he was made podestà of Ravenna, as were a number of other members of the Traversari family during his lifetime.

Guido di Carpigna's family seems to have been established in the district of Montefeltro in Ravenna as early as the tenth century. Dante is probably alluding to Guido the younger, who was podestà of Ravenna 1251. He was dead before 1283.

101. *a Fabbro . . . a Fosco:* Fabbro de' Lambertazzi was a Ghibelline leader of Bologna, whose family was said to have descended from the dukes of Ravenna in the twelfth century. In 1230 Fabbro was podestà in Faenza, and he held this office in other cities in northern Italy as well. He died in 1259.

Bernardo di Fosco was reputed by early commentators to have been of humble origin, but through his own merits, he distinguished himself to the point of being accepted by the nobility of his city of Faenza on their own level. He was podestà of Siena in 1249 and perhaps of Pisa in 1248, and in 1240 he played an important part in defending his native city against the Emperor Frederick II.

104. *Ugolin d'Azzo, Guido da Prata, too:* Ugolino of Azzo was a member of the powerful Ubaldini family, composed of such distinguished men as Ubaldino della Pila (*Purg.* XXIV, 29), Cardinal Ottaviano degli Ubaldini (*Inf.* X, 120), and the Archbishop Ruggieri degli Ubaldini (*Inf.* XXXIII, 14). He married Beatrice Lancia, who was the daughter of Provenzan Salvani, and by her he had three sons. He seems to have been a wealthy landholder who was well known in Romagna; he died in January of 1293.

Guido da Prata, who is mentioned in documents in the years 1222, 1225, 1228, also appears to have been a landholder of some importance in the vicinity of Ravenna. He died before 1245.

106. *Federigo di Tignoso:* A nobleman of Rimini, he was noted for his wealth and hospitality. He is believed to have lived in the first half of the thirteenth century, though there is no mention of him in any documents of the times.

107. *the Traversaro clan, the Anastagi:* The Traversaro clan was a powerful Ghibelline house of Ravenna, whose most distinguished member was Pier Traversaro (see note to XIV, 98).

The Anastagi were another powerful Ghibelline family in Ravenna, who were most active in politics and antagonistic toward the church. After 1258 the family declined, and by 1300 there was no longer any mention of them in Ravenna.

112. *Bretinoro:* A small town in Romagna (now Bertinoro), located between Forlì and Cesena. Initially controlled by the Malatesta family of Ravenna, it came under the lordship of the Ordelaffi of Forlì toward the end of the thirteenth century. According to the *Ottimo Commento,* the town was noted for the hospitality of its nobles.

115. *Bagnacaval:* The town of Bagnacavallo in Romagna was a stronghold of the Malvicini, a Ghibelline family that expelled Guido da Polenta and the Guelphs from Ravenna in 1249. By 1300 the Malvicini, counts of Bagnacavallo, were becoming extinct.

116. *and Castrocaro's wrong, and Conio more:* Castrocaro, now a village, was once a castle in Romagna belonging to the counts of Castrocaro, who, though Ghibellines, submitted to the church in 1282. Around 1300 the Ordelaffi of Forlì took possession of the castle. Benvenuto comments that in his day the counts of Castrocaro were no longer in existence.

The castle of Cunio in Romagna (near Imola), once owned by the counts of Conio, who were for the most part Guelphs, was totally destroyed soon after 1295.

118. *The Pagani's demon:* The Pagani were a noble Ghibelline family of Faenza and Imola. The "demon" among them was Maghinardo Pagano da Susinana, who ruled Faenza (1290), Forlì (1291), and Imola (1296) and died at Imola in 1302. Guido da Montefeltro refers to him (*Inf.* XXVII, 50) as "the lion of the white lair" (his coat of arms).

121–23. *Ugolin de' Fantolin:* Ugolino de' Fantolini, a Guelph, was podestà of Faenza (1253); he died in 1278. His sons died soon after—Ottaviano in 1282 at Forlì in a battle against Guido da Montefeltro; Fantolino, before 1291. Both died without heirs.

126. *our discourse has so wrung my sorrowing mind:* These are the last words of Guido del Duca, the most eloquent, impassioned speaker so far encountered in Purgatory. How deeply did his words impress the Pilgrim? The only reference in this canto to the Pilgrim's reaction occurs in verse 73, just after Guido has finished his dire prophecy to Rinieri about the latter's grandson. Later, however, it will become evident that Guido gave the Pilgrim food for thought on two other topics (XV, 44–45; XVI, 53).

131. *there came, like lightning:* Like the examples of Charity (the virtue opposed to Envy) in the previous canto, here the two examples of "Envy punished" will be offered by disembodied voices in the air.

133. *"I shall be slain":* The first voice is that of Cain, who, facing the punishment that God has visited upon him, cries out "I shall be a fugitive and a wanderer on the earth, and whoever finds me will kill me" (Gen. 4:13–14).

139. *I am Aglauros:* The second example of Envy is Aglauros, daughter of Cecrops, king of Athens. Out of jealousy she tried to prevent a rendezvous between her sister and Mercury and was, in consequence, turned to stone. Ovid tells the story in *Metam.* II, 737–832.

143. *That was the iron curb:* In the previous canto (XIII, 37–41), when the exempla of Charity had come to an end (Charity being the virtue directly opposed to the vice of Envy), Virgil had introduced the images of the whip and the curb. In that situation only the part played by the whip could be in question; as for the curb, Virgil told the Pilgrim that he would hear it soon. In verse 143, at the end of the illustrations of Envy punished, Virgil is reminding the Pilgrim of his prophecy as he applies the term curb to these exempla.

145. *But you men take the bait:* This tercet is devoted to Virgil's reproachful description of the blindness of mankind: though their experience is constantly offering "reins" or "curbs" in the form of deterrent examples, they will not learn from it; they swallow the hook with the bait and are reeled in. The tercet ends with a recapitulative reference to the "rein" and a shift to a new idea ("call"), which will be continued in the following tercet: the heavens revealing their beauty are constantly calling to men, who, however, insist on keeping their eyes fixed on the ground. Thus, they are punished, since they are neither deterred by the vices they see around them nor inspired by the beauty of the heavens calling them.

The "call" referred to in verse 148 is, in the original, a term of falconry (*richiamo*): the cry or whistle with which the falconer calls back his falcon. The technical implications of this image are surely not developed in the following tercet, but we cannot forget that they have been suggested, and it is surely not impossible to think of God as the falconer calling back His creature. In fact, it is precisely this image that will be presented five cantos later (*Purg.* XIX, 61–63). And is it not true that His penitents here on this Terrace of the Envious are like newly caught falcons whose eyes are stitched tight with iron thread to tame their restlessness? See the preceding canto, especially verses 70–72.

CANTO XV

THE PILGRIM IS stunned by the light emanating from the
Angel of Generosity, and Virgil explains that soon such a sight
will not be a burden to his eyes but a great joy. As they climb
past the angel, they hear from below the singing of the
beatitude "Blessed are the Merciful." At the Pilgrim's prompting, Virgil delivers a discourse on the difference between
earthly and heavenly possessions. When he has finished, the
two poets find themselves on the Third Terrace. Here, the
exempla of Meekness, the opposite of the sin of Wrath, present
themselves in the form of ecstatic visions. The first vision is of
the Virgin meekly questioning the Christ child as to why he has
remained behind in the temple, causing his parents so much
distress. The second vision is of Pisistratus, who, despite the
imprecations of his wife, refused to take revenge on the young
man who had embraced his daughter. The final example of
Meekness is taken from the life of St. Stephen, the first martyr.
The canto ends ominously with the menacing appearance of a
thick black cloud of smoke, which envelops the Pilgrim and his
guide.

The same amount of time it takes that sphere
   (which, like a child at play, is never still)
   to go from break of day to the third hour,   *3*

was left now for the sun to run its course
   toward night: mid-afternoon it was up there
   (and midnight here, where I am writing this).   *6*

Now, its late rays struck full upon our faces,
   for we had gone so far around the mount
   that we were walking due west toward the sun.   *9*

But suddenly I felt my brow forced down
   by light far brighter than I sensed before;
   my mind was stunned by what it did not know.   *12*

I placed both of my hands above my eyes
   and used them as a visor for my face
   to temper the intensity of light.   *15*

A ray leaps back from water or from glass,
    reflecting back the other way as it
    ascends in the same way it first came down,   18

forming an angle with the plummet-line
    exactly equal to the incidence—
    as theory and experiment both show;   21

in just this way it seemed I had been struck
    by light reflected just in front of me:
    and that is why I quickly looked aside.   24

"Dear father, what is this? There is no way
    for me to shield my eyes from such bright light;
    it's moving toward us, isn't it?" I asked.   27

"Don't be surprised if you can still be dazed
    by members of the Heavenly Court," he said.
    "This is our invitation to ascend.   30

Not long from now, a sight like this will prove
    to be no burden, but a joy as great
    as Nature has prepared your soul to feel."   33

Before the blessed angel now we stood.
    He joyfully announced: "Enter this way
    to stairs less steep by far than those below."   36

Past him we went, already climbing when
    Beati misericordes from behind
    came ringing, and "Conqueror, rejoice."   39

And while my guide and I in solitude
    were moving upward, I, hoping to learn
    from his wise words with every step we took,   42

turned toward him and began to question him:
    "What did that spirit from Romagna mean
    who spoke of 'partnership' and of 'denial'?"   45

"Knowing the price he pays for his worst fault,"
    he answered, "naturally he censures it,
    hoping that others will have less to bear.   48

Because you make things of this world your goal,
    which are diminished as each shares in them,
    Envy pumps hard the bellows for your sighs.   51

But if your love were for the lofty sphere,
    your cravings would aspire for the heights,
    and fear of loss would not oppress your heart;   54

the more there are up there who speak of 'ours,'
    the more each one possesses and the more
    Charity burns intensely in that realm."   57

"I hunger more for satisfaction now,"
    I said, "than when I held my tongue before,
    and new perplexities come to my mind.   60

How can one good that's shared by many souls
    make all those who possess it wealthier
    than if it were possessed by just a few?"   63

And he: "Since you insist on limiting
    your mind to thoughts of worldly things alone,
    from the true light you reap only the dark.   66

That infinite, ineffable true Good
    that dwells in Heaven speeds instantly to love,
    as light rays to a shining surface would;   69

just as much ardor as it finds, it gives:
    the greater the proportion of our love,
    the more eternal goodness we receive;   72

the more souls there above who are in love
    the more there are worth loving; love grows more,
    each soul a mirror mutually mirroring.   75

And if my words have not appeased your thirst,
    when you see Beatrice you will see
    all of your longings truly satisfied.   78

Strive hard for the quick disappearance now
    of the five wounds that suffering will heal,
    just as the other two have left no trace."   81

I was about to say "I'm satisfied,"
    but seeing that we had reached the next round,
    my eager eyes forgot about my tongue.   84

And, there, it seemed to me that suddenly
    I was caught up in an ecstatic trance:
    a temple filled with people I could see;   87

CANTO XV / 163

a lady at the entrance whispering,
  tenderly as a mother would, "My son,
  why hast Thou dealt with us this way? You see,   90

Thy father and I, both of us in tears,
  have searched for Thee." Silence. The vision then,
  quick to appear, as quickly disappeared.   93

And then, another lady I could see:
  her cheeks were streaked with tears distilled by grief—
  a grief born from the spirit of revenge.   96

She spoke: "If you are master of this town
  whose naming caused such strife among the gods,
  and which shines as the source of all the arts,   99

take vengeance on those wanton arms that dared
  embrace our daughter, O Pisistratus!"
  And then, it seemed, that lord replied to her,   102

his face serene, his words gentle and calm:
  "What shall we do to those who wish us harm
  if we condemn the ones who show us love?"   105

And then I saw a mob, raging with hate,
  stoning a boy to death, as all of them
  kept screaming to each other, "Kill him, kill!"   108

I saw him sinking slowly to his knees,
  the weight of death forcing him to the earth;
  but still his eyes were open gates to Heaven,   111

while he, in agony, prayed to his Lord
  for the forgiveness of his murderers,
  his face showing compassion for them all.   114

When finally my soul became aware
  of the reality that lay beyond,
  I recognized my error and its truth.   117

My leader, who saw I was in the plight
  of someone trying hard to wake from sleep,
  said: "What is wrong? Have you lost all control?   120

You have been walking for a good half-league
  like someone half-asleep or drunk on wine:
  your eyes about to close, unsteady legs."   123

"O my sweet father, listen: I will tell you
all of the things that did appear to me
while I could scarcely move my legs," I said.   _126_

And he: "Were you to put a hundred masks
upon your face, still you could never hide
from me the slightest thought that comes to you.   _129_

The things you saw were shown that you might learn
to let your heart be flooded by the peace
that flows eternally from that High Fount.   _132_

I did not ask, 'What's wrong?' as one who looks
with eyes that have no gift of insight might,
eyes doomed to blindness once the body dies;   _135_

I asked you this to give strength to your limbs;
so must the lazy man be spurred to put
the time of his reawakening to best use."   _138_

We walked along, with evening coming on,
into the splendor of the setting sun,
looking ahead as far as we could see.   _141_

Then gradually a cloud of smoke took shape;
slowly it drifted toward us, dark as night;
we were not able to escape its grip: _144_

it took away our sight, and the pure air.

NOTES

1–6

This canto opens with an obscure time periphrasis: literally, the poet is telling us that it is 3:00 P.M. (mid-afternoon) in
Purgatory and midnight in Italy ("here, where I am writing").
But the postmeridian time of Purgatory is expressed in terms
of a reversal of corresponding antemeridian time: that is, the
course remaining to the sun from the present moment until
sunset is equal to the course that the sun has completed, that
morning, from dawn until the third hour. Schematically expressed, the interval between the third hour and sunrise (figuring backwards) is equal to the interval between the present
moment and sunset (figuring forward). In each case it is a ques-

tion of three hours. Therefore, it is three hours before sunset in Purgatory.

Dante here is doing more than just telling time; he is introducing the important figure of the "mirror image." Evening time expressed as the "reverse image" of morning time serves to introduce the imagery of "reflection," which will dominate this canto. The "communication of goods" is expressed in terms of reflected light, in terms of angles of incidence and reflection. And light symbolizes the love of God, which can be shared— or "reflected"—by many, without being diminished.

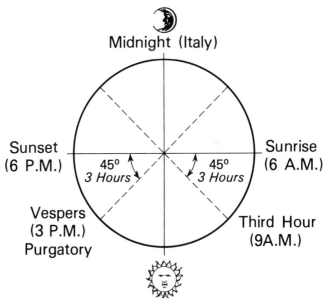

1. *The same amount of time it takes that sphere:* There has been much debate about the exact reference of the word *spera* in the original, which I have translated "sphere." But there can be no doubt that, in the opening lines, the sun's movement is seen from two points of view: the main concern is with the daily movement from dawn to sunset, but, in verse 2 ("which, like a child at play, is never still"), there must be a reference to the larger movement completed only in a year's time, allowing for the seasonal variation of the sun's position in the sky.

But why should this be compared to the movements of a frisky child? The seasonal changes of position are rigidly determined, with nothing of the spontaneity and abandon of a child at play. And to compare the glory and grandeur of the sun, the vastness of its course, to a mere child in its playground! Is this another glorification of innocent childhood (cf. the *anima semplicetta* of *Purg.* XVI, 87), and is Dante also suggesting in verse 2 that the sun is having fun? See Nardi (1953) for a reading of this canto.

9. *due west toward the sun:* This phrase prepares us for the coming of evening and for the Pilgrim's next dream.

11. *light far brighter than I sensed before:* For the third time in Purgatory proper the Pilgrim is dazzled by the radiance of an angel. This time the light is far brighter than before—and much more startling for the Pilgrim, who has not yet seen the angel, the source of this light.

16. *A ray leaps back from water:* The poet describes, in the erudite terms of optics, the phenomenon of the reflection of a ray of light. The ray, striking a horizontal surface (water or glass) will be reflected from it at precisely the same angle at which it struck: the angle of reflection is equal to the angle of incidence. Just how this highly technical description of a commonplace phenomenon serves to explain the Pilgrim's exceptional experience is none too clear.

34. *Before the blessed angel:* After his shattering experience, the Pilgrim sees the prescribed pattern renewing itself: the "blessed angel" welcoming him to the stairs leading to the next ' Terrace: that of the Wrathful.

38. *Beati misericordes:* "Blessed are the Merciful." Having passed beyond the Terrace of the Envious, the Pilgrim hears from behind the beatitude praising the opposing virtue of Mercy or Generosity. This is from the fifth beatitude (see Matt. 5:7): "Beati misericordes, quoniam ipsi misericordiam consequentur." Since none of the beatitudes refers to Charity, the virtue that best opposes Envy (see Thomas Aquinas, *Summa theol.* II–II, q. 36, a. 3, ad 3: "Unde invidia misericordiae opponitur et charitati ["so that envy is contrary to pity and charity"]), Dante the Poet selects the one that speaks of mercy or compassion for others.

39. *"Conqueror, rejoice":* There is no exact biblical or liturgical source for these words, although some commentators see in

them a reflection of the conclusion of all the beatitudes (Matt. 5:12): "Rejoice and be glad, for your reward is great in heaven." See Singleton (1973), p. 322.

44. *spirit from Romagna:* The Pilgrim is referring to the words of Guido del Duca (*Purg.* XIV, 86–87), who reproached mankind for placing its hopes "where partnership must always be denied." Here we have the first of the two indications mentioned earlier (*Purg.* XIV, 126) that the Pilgrim's interest has been stirred by certain words of Guido del Duca, to which he did not react at the time.

49. *Because you make:* The "you" here is plural—Virgil is speaking of all mankind. Men desire worldly goods, those goods which are diminished when shared. The discourse that follows will point out the difference between earthly goods and heavenly possessions.

52. *But if your love were for the lofty sphere:* Here Virgil states the essential characteristic of heavenly love: the more the love of God is shared, the more each one of those who share possesses. The sharing in no way diminishes the quantity of love but actually increases it. Such a concept is frequently found in medieval Christian writers: cf. Augustine, *De civ. Dei* XV, 15; Gregory the Great, *Moral.* IV, 31.

61. *How can one good that's shared by many souls:* The Pilgrim's question is intended to reveal not only his great perplexity but also the magnitude of the problem. How many readers would have asked themselves the question, if the Pilgrim had not?

69. *as light rays to a shining surface would:* This verse cannot fail to remind the reader of the earlier passage (16–21) describing the reflection of light. But what was Dante's purpose in reminding us? Here we have to do not with the reflection of light but with, supposedly, the attraction of light. Moreover, the phenomenon mentioned in verse 69 is hardly demonstrable by "theory and experiment": it is surely not true that a shining body attracts light. We have to do with a very loose application of the idea of "affinity": like attracts like. In verse 75, however ("each soul a mirror, mutually mirroring"), there is, very probably, a reference to the reflection of light—the light of love. This is an important concept in the *Paradiso*.

76. *your thirst:* This corresponds to Dante's earlier reference to his own hunger for knowledge (58).

79–81. *Strive hard for the quick disappearance:* We are informed that the Pilgrim has now had the second of the *P*'s removed from his forehead (those which represent Pride and Envy), and that five remain to be purged. We were not, however, told about the removal of the second *P* at the time it actually occurred.

86–87. *I was caught up in an ecstatic trance:* Here is offered the first member of the third pair of exempla appropriate to the Terrace of the Wrathful (the virtue of Meekness). On the Terrace of the Proud, the pair took the form of sculptures, appealing to the sense of vision; on the Terrace of the Envious, the exempla were represented by means of disembodied voices, appealing to the sense of hearing. Now, on the Terrace of the Wrathful, they take the form of an inner vision experienced by the Pilgrim (and by the Penitents as well?).

89–90. *"My son, / why hast Thou dealt with us this way?":* The first example of Meekness, the virtue opposed to the vice of Wrath (taken, as always, from the life of Mary) is the episode in which Mary and Joseph, having left Jerusalem and travelled an entire day, discover that the boy Jesus is not in their company. Upon returning to Jerusalem they find him in the temple with the teachers and the learned men, listening to them and asking them questions. Mary's meekness is apparent in her first words to her son, whose absence indeed must have caused her considerable consternation and anxiety. But despite the distress that she must have suffered, she speaks to Jesus gently, without a trace of anger. See Luke 2:40–48.

97. *"If you are master of this town":* The allusion here is, of course, to Athens. Legend has it that both Neptune and Athena desired to give their name to this newly founded capital. A contest ensued, and from it the city came to be called Athens. The nature of the contest, which was presided over by the gods, was to see which of the two contestants could present the gift most useful to mankind. Neptune, striking the ground with his trident, brought forth water. Athena, however, planted an olive tree, which the gods decided to be the more useful. See Ovid, *Metam.* VI, 70–82, and Augustine, *De civ. Dei* XVIII, 9.

103. *his face serene, his words gentle and calm:* The second example of Meekness is Pisistratus, the benevolent tyrant of Athens from 560–527 B.C.; he was famous for his ability to turn away wrath with a soft answer. Valerius Maximus (*Facta et Dicta* V, i) relates how Pisistratus cooled the wrath of his wife, who had become angered at seeing her daughter embraced in public by a suitor who had not won parental approval. To his wife's vengeful imprecations Pisistratus calmly replied, "If we slay those who love us, what shall we do with those who hate us?"

106–14. *And then I saw a mob:* The third example of Meekness is from the life of St. Stephen, the first Christian martyr. Stephen was stoned to death by an angry crowd, but, even in his final agony, he asked the Lord to forgive his persecutors (Acts 7:54–60).

117. *my error and its truth:* What the Pilgrim had seen was not objectively present, but it was not false either. The truth of the visions resides in their inner, subjective reality and their exemplary moral value as God-given lessons.

131. *to let your heart be flooded:* These peaceful waters that flow from the eternal High Fount of God are such as to quench any tendency toward Wrath, the sin being punished on this terrace. With these waters there flowed into the Pilgrim's heart the three exempla of Meekness forming his three visions.

134. *eyes that have no gift of insight:* Virgil's reference to his "eyes" should be seen in connection with the preceding two tercets: he has understood that the Pilgrim's sleepy attitude was due to the visions he had been experiencing. He knows what the Pilgrim has seen and why he was allowed to see them. But now that the visions have come to an end, he must urge the Pilgrim to resume his journey with zeal. For an entirely different interpretation of this passage, see Singleton (1973, p. 339), who quotes Torraca (1921).

142. *Then gradually:* The canto ends with the unexpected introduction of a new element, which leaves the reader in suspense.

CANTO XVI

THE PILGRIM IS blinded by the smoke and clings tenaciously to his guide. He hears the voices of the Wrathful singing the *Agnus Dei* in perfect concord. One of the souls, Marco the Lombard, comes forward to speak with the Pilgrim and, at his invitation, accompanies him (and Virgil) to the end of the smoke-filled space, discussing the problems connected with the present-day corruption of society. He belittles the influence of the stars on human affairs, affirms the existence of Free Will, and laments the lack of good leadership in church and state.

The gloom of Hell or of a night bereft
   of all its planets, under barren skies,
   and totally obscured by dark, dense clouds,   *3*

never had wrapped my face within a veil
   so thick, made of such harsh and stinging stuff,
   as was that smoke that poured around us there.   *6*

It was too much for open eyes to bear,
   and so my wise and faithful guide drew near,
   offering me his shoulder for support.   *9*

Just as the blind man walks close to his guide
   in order not to stray, or to collide
   with something that could hurt or even kill him,   *12*

so I moved through that foul and acrid air,
   hearing my guide keep telling me: "Watch out!
   Be very careful not to lose me here."   *15*

I could hear voices, which all seemed to pray
   the Lamb of God Who takes away our sins
   that He be merciful and grant them peace.   *18*

Each prayer they sang began with *Agnus Dei;*
   the same words, sung in unison, produced
   an atmosphere of perfect harmony.   *21*

"Master, those voices—are they shades I hear?"
   I asked. And he to me, "Yes, you are right,
   and they are loosening the knot of Wrath."   *24*

"And who are you whose body cleaves our smoke?
    You speak of us as though you still belonged
    with those who measure time by calendars."   27

I heard a voice, somewhere, that spoke these words.
    My master said: "Answer his question, first,
    then ask him if this is the right way up."   30

And I: "O creature, you who cleanse your soul
    to give it back, made beautiful, to God,
    you will hear wonders if you come with me."   33

"I'll come as far as I'm allowed," he said,
    "and if we cannot see each other's face,
    we can at least hear one another's words."   36

Then I began: "Still wrapped in mortal bonds
    that death has yet to loose, I climb to Heaven;
    and through the pains of Hell I have come here.   39

Since God has given me the special grace
    of His desire that I should see His court
    by means unknown to men of our own day,   42

please tell me who you were before you died,
    and tell me, too: is this the way to reach
    the passage up? Your words shall be our guide."   45

"I was a Lombard, Marco was my name;
    I knew about the world, I loved that good
    at which men now no longer aim their bows.   48

The path you're on will lead you to the stairs."
    Thus he replied, then added: "Now, I pray
    that you will pray for me when you're above."   51

"I promise you to do what you have asked,"
    I said. "But there's a problem haunting me:
    I can no longer keep it to myself.   54

I first was made aware of it below,
    and now it plagues my mind a second time,
    for your words second what I first heard there: 57

the world, indeed, as you have just declared,
    is destitute of every virtue known,
    swarming with evils, ever breeding more.   60

What is the cause of this? Please make it clear
    that I may teach the truth to other men;
    some see it in the stars, some on the earth."   63

A deep sigh, wrung by grief into "Alas!"
    came first, and then: "The world, brother, is blind,
    and obviously the world is where you're from!"   66

You men on earth attribute everything
    to the spheres' influence alone, as if
    with some predestined plan they moved all things.   69

If this were true, then our Free Will would be
    annihilated: it would not be just
    to render bliss for good or pain for evil.   72

The spheres initiate your tendencies:
    not all of them—but even if they did,
    you have the light that shows you right from wrong,   75

and your Free Will, which, though it may grow faint
    in its first struggles with the heavens, can still
    surmount all obstacles if nurtured well.   78

You are free subjects of a greater power,
    a nobler nature that creates your mind,
    and over this the spheres have no control.   81

So, if the world today has gone astray,
    the cause lies in yourselves and only there!
    Now I shall carefully explain that cause.   84

From the fond hands of God, Who loves her even
    before He gives her being, there issues forth
    just like a child, all smiles and tears at play,   87

the simple soul, pure in its ignorance,
    which, having sprung from her Creator's joy,
    will turn to anything it likes. At first   90

she is attracted to a trivial toy,
    and though beguiled, she will run after it,
    if guide or curb do not divert her love.   93

Men, therefore, needed the restraint of laws,
    needed a ruler able to at least
    discern the towers of the True city. True,   96

the laws there are, but who enforces them?
   No one. The shepherd who is leading you
   can chew the cud but lacks the cloven hoof.   99

And so the flock, that see their shepherd's greed
   for the same worldly goods that they have craved,
   are quite content to feed on what he feeds.   102

As you can see, bad leadership has caused
   the present state of evil in the world,
   not Nature that has grown corrupt in you.   105

On Rome, that brought the world to know the good,
   once shone two suns that lighted up two ways:
   the road of this world and the road of God.   108

The one sun has put out the other's light;
   the sword is now one with the crook—and fused
   together thus, must bring about misrule,   111

since joined, now neither fears the other one.
   If you still doubt, think of the grain when ripe—
   each plant is judged according to its seed.   114

The region of the Po and Adige
   flowed with true worth, with honest courtesy,
   until the time of Frederick's campaign;   117

but now, the kind of man who is ashamed
   to talk with, even meet with, honest folk,
   may travel there completely reassured!   120

There, three old men still live in whom the past
   rebukes the present. How those three must yearn
   for God to call them to a better life!—   123

Currado da Palazzo, good Gherardo,
   and Guido da Castel—who's better named
   'the simple Lombard,' as the French would say.   126

Tell the world this: The church of Rome, which fused
   two powers into one, has sunk in muck,
   defiling both herself and her true role."   129

"Well argued, my dear Marco," I replied,
   "and now I understand why Levi's sons
   were not permitted to inherit wealth.   132

But who is this Gherardo whom you give
    as an example of a race extinct,
    whose life rebukes this barbarous age of ours?"   *135*

"Your words are meant to trick me or to test me!"
    he said. "How can you speak the Tuscan tongue
    and not know who the good Gherardo is?   *138*

I know him by no other name than this,
    unless he's known as Gaia's father, too.
    God be with you! And now I must go back: *141*

see how the rays of light through the thick smoke
    grow brighter now? The angel's near, and I
    must leave before he sees me." And he turned,   *144*

not giving me a chance to ask him more.

NOTES

9. *offering me his shoulder for support:* Evidently Virgil is offering his shoulder as a support for the Pilgrim's hand. The
Pilgrim, then, would be walking behind his master.

15. *Be very careful not to lose me here:* Virgil, evidently, can
"see" in the smoke. He is here acting out his symbolic role of
Reason, guiding the Pilgrim. The smoke on this terrace, the
Terrace of the Wrathful, symbolizes the bitter, smoky passion
of Wrath, which blinds the mind to reason.

19. *Agnus Dei:* Lamb of God. This prayer is taken from the
canon of the Mass. It is significant that the Wrathful are singing
to the *Lamb of God,* to Jesus, the meek One.

20–21. *in unison . . . / perfect harmony:* Such harmony is indeed surprising among the Wrathful!

22. *"Master, those voices —are they shades I hear?":* I think we
are meant to be startled by the Pilgrim's words to Virgil: he
seems not quite sure that the voices he has heard in prayer are
those of the Penitent. But earlier he had heard two other
groups chanting the prayer of their respective terraces, and
whom else would he expect to find on the mountain of Purgatory? Perhaps the Pilgrim has been so unnerved by his experience of walking blindly, clutching Virgil's shoulder, in the ac-

rid, stinging smoke that, for a moment, he is not quite sure where he is (he had been reminded of the darkness of Hell: verse 1)! And perhaps Virgil knows this and that is why he gives him such encouraging corroboration that he has guessed the truth: "Yes, you are right."

25. *And who are you:* Canto XV had opened with a question, "Who is this man?" spoken by a shade still hidden to the reader; here, we have the question "and who are you?" spoken by a shade invisible to the Pilgrim himself. It is fitting that in the presentation of the two most important speakers so far encountered in the *Purgatory,* dramatic stress should be laid upon their voices. It is also fitting that both questions show an interest in the Pilgrim, since it is he whom the two speakers take it upon themselves to teach.

27. *calendars:* Calends is the first day of the month, according to the ancient Roman calendar. The voice, in saying, "you speak as though you reckon time by earthly measurements," is saying, " . . . as though you were still alive." And if we wonder why Marco chooses precisely "measurement of time" as characteristic of those still living on earth, it could indeed be that such measurements are completely meaningless to the Penitents. It is not in months and years that the term of their purgation can be measured but in the intensity of their penance.

46. *I was a Lombard, Marco was my name:* Though we know nothing certain regarding Marco (not even his exact name), it is speculated that he was a Knight of Venice and may have been a member of the Venetian Lombardi family; that he was from Lower Lombardy (specifically the March of Treviso) and was on cordial terms with the noblemen of Lombardy, for whom he arranged treaties, pacts, etc.; and that he frequented Paris. He was reputed to have had a stubborn temperament, but also to have been very generous. On his identity, see Maggini. Zaccagnini cites a document of the Archivio di Stato di Bologna, dated January 5, 1267, which mentions a "dominus Marchus Lombardus."

47. *I knew about the world:* That the world is no longer disposed toward virtue, we remember from the vituperative words of Guido del Duca (*Purg.* XVI). The figure of speech that Marco will use here, that of the slackened bow, is appropriate

for the world's degeneracy: no one is "aiming" at valor any longer.

51. *pray for me:* Once more the Pilgrim is an instrument of grace for the souls in Purgatory. Marco Lombardo is the second spirit in Purgatory proper (after Sapìa in XIII, 147) who asks Dante to pray for him. He, however, wants the Pilgrim not to wait until his return to earth but to pray for him when he reaches Heaven.

53–63

Here we have the second belated indication (see note to *Purg.* XIV, 126) of the effect on the Pilgrim of Guido's preachments—an effect that has just been increased by the words of Marco, to whom the Pilgrim now turns for an explanation. That he is deeply concerned, and sorely perplexed, is clear.

It is interesting to look back a few tercets to see precisely what leads to Marco's ensuing words. The Pilgrim has asked Marco two questions: "Who are you?" and "Is this the right way up?" (43–45). Marco answers the first question in verse 46 and the second in 49; between the two answers he inserts a passing reference to present-day corruption (47–48) and concludes with a request for the Pilgrim's prayers. The reader gets the impression that Marco has said everything he had on his mind: his words are far removed from suggesting the introduction to a "speech." But, because of his brief allusion in verses 47–48, which inspires the Pilgrim's plea for instruction (52–63), he will end up delivering a discourse of sixty-six uninterrupted lines (64–129).

63. *Some see it in the stars, some on the earth:* Some people say that the influence of the stars causes corruption; others say that the cause is to be found in men themselves (on earth).

64. *A deep sigh, wrung by grief into "Alas!":* Is grief alone expressed in Marco's following words, or does he give way to impatience with the Pilgrim's blindness, as in verse 66? See also verse 97.

71. *it would not be just:* The idea that the concept of justice, the meaning of reward and punishment, depends on the existence of Free Will had been brilliantly discussed by Boethius (*Consol. philos.* V, 2:1–127).

73. *The spheres initiate your tendencies:* Marco destroys the idea that the stars are the cause of corruption. The heavens or spheres initiate (some of) men's movements, but men are responsible, because they have Free Will and an understanding of good and evil. Thomas Aquinas explains how the heavens may have an indirect effect on man's actions in *Summa theol.* I–II, q. 9, a. 5, resp., and II–II, q. 95, a. 5, resp.

85. *From the fond hands of God:* Following the doctrinal exposition of Free Will and leading up to the discourse on the necessity of laws and leadership comes this exquisitely lyrical passage with its famous description of the new-born soul. Actually, the passage 85–93 forms a most important link between the two parts of Marco's discourse. The first part ended with the statement that, if the world has gone astray, the cause is to be found not in the stars but in man (83). Then, lest the reader misunderstand him, lest he attribute the cause of present evils to the depravity of human nature, he insists (tenderly) that the soul is born innocent—innocent but in great need of guidance. And it is due to the lack of such guidance that the present state of evil has come about—"not Nature that has grown corrupt in you" (105). But the "bad leaders" (who were born innocent) may have had bad leaders—what is the ultimate cause?

98–99. *shepherd . . . cud . . . hoof:* Jewish dietary law states, in Lev. 11:3: "Any animal that has hoofs you may eat, provided it is cloven footed and chews the cud." Medieval biblical scholarship, interpreting this verse allegorically as referring to the "just man," took "chewing the cud" to mean meditation and understanding, while the "cloven foot" symbolized the powers of judgement and discrimination. In these verses Dante is voicing (through Marco Lombardo) a critique of papal power in terms of this traditional biblical image: the shepherd, of course, is the present pope, Boniface VIII (whom Dante despised; cf. *Inf.* XIX, 53). When Dante says that he can "chew the cud," he probably means that he has a knowledge and understanding of the law and his high position, but, lacking the cloven hoof, he is unable to discriminate either between good and evil or, more likely, between temporal and spiritual power. The result, of course, is defective leadership, which Dante goes on to discuss further in the next tercet.

107. *two suns:* The emperor and the pope were once two suns, that is, two independent and equal authorities. Here Marco is expressing an ideal peculiar to Dante, which he treats in *De monarchia,* III, iv. Most of Dante's contemporaries had presented the papacy and the empire as symbolized by the sun and the moon respectively. Dante objected to the idea that the empire could receive no light of its own but only that reflected by the papacy. Hence, the unusual concept of "two suns." See Kantorowicz, p. 231.

112. *since joined, now neither fears the other one:* With these words Marco brings to an end the second of his two main topics. Though he has had occasion in his discourse to the Pilgrim to deal with human sinfulness and with the role of the church, nothing that he says shows any concern for theological values or problems. Nothing is said about Original Sin or about the need of grace or about the salvation of the soul. It is above all a picture of social disorder that he offers.

115. *The region of the Po and Adige:* This phrase loosely designates a region, as Marco goes on to say, that is characterized by the degeneracy of its inhabitants—as were, according to Guido del Duca, the lands of Tuscany and Romagna.

116. *with true worth, with honest courtesy:* This verse echoes the nostalgic note with which Guido del Duca had ended his "Ubi sunt" lament: "which love and courtesy did once inspire" (*Purg.* XIV, 110).

117. *until the time of Frederick's campaign:* Emperor Frederick II, last of the emperors, according to Dante's view, was involved in successive conflicts with the papacy: he met resistance from Popes Honorius III, Gregory IX, and Innocent IV.

124. *Currado da Palazzo, good Gherardo:* Currado was a Guelph from Brescia and acted as vicar to Charles of Anjou in Florence in 1276; he was podestà of Piacenza in 1288. Benvenuto reports that Currado, who was standard-bearer in a battle, had both hands hacked off, yet kept the standard waving by hugging the staff with the stumps of his arms.

Gherardo da Camino, son of Biaquino da Camino and India da Camposampiero, born ca. 1240, was the captain-general of Treviso from 1283 to 1306, the year he died. Dante cites Gherardo as an example of true nobility in *Conv.* IV, xiv, 12.

125. *Guido da Castel:* A nobleman of Reggio Emilia, born in 1235 and still living in 1315. He is cited for his nobility by Dante in *Conv.* IV, xvi, 6. Guido was a vernacular poet and was one of Dante's hosts during the latter's exile.

126. *'the simple Lombard,' as the French would say:* All scholars are agreed that the epithet *simple* is used in a highly laudatory sense, but two reasons are offered for the creation of Marco's French nickname. Some believe it originated in appreciation of the great generosity he showed to French travellers whom he entertained; others see in it a witticism, a contradiction in terms: since all Italians were called "Lombards" by the French and all were considered to be shrewd and unscrupulous, this honorable man would be seen as an exception to the rule. This latter interpretation seems dubious to me, since it is put into the mouth of Marco, a self-declared Lombard.

131. *Levi's sons:* The Levites, members of the tribe of Levi, were designated to serve the Temple, and, in order to prevent corruption and distraction in the performance of their sacred function, Jewish law prohibited them from owning property.

140. *Gaia's father:* Gaia was Gherardo's daughter by his second wife, Chiara della Torre of Milan. She married Tolberto da Camino, a relative, and she died in 1311. Although the Anonimo fiorentino states that she was noted for her beauty and virtue, Benvenuto affirms that she was notoriously promiscuous and even offered to procure beautiful girls for her brother, Rizzardo, if he would return the favor with young suitors for her. Perhaps Marco, who has just reproached the Pilgrim for not knowing more about "the good Gherardo," is pretending, in verse 140, to be equally ignorant—in order to suggest that the notoriety of the wanton daughter was more extensive than the good reputation of her father. Finally, the mention of the notorious Gaia introduces the theme of wanton women, which will be developed in later cantos.

143. *The angel's near:* This is the angel of Meekness, who will erase the third *P* from the Pilgrim's brow and pronounce the appropriate beatitude.

CANTO XVII

As THE PILGRIM emerges from the cloud of smoke that surrounds the Wrathful, the sun is about to set. He experiences three more visions that offer exempla of Wrath. They center on the stories of Procne, Haman, and Amata, the wife of King Latinus. The angel of Meekness then appears and points to the way by which the two poets may continue their ascent. As they move toward the indicated stairway, they hear the words of the beatitude "Blessed are the Peacemakers." Upon reaching the Fourth Terrace, the Pilgrim feels that all strength has left his limbs, and both he and his guide rest from their journey: they have reached the Terrace of the Slothful, and night is about to fall. Virgil takes advantage of this pause to discourse on the nature of love, showing that all the sins purged in Purgatory spring from one of three perversions of love. His words bring the canto to a close.

Reader, if ever you have found yourself
   caught in a mountain fog, trying to see
   your way through it, as sightless as a mole,   *3*

remember how at last the damp, dense air
   starts to dissolve, and how the sun's pale disc
   feebly begins to penetrate the mist,   *6*

and you will find it easy to recall
   what it was like when finally I saw
   the sun again, the sun about to set.   *9*

Matching the faithful footsteps of my guide,
   I walked out of that cloud into the light
   whose rays had died out on the shore below.   *12*

O power of fantasy that steals our minds
   from things outside, to leave us unaware,
   although a thousand trumpets may blow loud—   *15*

what stirs you if the senses show you nothing?
   Light stirs you, formed in Heaven, by itself,
   or by His will Who sends it down to us: *18*

In my imagination there took shape
     the impious deed committed by that being
     transformed into the bird that lives to sing;   21

my mind became, at this point, so withdrawn
     into itself that the reality
     of things outside could not have entered there.   24

Then poured into my soaring fantasy,
     a figure crucified, whose face revealed
     contempt and fury even as he died.   27

By him the great Ahasuerus stood,
     Esther his wife, and the just Mordecai,
     integrity in word and deed was his.   30

Then, when this image of its own accord
     burst like a bubble when the watery film
     around it breaks—another vision rose   33

in my imagination: a young girl
     bitterly weeping, saying: "O my queen,
     why did you let your rage destroy your life?   36

You killed yourself rather than lose Lavinia?
     Now you have lost me! I am she who mourns
     your death, Mother, before another's ruin!"   39

When suddenly closed eyes are struck by light,
     our sleep is broken, though it lingers on
     a little while before it fully dies,   42

just so my vision slipped away from me
     when I was struck by light across my eyes,
     a light far brighter than is known on earth.   45

Looking around to find out where I was,
     I heard a voice: "Here is the place to climb."
     This drove all other thoughts out of my mind   48

and left me burning with desire to see
     the one who spoke—a wish that will not cease
     till it comes face to face with its desire;   51

but, as if looking at the burning sun
     whose brilliance overwhelms the sight and veils
     its very form, I felt my powers fail.   54

"This is an angel of the Lord who comes
  to show us the ascent before we ask,
  and hides himself in his own radiance.   57

He treats us as a man would treat himself:
  who sees the need but waits for the request,
  already is half-guilty of denial;   60

so, let our feet obey his call, and climb
  as far as possible while there is light,
  for we may not ascend once it grows dark."   63

These were my leader's words; and then, as one,
  the two of us went over to the stairs.
  As soon as I had taken one step up,   66

I felt what seemed to be a wing that moved
  and fanned my face; I heard the words: *"Beati
  pacifici,* who feel no sinful wrath."   69

The day's last rays, which night would follow soon,
  already were so high above us now
  that stars began to show through, here and there. 72

"Why is my strength fading away like this?"
  I kept repeating to myself, as I
  felt all my forces draining from my legs.   75

We had just reached the last step of the stairs,
  and there we found ourselves immobilized,
  just like a vessel having run ashore.   78

I waited for a moment, listening
  to hear some sound come from this unknown round;
  then, turning to my master, I inquired: 81

"O my sweet father, what offense is purged
  here on this terrace? Though our steps have stopped,
  don't you stop speaking to me." So he said: 84

"That love of good which failed to satisfy
  the call of duty, here is fortified:
  the oar once sluggish now is plied with zeal.   87

But if you want to better understand,
  give me your full attention: you will reap
  excellent fruit from this delay of ours.   90

Neither Creator nor his creatures ever,
   my son, lacked love. There are, as you well know,
   two kinds: the natural love, the rational.   93

Natural love may never be at fault;
   the other may: by choosing the wrong goal,
   by insufficient or excessive zeal.   96

While it is fixed on the Eternal Good,
   and observes temperance loving worldly goods,
   it cannot be the cause of sinful joys;   99

but when it turns toward evil or pursues
   some good with not enough or too much zeal—
   the creature turns on his Creator then.   102

So, you can understand how love must be
   the seed of every virtue growing in you,
   and every deed that merits punishment.   105

Now, since it is a fact that love cannot
   ignore the welfare of its loving self,
   there's nothing in the world can hate itself;   108

and since no being can be conceived as being
   all in itself, severed from the First Being,
   no creature has the power to hate his God.   111

And so it follows, if I argue well,
   the evil that man loves must be his neighbor's.
   This love springs up three ways in mortal clay: 114

There is the man who sees his own success
   connected to his neighbor's downfall; thus,
   he longs to see him fall from eminence.   117

Next, he who fears to lose honor and fame,
   power and favor, if his neighbor rise:
   vexed by this good, he wishes for the worst.   120

Finally, he who, wronged, flares up in rage:
   with his great passion for revenge, he thinks
   only of how to harm his fellow man.   123

This threefold love is purged by those below.
   Now, I would have you know the other kind:
   love that without measure pursues its good.   126

All of you, vaguely, apprehend and crave
    a good with which your heart may be at rest;
    and so, each of you strives to reach that goal.   *129*

If you aspire to it or grasp at it
    with only lukewarm love, then on this ledge
    you will be punished, once you have confessed.   *132*

Another good there is: it brings not joy,
    not perfect joy, for it is not the True
    Essence, the fruit and root of every good;   *135*

the love that yields excessively to this
    is purged above us on three terraces,
    but how the nature of such love is threefold,   *138*

I would have you discover for yourself."

NOTES

1–53

In the first two tercets the reader is in the mountain fog
with the Pilgrim, sharing his experience; in the third tercet he
emerges with him into the light; throughout he has been somehow inside the Pilgrim. In the fourth tercet (10–12), we are
back to pure narrative, and, separate from the Pilgrim, we see
him walking with confidence beside his guide. Then, in the
next line, and for forty lines without interruption, we are again
"inside" the Pilgrim, learning his thoughts, seeing his visions.
This is the most extensive use of the narrative device of "sharing with the protagonist" that has been encountered so far in
the *Comedy*.

1. *Reader:* With this "Address to the Reader" Dante begins
Canto XVII, which is exactly in the middle of the thirty-three
cantos of the *Purgatory* and thus is at the center of the entire
Divine Comedy. In this canto, through Virgil, Dante explains
love as the motivating force of all human actions. Quite fittingly, this discourse of central importance is placed at the very
heart of the poem.
Virgil will continue his discussion of love in the following
canto; if we consider Marco Lombardo's description of the
new-born soul in *Purg.* XVI, 85–93, as also concerned with

love, then it could be said that love is treated in the three central cantos of the *Purgatory* (and, hence, of the *Comedy*).

3. *mole:* In antiquity and the Middle Ages it was commonly believed that the mole was blind, or could see only very dimly, its eyes being covered by a membrane.

9. *the sun about to set:* Thus, the Pilgrim's second day on Mount Purgatory, Easter Monday, is drawing to a close. He will have his second dream on the Terrace of the Slothful in the early morning of the next day.

10. *Matching the faithful footsteps of my guide:* Having come out from the cloud of smoke into the light, the Pilgrim, no longer clinging to Virgil's shoulder, can now match his pace to that of his guide, walking by his side.

13. *O power of fantasy:* Since the exempla of Meekness had been presented as an inner vision experienced by the Pilgrim, it is inevitable that the exempla of Wrath would be presented in the same way. Why is the nature itself of such a vision discussed only here? Perhaps Dante felt it would be more effective to present the first set of visions in a matter-of-fact way; then, once the reader has accepted the event as a fact and is prepared for its repetition, he is in a better mood to ponder the significance of such a phenomenon.

16. *what stirs you if the senses show you nothing:* In the answer to this question, contained in the two following lines, most scholars believe that Dante is offering two mutually exclusive explanations for the occurrence of inner visions. In the first case the vision would be formed without divine intervention, influenced by the physical heavens, the vision descending in the form of light coming from the stars; in the second case, the vision would be inspired by God, who directs it downward to the human mind. If we accept this dichotomy, the visions experienced by the Pilgrim are surely of the second type.

21. *transformed into the bird that lives to sing:* This is the first of the three exempla of Wrath, which, like those of Meekness, will be presented as visions in the Pilgrim's mind. In these lines the poet alludes again to the story of Procne (see note to *Purg.* IX, 15), who, angered over her husband's rape of her sister, savagely killed her son and fed him to his father. For this crime she was transformed (according to Dante) into a nightingale.

26. *a figure crucified:* Haman, minister of Ahasuerus, king of Persia, enraged that the Jew Mordecai refused to do him homage, persuaded the king to decree the death of all the Jews in the land: a cross (or more likely a gibbet) was constructed especially for Mordecai. Esther, Mordecai's niece, however, dissuaded Ahasuerus, who, finally convinced of Haman's wickedness, condemned him to suffer the same penalty originally decreed for Mordecai. See Esther 3:7.

35. *queen:* Queen Amata, wife of Latinus and mother of Lavinia. Amata hoped that Turnus would kill the invader Aeneas and marry her daughter, but when she heard a false report that Turnus had died in battle, she killed herself in a rage *(Aen.* XII, 593–607). Turnus was later killed by Aeneas, who married Lavinia, as was decreed by fate. That Amata could be presented along with the vicious figures of Procne and Haman is surely due to Dante's unlimited admiration of Aeneas and to his association of the Trojans with the Romans in carrying out God's will. God Himself had planned that Aeneas should found Rome in Latium, which would become the site of the church. Thus, Amata's wrath against Aeneas was an example of sacrilegious wrath.

40. *When suddenly closed eyes are struck by light:* The simile describing the cessation of the Pilgrim's vision compares the process to an awakening from sleep, when one is struck by an intense light. The light in this case comes from the angel of Meekness, whom the Pilgrim is now approaching—and whose presence had already been anticipated by Marco at the end of the previous canto.

58. *He treats us as a man would treat himself:* Most men are quick and zealous to satisfy their own desires; the angel has been quick to satisfy what he knew the pilgrims desired, without waiting for their request.

61. *so, let our feet obey his call:* Virgil enjoins speed—to match the angel, who had indicated the ascent without waiting for a request, and also, perhaps, in anticipation of the "speedy" Slothful in the next canto.

67. *a wing that moved:* Another *P* is removed, leaving four more to be erased.

68–69. *Beati / pacifici:* The Beatitude for the Terrace of the Wrathful: "Blessed are the Peacemakers." "Who feel no sinful wrath" is a gloss added by Dante to the biblical text.

69. *who feel no sinful wrath:* The phrase "sinful wrath" is not tautological. The distinction was frequently drawn between righteous anger and the sin of Wrath. For *mala ira* as opposed to *bona ira,* see Thomas Aquinas, *Summa theol.* II-II, q. 158, a. 2, resp.

78. *just like a vessel having run ashore:* Again, a reminder that the Pilgrim's journey is like a sea voyage—and one marked by continuous success, unlike that of the ill-fated Ulysses. The two travellers have arrived at the top step, where we must assume they sit with their backs to the mountain wall of the Fourth Terrace: they have arrived at their goal for the moment; the Pilgrim is suddenly exhausted; and it will soon be dark (when they see the Slothful much later, the moon will have risen). Now, the image of the ship having reached port suggests success and independence, but there are two suggestions to the contrary: the physical condition of the Pilgrim is not described as normal fatigue but as a sudden cessation of his powers of movement, as a paralysis; the verb used to announce their stop suggests that they have been somehow prevented from going farther.

In this connection, some scholars speak of the working of the spell of Slothfulness, now that Virgil and the Pilgrim have reached the Terrace of the Slothful; others are reminded of the Law of the Mountain, which forbids ascent after sunset. (As concerns the latter point, of course, there is no question at this moment of further ascent: Virgil and the Pilgrim want to stay on this terrace and observe the operations of the Slothful.) In any case, there seems to be implied a restraint imposed upon the two travellers.

82–139

In the first tercet the Pilgrim asks Virgil a simple question: "What offense is purged here on this round?" In the next Virgil's answer contains a definition of Sloth as deficient love of good. But Virgil is far from finished. In the next fifty-two verses he offers a classification of the Seven Capital Sins punished on the seven terraces of Purgatory proper—analyzing them all within the same framework in which he had presented Sloth: that is, in terms of a wrong kind of loving.

Wrong love, which can only lead to sin, falls into two main types: in the one case it is the goal that is wrong; in the other, where the goal is good, the flaw lies in the lack of proper measure. That love which is wrongly directed aims always at harm for one's neighbor and reveals itself in one of three ways: as Pride, as Envy, as Wrath. These are the three sins purged on the first three terraces above the gate. That love which is marked by lack of measure may be either insufficient or excessive love. Insufficient love, as we already know, is Sloth (purged on the terrace where we are). Excessive love, purged on the last three terraces, reveals itself in three ways: as Avarice, as Gluttony, as Lust. (Virgil does not list the last three sins, telling the Pilgrim he must make his own threefold definition.)

Actually, there are three kinds of goals: the absolutely bad, as represented by the first three sins; the absolutely good, which can lead to sin by insufficient love (Sloth); the relatively good, which leads to sin through excessive love (Avarice, Gluttony, Lust). There can be no doubt that the good Virgil refers to in his second discussion of Sloth (127–32) is the maximum good: God Himself.

93. *two kinds: the natural love, the rational:* Of the two kinds of love Virgil mentions, he will discuss in this canto only the second (and that only in terms of being the source of sin); natural love is reserved for the next canto, where it will be considered in connection with Free Will.

108. *nothing in the world can hate itself:* Dante is here following Aquinas in stating that no man can hate himself, since every man naturally desires only good for himself (see *Summa theol.* I-II, q. 29, a. 4, resp.). Even in the exteme case of suicide, the desired death is envisioned as a good, since it will put an end to some unhappiness or pain.

120. *vexed by this good, he wishes for the worst:* with these words Virgil concludes his treatment of Envy, which he contrasts with Pride. The proud man, according to Virgil, is constantly hoping that his neighbor will fail; the envious man is vexed when he sees his neighbor rise, and hopes for a reversal of his fortunes. It is difficult to see a basic difference between the two attitudes.

128. *a good in which your heart may be at rest.* This good is, of course, God. These words reflect the famous Augustinian formulation that is never far from the thematic surface of the *Divine Comedy:* "Our hearts are restless till they rest in Thee" (*Conf.* I, i).

139. *I would have you discover for yourself:* What the Pilgrim must discover for himself (and what Virgil well knows) is that on the last three terraces of Purgatory are purged the sins of Avarice, Gluttony, and Lust. The sins that are purged in Purgatory are classified somewhat differently, and in far less detail, than those that are punished in Hell; here Dante is following the conventional theological divisions into the Seven Capital Sins.

The reader may tend to be amazed that Virgil is so familiar with the purgatorial system on the mountain. But if we grant that he may have become familiar with the Seven Capital Sins and the relative degree of their gravity from Pride to Lust, it is not surprising that he is able to locate the ascending sites of their purgation on the mountain.

How could Virgil have learned about the Seven Capital Sins? We must remember that in Limbo he witnessed the Harrowing of Hell and learned the great significance of the birth of Christ. Moreover, he seems to be aware, when speaking to the Pilgrim about Beatrice, of what she stands for in the divine plan.

CANTO XVIII

IN RESPONSE TO the Pilgrim's request, Virgil continues his lecture on love. More than satisfied with the explanations of his guide, the Pilgrim lets his thoughts wander aimlessly and sleepily, when, suddenly, a group of souls rushes upon them from behind. These are the Slothful. Two souls out in front of the frenzied pack shout out two exempla of the virtue of Zeal, one involving the Virgin Mary, the other, Julius Caesar. As the crowd rushes by, one soul, the Abbott of San Zeno, exchanges a few hasty words with Virgil. The exempla of Sloth are proclaimed by two souls at the rear of the rapidly moving group: they involve the recalcitrant Israelites wandering with Moses in the desert, and certain companions of Aeneas who refused to continue the voyage to Latium with him.

When he had brought his lecture to an end,
　　the lofty scholar looked into my face,
　　searching to see if I seemed satisfied;　　　　　　3

and I, already thirsting for more drink,
　　kept silent, wondering: "Could he, perhaps,
　　be tired of all this questioning of mine?"　　　　6

But that true father, sensing my desire,
　　which was too timid to express itself,
　　spoke first, and thus encouraged me to speak.　　9

I said: "Master, the light you shed has made
　　my sight so keen that now I clearly see
　　all that your words mean or what they imply.　　12

So I beseech you, father, kind and dear,
　　define love for me, please, which is, you say
　　the source of every virtue, every vice."　　　　15

"Now focus your mind's eye on what I say,"
　　he said, "and you will clearly understand
　　the error of the blind who lead the blind.　　　18

The soul at birth, created quick to love,
　　will move toward anything that pleases it,
　　as soon as pleasure causes it to move.　　　　21

From what is real your apprehensive power
    extracts an image it displays within you,
    forcing your mind to be attentive to it;   24

and if, attentive, it inclines toward this,
    that inclination is love: Nature it is
    which is through pleasure bound anew in you.   27

Just as a fire's flames always rise up,
    inspired by its own nature to ascend,
    seeking to be in its own element,   30

just so, the captive soul begins its quest,
    the spiritual movement of its love,
    not resting till the thing loved is enjoyed.   33

It should be clear to you by now how blind
    to truth those people are who make the claims
    that every love is, in itself, good love.   36

They think this, for love's substance, probably,
    seems always good, but though the wax is good,
    the impression made upon it may be bad."   39

"Thanks to your words and my keen interest,
    I know what love is now," I answered him,
    "but knowing this brings more uncertainty: 42

if love comes from a source outside of us,
    the soul having no choice, how can you praise
    or blame it for its love of good or bad?"   45

And he to me: "I can explain to you
    as much as reason sees; for the rest, wait
    for Beatrice—it is the work of faith.   48

Every substantial form, being distinct
    from matter, yet somehow conjoined with it,
    contains within itself a certain power   51

not visible except as it is made
    manifest through its workings and effects:
    as life in plants is proved by their green leaves.   54

So, man cannot know where his cognizance
    of primal concepts comes from—or his bent
    for those primary objects of desire;   57

these are a part of you, just like the zeal
    of bees for making honey; the primal will
    is neither laudable nor blamable.   60

That other wills conform to this first one,
    you have the innate faculty of reason,
    which should defend the threshold of consent.   63

This is the principle on which is based
    the judgment of your merit—according as
    it winnows out the good love from the bad.   66

Those men who with their reason probed the depths,
    perceived this liberty innate in man,
    thereby bequeathing ethics to the world.   69

Let us assume that every love that burns
    in you arises through necessity;
    you still have power to restrain such love.   72

This noble power Beatrice knows
    as Freedom of the Will: remember that,
    if ever she should mention it to you."   75

The moon was shining close to midnight now,
    like a brass bucket burnished bright as fire,
    and, thinning out the stars that we could see,   78

was following that course against the sky
    made fiery by the sun, when Romans see
    it set between the Sards and Corsicans.   81

That noble shade, who had made Pietola
    renowned above all Mantuan towns, was now
    free of the burden I had laid on him,   84

and I, having been privileged to reap
    such clear, plain answers to my questioning,
    let my thoughts wander vaguely, sleepily;   87

but this somnolent mood did not last long,
    for suddenly we heard a rush of souls
    coming around the mount behind our backs: 90

And as Ismenus and Asopus saw
    in ancient times at night along their banks
    the rush and rage of Theban bacchanalia,   93

just such a frenzied urge I thought I saw
   when that thick rush of souls curved round the bank
   spurred in their race by good will and just love.   *96*

And then they were upon us—that entire,
   enormous mass of spirits on the run;
   two out in front were shouting as they wept: *99*

"Mary in haste ran to the hills," cried one,
   the other: "Caesar, Ilerda to subdue,
   thrust at Marseilles, and then rushed down to Spain."   *102*

"Faster! faster, we have no time to waste,
   for time is love," cried others from behind,
   "strive to do good, that grace may bloom again."   *105*

"O souls in whom keen eagerness atones,
   perhaps, for past delay and negligence,
   induced by lukewarm love of doing good—   *108*

this man, who is, I swear to you, alive,
   would like to climb above when day returns;
   show us the nearest way to reach the cleft."   *111*

These were my leader's words. One of the shades
   called out as he rushed by: "Follow our path,
   and you will find the passage by yourself.   *114*

We cannot stop; desire to race keeps on
   running through us; we beg your pardon, then,
   if penance seems to be discourtesy.   *117*

I was San Zeno's abbott in Verona,
   when the good emperor Barbarossa reigned—
   of him Milan still speaks with bitterness.   *120*

There is a man with one foot in the grave
   who soon will have good cause to rue the power
   he wielded once over that monastery: *123*

in place of its true pastor he has put
   as head a bastardly born son of his,
   deformed in body and maimed worse in mind."   *126*

If he said more, I did not hear the words,
   the two of us were left so far behind;
   but I was glad to hear as much as this.   *129*

And he who always was my help in need
   said: "Turn around, look at those racing souls
   straining themselves to put the curb on Sloth."   *132*

Two at the end were shouting: "All of those
   for whom the Red Sea's waters opened wide
   were dead before the Jordan saw their heirs;   *135*

and those who found the task too difficult
   to keep on striving with Anchises' son,
   gave themselves up to an inglorious life."   *138*

Then, when those souls had sped so far ahead
   that they were now completely out of sight,
   a new thought started forming in my mind,   *141*

creating others, many different ones:
   from one to another to another thought
   I wandered sleepily, then closed my eyes,   *144*

letting my floating thoughts melt into dreams.

NOTES

14. *define love for me, please, which is, you say:* In his first discourse on love, with which Canto XVII ended, Virgil has discussed love from a very limited point of view. His practical
purpose had been to classify the Seven Capital Sins and to locate the terraces on which these are purged; he had chosen to
do so by presenting them as the result of a wrong kind of loving. He had discussed only one kind of love: the rational as
distinct from the natural; he had discussed only its harmful effects and, at the most, treated only the operation of (certain
kinds of) love and not love's essence. It is this essence that the
Pilgrim now asks him to describe.

18. *the error of the blind who lead the blind:* Later on in this
canto (34–36) there is a second reference to "blind teachers,"
where their error is specifically stated: the false idea that all
loves are in themselves good (a doctrine of the Epicureans and
their followers). Surely the false teachers of verse 18 and verse
35 are the same; thus, Virgil would begin and end the first part
of his discourse with the warning that not all loves are good.

The Pilgrim, of course, cannot know, at this point, just what Virgil is hinting at.

19. *The soul at birth, created quick to love:* It should be clear from this verse with which Virgil's analysis begins that he is speaking here only of natural love: that potentiality of loving, that instinct innate in mankind—that love which Virgil in the previous canto had declared (before dismissing it) to be always without fault. In this tercet there is summed up that threefold "movement of love" which will be elaborated upon in the next four tercets.

22—33

The first tercet describes a stage preparatory to the initiation of love: from something that exists in outside reality, the apprehensive faculty offers an image that the mind is encouraged to focus upon. With preliminary love, it must be love of an image and not of the object itself that is involved. In the next tercet (25—27) comes the mind's recognition that it is receiving pleasure from the sight of what has been shown it. This condition is the first stage of love. Before proceeding to the second stage, i.e., the movement of the soul toward what gives it pleasure, Virgil describes (28—30) the inevitable upward movement of a flame seeking to reach the sphere of fire that is its natural resting place (the first of three similes involving natural phenomena, brought in to stress the naturalness of the soul's operation). The last tercet (31—33) describes the beginning of the soul's "movement toward" and also suggests the successful conclusion; it includes the second and third stages.

27. *which is through pleasure bound anew in you:* If the inception of a specific love represents a "new" bond with Nature, the first bond must be simply represented by that instinct for love with which every creature is born.

34. *It should be clear to you by now how blind:* Having described the stages of love, Virgil now speaks as if his words had made clear that not every love is a good love. But he has not made this clear at all. In the preceding canto Virgil had shown that love could be the source of every sin, but such a love was the rational love as opposed to the natural love, which is, supposedly, always without error. And he has allowed the Pilgrim to understand in verse 19 of this canto that it was only this love, this supposedly flawless love, that he was concerned with.

35. *those people:* The philosophers, particularly the Epicureans, and their followers (the "blind" of verse 18), who maintain that every kind of love is praiseworthy because it is a natural tending to the good.

38–39. *but though the wax is good:* That is to say: as a poor seal may stamp on good wax a bad imprint, so some object that is unworthy may kindle the good instinct of love to a wrongful passion. See Grandgent, p. 466.

44. *the soul having no choice, how can you praise:* The Pilgrim's question suggesting that it would be wrong to praise or blame the soul for its choice of a good or a bad love surely seems justified: Virgil had described the three stages of love as proceeding inevitably, necessarily—"the soul having no choice."

Virgil's answer to this objection of the Pilgrim occupies the next ten tercets, which begin (46–48) and end (73–75) with a reference to Beatrice—the first reference praising her knowledge as being superior to his own (since the question of faith is involved). Of the eight intervening tercets, it is only in the last four, it seems to me, that he faces directly the Pilgrim's problem. For the first time, he mentions reason, "which should defend the threshold of consent"; for the first time, he mentions the soul's power of restraint (72); for the first time, he mentions free will. If we now try to fit what Virgil is saying here back into his description of the three stages of love, it would appear that it is between the first stage (the soul's pleasurable sensation stirred by the image that the apprehensive faculty shows it) and the second (when it starts its movement toward the image) that the faculty of reason should come into play, to "defend the threshold of consent"—at which moment natural love becomes rational love (?).

49. *substantial form:* In scholastic terminology, substantial form is that which gives to anything its own particular essence. The substantial form in man is, of course, his intellectual soul. And this soul contains within it a certain virtue that is made manifest only in its workings or in its effects (51–54). The basic components of the soul, then, cannot be known directly. Man cannot arrive at the source of his primal knowledge or primal desire. They are instinctive (and knowable only in their effects). Natural, instinctive love, then, since it is a part of man,

a "given" in his makeup, is a neutral factor, worthy of neither praise nor blame.

61. *That other wills conform to this first one:* The "other wills," on a more intellective plane, should have the innocence of the primal instinctive will.

67. *Those men:* Plato and Aristotle—those philosophers who, using their reason, perceived the free will innate in man and founded the study of ethics or the science of morality.

72. *you still have power to restrain such love:* Just as Marco Lombardo in Canto XVI had assured the Pilgrim that free will could protect him from exterior forces (e.g., astral influences), so Virgil points out that, possessing free will, man need not be the victim of inner forces (e.g., his own temperament).

79. *was following that course against the sky:* That is, following its monthly course in the direction from west to east. In the complicated astronomical figure contained in this tercet, we are told that the moon was in the same path of the Zodiac that the sun follows when the people of Rome see it setting on a line between Sardinia and Corsica. According to Moore (1887, pp. 104–105), this happens in late November, when the sun is in Sagittarius, and this is exactly where the moon would be on this night of April in Purgatory.

82–83. *Pietola . . . above all Mantuan towns:* The noble shade is Virgil, who, according to legend, was born at Pietola, a village near Mantua. The fame and glory of the poet has caused his birthplace to outshine all the other surrounding Mantuan towns.

87. *let my thoughts wander vaguely, sleepily:* Virgil's "clear, plain answers" (86) to the Pilgrim's questions have produced in his ward a state of vague mental preoccupation. This mood will be immediately broken when he hears the "rush of souls" (89) but will be resumed as soon as the last slothful soul disappears—thereby serving as a frame for the performance of the Slothful.

89. *a rush of souls:* This group is the Slothful; they are the first Penitents to appear whose purgation takes the form of practicing the virtue opposed to their sin. That virtue is Zeal, and it is illustrated in two ways: first, in the swiftness of their

movement; second, in the fact that all are shouting words in praise of Zeal. There are the two in front who offer the exempla of this virtue and the two in back who provide the exempla of the vice, and, in between, all the souls seem to be crying out admonitions both to themselves and to their companions to waste no time. It is a bedlam of "zeal" that is offered.

The image of the Penitents rushing by is reinforced on a more subtle level: Dante the Poet speeds up the narrative itself to a remarkable degree. The interval between the first appearance of the Slothful (89) and their disappearance (140) occupies only fifty-two verses, and this interval includes both sets of exempla. For the Terrace of the Proud, however, more than two cantos intervened between the beginning of the first exempla and the conclusion of the last.

91. *Ismenus . . . Asopus:* Two rivers of Bretia near Thebes, along which the orgiastic rites of the god Bacchus were observed.

99. *two out in front were shouting as they wept:* Here on the Terrace of the Slothful, as earlier, on the Terrace of the Envious, the exempla of both virtue and vice are presented verbally. But now it is not disembodied voices that are heard but the voices of the Penitents themselves.

100. *"Mary in haste ran to the hills":* This biblical exemplum refers to Mary's visit to Elizabeth, wife of Zachariah (who lived in the hill country), soon after the angel of the Annunciation had appeared to her. As Elizabeth, herself with child, listened to the glad news, the babe in her womb lept up. He was to be the beloved disciple of Christ, John the Baptist. What a difference between this beautiful, spiritual exemplum (Mary, eager to proclaim the existence of the Savior before he was born) and that of Julius Caesar (101), the experienced, indefatigable military strategist!

101. *Caesar, Ilerda to subdue:* On his way to Ilerda (today Lerida) in Spain, Caesar began the siege of Marseilles; then, leaving part of his army there under Brutus to complete the task, he hurried on to his main goal.

108. *induced by lukewarm love of doing good:* For the third time, Virgil defines the sin of Sloth, this last time addressing the practitioners of this vice themselves. His use of the word

"perhaps" in the preceding verse may be taken as a courteous attempt to avoid being dogmatic.

This is the only time that Virgil takes it upon himself to ask the way to the next terrace. Before, he had always told the Pilgrim to do so. Perhaps the explanation lies in the fact that Dante wanted the sin of Sloth to be defined three times, and only Virgil was the proper person to offer such a definition.

114. *and you will find the passage by yourself:* Though Virgil in asking for information had said "show *us*," the soul in answering speaks only to Virgil. What is much more striking is his apparent unconcern at the announcement that Virgil's companion is alive.

115. *We cannot stop:* Could this refusal to stop running be the reason that no prayer is offered on the Terrace of the Slothful? This could hardly be the case: these Penitents were able to shout out exempla as they rushed on. For some artistic reason, it has seemed appropriate to Dante that no prayer be uttered (or heard) on the Terrace of the Slothful.

118. *I was San Zeno's abbott in Verona:* Though he has not been positively identified, this abbot was probably a certain Gherardo II, who died in 1187 and was abbot of the church of San Zeno in Verona during the time of Emperor Frederick I.

119. *Barbarossa:* Emperor Frederick I, who ruled from 1152 to 1190 and was in conflict with Pope Alexander III, by whom he was excommunicated. He destroyed Milan in 1162, razing the city, plowing its ruins into the ground, and sowing the site with salt so nothing would grow there. In his impatience to cross a river in Armenia during the Crusade of 1190, he drowned.

121. *There is a man with one foot in the grave:* Alberto della Scala, Lord of Verona, who died in 1301, and hence, in 1300, had one foot in the grave.

124. *in place of its true pastor:* Alberto's illegitimate son, Giuseppe (1263–1313), despite being mentally retarded, crippled, and a bastard, served as the abbot of San Zeno from 1292 to 1313. (Except under special circumstances a candidate for priesthood cannot be ordained if illegitimate, mentally unqualified, or physically handicapped.) Another illegitimate son of

Alberto's, Can Grande, was Dante's host at Verona, and it is to him that Dante was to dedicate the *Paradiso*.

126. *deformed in body and maimed worse in mind:* The abbot of San Zeno, without slackening his pace, has spoken almost fourteen verses. (A good deal to say for someone on the run!) While his brief answer to Virgil's question (113–14) could easily have been intelligible as he rushed by, it is impossible to assume this clarity for the whole of his speech—unless, of course, he spoke with the rapidity of a machine gun, shouting at the top of his lungs.

Apart from this problem of narrative realism, there is something puzzling about the content of the abbot's words. That he should take pains to apologize for his speed is slightly strange under the circumstances; but that he should be interested in telling his interlocutor of Barbarossa's cruelty to Milan, or of the sin and forthcoming punishment of the second person mentioned, is most difficult to understand—all the more so since the abbot was so preoccupied with the performance of his duty that he paid no attention to Virgil's astonishing announcement that his companion was a living man. The treatment of the Slothful finds no parallel in the descriptions of the other terraces.

133–35. *All of those / . . . saw their heirs:* The first exemplum of Sloth, taken from the Bible (Num. 14:1–39), is that of the Israelites, who were sluggish in crossing the desert with Moses after the Lord had opened up the Red Sea so that they could escape from Egypt. They were punished by not being allowed to cross the Jordan (with the exception of Joshua and Caleb); only their children born in the desert were allowed to enter the Promised Land.

136–38. *and those who found the task too difficult:* The second exemplum, from classical lore, indicts the followers of Aeneas, who, instead of following him to Latium, stopped and settled with Akestes in Sicily, thus giving up their share of the glory of founding Rome (*Aen.* V, 605–40).

CANTO XIX

Just before dawn the Pilgrim dreams of a hideous female, stuttering, cross-eyed, maimed, and with sallow skin. But as he stares intently at her, she loses all her deformity and takes on a very desirable aspect. She is a Siren, and her singing captivates the Pilgrim and holds him entranced, until a saintly lady appears and rouses Virgil to go to the aid of his charge. Virgil rips open the Siren's garment, to reveal her belly, the stench from which startles the Pilgrim from his dream. As the two poets begin to climb again, the angel of Zeal appears to show them the way and pronounces the beatitude "Blessed are they who mourn." When the two pilgrims reach the next terrace, they see souls everywhere stretched out upon the ground, weeping and sighing as they recite the psalm *Adhaesit pavimento anima mea*. This group is the Avaricious. The Pilgrim's attention is attracted by one of the souls, and, with Virgil's consent, he goes over to speak to him. It is the shade of the former Pope Adrian V, who explains that since the Avaricious turned their backs on Heaven and fixed their eyes on earthly goods, so Justice has here bound them face down to the ground. He rebukes the Pilgrim for kneeling to him, citing a verse from the gospels to indicate that earthly relationships no longer hold in the spiritual realm, and finally expresses the desire that his niece Alagia be preserved from the corruption surrounding her.

It was the hour when the heat of day,
   quenched by Earth's cold (at times by Saturn's too),
   cannot prevail against the lunar chill—   *3*

when geomancers see far in the east
   Fortuna Major rise before the dawn
   along a path soon to be bathed in light.   *6*

There came into my dream a woman, stuttering,
   cross-eyed, stumbling along on her maimed feet,
   with ugly yellow skin and hands deformed.   *9*

I stared at her. And as the sun revives
   a body numbed by the night's cold, just so
   my eyes upon her worked to free her tongue   *12*

and straighten out all her deformities,
    gradually suffusing her wan face
    with just the color Love would have desired.   15

And once her tongue was loosened by my gaze,
    she stared singing, and the way she sang
    captured my mind—it could not free itself.   18

"I am," she sang, "the sweet Siren, I am,
    whose song beguiles the sailors in mid-sea,
    enticing them, inviting them to joy!   21

My singing made Ulysses turn away
    from his desired course; who dwells with me
    seldom departs, I satisfy so well."   24

Her lips had not yet closed when there appeared
    a saintly lady standing at my side,
    ready to foil the Siren's stratagem.

"Virgil, O Virgil, who is this?" she cried
    with indignation. Virgil moved toward her,
    keeping his gaze fixed on that noble one.   30

He seized the other, ripped her garment off,
    exposing her as far down as the paunch!
    The stench pouring from her woke me from sleep.   33

I looked at my good master, and he said:
    "Three times at least I called you. Get up,
    come, let us find the passageway for you."   36

So, I stood up. Daylight had now spread out
    through all the circles of the sacred mount
    as we moved on, the new sun at our back.   39

Following in his footsteps, brow bent low,
    so heavy with my thoughts (I must have looked
    like half a bridge's arch), I suddenly   42

heard a voice say, "Come here, here is the pass,"
    words spoken in soft tones of graciousness,
    tones never heard within our mortal bounds.   45

Then angel's wings, that could have been a swan's
    outstretched, invited us to make our way
    upward between the two high hard stone walls,   48

and then he moved his wings and fanned us both,
  declaring those *qui lugent* to be blest,
  for consolation shall be theirs in Heaven.   51

"What is it that disturbs you?" said my guide,
  "what causes you to stare so at the ground?"
  (By then we had climbed past the angel's post.)   54

I said: "It is that strange dream which I had,
  a vision that still fills me full of dread —
  I cannot get the thought out of my mind."   57

"You saw," he said, "that ageless sorceress
  for whom alone the souls above must weep;
  you also saw how men escape from her.   60

Let these words be enough. Move faster, now,
  and look up at the lure of mighty spheres
  that the Eternal King forever spins."   63

The hawk who has been staring at its feet
  will, when he hears the cry, stretch wide his wings
  ready to soar toward food he knows is there;   66

I did the same: I strained to reach the end
  of the ascending passage in the rock,
  and enter on another circling ledge.   69

When I came out and stood on the Fifth Round,
  I saw spirits stretched out upon the dust,
  lying face downward, all of them in tears.   72

Adhaesit pavimento anima mea,
  I heard, accompanied with heavy sighs
  that almost made the words inaudible.   75

"O souls elect of God, whose sufferings
  Justice and Hope make easier to bear,
  tell us the way to reach the higher stairs."   78

"If you have been exempt from lying prone,
  and wish to find the quickest way to go,
  be sure to keep your right side to the edge."   81

Thus did the poet ask, and thus I heard,
  from somewhere close in front of us—so close,
  I could make out the hidden face that spoke.   84

I fixed my eyes upon my master's eyes,
  and there I saw the joy of his consent
  to the desire he saw in mine. And then,   87

once free to do exactly as I wished,
  I walked ahead and stood above that soul
  whose voice caught my attention earlier;   90

I said, "Spirit in whom weeping makes ripe
  that without which no one returns to God,
  I beg you, interrupt your greater task   93

a moment: tell me who you were and why
  you all lie prone. Is there some way that I
  can help you in the world I left alive?"   96

"Why Heaven has made us turn our backs to Heaven,"
  the spirit said, "you soon shall know, but first:
  scias quod ego fui successor Petri.   99

Between Sestri and Chiaveri descends
  a lovely stream, and from its name derives
  the noble title of my family.   102

In hardly more than one month's time I learned
  how the Great Mantle weighs on him who wants
  to keep it clean—all else is feather weight!   105

I was, alas, converted very late:
  only when I became Shepherd of Rome,
  did I perceive the falseness of the world.   108

Man's heart, I saw, could never rest down there;
  nor in that life could greater heights be reached,
  and so, I came to love the other life.   111

Until that time I was a wretched soul,
  servant of Avarice, cut off from God;
  here, I am punished for it, as you see.   114

What Avarice does is declared in this
  purgation as conversion to the ground—
  the mountain knows no harsher penalty.   117

Just as our eyes, attached to worldly goods,
  would never leave the earth to look above,
  so Justice, here, has forced them to the ground.   120

Since Avarice quenched all our love of good,
  without which all our labors were in vain,
  so here the force of Justice holds us fast,   *123*

our feet and hands bound tight within its grip;
  as long as it shall please the righteous Lord,
  so long shall we lie stretched out, motionless."   *126*

I was by then already on my knees;
  I started speaking; he, at my first words,
  guessed from their tone the form of my respect.   *129*

"Why are you kneeling at my side?" he asked,
  and I replied, "Your dignity commands.
  My conscience would not let me stand up straight."   *132*

"Up on your feet, my brother," he replied.
  "You should not kneel: I am a servant, too,
  with you and all the others, of One Power.   *135*

If you have ever understood the words
  sounded by holy gospel: *Neque nubent,*
  you will know why I answer as I do.   *138*

Do not stay any longer. Leave me now;
  your presence here prevents the flow of tears
  that ripens what you spoke about before.   *141*

I have a niece on earth, by name Alagia,
  a good girl—may she not be led astray
  by all the bad examples of our house—   *144*

and she is all I have left in the world."

NOTES

1–6

  This passage offers a periphrastic indication of time intended to prepare the reader for the Pilgrim's second dream; it
is much less pictorial than the time periphrasis leading up to
the first dream of the Pilgrim in Canto IX.

  3. *lunar chill:* It was the medieval belief that the rays from
the moon cast a chill upon the earth, already chilled by the loss
of the heat of the day. Saturn, when close to the horizon, could
have the same influence.

4. *geomancers:* Those who foretold the future by reading random arrangements of points on a surface and attempting to match them with certain configurations of stars. One of the figures used in their divinations was *Fortuna Major,* which resembles the pattern formed by the last stars in the constellation of Aquarius and the first stars of Pisces. These two constellations would be seen in the east just before sunrise, at the alleged time of Dante's journey. (The mention of geomancers anticipates the ancient witch who will appear in Dante's dream.)

Despite the cold and somewhat ominous opening tercet, this second tercet is radiantly optimistic, bringing in *Fortuna Major* (good luck), the dawn, and the "path soon to be flooded with light." The Poet may, in these two tercets, be reflecting the fact that after the upsetting dream, the Pilgrim's journey will indeed prosper—along a path flooded with light.

7-33

There comes into the Pilgrim's dream a hideously ugly woman, whose deformities are clearly described. It would seem evident that the picture presented to the reader represents objective perception on the part of the Pilgrim. He stares at her, surely (at least at the beginning) shocked and repulsed; then he watches as his own gaze effects her transformation from hideous to beautiful. Not once have the Pilgrim's emotions been described; when the woman begins to sing in verse 17 we do learn that he was spellbound "by the way she sang." It is not said that she sang sweetly; again, we do not know the Pilgrim's exact emotion.

It is very difficult to see the Pilgrim here in the role of a spellbound lover, whose eyes play a part in stirring his imagination. Here the eyes are not presented as receptive; nor do we know that his emotions are stirred. His eyes, we are told, project something outward: a steady gaze that has a miraculous effect on the woman at whom he is gazing.

And even though the effect is that of transforming the ugly into the beautiful, this does not mean that it is relevant to quote Andreas Capellanus, who says that often the lover sees a base and homely woman as noble and beautiful. It is, of course, conceivable that a man's desire to love (but have we been made aware of any such desire on the part of the Pilgrim?) may blind him to the ugliness of the one he craves to love and may stimulate his imagination into creating a false image of beauty according to preconceived ideas. But the Pilgrim is not blind (at the beginning at least): he is acutely aware of every detail of the woman's hideousness. No such moment of objective appraisal of a woman's ugliness, as a first stage of falling in love, is conceivable within the tradition of courtly love. And we hardly have the right to recur to Freud.

More credible is the parallel adduced by Carroll (p. 247), who quotes the following lines from Pope's *Essay on Man* (ii, 217–20): "Vice is a monster of such hideous mien / As to be hated needs but to be seen. / Yet seen too oft, familiar with her face, / We first endure, then pity, then embrace." This passage contains an allusion to that first moment of horror caused by looking squarely into the face of vice—a moment followed by a change of attitude. But this change takes place slowly, in a number of stages, and perhaps over a number of years. What is concerned here is the individual's adjustment to society, his gradual acquiescence (perhaps influenced by the attitudes of those with whom he associates in society) to the vices characteristic of his age.

7. *There came into my dream a woman:* This loathsome female, as we shall learn later, symbolizes the vices of Avarice, Gluttony, and Lust, which the Pilgrim will see being purged on the upper three terraces.

15. *with just the color Love would have desired:* This color, replacing the ugly yellowness of the woman's face, is probably that blend of rose and white mentioned by the poets of courtly love in Dante's time and earlier. Is this judgment intended to betray the Pilgrim's admiration, or does it simply represent a cool appraisal of the transformation wrought?

17. *the way she sang:* For the third time in the *Purgatory* the Pilgrim listens spellbound to music being sung. In Canto II Casella sang a love poem of a worldly, refined nature; in Canto VIII, at the hour of compline, one of the devout souls in the valley leads his companions in the singing of the Ambrosian hymn *Te lucis ante.* Here the Siren sings, inviting to lewdness.

In the first case the music the Pilgrim heard was sweet:

Amor che nella mente mi ragione,
    began the words of his sweet melody—
    the sweetness still is sounding in my soul.   (II, 112–14)
And while we stood enraptured by the sound
    of those sweet notes. . . .   (II, 118–19)

And in the second case reverent and melodious:

> *Te lucis ante,* with such reverence,
>   and so melodiously, came from his lips,
>   that I was lost to any sense of self;
>
> the rest, then, reverently, in harmony,
>   joined in to sing the hymn through to the end. . . . (VIII, 13–17)

But it is not said specifically how the Siren sang. We do not
know how the Pilgrim's soul was stirred as he listened to her
seductive words.

22. *My singing made Ulysses turn away:* Again a reference to
Ulysses and his ill-fated journey, which should always be a reminder of the Pilgrim's own successful journey. But Ulysses'
fate can also be seen in contrast to that of Aeneas; and it is
surely no chance that at the end of the last canto the name of
Aeneas was mentioned in order to indict the slothful Trojans
who abandoned his noble enterprise.

As for the information offered by the Siren about Ulysses, it
is, of course, false: though Ulysses did yield to Circe (of his
own free will) he resisted the Sirens by having himself lashed to
the mast of his ship. Dante did not know Homer firsthand, and
commentators have assumed that he is here confusing the two
narratives. The theory of Moore (1896, p. 264), that Dante was
misled by reading in Cicero (*De Fin.* V. xviii. par. 49) the Latin
translation of a few lines from Homer, I do not find convincing.

26. *a saintly lady standing at my side:* In attempting to determine the exact identity of the woman who appears at the
end of the hag-siren's song, we must not fail to take into consideration that what is described in these lines is not a physical
event in the Pilgrim's journey up the mountain of Purgatory
but a dream, which the narrator has carefully indicated as
originating in the Pilgrim's thoughts. Just as the hag-siren is a
particularization of the archetypal witch-seductress, the saintly
woman of the Pilgrim's dream is not any one woman. She is
grace; she is the Virgin Mary, who told St. Lucy that the Pilgrim had need of her (*Inf.* II, 94–99); she is St. Lucy, who
dispatched Beatrice to seek Virgil's help for the trapped Pilgrim and who actually transported the sleeping Pilgrim from
the Valley of the Princes to Purgatory proper (IX, 1–69); she is
Beatrice, who sent Virgil to the Pilgrim and who will soon
reappear in the Earthly Paradise to act henceforth as the Pilgrim's guide in all but the very highest regions of Paradise.

31. *He seized the other, ripped her garment off:* As my translation shows, I believe it was Virgil who exposed the ugly body of the Siren. The original text is ambiguous (the subject not being supplied: "l'altra prendea"). Poletto (p. 442), for one, believes it was the saintly lady who performed this brutal act. Although it is true that Virgil was goaded into action by the saintly lady, the symbol of grace, it is the Pilgrim who has dreamed up this figure, allowing Virgil to be inspired, secondarily, by the grace that he could never know directly.

33. *woke me from sleep:* Now that the Pilgrim's second dream has come to an end, a comparison with the first dream would seem in order. Both are prophetic, pointing to the Pilgrim's experiences that still lie ahead. In the first dream, the whole of the Pilgrim's journey is encompassed in one sudden, upward rush; in the second dream the Siren anticipates the last three stages of the Pilgrim's ascent of the mountain of Purgatory, while the saintly lady prefigures Beatrice, who will lead him through the Paradise. There is one great difference between the two dreams: in the first, a dream mood (entirely absent from the second) is evoked; this makes for a high degree of "sharing with the protagonist" on the part of the reader. We follow his thoughts, we feel his moods, we experience his sensations. But in the second dream, if we try to share the Pilgrim's feelings, we are only frustrated. There is a second difference, which initially would seem to distinguish the two most sharply. In the dream with the eagle the Pilgrim was seen as a victim, an unresisting victim; in the dream with the Siren the Pilgrim has the power to transform the being that has entered his dream. But this contrast is ambiguous: if the Pilgrim let himself be a victim of the eagle, he was yielding to God Himself; and if he had the power to effect the transformation of the hideous female, that transformation meant that he ran the risk of becoming, and perhaps did briefly become, the victim of her false charms.

40–41. *brow bent low, / so heavy with my thoughts:* The Pilgrim is pensive after his thought-provoking dream. His stooped figure and downcast gaze contrast strikingly with the magnificent figure of the angel of Zeal, who, with outstretched, swanlike wings, directs the two travellers upwards. His stooping may also be an anticipation of the Avaricious, who are stretched out, face down to the ground.

49. *fanned us both:* It goes without saying that with this gesture, the angel removes another *P* from the Pilgrim's forehead.

50. *qui lugent:* The beatitude chosen for the Fourth Terrace is, "Blessed are they who mourn, for they shall be comforted" (Matt. 5:4). Just why this beatitude should be appropriate to the purgation of the particular sin of Sloth is not too clear. Perhaps it is inevitable that Dante's decision to apply so many beatitudes to so many terraces could not be realized convincingly in every case.

53. *stare so at the ground:* Once again, the Pilgrim is anticipating the punishment of the Avaricious.

58. *that ageless sorceress:* In this tercet Virgil explains to the Pilgrim the meaning of his dream. He tells him that the ugly woman represents the three vices that are purged on the terraces above them, Avarice, Gluttony, and Lust. (Had the Pilgrim realized this?) In addition he reminds the Pilgrim that he has learned how to escape from these vices. Is Virgil reminding him of the fact that one may need more than reason (may need that which the "saintly lady" represented in his dream)?

62. *look up at the lure of mighty spheres:* Canto XIV offered a description (148–50) of the heavens calling to man, inviting him to enjoy the beauty they revealed—a faint suggestion of falconry being found in the preceding line of reproach (and mixed metaphor): "both rein and call (*richiamo*) are valueless to you." And here we have a clear reference to God the Falconer: "the lure of mighty spheres / that the Eternal King forever spins."

64. *The hawk who has been staring at its feet:* Here there is a shift from the reference to God as falconer to a *terre-à-terre* description of a stage in the falcon's training. Staring at his feet, still bound with jesses to the falconer's wrist, the falcon waits to be released and hear the signal sending him aloft in pursuit of the quarry, which, once seized and brought back to the falconer, will serve as food (66) for him as well as his master. This is the first stage in the falcon's obedience to his master; later, he will be called back, or lured back, with the captured quarry. It is this later stage that is envisaged in the preceding tercet with God the Falconer; it is the first stage that will be illustrated by the Pilgrim's following act: "I did the same: I strained to reach the end / of the ascending passage . . ." (67–68).

73. *Adhaesit pavimento anima mea:* "My soul cleaveth unto the dust." The Fifth Terrace opens with a prayer taken from Psalm 119:25.

79. *If you have been exempt:* This is the first indication that the souls in Purgatory are not necessarily required to spend time on each terrace: if their addiction to a particular sin has been slight, they may pass through the terrace on which the sin is expiated and climb up to the next one. Thus in verses 79–81, Dante is mistaken for a soul assigned to Purgatory who is in search of a terrace higher up, a shade who does not have to atone for the sin of Sloth.

92. *that without which no one returns to God:* There is no return to God without self-purification, and this process is "ripened" by the penitent's tears.

99. *scias quod ego fui successor Petri:* "Know that I was a successor of Peter." The speaker is Pope Adrian V (Ottobuono de' Fieschi of Genova), a nephew of Innocent IV, who succeeded Innocent V on July 11, 1276, and died thirty-eight days later, on August 18.

101. *a lovely stream, and from its name derives:* The river is the Lavagna, flowing between Sestri and Chiaveri, coastal towns near Genova. Adrian was of the line of the counts of Lavagna.

109. *Man's heart, I saw, could never rest down there:* Once again we are reminded of the Augustinian theme of the unquiet heart ("Our hearts are restless till they rest in Thee"). Adrian has seen that there can be no hope of satisfaction in worldly goods, and, while still on earth, his love for the eternal life was kindled. Notwithstanding the nobility of his family and the grandeur of his papal office, Adrian's speech is among the most humble of those we hear in Purgatory.

110. *nor in that life could greater heights be reached:* That is, no higher post than that of the papacy exists on earth.

115. *What Avarice does:* Here Adrian explains a *contrapasso.* As the eyes of the Avaricious were always fixed on earthly goods and their minds on the rewards of wealth and its attendant power, so now, in Purgatory, they must lie face down, their eyes forcibly riveted to the earth and their minds thus constrained to contemplate the state in which their greed has landed them.

116. *conversion to the ground:* This verse in the original reads simply "(in this purgation of) the converted souls." If I translate "conversion *to the ground*" it is because I see in this verse an echo of verse 106, in which the word is used in its conventional, theological sense. Dante would be playing on the word "convert" with its literal meaning, "to turn."

117. *no harsher penalty:* Every true penitent is apt to believe that his besetting sin is worse than the others, and if his punishment is such as to recall vividly that sin, he will consider the punishment to be the most harsh. The Avaricious in life had refused to look up at God's heavens, preferring to look down and keep their eyes fixed on the things of this earth. Thus, the physical position they are forced to maintain on their terrace is an imitation, hence a most painful reminder, of their sin.

137. *Neque nubent:* These words begin the quotation "They neither marry nor are given in marriage," which can be found in the gospels of Matthew (22:23–30), Mark (12:18–25), and Luke (20:27–35). The quotation represents Jesus' answer to a group of Sadducees who, in an attempt to demonstrate the absurdity of the concept of the resurrection of the flesh, hypothesized the situation of a woman who had married successively seven brothers and asked who should have her as wife at the Resurrection. Jesus answered that those who are to participate in the Resurrection "neither marry nor are given in marriage," but would be as angels in heaven.

But what Adrian surely had in mind here were the symbolic marriages consecrated by the church between bishops (all bishops, including the pope) and their dioceses, and between nuns and Christ. Both bishops and nuns wear rings as symbols of these unions. At death, however, such marriages are dissolved: in the Afterlife the office of pope is meaningless and thus the Pilgrim's act of kneeling was uncalled for.

141. *that ripens what you spoke about before:* See note to 92.

142. *Alagia:* Adrian's niece is Alagia de' Fieschi, daughter of Niccolò de' Fieschi, the imperial vicar in Italy, and the wife of Morello Malaspina, Dante's friend, by whom she had three sons. Benvenuto comments that Dante means to imply that the women of the Fiesco house were *nobiles meretrices,* "noble whores."

CANTO XX

As THE PILGRIM and Virgil pick their way through the prostrate souls of the Avaricious, someone ahead of them begins to call out the exempla of the virtue opposed to Avarice. He proclaims the poverty of Mary, evidenced by the place where she gave birth to her son; he then cites the Roman consul Fabricius, who preferred virtuous poverty to the luxury of vice, and finally, St. Nicholas, whose generosity saved the three maidens from lives of shame. The speaker is Hugh Capet, who established the Capetian dynasty. Addressed by the Pilgrim, he identifies himself and goes on to denounce his descendents for their avarice. Hugh explains that as long as daylight lasts, all the souls, with greater or lesser force, recite the exempla of virtue, and that during the night, they cry out condemnations of Avarice: they cite the greed of Pygmalion, Midas, Achan, Sapphira, Heliodorus, Polymnestor, and Crassus. As the Pilgrim and his guide take leave of Hugh, they suddenly feel the entire mountain tremble, and they hear shouts of *Gloria in excelsis Deo.* Anxious to know what has happened, and puzzled, they continue their journey in silence.

The lesser will yields to the greater will:
   to satisfy him, I, unsatisfied,
   withdrew my sponge unfilled, and turned away.   3

My master moved ahead close to the cliff,
   wherever there was space—as one who walks
   along the ramparts hugs the battlements: 6

the mass of souls whose eyes were, drop by drop,
   shedding the sin which occupies our world
   left little room along the terrace edge.   9

God damn you, ageless She-Wolf, you whose greed,
   whose never-sated appetite, has claimed
   more victims than all other beasts of prey!   12

You heavens, whose revolutions, some men think,
   determine human fate—when will he come,
   he before whom that beast shall have to flee?   15

Slowly we moved along with cautious steps,
   and I could think of nothing but those shades
   who grieved and sobbed so piteously there.   18

Then, somewhere up ahead of us, I heard
   a voice wailing, "Sweet Mary!" and the cry
   was like that of a woman giving birth;   21

the voice went on: "How very poor you were
   is clear to all men from the place you found
   to lay your holy burden down." And then   24

I heard: "O good Fabricius, you who chose
   to live with virtue in your poverty,
   rather than live in luxury with vice."   27

Those words pleased me so much I rushed ahead
   to where I thought the voice was coming from,
   eager to know that spirit who just spoke;   30

he kept on speaking—now, of the largesse
   bestowed by Nicholas on the three girls
   that they might live their young lives virtuously.   33

"O soul," I said, "who speaks of so much good,
   tell me who you were, and why no one else
   joins in to praise the praiseworthy with you.   36

Your answer will not go without reward,
   if I return to finish the short road
   of life that races on to its quick end."   39

"I'll answer you," he said, "not out of hope
   for any help from your world, but because
   God's grace shines in your living presence here.   42

I was the root of that malignant tree
   which overshadows all of Christendom,
   so that good fruit is seldom gathered there;   45

but if Douai and Lille and Ghent and Bruges
   were strong enough, vengeance would soon be theirs—
   and that it may, I beg of God the Judge!   48

On earth beyond I was called Hugh Capet;
   from me have sprung the Louises and Philips,
   rulers of France up to the present day.   51

My father was a Paris cattle man.
　　When the old line of kings had all died out,
　　except for him who wore a monk's grey robe,　　　　54

I found I held the reins of government
　　in my firm grip, and that all my new wealth
　　gave me such power, made me so rich in friends,　　57

that for the widowed crown of France my own
　　son's head was chosen, and it was from him
　　that those anointed bones were to descend.　　　　60

While my descendents kept their sense of shame,
　　they, though worth little, did no harm. Then came
　　their scheme to get the dowry of Provence.　　　　63

With this bloomed their rapacity, their use
　　of force and fraud. Later, to make amends,
　　they seized Ponthieu, Normandy, Gascony.　　　　66

Charles came to Italy; to make amends
　　he made of Conradin his victim; then,
　　sent Thomas off to Heaven, to make amends.　　　　69

I see a time, and not too far away,
　　when there shall come a second Charles from France,
　　and men shall see what he and his are like.　　　　72

He comes bearing no arms, save for the lance
　　that Judas jousted with and, taking aim,
　　he bursts the guts of Florence with one thrust.　　　75

From this he gains not land but sin and shame!
　　And worse is that he makes light of the weight
　　of all his crimes, refusing all the blame.　　　　78

The third, once hauled a captive from his ship,
　　I see selling his daughter, haggling the price,
　　as pirates do, over their female slaves.　　　　81

O Avarice, what more harm can you do?
　　You have so fascinated all my heirs,
　　they have no care for their own flesh and blood.　　84

That past and future crimes may seem as naught,
　　I see the *fleur-de-lis* enter Alagna
　　and in His vicar Christ made prisoner.　　　　87

I see the gall and vinegar renewed;
   I see Him being mocked a second time,
   killed once again between the living thieves.   90

I see this second Pilate so full of spite
   that, still unsatisfied, his greedy sails
   he drives, unchartered, into Holy Temple.   93

O Lord, when shall I have the joy to see
   that retribution which, now lying hid,
   makes sweet Thy wrath within Thy secret will?   96

The words that I recited earlier
   about the one Bride of the Holy Ghost
   (which brought you to me that I might explain)   99

make up the prayers that we here must recite
   as long as daylight lasts; when night comes, though,
   our litany is just the opposite: 102

then, we cry out against Pygmalion,
   how he turned traitor, thief, and parricide
   through his unsated appetite for gold;   105

and avaricious Midas, whose request,
   moved by his greed, made him a starveling wretch,
   the butt of ridicule through centuries;   108

then we recall the foolishness of Achan,
   who stole the spoils, and stirred Joshua's wrath—
   which seems, as we recite, to sting him still.   111

Next we accuse Sapphira with her mate;
   we hail the hoofs that kicked Heliodorus;
   and, all around the mount, echoes the shame   114

of Polymnestor slaying Polydorus;
   the last cry heard is 'Crassus, tell us, now,
   what does gold taste like? *You* should surely know!'   117

At times we cry out loud, at times speak soft,
   according as our feelings spur us on,
   sometimes with greater, sometimes lesser force.   120

So, I was not the only one to cry
   the good we praise by day; it was by chance
   no other spirit nearby raised his voice."   123

We had already taken leave of him
   and we were striving to cover as much
   ground as those prostrate souls allowed us to,   *126*

when, suddenly, I felt the mountain shake
   as if about to crumble, and I felt
   my body numb, seized by the chill of death.   *129*

Delos, before Latona nested there,
   in order to give birth to those two eyes
   that shine in Heaven, was never shaken more.   *132*

Then on all sides a shout rose up, so loud
   my master drew close to my side and said:
   "You need not fear while I am still your guide."   *135*

Gloria in excelsis, all sang, *Deo* —
   at least, this is what those close by sang out,
   whose words I could hear clearly as they cried.   *138*

As had the shepherds who first heard that song,
   we stood fixed with out souls suspended there
   until the hymn ended, the tremor ceased.   *141*

Then we continued on our sacred road:
   beneath our eyes the prostrate souls once more
   were wholly given up to their laments.   *144*

Never before, unless my memory errs,
   had my blind ignorance stirred up in me
   so violent a desire for the truth   *147*

as I felt now, racking my brain to know.
   I dared not slow our pace with questioning,
   and I could see no explanation there.   *150*

I walked along, timid, deep in my thoughts.

NOTES

1. *The lesser will yields to the greater will:* The Pilgrim, although he wants to hear more from Adrian, withdraws, thus allowing him to continue his penance.

10–12. *God damn you, ageless She-Wolf, you whose greed:* With this tercet the Poet recalls to his reader's mind the She-Wolf of the opening canto of the *Inferno*, the beast that blocked the Pilgrim's way up that other mountain in the prologue scene to the *Divine Comedy*. The reader is also reminded of the avaricious Plutus, who guards over the Miserly and Prodigal in Hell (see note to *Inf.* VII, 8). We may even be reminded of the "ageless sorceress" in the preceding canto (*Purg.* XIX, 58). All are closely associated with the sins of Incontinence.

14. *when will he come:* These words are reminiscent of the prophecy, in the opening canto of the *Comedy*, of the coming of the Greyhound (*Inf.* I, 101), who one day will track down the She-Wolf, the personification of Avarice (and the other sins of Incontinence).

19-33

Again, as on the second and fourth terraces, the exempla are presented orally. But here, rather than disembodied voices in the air or the voices of a group of Penitents, it is a single individual who praises the virtue opposed to Avarice—or so it seems to the Pilgrim and the reader at this point. Only later will we receive an explanation of the unique way in which the exempla are regularly presented on the Terrace of the Avaricious (97-123).

The first two exempla that the Pilgrim and the reader hear are in the form of direct discourse (the first time we have encountered this vivid device): "Sweet Mary," "Oh, good Fabricius"; the third the Pilgrim surely heard as, "Oh, Saint Nicholas," but Dante has chosen to present this direct address in the form of a summary. Thus we have the stylistic variation of direct discourse followed by indirect discourse. We will see still another stylistic variation in the treatment of the second set of exempla (97-123).

21. *was like that of a woman giving birth:* The juxtaposition of Mary's name and the image of a woman giving birth recalls the birth of the Savior (which will be explicitly mentioned in the following tercet). The soul who calls out in praise of the Virgin wails like a woman in labor, and he is none other than the Hugh who gave birth to the Capetian line of kings, famous for their avarice.

22-24. *How very poor you were:* The first example of a virtue opposed to the sin of Avarice—taken, as always, from the life of the Virgin—apparently extols poverty: the poverty that Mary accepted without complaint when she gave birth to her glorious son in a stable.

25. *Fabricius:* The second example of the virtue opposing Avarice again has to do with poverty, poverty as the result of asceticism, deliberate self-denial. Fabricius Caius Luscinus, consul of Rome in 282 and 278 B.C., censor in 275 B.C., refused throughout his public career to accept bribes, as was the custom of his day. He also resisted the greed and luxury of the Romans, so much so that he died a pauper and had to be buried by the state (which also had to provide his daughters with dowries).

32. *Nicholas:* Here the virtue praised is that of generosity. St. Nicholas, bishop of Myra in Lycia, Asia Minor, who lived under Constantine and was present at the Council of Nicaea in A.D. 325, is venerated as a saint by both Greek and Roman churches and is considered the patron of virgins, sailors, thieves, merchants, and travellers, not to mention children (Santa Claus). Dante alludes to the legend in which Nicholas, to prevent an impoverished local nobleman from prostituting his daughters, threw a bag of gold, on three different nights, through the nobleman's window as dowries for the girls.

43–60

In these verses the speaker is introducing himself to the Pilgrim and telling him something of his career, but his identity has not yet been clearly established. Some scholars believe that the speaker is Hugh I (usually called Hugh the Great), the powerful nobleman who was the *de facto* ruler of France during the reign of Louis IV (936–54) and for the first two years of the reign of Lothair (954–86). He died in 956. Others believe that the speaker is Hugh II (usually called Hugh Capet), son of Hugh I, who in 987, on the death of Louis V (Lothair's successor), became the first king of France of the Capetian line. All are agreed that Dante, like many of his contemporaries, had confused the two figures, and also that his knowledge of late tenth-century French history was inadequate.

Verse 43 ("I was the root of that malignant tree") would seem to apply most naturally to Hugh II, the first of the Capetian line; the possibility is not, however, excluded that Hugh I, as the father of the first king, could think of himself as the "root." The name that appears in verse 49, Hugh Capet, is for some scholars conclusive evidence that Hugh II is involved, Poletto (p. 464) insisting that the sobriquet *Capet* was never applied to the father, Hugh I—and this is the practice of most modern commentators. A few, however, who for other reasons believe the speaker to be Hugh I, ignore this evidence.

The reference in verse 52 ("My father was a Paris cattle man") is obviously true neither of Hugh I nor of Hugh II. Dante here must be following a popular tradition. But to whom did this tradition apply? Of the earlier commentators who mention this tradition, Buti is completely confused, having telescoped the two figures. Villani, however, states clearly that it was Hugh II, whose father was said to be "a very rich and powerful burgher of Paris who had originally been a butcher or a cattle merchant" (*Cron.*, IV, 4). Thus, the cattle dealer would have been Hugh I and not the father of Hugh I, as a number of scholars believe (see Singleton [1973, pp. 476–77], who, curiously enough, quotes Villani in support of his theory).

In the passage 53–60 the speaker states that when the Carolingian line came to an end (except for one who had become a monk) he had acquired such influence that he was able to have his son crowned king of France. The Carolingian line came to an end in the year 987; in that year Hugh I had been dead for thirty-one years and could not have seen his son crowned. But it is equally impossible for the words to apply to Hugh II: it is true that he was alive in 987, but the one who was crowned king of France was not Hugh II's son (Robert) but Hugh II himself.

As for the first three bits of evidence discussed, the first two seem clearly to support the choice of Hugh II as speaker (though not actually excluding Hugh I as a possibility); the third, *if* we trust Villani, points exclusively to Hugh II. But since the last passage can apply to neither of the two candidates, I think it is pointless to try to choose between them. For a discussion of the problem, see Rajna.

43. *that malignant tree:* The "malignant tree" is the Capetian monarchy.

46. *but if Douai and Lille and Ghent and Bruges:* These are the foremost cities of Flanders, representing that region as a whole. The revenge that Hugh seems to long for so eagerly will indeed take place in the year 1302, when the Flemish defeat

the French at the battle of Courtrai. As for the grievances that made the Flemish seek revenge, see Singleton (1973), pp. 475–76.

50. *from me have sprung the Louises and Philips:* From the year 1060 to the fictional date of the *Comedy* (and even beyond), all the Capetian kings were named either Louis or Philip.

54. *except for him who wore a monk's grey robe:* When Louis V died in 987, after a brief reign, the only living representative of the Carolingian line was Charles, Duke of Lorraine, son of Louis IV, brother of Lothair and uncle of Louis V. But he did not become a monk. He was put in prison by Hugh, against whom he had armed himself. Many scholars believe that Dante is confusing the last of the Carolingians with the last of the Merovingians, Childeric III, who did become a monk after his deposition in 752.

60. *that those anointed bones were to descend:* In the coronation ceremony of the Capetian kings (a solemn ceremony in the Cathedral of Rheims), the person of the king was anointed with holy oil.

63. *dowry of Provence:* The kingdom of Provence was annexed to the French crown through the marriage of Charles of Anjou (brother of Louis IX of France) to Beatrice, daughter and heiress of Raymond Berenger IV of Provence. Berenger, in giving his daughter to Charles, was breaking his promise to Count Raymond of Toulouse, to whom she had first been betrothed.

66. *Ponthieu, Normandy, Gascony:* Normandy was taken from England in 1202 by Philip II; both Ponthieu and Gascony were taken from England in 1295 by Philip the Fair.

67–68. *Charles came to Italy:* Charles of Anjou, invited by Urban IV to assume the crown of Naples and Sicily, came into Italy in 1265; in 1266 he defeated Manfred at Benevento and was crowned in the same year.

Conradin, the rightful heir (see *Purg.* III, 112), attempted to wrest the throne from Charles, but was defeated at Tagliacozzo in 1268 and executed in Naples in October of the same year.

69. *sent Thomas off to Heaven, to make amends:* The legend, current in Dante's time, that Charles had poisoned St. Thomas

Aquinas is unfounded. Thomas died in 1274 during a journey to the Council of Lyons, to which he had been summoned by Gregory X.

The phrase "to make amends" is repeated three times (65, 67, 69), and in rhyme position. It is obviously intended to be heavily ironic, since the French seem to make amends by adding villainy to villainy.

71. *a second Charles:* This is Charles of Valois (1270–1325), who was called to Italy by Boniface VIII as a peacemaker (i.e., to destroy those who opposed the papacy). Charles arrived in Florence on All Saints' Day, 1301; as a result of his intervention, the city was delivered over to the Black party, and all of the Whites, including Dante himself, were exiled from Florence.

73–74. *the lance / that Judas jousted with:* This lance must symbolize Judas's "weapon" of betrayal.

76. *From this he gains not land but sin and shame:* Charles had already been known by the nickname "Charles Sansterre," since he had inherited no land.

79. *The third:* This is a reference to the "third Charles." Charles II, king of Naples (1243–1309), son of Charles of Anjou, was defeated in a naval battle by Peter III of Aragon in 1284 and was taken from his own ship. In 1305 Charles married off his young daughter, Beatrice, to the much older Azzo VIII of Este in exchange for a large sum of money.

87. *and in His vicar Christ made prisoner:* The vicar of Christ here mentioned is Pope Boniface VIII. In September 1303, at the culmination of a long dispute, Philip the Fair, king of France, about to be excommunicated, sent an armed force under Sciarra Colonna and William of Nogaret to Anagni ("Alagna," 86). These troops seized the pope, ransacked his palace, and subjected him to every manner of abuse for three days, threatening to carry him off in chains to his execution. Boniface's captors were expelled by the good people of Anagni and the pope was taken to Rome, where he died a month later of "hysterical seizures." Dante compares Philip's act to Pilate's turning Christ over to his persecutors (91).

92–93. *still unsatisfied, his greedy sails / he drives:* This strange mixed metaphor refers to the persecution and destruction by Philip the Fair of the Knights Templar, which was one of the military orders founded in the twelfth century, with the approval of Pope Honarius II, to defend the Latin kingdom of Jerusalem. Their headquarters was in the palace of the Latin kings on Mount Moriah (also known as Solomon's temple). In 1307 Philip accused the order of heresy and other hideous offenses and began arresting them, torturing them, and extracting from them false confessions. This he did without papal decree or permission of the church—as the Italian text states, "sanza decreto," which I have translated as "unchartered" (93). Five years later Philip succeeded in having Clement V condemn them and in having their grand master, Jacques de Molay, burned at the stake in Paris in the royal presence. The main reason for Philip's destruction of the Templars was, of course, to take possession of the enormous wealth that this order had accumulated over the years.

97–123

After having answered the Pilgrim's first question (43–96), Hugh proceeds to answer the second question: why he was alone in reciting the first set of exempla. In his explanation we have for the first time the situation in which one of the Penitents explains to the Pilgrim the habitual practices of the whole group. This setup involves another variation on the manner in which the exempla are presented. We have seen that the first set of exempla offers direct discourse followed by indirect; now, with the second set, as Hugh speaks of Pygmalion and the rest of the avaricious crew, his description is offered in the first person: "We cry out" (103), "We accuse" (112). The Pilgrim will never hear the group of souls cry out these exempla; he is only allowed to hear the themes summarized by a single Penitent.

These nine tercets offer a well-organized structural unit in themselves, as well as suggesting the larger unit beginning with Hugh's first words ("Sweet Mary": 20). In the first two tercets, we have the beginning of Hugh's answer to the Pilgrim's second question, which contains a reminder of the first set of exempla. This introduction is followed by the five tercets that offer the second set of exempla. In the last two tercets he gets closer, verse by verse, to giving the precise answer to the Pilgrim's question: "no other spirit nearby raised his voice."

97. *The words that I recited earlier:* Though Hugh's reference here is limited to his apostrophe to the Virgin Mary (the first of the three exempla he had recited), we can only assume that it is all three exempla that "make up the prayers that we here must recite" (100).

100. *the prayers that we here must recite:* For the first and only time the exempla are referred to as "prayers." The single prayer assigned to this terrace is, of course, *Adhaesit pavimento anima mea* (XIX, 73), which the Pilgrim heard before his meeting with Adrian.

101. *as long as daylight lasts; when night comes, though:* That one set of exempla should be recited in the day, another set at night, represents a striking exception to the general practice of the mountain. Moreover, the reader receives the impression that *all* day and *all* night the Penitents were (off and on) given up to such recitations. There is clearly an extraordinary emphasis on continuous effort on the part of the prostrate souls to keep in mind those figures of virtue and vice.

103. *Pygmalion:* Not to be confused with Pygmalion the sculptor, of Greek legend, who fell in love with one of his own statues, this Pygmalion, king of Tyre, was the brother of Dido. He murdered her husband, Sichaeus, for his wealth. Dido, advised of this in a dream, fled secretly from Tyre with the treasure and went to Africa, where she founded the city of Carthage.

106. *Midas:* King of Phrygia, to whom Bacchus granted one request in exchange for his kindness to Silenus, Bacchus's instructor. Midas, in his greed, asked that all he touched be turned to gold. However, after the wish was granted, Midas discovered that even the food he touched became gold, and so he implored Bacchus (successfully) to take his favor back.

109. *Achan:* The son of Carmi, who stole and hid some of the Spoils of Jericho, which Joshua had ordered to be consecrated to the Lord. He was later discovered, and, at the order of Joshua, he and his family were stoned to death (Josh. 6:17–19; 7:1–26).

112. *Sapphira:* She and her husband, Ananias, sold some property held in common by the apostles but returned to them only part of the price they had received. When St. Peter re-

buked them for their greed, they collapsed dead at his feet (Acts 5:1–11).

113. *Heliodorus:* Sent by the king of Syria to steal treasures from the temple in Jerusalem, Heliodorus was driven away and nearly kicked to death by a horse who appeared mysteriously, ridden by a man in golden armor. This story is taken from the Old Testament Apocrypha: II Mach. 3:25–27.

115. *Polymnestor:* Before the fall of Troy, Priam entrusted Polymnestor, a king of Thrace, with his son Polydorus and a large sum of money. After Troy fell, Polymnestor killed the boy and took the money for himself. (See Ovid, *Metam.* XIII, 429–38).

116. *Crassus:* The greedy Marcus Licinius Crassus, consul with Pompey in 70 B.C. and later triumvir with Pompey and Caesar, was defeated and beheaded by the Parthians in 53 B.C. The victors sent the head, along with the right hand, to their King, Hyrodes, who, in mockery of Crassus's thirst for wealth, had molten gold poured down his throat.

118. *At times we cry out loud, at times speak soft:* Just why such vocal fluctuations should be particularly fitting for the Penitents on the Terrace of Avarice is not too clear; it must be connected somehow with the emphasis on the persistence of their recitation.

123. *no other spirit nearby raised his voice:* This must mean that no other spirit was crying out in a loud voice—not that all the rest nearby were absolutely silent.

125–26. *as much / ground as those prostrate souls:* This is the fourth reference (see also verses 5, 9, 16) to the difficulty experienced by the Pilgrim and his guide in making their way around the bodies of the Penitents on this terrace. That means the fourth reference to the quantity of souls occupying the Terrace of Avarice and, also, to their abject form of punishment, which had caused Adrian to say in the previous canto (XIX, 117): "the mountain knows no harsher penalty."

130. *Delos:* An island in the Cyclades, where Latona went to escape the wrath of Juno and to bring forth her two children by Jupiter: Apollo and Diana. According to one legend, Delos was

a floating island tossed about by waves, until Jupiter fixed it in place as a refuge for Latona. It is fitting that this should be compared to Purgatory and its tremors, since Purgatory, too, is an island.

136. *"Gloria in excelsis," all sang, "Deo":* The song "Glory to God in the Highest" was sung by the angels on the eve of the Nativity and heard by the shepherds (139) in the fields. This reference to the birth of Christ, as well as the reference earlier to the birth of Apollo and Diana (also "divine beings" according to pagan lore), clearly points ahead to the appearance of Statius, since the mountain is giving rebirth to his soul. But this reference to the birth of Christ points not only ahead but back: to the first exemplum of Poverty (illustrated by the poverty of the stable in which Christ was born).

CANTO XXI

As THE PILGRIM and Virgil walk along the Terrace of the Avaricious, a shade appears and speaks to them. Virgil explains that the Pilgrim is still alive, and he relates the nature and purpose of their journey, finally asking the shade why the mountain has just trembled. The shade explains that the mountain of Purgatory is not subject to the vicissitudes of Nature such as rain, wind, and lightning, but that when a soul feels that the time of its purification has come to an end and it is ready to ascend to heaven, then the mountain shakes and voices shout praises to God. The shade speaking is the one who has just experienced this release after more than five hundred years of purgation. He identifies himself as Statius, the author of the *Thebaid* and the unfinished *Achilleid*. Statius claims that he has derived his poetic inspiration from the *Aeneid*, and he expresses his ardent wish to have lived when Virgil was alive, and to have met the great poet. At these words the Pilgrim smiles knowingly, and with his guide's permission, reveals to Statius that he is standing in the presence of his mentor. Forgetting himself, Statius bends down to embrace Virgil's knees, but is gently reminded by that prince of poets that they are only empty shades.

The natural thirst which nothing satisfies
   except that water begged for long ago
   by the poor woman of Samaria								3

tormented me, and haste was urging me
   along the crowded path, and I was still
   grieving at the just pain those souls must pay,				6

when suddenly—just as we read in Luke
   that Christ, new-risen from the tomb, appeared
   to the two men on the Emmaus road—						9

a shade appeared! He had come from behind
   while we were trying not to step on shades,
   quite unaware of him until he spoke:							12

"May God, my brothers, give you peace." At that,
   we quickly turned around, and Virgil then
   responded to his words appropriately,						15

and said: "May God's True Court which sentenced me
    to eternal banishment, lead you in peace
    into the Congregation of the Blest."   18

"What's that?" he said as we kept forging on.
    "If you are souls whom God will not receive,
    who let you climb His stairway this far up?"   21

And then my teacher said: "If you observe
    those marks the angel has traced on his brow,
    you'll see that he must dwell among the Just.   24

But she who labors spinning day and night,
    had not spun out for him the flax which Clotho
    packs on her distaff for each one of us;   27

therefore, his soul, sister to yours and mine,
    in coming up, could not come by itself,
    because it does not see as our eyes do.   30

And so I was brought up from Hell's wide throat
    to serve him as a guide, and guide I shall
    as far as my own knowledge will permit.   33

But can you tell me why the mountain shook
    so hard just now, and why all of the souls
    down to its marshy base, cried out as one?"   36

My leader's question pierced the needle's eye
    of my desire, and with the eager hope
    that this aroused, I felt my thirst relieved.   39

The shade said: "Sacred laws that rule this mount
    will not let anything take place that is
    uncustomary or irregular.   42

This place is not subject to any change:
    what Heaven takes from itself into itself,
    and nothing else, can serve as cause up here;   45

therefore no rain, no hail, no snow can fall,
    nor dew nor hoarfrost form at any point
    beyond the three-step stairway down below.   48

There are no clouds, misty or dense, no sign
    of lightning or of Thaumas' daughter, she
    who often moves from place to place below;   51

nor can dry vapors rise beyond the height
   of those three steps of which I just now spoke,
   whereon Saint Peter's vicar rests his feet.   54

Quakes may occur below, slight or severe,
   but tremors caused by winds hid in the earth
   (I know not why) have never reached this high.   57

Up here the mountain trembles when some soul
   feels itself pure enough to stand erect
   or start at once to climb—then, comes the shout.   60

The will to rise, alone, proves purity:
   once freed, it takes possession of the soul
   and wills the soul to change its company.   63

It willed to climb before, but the desire
   High Justice set against it, inspired it
   to wish to suffer—as once it wished to sin.   66

And I, who for five hundred years and more,
   have lain here in my pain, felt only now
   will free to raise me to a higher sill.   69

That's why you felt the quake and why you heard
   the pious dwellers on the mount praise God.
   May He soon call them up to be with Him."   72

This was his explanation. And my joy
   was inexpressible: the more the thirst,
   the more enjoyable becomes the drink.   75

And my wise leader: "Now I see what net
   holds you bound here, and how the mesh is torn,
   why the mount shakes, why you rejoice as one.   78

Now, if it please you, I would like to know
   who you once were, and learn from your own words
   why you have lain so many centuries here."   81

"During the rule of the good Titus, who,
   assisted by the King of Kings, avenged
   the wounds that poured forth blood which Judas sold,   84

I bore the title that endures the most
   and which is honored most," that soul replied;
   "renown I had, not yet the Christian faith.   87

The spirit of my verses was so sweet
    that from Toulouse, Rome called me to herself,
    and judged me worthy of the myrtle crown.   90

My name is Statius, still well known on earth.
    I sang of Thebes, then of Achilles' might,
    but found that second weight too great to bear.   93

The spark that kindled my poetic ardor
    came from the sacred flame that set on fire
    more than a thousand poets: I mean the *Aeneid*.   96

That was the mother of my poetry,
    the nurse that gave it suck. Without that poem,
    my verses would have not been worth a thing.   99

And if only I could have been alive
    when Virgil lived, I would consent to spend
    an extra year of exile on the mount."   102

At these words Virgil turned to me. His look
    told me in silence: "Silence!" But the power
    of a man's will is often powerless: 105

laughter and tears follow so close upon
    the passions that provoke them that the more
    sincere the man, the less they obey his will.   108

I smiled and unsmiled quicker than a blink,
    but he stopped speaking; staring straight at me,
    into the eyes, where secrets are betrayed: 111

"So may your toiling win you grace," he said,
    "tell me the reason for your smile just now—
    that smile that quickly came and quickly went."   114

Here I am caught between opposing sides:
    the one tells me be quiet, the other bids
    me to speak up. And so, I sigh. My guide   117

perfectly understood: "Don't be afraid
    to speak," he said: "speak to him, answer now
    the question he has asked so earnestly."   120

"You seem to find my smiling very strange,"
    I said to him, "O ancient spirit, but
    I have to tell you something stranger still: 123

This shade here who directs my eyes to Heaven
    is the poet Virgil, who bequeathed to you
    the power to sing the deeds of men and gods.   126

In truth, the only reason for my smile,
    is that you chose to mention Virgil here:
    your very words are guilty of my smile."   129

Already he was bending to embrace
    my teacher's feet, but Virgil: "Brother, no!
    You are a shade; it is a shade you see."   132

And Statius, rising: "Now you understand
    how much my love for you burns deep in me,
    when I forget about our emptiness   135

and deal with shadows as with solid things."

NOTES

1. *The natural thirst which nothing satisfies:* Note the statement of Aristotle "All men naturally desire knowledge"
(*Metaphys.* I, 1, 980a); Dante refers to this passage in *Conv.* I, i, 1.

3. *the poor woman of Samaria:* The story of Jesus and the
Samaritan woman at the well is told in John 4: 5–15. But there
the water that Christ says he is able to give and that she then
asks for is declared to be the water of everlasting life. Christ is
offering her the possibility of salvation: "Jesus said to her,
'Everyone who drinks of this water will thirst again. He, however, who drinks of the water that I will give him shall never
thirst; but the water that I will give him shall become in him a
fountain of water springing up into everlasting life.'"

6. *grieving at the just pain those souls must pay:* The "just
pain" is the humiliating punishment of the Avaricious, mentioned for the last time at the end of the preceding canto (XX,
143–44). As a matter of fact, the Pilgrim is preoccupied by
three things as he starts once more on his journey: his curiosity
to know the cause of the mountain's tremor, the need to hurry,
and the sight of the prostrate Penitents. The same three preoc-
cupations, though not in the same order, are listed at the end of
the preceding canto (XX, 143–51).

10. *a shade appeared:* The shade, as we will learn, is the

Roman poet Statius (whom Dante will present as having been converted to Christianity). From this point on, until the Pilgrim meets Beatrice, Statius will serve as the Pilgrim's second guide; thus, he represents a transition from Virgil (reason and classical culture) to Beatrice (grace and revelation). The fictional identity that Dante has constructed for Statius (pagan become Christian) makes him eminently suited to such a role. And by virtue of the fact that he has already been released from Purgatory, he naturally points ahead to the top of the mountain (and to Paradise). Furthermore, Statius appears here like the risen Christ, Virgil and the Pilgrim being like the two apostles surprised on the road to Emmaus (Luke 24:13–16). And the Christ figure Statius anticipates Beatrice, who is also a Christ figure. On the prophetic role of Statius in the *Purgatory* see Heilbronn (1977).

15. *responded to his words appropriately*: The Italian text reads, "rendèli 'l cenno ch'a ciò si conface" ("answered him with the greeting that is fitting thereto"). No one has as yet proposed an entirely satisfactory explanation as to what this specific gesture of greeting might be. However, in the liturgy, the proper response to *Pax vobis* (Statius's greeting or salutation of peace in verse 13) is the kiss of peace.

20. *If you are souls whom God will not receive*: Though Virgil had spoken only of his own fate and had said nothing about the condition of the Pilgrim, Statius evidently assumes that the Pilgrim is also a dead soul. Since the two travellers are on the western side of the mountain, the Pilgrim's body can cast no shadow signifying that he is alive.

22. *If you observe*: Statius has just shown by his question (19–21) that he has made two false assumptions: that the Pilgrim is dead and that he has been damned. Virgil corrects the first by pointing out to Statius the marks traced on the Pilgrim's brow by the angel at the gate of Purgatory as a sign of heavenly favor. In the following tercet he will correct the second one.

25–27. *But she who labors spinning day and night*: Lachesis, one of the three Fates. Lachesis spins the thread of a man's life from a certain quantity of wool, which her sister, Clotho, has loaded onto the distaff. Naturally, the quantity of the wool determines the length of the particular life. (A third sister, Athropos, cuts the thread when it is finished.) With this rather elaborate image taken from classical mythology, Virgil the poet is telling Statius, another poet, that Dante is still alive.

30. *because it does not see as our eyes do*: The Pilgrim still sees with the eyes of the flesh and not as spirits see. We are reminded here of the distinction Virgil made earlier (*Purg.* XV, 134–35) between the vision of spirits and mortal eyesight ("eyes doomed to blindness once the body dies").

50. *Thaumas' daughter*: The daughter of the centaur Thaumas and Electra was Iris, the personification of the rainbow, and Juno's messenger. Since the rainbow is seen in different parts of the sky, always opposite the sun, Iris "moves from place to place."

56. *tremors*: According to Dante's medieval geology, earthquakes were caused by winds trapped underground.

61–66. *The will to rise*: Grandgent (p. 493) explains this passage as follows:

> When we sin, we follow, not our absolute, but our conditioned will, which has been perverted by false appearances. So when we make atonement, it is not the absolute will that seeks punishment, but the conditioned will, shaped by the knowledge that good can come through penance alone. A soul in Purgatory is held there only by its own conditioned will. As soon as this conditioned will, or desire, coincides with the absolute and eternal inclination to seek blessedness, the penitent knows that his expiation is over and he is at liberty to rise.

82. *Titus*: Son and successor of Vespasian, Titus served as Roman emperor from A.D. 79 to A.D. 81. His destruction of Jerusalem and defeat of the Jews in A.D. 70 was regarded by Dante as just vengeance for the crucifixion of Christ. This idea was first expressed by Orosius (see *Hist.* VII, iii, 8 and ix, 9).

91. *Statius*: Publius Papinus Statius, born in Naples ca. A.D. 45, died A.D. 96. (Dante confuses him in line 89 with Lucius Statius Ursulus, a rhetorician of Toulouse.) He was the major poet of the Silver Age of Latin literature and spent most of his life in Rome. His best work is an epic in Latin hexameters, the *Thebaid*, which, in twelve books, narrates the expedition of the Seven against Thebes and the dispute between Eteocles and Polynices. A second epic, the *Achilleid*, based on the life of Achilles and the Trojan War, was left unfinished at his death.

His conversion to Christianity has no historical basis and appears to be Dante's invention.

93. *but found that second weight too great to bear:* Statius died before completing his second major work, the *Achilleid.*

94–99. *The spark that kindled my poetic ardor:* Statius acknowledges his debt as a poet to the poet Virgil. With the entrance of Statius, Dante brings into focus the themes of poetry and poet ("the title that endures the most," 85), which will be important in the cantos still to come.

100. *And if only I could have been alive:* Statius impulsively claims that he would gladly have spent another year in Purgatory, if he could have been a contemporary of Virgil's in this life—a spiritual incongruity for a soul already free to rise to Heaven?

132. *You are a shade; it is a shade you see:* Virgil's admonitory words to Statius here have generally been taken to mean that it is physically impossible for shades to embrace each other. That this act is quite possible, however, has been proven in Cantos VII and VIII of *Purgatory:* Sordello embraces Virgil three or four times and later clasps his legs. And I do not agree with those critics who believe that Dante has conveniently "forgotten" Sordello's elaborate embrace.

It is far more likely that Virgil is suggesting to Statius that an embrace would not be fitting between the two. The relationship between Sordello and Virgil was on a worldly plane: the first embrace was prompted by Sordello's recognition of the fact that the two were born in the same town; the second, when Sordello realized that the shade before him was the most famous of all Roman poets. But Statius loved Virgil; he was drawn to him for reasons far deeper and more personal: moral, poetic, and spiritual reasons. Through Virgil's words on Avarice he was led to examine his system of ethical values; through Virgil he was able to develop his own poetic talent; through Virgil he was led to Christ. Surely a worldly embrace would be inappropriate.

But why did Virgil, who did not believe that all embraces between shades were inappropriate, not deter Statius by a reference to the particular relationship between the two? Perhaps he felt that to remind Statius that he was a shade (who had just been accepted by Heaven) would remind him of all the rest.

CANTO XXII

LEAVING THE FIFTH Terrace, the Pilgrim and Virgil, now
accompanied by Statius, are directed to the next ledge by an
angel who removes another *P* from the Pilgrim's forehead and
pronounces those blessed who thirst for righteousness. Virgil
tells Statius that he has felt a great deal of good will toward him
ever since Juvenal had come down to Limbo with the report of
Statius's love and admiration for Virgil. But he is puzzled as to
how such a magnanimous spirit could find room in its heart for
avarice. Statius explains that his sin was not Avarice, but Prodigality, and that whenever two sins are the immediate opposite
of one another, they are purged together on the same terrace
of the mountain of Purgatory. Virgil then asks Statius how he
came to be a Christian, and Statius replies that it was Virgil's
Fourth Eclogue that eventually led him to give ear to the Christian preachers. Once converted however, he kept his faith a
secret, and for this lack of zeal was consigned to spend four
hundred years on the Terrace of the Slothful. As the poets
finish their conversation, they step out onto the Sixth Terrace,
where they encounter a tree with sweet-smelling fruit in the
middle of the road. A cascade of clear water rains down on its
uppermost leaves. As they draw closer to the tree, a voice from
within the branches shouts the exempla of the virtue opposed
to gluttony.

By now we had already left behind
　　the angel who directs to the Sixth Round
　　and from my brow erased another scar,　　　　　　　*3*

saying that all who looked for righteousness
　　are blest—omitting the *esuriunt*,
　　and predicating only *sitiunt*.　　　　　　　　　　*6*

And I, lighter than I had felt before
　　at any other stairs, moved easily
　　upward, behind those swiftly climbing shades.　　　*9*

Now, Virgil was already speaking: "Love,
　　kindled by virtue, always kindles love,
　　if the first flame is clearly visible;　　　　　　　*12*

thus, ever since the day that Juvenal
    came down to Hell's Limbo to be with us,
    and told me of the love you felt for me,   *15*

I have felt more good will toward you, more than
    was felt toward any person not yet seen;
    and so, these stairs will seem much shorter now.   *18*

But tell me—speak to me as to a friend,
    and as a friend, forgive me if I seem
    too bold in slackening decorum's reins—   *21*

how could your heart find room for avarice,
    with that abundant store of sound, good sense
    which you acquired with such diligence?"   *24*

These words of Virgil brought to Statius' lips
    a briefly lingering smile; then he replied:
    "All you have said reveals your love for me.   *27*

Appearances will often, it is true,
    give rise to false assumptions, when the truth
    to be revealed is hidden from our eyes.   *30*

Your question makes it clear to me that you
    believe my sin on earth was Avarice—
    perhaps because you found me where you did.   *33*

In truth, I had no part of Avarice;
    in fact, too little! The sin I purged below,
    thousands of months, was Prodigality.   *36*

And if I had not come to change my ways
    while meditating on those lines you wrote,
    where you, enraged by human nature, cry: *39*

'To what extremes, O cursèd lust for gold
    will you not drive man's appetite?'—I would
    be rolling weights now in the dismal jousts.   *42*

But when I understood how hands could spread
    their wings too wide in spending, then that sin,
    and all my others, I repented of.   *45*

How many shall rise bald the Final Day
    through ignorance of this vice, forbidding them
    repentance during life or on death's bed?   *48*

And know that when the vice of any sin
  is the rebuttal of its opposite,
  the two of them wither together here.   51

So, though to purge myself I spent my time
  among those souls who weep for Avarice,
  my sin was just the opposite of theirs."   54

"Now, when you sang about the bitter strife
  of the twin sources of Jocasta's grief,"
  the bard of the *Bucolics* said to him,   57

"from what you wrote in Clio's company,
  it does not seem that you were faithful then
  to that faith without which virtue is vain.   60

If this be so, tell me what heavenly sun
  or earthly beam lit up your course so that
  you could set sail behind the Fisherman."   63

Statius said: "It was you directed me
  to drink Parnassus' waters—it was you
  whose radiance revealed the way to God.   66

You were the lonely traveller in the dark
  who holds his lamp behind him, shedding light
  not for himself but to make others wise;   69

for you once wrote: 'The world is born again;
  Justice returns, and the first age of man,
  and a new progeny descends from heaven.'   72

Through you I was a poet, through you, a Christian.
  And now, to show you better what I mean,
  I shall fill in my outline with more color.   75

By then, the world was laboring in the birth
  of the true faith, sown by the messengers
  of the Eternal Kingdom; and your words,   78

which I just quoted now, so harmonized
  with what the new preachers were saying then,
  that I would often go to hear them speak.   81

These men became so holy in my eyes
  that when Domitian persecuted them,
  I wept, as they wept in their suffering,   84

and, for as long as I remained alive,
    I helped them, and their righteous way of life
    taught me to scorn all other faiths but theirs.   87

Before I brought the Greeks to Theban streams
    with my poetic art, I was baptized,
    but was a secret Christian out of fear,   90

pretending to be pagan many years;
    and for this lack of zeal, I had to run
    four hundred years on the Fourth Circle. Now,   93

please tell me, you who did remove the veil
    that once concealed from me the good I praise,
    tell me, while there is still some time to climb,   96

where is our ancient Terence, do you know?
    And Plautus, and Caecilius and Varius?
    Have they been damned? If so, where are they lodged?"   99

"They all, along with Persius and me
    and others," said my guide, "are with that Greek
    the Muses suckled more than all the rest,   102

in the First Round of Hell's unlighted jail.
    We often talk about the mountain slope
    where our nine nurses dwell eternally.   105

Euripides walks with us; Antiphon,
    Simonides, and Agathon are there,
    and other Greeks who wear the laurel crown.   108

With us are many of your people too:
    Antigone, Deïphyle, Argia,
    Ismene, sad as she has ever been,   111

and she who showed Langia to the Greeks,
    and Thetis, and the daughter of Tiresias,
    Deïdamia with her sisters, too."   114

The poets now were free of walls and stairs,
    both of them standing silent on the ledge,
    eager again to gaze at everything.   117

Already the four handmaids of the day
    were left behind, and at the chariot-pole,
    the fifth was tilting up the blazing tip,   120

when my guide said: "I think we ought to move
    with our right shoulders to the outer edge,
    the way we always have gone round this mount." 123

So, habit was our guide there, and we went
    our way with much less hesitation now,
    since worthy Statius gave us his assent. 126

They walked ahead and I, behind, alone,
    was paying close attention to their words,
    which taught me things about the art of verse. 129

But then, right in the road a tree appeared,
    laden with fruit whose fragrance filled the air,
    and instantly that pleasant talk was stopped! 132

Just as a fir tree tapers toward the top
    from branch to branch, so this one tapered down,
    to keep the souls from climbing, I suppose. 135

On that side where our way was bounded, poured
    clear water from the high rock to the tree,
    sprinkling the topmost leaves in its cascade. 138

As the two poets drew close, there came a voice
    that shouted at us from within the tree:
    "This fruit and water is denied to you." 141

Then the voice said: "Mary was more intent
    on gracing the wedding feast with plenitude
    than on her own mouth, which now pleads for you! 144

In ancient Rome the women were content
    with water as their drink! And Daniel, too,
    acquired wisdom by despising food! 147

Mankind's first age was beautiful as gold,
    and hunger made the acorns savory,
    and thirst made nectar run in every stream! 150

Locusts and honey were the only foods
    that fed the Baptist in the wilderness;
    to that he owes his glory and his fame, 153

which in the Gospel is revealed to you!"

NOTES

1. *we had already left behind:* The narrative is here speeded up: the angel is *already* left behind, the erasure of another *P* has been accomplished, and the poets are pushing ahead toward the Sixth Terrace.

5. *omitting the* esuriunt: The angel, as always, recites a beatitude. The entire beatitude is, "Blessed are they who hunger and thirst after righteousness, for they shall be satisfied" (Vulgate: Beati qui *esuriunt* et *sitiunt* justitiam . . .). Here, the verse is recited only with *sitiunt,* the other part, *esuriunt,* being omitted: "Blessed are they who thirst after righteousness." "Hunger" is saved for use on the Terrace of the Gluttons.

Grandgent attributes this "splitting" of the beatitude to Dante's attempt to "get the requisite number of appropriate beatitudes," and Ciardi remarks, "Dante was forced into some such device if he was to make six Beatitudes do for seven circles." But since there are not six but eight beatitudes in the Bible, then Dante's technical problem would have been the opposite: to squeeze two beatitudes into one circle. Where are the Meek? Where are those who suffer persecution?

It would appear that Dante's intention was to use a beatitude in each circle, but that he was not committed to ruthlessly and programmatically exploiting all eight of them. Perhaps the "split" beatitude is the result of attention to thematic concerns. The "thirst" motif has been one of the central metaphors of the *Purgatory* and has been receiving particular emphasis in the last few cantos. Both Cantos XX and XXI (as well as XXII) begin with reference to thirst. We can see that the "splitting" of the beatitude enables the poet to maintain a sharper focus on the idea of "desire." He now has not only "thirst" but "hunger" to exploit, as well as to keep the Pilgrim's ever-increasing desire before us.

9. *behind those swiftly climbing shades:* Dante's position is now, and will continue to be for the entire canto, *behind* the two masters—he is the student, the disciple, and he will learn from them.

10–11. *Love, / kindled by virtue, always kindles love:* This is Virgil's answer to Statius's attempt to demonstrate his affection and reverence at the end of the last canto. Virgil's words about the inevitability of "loving back" may remind us of Francesca's words (*Inf.* V, 103): "Love, that excuses no one loved from loving." But the law proclaimed by Virgil depends upon an important condition: that the first love be kindled by virtue—a condition that the passionate Francesca ignored.

13. *Juvenal:* Decimus Junius Juvenalis (ca. A.D. 60–ca. A.D. 140), Roman satirical poet and author of the *Satires.* Juvenal mentions in his *Seventh Satire* the poverty of Statius, his contemporary.

22. *how could your heart find room for avarice:* It may seem strange that Virgil, who in Canto XVII showed a knowledge of the purgatorial system, which he need not have been expected to possess, here seems totally ignorant of the fact that Prodigality is punished on the same terrace with Avarice—since in Hell we find the same arrangement.

40. *To what extremes, O cursèd lust for gold:* As I have translated Dante's words (whose words are a translation of Virgil's in *Aen.* III, 56–57), it is clear that we have to do with a direct attack on Avarice and Avarice alone. Yet Statius tells us in the next tercet that reading these lines made him repent of his prodigality. And so critics have decided that Dante's translation of Virgil (who himself was concerned only with Avarice) involves a reinterpretation, and they manage to water down Dante's words to represent an attack on the abuse of wealth whether through Avarice or Prodigality. For a description of their results, see Sayers's essay (pp. 343–45).

But I see no difficulty whatsoever in interpreting Dante's words put into the mouth of Statius exactly in the sense of Virgil's lines, and no one has doubted that in the *Aeneid* only Avarice is involved. Aeneas, at the tomb of Polydorus, is reminded of the hideous crime of Polymnestor, who, entrusted with the son of his friend who came with part of his father's treasure, slew the youth and took possession of the treasure. At this point Virgil exclaims, "Quid non mortalia pectora cogis, / auri sacra fames!" On reading these lines Statius would naturally be shocked, as was Virgil, at the harmful results of Avarice. Then, perhaps congratulating himself on the fact that he was entirely free of that sin, he began reflecting in a more general way on the proper attitude toward wealth, and came to see that his own attitude was also a sin. He repented of his prodigality and all his other sins. For a different interpretation of these verses, see Shoaf, who treats them in relationship to the evocation of the Age of Gold at the close of this canto (148–50) and translates *auri sacra fames* as "sacred hunger for gold."

42. *rolling weights now in the dismal jousts:* That is, Statius would be in Hell, where the Prodigal sinners roll great stones about, clashing (jousting) with the Avaricious (cf. *Inf.* VII, 25–30).

44. *wings too wide:* Wings have consistently been associated, positively, with the ascent in *Purgatory*. Here they are used in a warning against lack of moderation, perhaps suggestive of the figure of Icarus (*Inf.* XVII, 109) and the "mad flight" of Ulysses (*Inf.* XXVI, 125).

46. *How many shall rise bald:* We are told (*Inf.* VII, 56–57) that on the day of the Last Judgment the Prodigal will appear with little or no hair on their heads.

51. *the two of them wither together here:* Finally Statius tells us that a sin and its opposite are purged on the same terrace, but the Fifth Terrace would appear to be unique in this respect: nowhere else in the *Purgatory* does Dante make mention of such a case.

Perhaps Statius resorts here to a generalization in order to point to an obvious truth that will convince Virgil that his sin need not have been that of Avarice. In the tercet 49–51 he is saying, as it were, "It is only natural that two sins which are the exact opposite of each other should be punished on the same terrace. This happens to be the case with Avarice and Prodigality: you should not be surprised if I lay claim to the second sin."

56. *twin sources of Jocasta's grief:* Jocasta was the mother of Oedipus, whom she later unwittingly married, giving birth to Eteocles and Polynices. In the struggle for the throne of Thebes, these two brothers killed one another, thus producing the twin sorrows of their mother. This fratricidal conflict was the subject of Statius's *Thebaid*. Statius is here addressed, in effect, as the author of the *Thebaid*, the way Virgil, in the following verse, will be identified as the author of the *Eclogues*.

57. *the bard of the* Bucolics: The *Bucolics* of Virgil contain the *Eclogues*, from which there will be a quotation in verse 70.

58. *Clio:* The Muse of history, whom Statius invokes at the beginning of the *Thebaid.*

60. *to that faith without which virtue is vain:* Virgil implicitly acknowledges here the reason for his own damnation: his good actions during life did not suffice for salvation, because he lacked faith.

63. *you could set sail behind the Fisherman:* The sea voyage, the ship with its sails, has been one of the metaphors used throughout the *Comedy* for the Pilgrim's journey toward God and salvation.

64. *It was you directed me:* Virgil not only taught Statius poetry (and morality) but also directed him toward the Christian faith, like one who carries a light behind him and illuminates the way for others but not for himself. Statius, in saying that Virgil led him to Parnassus (the mountain of Apollo and the Muses, hence poetry) and also led him to God, is making an important connection between the two things—hinting at the "sacred" role with which Dante invests poetry.

72. *a new progeny descends from heaven:* The tercet 70–72 represents a translation, by way of Dante, who paraphrases slightly, of verses 5–7 of Virgil's Fourth *Eclogue*, which the Middle Ages considered a prophecy of the birth of Christ:

Magnus ab integro saeclorum nascitur ordo.
Iam redit et Virgo, redeunt Saturnia regna;
iam nova progenies caelo demittitur alto.

The great line of the centuries is born anew.
Now the Virgin returns, the reign of Saturn returns;
now a new progeny descends from high heaven.

Scholars can only guess at the identity of the newborn infant that Virgil had in mind: the son of Octavian or Antony, or of Asinius Pollio, consul at the time the poem was written (between 42 and 34 B.C.). What is most important is that Virgil's poem is announcing the return of a Golden Age, which can be seen to coincide with Christian ideas about the age instituted by Christ. The idea of a Roman prophecy of the birth of Christ is one, needless to say, that would appeal particularly to Dante.

73. *Through you I was a poet, through you, a Christian:* As pointed out above (note to 64), there seems to be an implicit

connection between poetry and Christianity. Nowhere is this connection more emphatic than in this one terse line.

83. *Domitian:* Domitian (Titus Flavius Domitianus Augustus) succeded his brother Titus as emperor of Rome in A.D. 81 and was murdered in A.D 96. Statius's *Thebaid* is dedicated to him. Tertullian, Eusebius, and Orosius mention him as a relentless persecutor of Christians.

88. *Before I brought the Greeks to Theban streams:* The Greeks draw near the Theban rivers, the Ismenus and the Asopus, in the seventh book of the *Thebaid;* it was before Statius had reached that point in writing his first epic that he was baptized.

93. *four hundred years on the Fourth Circle:* Because Statius, out of fear, had kept his conversion a secret, he was forced to spend more than four hundred years on the Fourth Terrace, among the Slothful. If we add these "more than four hundred years" to the "more than five hundred years" spent on the Fifth Terrace, this would account for roughly a thousand years. But by the year 1300 Statius had been dead for 1204 years; he must have spent the extra time somewhere below the Fourth Terrace.

97–98. *where is our ancient Terence, do you know:* In Statius's question we find the *ubi sunt* motif once more, but without the pathos and the sociological implications of Guido del Duca's lament over the dead Romagnols (*Purg.* XIV, 97). Statius simply wants to know where in the Afterworld the souls of certain Latin poets have been assigned. Of the four names he mentions, the first three are comic playwrights belonging to the early period of Latin literature (third and second centuries B.C.), and Varius is a writer of tragedies and epics.

100. *Persius:* Aulus Persius Flaccus was a Roman satirist (A.D. 34–62).

101. *that Greek:* The reference is, of course, to Homer (see *Inf.* IV. 86–88).

105. *nine nurses:* These are the nine Muses. We have already seen poetic influence or poetic inspiration characterized by the "nursing" metaphor (*Purg.* XXI, 97–98: the *Aeneid* was Statius's mother and nurse). See also the reference to Homer in verse 102: "the Muses suckled more than all the rest."

106–107. *Euripides walks with us:* Virgil proceeds to mention four Greek poets that are with him in Limbo: Euripides (485 B.C.?–406 B.C.) was a Greek playwright, eighteen of whose tragedies have survived in more or less completed form. Antiphon was a Greek tragic poet, whom Plutarch mentions among the great tragic authors; only fragments of three of his tragedies survive. Simonides, a Greek lyric poet, was born ca. 556 B.C. and died 467 B.C. None of the works of Agathon (ca. 448 B.C.–ca. 402 B.C.), a Greek tragic poet, has survived.

109–14. *many of your people:* In the following list, the first six names are characters from the *Thebaid,* the last two, from the *Achilleid.* It is interesting to note that Dante jumps with the greatest of ease from *real* authors to *fictional* characters. What both groups have in common, however, is their connection with literature, and at this point Dante wants to keep literature in our minds, in order to prepare for the discussions of poetry which will take place on the terraces of Gluttony and Lust.

Of the eight characters, *Antigone* (110) and her sister *Ismene* (111) were daughters of Jocasta and Oedipus. *Deïphyle* (110) and her sister *Argia* (110) were daughters of Adrastus, King of Argos. Argia was the wife of Polynices, and wore the necklace of Harmonia (see *Purg.* XII, 50–51). *She who showed Langia to the Greeks* (112) was Hypsipyle, who conducted Adrastus and other Greek kings and their forces to the fountain of Langia when they were dying of thirst. *The daughter of Tiresias* (113) was the soothsayer Manto, whom, contrary to what is said here, Dante has placed in Hell's fourth *bolgia* (see *Inf.* XX). *Thetis* (113) was the sea-goddess wife of Peleus and mother of Achilles. *Deïdamia* (114) was one of the daughters of King Lycomedes, with whom Thetis hid her son Achilles, disguised as a girl (cf. *Inf.* XXVI, 62).

114. *Deïdamia with her sisters, too:* This is Virgil's final account of Limbo, completing the enumerations in *Inf.* IV, 88–90, and 121–44. Because this list consists of literary figures, it looks ahead to the discussions on poetry that will take place on the terraces of Gluttony and Lust.

118. *Already the four handmaids of the day:* In *Purg.* XII, 80–81, we learned that the "handmaids" of the day were the twelve hours of the day; here, they are represented as driving, in succession, the chariot of the sun. Since the fifth handmaid is

at her post, and the sun rises at 6:00, it is now between 10:00 and 11:00 A.M.

128. *was paying close attention to their words:* Virgil and Statius are speaking of poetry. The tercet looks ahead to Canto XXIV, on poetry, when the Pilgrim will discuss poetry with one of the shades.

Dante's position—alone, behind the other two—is symbolic. Both poets are his predecessors: Virgil, a pagan poet; Statius, a pagan poet who became a Christian (but not a Christian poet); and Dante, a Christian poet.

129. *which taught me things about the art of verse:* Dante, following the two poets and listening to them, learns about poetry. But this verse ("ch'a poetar mi davano intelletto") implies something more than hexameters and hendecasyllables. Dante is given *understanding* of writing poetry. I take this "intelletto" to be connected with the "right" function of poetry (see note to 73), which is an integral part of Dante's poetic education.

130–41. *a tree appeared:* The tree looks something like a fir tree turned upside down, that is, with the small branches at the bottom and the larger branches at the top, so that one cannot climb up. As such, the fruit of the tree would be unattainable, and this point is made, explicitly, by the voice from within the branches (141). It has also been suggested that verses 130–35 are informed by a widespread medieval conception of the configuration and moral significance of the palm tree (see Hill).

Since the tree is clearly associated with Eden—by its luxuriance, its paradisiacal fruit, and by the waters that flow down on it from above (from the Earthly Paradise)—it is easy to see in the words "This fruit and water is denied to you (141) an echo of God's first prohibition.

142–54

Again the exempla are presented verbally, and in a way that reminds us particularly of the Terrace of Envy, where disembodied spirits in the air called out the names.

142. *Mary was more intent:* This is the second example from the wedding feast at Cana. *Purg.* XIII, 29, shows the generosity of Mary; here we see her temperance.

144. *than on her own mouth, which now pleads for you:* Mary's mouth now prays to God for us—that is what a mouth should do, pray, and not be concerned with stuffing itself with food and drink (cf. *Purg.* XXIII, 11).

145. *In ancient Rome the women were content:* The Roman matrons are reputed to have been content with drinking water. According to Valerius Maximus, as cited by Thomas Aquinas (*Summa theol.* II-II, q. 149, a. 4, resp.), the ancient Roman women drank no wine.

146–47. *And Daniel, too, / acquired wisdom by despising food:* Daniel (Dan. 1:3–20) spurned the meat and drink of the king's table and was given by God the gift of interpreting visions and dreams. See Kleinhenz, who connects these verses with the next two cantos (*Purg.* XXIII and XXIV).

151. *Locusts and honey were the only foods:* See Matt. 3:4.

154. *which in the Gospel is revealed to you:* "Amen, I say unto you, among those born of women there has not risen a greater than John the Baptist" (Matt. 11:11).

CANTO XXIII

As the three poets turn from the tree, they hear the tones of the psalm *Labia mea Domine*. Soon a quickly moving band of emaciated spirits with famished faces comes from behind them. These are the Gluttonous. The Pilgrim recognizes one of these souls by his voice—his features have been so altered by starvation—as his old friend Forese Donati. Although a late repentent and dead only five years, Forese has been able to advance so far up the mountain on account of the prayers of his widow, Nella. The thought of the virtuous Nella provokes from Forese a diatribe against the shameless women of Florence. The canto ends with the Pilgrim describing to his old friend the nature of the journey he has undertaken.

While I peered up through that green foliage,
   trying to see what might be hidden there,
   like one who wastes his lifetime hunting birds,   *3*

my more than father called to me : "Dear son,
   come with me now; the time allotted us
   ought to be spent more profitably." So,   *6*

I quickly turned and, just as quickly, moved
   to follow the two poets whose talk was such
   that every step I took cost me no strain.   *9*

Then suddenly we heard the tearful chant
   of *Labia mea Domine*, in tones
   inspiring a sweet blend of joy and pain.   *12*

"Dear father, tell me, what is this I hear?"
   I asked, and he replied: "They may be shades
   loosing the knot of their great debt to God."   *15*

As pilgrims wrapped in meditation pass
   someone they do not know along the road
   and turn to stare and then go quickly on,   *18*

so, from behind us, moving swiftly, came
   and passed us by with a quick look of doubt,
   a band of spirits, silent and devout,   *21*

their eyes dark-shadowed, sunken in their heads,
    their faces pale, their bodies worn so thin
    that every bone was molded to their skin.   *24*

I do not think that wretched Erysichthon
    had come to such a state of skin and bones,
    not even when he feared starvation most.   *27*

And I said to myself, "Look at those souls!
    They could be those who lost Jerusalem,
    when Miriam sunk her beak into her son."   *30*

The sockets of their eyes were gemless rings;
    one who reads *omo* in the face of men,
    could easily have recognized the *m*.   *33*

Who would believe, ignorant of the cause,
    that nothing but the smell of fruit or spring
    could bring them to this withered greediness?   *36*

I was still marvelling at their famishing,
    since I did not yet understand what caused
    their leanness and their scabby shrivelling,   *39*

when suddenly a shadow turned his eyes
    toward me and stared from deep within his skull,
    then cried: "What grace has been bestowed on me!"   *42*

I never would have known him by his looks,
    but in his voice I clearly recognized
    the features that his starving face disguised.   *45*

This spark rekindled in my memory
    the image of those features now so changed,
    and I could see again Forese's face.   *48*

"Oh, please forget about the crusty scurf
    discoloring my sickly skin," he begged,
    "pay no attention to my shrivelled flesh;   *51*

tell me about yourself. And those two with you,
    tell me who they are too. Please answer me,
    do not withhold from me what I desire!"   *54*

"When death was on your face, I wept," I said,
    "and now the grief I feel is just as great,
    seeing your face so piteously disfigured.   *57*

In God's name tell me what strips you so bare.
    Do not ask me to speak, I am benumbed!
    And one speaks ill whose thoughts are somewhere else." 60

And he: "From the Eternal Mind a power
    descends into the water and the tree
    that you just passed: this is what makes me lean. 63

All of us here who sing while we lament
    for having stuffed our mouths too lovingly,
    make ourselves pure, thirsting and hungering. 66

The fragrance of the fruit and of the spray
    that trickles down the leaves stirs up in us
    a hungering desire for food and drink— 69

and not just once: as we go running round
    this road, our pain is constantly renewed.
    Did I say pain? Solace is what I mean! 72

For that same will that leads us to the tree
    led Christ to cry out joyously, 'Eli,'
    when he delivered us with His own blood." 75

And I: "Forese, since that day when you
    abandoned our world for a better life,
    less than five years from your last day have passed! 78

If, when you knew that moment of sweet grief
    that weds the soul to God again, you were
    close to your death, able to sin no more— 81

how have you climbed so high up on the mount?
    I thought, surely, to find you down below
    where souls who wasted time must pay with time." 84

"It was my Nella with her flowing tears,"
    he answered me, "who brought me here so soon
    to let me drink the sweet wormwood of pain. 87

It was her pious prayers and her laments
    that raised me from the slope where souls must wait,
    and set me free from all the other rounds. 90

All the more dear and pleasing to the Lord
    is my sweet widow that I greatly loved,
    the more she is unique in doing good; 93

CANTO XXIII / 251

for the Barbagia of Sardinia counts
  among its women many far more chaste
  than those in the Barbagia where she lives.   96

My dear brother, how can I tell you this:
  I see a future time—it won't be long—
  in which bans from the pulpit shall clamp down   99

on those ladies of Florence who, bold-faced,
  now walk our city streets as they parade
  their bosom to the tits! What barbarous girl,   102

what female Saracen, had to be taught
  spiritual discipline, or anything,
  to keep her body decently concealed?   105

But if these shameless creatures only knew
  what the swift heavens have in store for them,
  they would by now be screaming their heads off!   108

For if our foresight here does not deceive,
  they shall have cause to grieve before the cheeks
  of those now soothed by lullabies grow beards.   111

My brother, now tell me about yourself.
  You see how everyone, including me,
  is staring there where you block out the sun."   114

I answered him: "Whenever you recall
  what we were like together, you and I,
  the memory of those days must torture you.   117

From that life I was called away by him
  who leads me here—just a few days ago,
  when his sister (I pointed to the sun)   120

was shining full. Still wearing this true flesh
  I came into and through the darkest night
  of the true dead with this soul as my guide;   123

from there, sustained by him, I came up here
  climbing and ever circling round this mount
  which straightens in you what the world has bent.   126

He says that I shall have his company
  until I am where Beatrice is—
  and from then on, without him I must go.   129

Virgil (I pointed to him) told me this.
The other spirit standing over there
is he for whom this mountain's terraces
trembled just now, releasing him to Heaven."

NOTES

3. *wastes his lifetime hunting birds*: Such an occupation would mean in general the pursuit of a lesser good, which indeed fits into the theme, running throughout the *Purgatory*, of the Pilgrim's tendency to become distracted from his journey. But the bird image here also serves to foreshadow the bird image involved in the disappearance of the flock of the Gluttonous in the next canto (XXIV, 64–69).

11. *Labia mea Domine*: This is the prayer of the Gluttonous, who are punished on the Sixth Terrace of Purgatory. It is taken from the *Miserere* (Psalm 50), and the verse that Dante evokes here is the following: "Open my lips, O Lord, and my mouth shall proclaim your praises." The application of the prayer to the predicament of the Gluttonous is obvious: the mouth is not only an organ of eating and drinking but a means of praising the Lord.

16. *As pilgrims*: Like pilgrims, the souls of the Gluttonous pass quickly by, intent on the goal of their journey and not yielding to momentary distraction. They have learned the lesson of Purgatory.

20. *and passed us by with a quick look of doubt*: The look of doubt or wonder was probably due to the fact that the spirits could see the shadow cast by the Pilgrim. In any case, after one quick look they return to their pious concerns, unlike the souls in the Antepurgatory, who concentrated their attention on the spectacle that the Pilgrim's body offered.

21. *a band of spirits, silent and devout*: A moment before, we had heard the same spirits singing *Labia mea Domine* (11), yet it is in silence that they pass by the three poets. Porena suggests that we have here an imitation of the practice of actual pilgrims, who alternate song and silence—therefore affording a better reason for the simile in verse 16 ("As pilgrims who") than that made explicit by Dante.

25. *Erysichthon*: Son of King Triopas, Erysichthon committed an outrage against the goddess Ceres by cutting trees in her sacred grove. Ceres then afflicted him with a ravenous hunger, which drove him to sell his own daughter for food and, finally, to devour his own flesh. (See Ovid, *Metam*. VIII, 738–878.)

30. *Miriam*: Josephus (in *The Jewish War* VI, 3) reports that during the Roman siege of Jerusalem (A.D. 70), a certain Miriam, driven by hunger, killed and ate her own infant son. Dante describes her as sinking "her beak into her son," as though she were some horrible bird of prey.

32. *one who reads "omo" in the face of men*: The word *omo* (Latin *homo*, "man") can be "read" on the face of a man, if the eyes are the *o*'s, and the *m* is formed by the nose, eyebrows, and cheek bones. It was believed in the Middle Ages that God had thus signed and identified his creation. Actually, Dante has reduced to one word the phrase used in a more extensive "reading": *omo dei* ("man [is] of God"); in *dei*, the ears would represent the *d*, the nostrils, the *e*, and the mouth, the *i*.

42. *What grace has been bestowed on me*: Forese's exclamatory greeting is reminiscent of the glad cry uttered by Brunetto Latini when he sees the Pilgrim among the Sodomites in Hell (*Inf*. XV, 24): "How marvelous!"

48. *Forese*: Dante's friend Forese Donati, also known as Bicci Novello, engaged with him in a facetious poetical correspondence consisting of six sonnets. In one of the sonnets of the *tenzone*, which is a rather good-natured, though strong-worded, contest of insults, Dante accuses Forese of Gluttony; he is also accused of being a thief, a bastard, and a negligent (or impotent) husband. Even Forese's wife serves as a target for ridicule: she has a constant cold, due to the constant negligence of her husband. See Foster and Boyde for the text of the sonnets with English translations and commentary. See also Barbi (1956, 1932) and Contini (1965) for further discussions of the exchange of sonnets.

73. *that same will that leads us to the tree*: The three poets have already seen one tree (*Purg*. XXII, 130–155), from which a voice uttered exempla of abstemiousness; no Penitents were visible. They will see a second tree in the next canto (XXIV, 103–129), before which are gathered a group of Penitents

mutely begging the tree for its fruits; they will finally retreat disappointed. A voice from the tree will then address the Pilgrim and his companions, giving its history and presenting exempla of Gluttony. Of the two trees, that one which renews their pain would seem to be the second tree.

74. *Eli*: Cf. Matt. 27:46: "But about the ninth hour Jesus cried out with a loud voice, saying 'Eli, Eli, lema sabachthani,' that is, 'My God, my God, why hast thou forsaken me?'."

83. *I thought, surely, to find you down below*: Forese died in 1296. The Pilgrim expected him to be in the Antepurgatory because of his late repentance.

85. *Nella*: Forese's virtuous wife, Giovanella.

92. *my sweet widow that I greatly loved:* Dante the Poet, it would appear, is making amends for the insults he wrote about Forese's wife and Forese's neglect of her, by having Forese speak of her with deep love and respect.

94. *The Barbagia*: The Barbacini, a clan of bandits said to have descended from a settlement of prisoners established by the Vandals, inhabited a wild, mountainous region (the Barbagia) of Sardinia. They were proverbial in the Middle Ages for living like animals and being lascivious—particularly the women, who were said to go bare-breasted.

99. *bans from the pulpit:* No pulpit interdict concerned with immodest attire on the part of women has been recorded; Villani (IX, 245; X, 11, 150), however, has several references to laws directed against sumptuary extravagance. On the problem of the interdict, see Cassell.

111. *those now soothed by lullabies grow beards:* That is, within the space of about fifteen years, the amount of time it would take a child to reach puberty, to progress from "lullabies" to a "beard." Indeed, between 1300 (the time of Dante's journey) and 1315, several disasters had befallen Florence, including the invasion of Charles of Valois (1301), a famine (1302), an interdict (1303), and finally, in 1315, the disastrous defeat of the Florentine Guelphs at Montecatini.

117. *the memory of those days must torture you:* The Pilgrim mentions only the regret that the memories of "those days"

bring his friend. But there is surely implied regret on the part of the Pilgrim too. What has caused them such remorse? History supports the interpretation that Dante is referring to their foolish, vulgar exchange of sonnets: he would seem to be offering a condemnation of the kind of poetry that should never have been written. But the fact that Forese resides among the Gluttonous, combined with the dramatic wording of the verse ("must *torture* you"), implies that the memories the Pilgrim evokes involve other shared excesses. One has an image of the two of them carousing together, overindulging in food and drink. This impression is strengthened by Dante's reference in the following verse (118) to "that life" from which he was called away to his journey. Surely he is thinking of more "sinful" acts than the writing of wrongheaded poetry.

118–30

The Pilgrim gives a condensed version of his story—the whole journey, beginning with his entrance into the Dark Wood on the moonlit night of Holy Thursday, where he met Virgil, to the end, when he will meet Beatrice. This is the only time he gives such a complete summary.

All the shades gathered near must be able to overhear him, and that one of them took his words to heart will be made clear in the next canto.

121. *was shining full:* The Pilgrim is referring to the full moon that was shining on the night of Holy Thursday, when he entered the Dark Wood, in the opening canto of the *Comedy*.

CANTO XXIV

THE PILGRIM AND Forese continue their conversation. Forese says that his sister, Piccarda, has already been taken up into Heaven, and then he points out a number of the souls of the Gluttonous, among them Bonagiunta Orbicciani of Lucca, Pope Martin V of Tours, Ubaldino della Pila, Boniface de' Fieschi, archbishop of Ravenna, and the Marchese degli Orgoliosi of Forlì. The Pilgrim chooses to speak to the shade of Bonagiunta, who seems particularly anxious to approach him. Bonagiunta prophesies that a woman named Gentucca will someday make the Pilgrim appreciate the city of Lucca. He then asks Dante if he is the author of the poem "Ladies who have intelligence of Love," and a brief discussion of the "dolce stil nuovo" ensues. As this discussion comes to an end, the souls of the Gluttonous turn and speed away. Only Forese remains behind to converse further with the Pilgrim, and he prophesies the ignominious death of his brother, Corso Donati. When Forese has departed, the Pilgrim encounters a second tree, from whose branches a voice shouts exempla of Gluttony; these include the drunken centaurs at the wedding feast of Theseus and the unworthy soldiers of Gideon's band, who drank greedily, putting their faces in the water. Finally the angel of Abstinence shows the three poets the way to the next terrace.

Talking did not slow down our walk, nor did
   walking our talk: conversing, on we sped
   like ships enjoying favorable winds.   *3*

And all those shades, looking like things twice dead,
   absorbed the miracle through caved-in eyes:
   this was a living man which they beheld!   *6*

And I, continuing where I left off,
   said: "He is climbing at a slower pace
   because of his companion, I suppose.   *9*

If you can, tell me where Piccarda is.
   And, are there any here that I should know
   among these shades that stare at me like this?"   *12*

"My sister, who was just as virtuous
    as she was lovely, is in triumph now
    on High Olympus, joyful in her crown."   15

This he said first, and then: "No reason why
    I should not tell their names—especially
    since abstinence has milked our features dry.   18

There"—and he pointed—"Bonagiunta goes,
    the Luccan Bonagiunta; the one behind—
    see that face withered more than all the rest—   21

once held within his arms the Holy Church:
    he was from Tours, and here he fasts to purge
    Bolsena's eels cooked in Vernaccia wine."   24

Then, many others he named, one by one,
    and all seemed quite content at being named—
    no one, at least, gave him an angry look.   27

I saw two souls for hunger chewing air:
    Ubaldino della Pila, Boniface,
    who with his crook led multitudes to graze.   30

I saw Milord Marchese. He, in Forlì,
    drank endlessly and with less thirst than here—
    yet no one ever saw him satisfied.   33

Often a face will stand out in a crowd;
    this happened here: I singled out the shade
    from Lucca, who seemed interested in me.   36

He mumbled something—something like "Gentucca"
    I heard come from his lips, where he felt most
    emaciating Justice strip him bare.   39

"O, soul," I said, "you seem so much to want
    to talk to me; speak up so I can hear;
    that way your words can satisfy us both."   42

"A woman has been born," he said, "and she
    is still unmarried, who will give you cause
    to love my city, which all men revile.   45

Remember well this prophecy of mine,
    and if the words I muttered are not clear,
    future events will clarify their sense.   48

But, tell me, do I not see standing here
  him who brought forth the new poems that begin:
  'Ladies who have intelligence of Love.'"   51

I said to him, "I am one who, when Love
  inspires me, takes careful note and then,
  gives form to what he dictates in my heart."   54

"My brother, now I see," he said, "the knot
  that held Guittone and the Notary
  and me back from the sweet new style I hear!   57

Now, I see very clearly how your wings
  fly straight behind the dictates of that Love —
  this, certainly, could not be said of ours;   60

and no one who examines the two styles
  can clarify the difference more than I."
  Then, pleased with what he said, he said no more.   63

As birds that winter down along the Nile
  take flight massed close together in the air,
  then, gaining speed, will fly in single file —   66

just so that mass of spirits lined up straight,
  and then, light with their leanness and desire,
  all of a sudden, sped away from us.   69

And as a weary racer slows his pace,
  allowing all the rest to pass him by,
  until the heaving of his chest subsides,   72

so did Forese let that holy flock
  rush by him while he still kept step with me
  as he inquired: "When shall we meet again?"   75

"How long my life will last I do not know,"
  I said, "but even if I come back soon,
  my heart already will have reached the shore,   78

because the place where I was born to live
  is being stripped of virtue, day by day,
  doomed, or disposed, to rip itself to ruin."   81

He said, "Take heart. The guiltiest of them all
  I see dragged to his death at a beast's tail
  down to the pit that never pardons sin.   84

The beast with every stride increases speed,
    faster and faster, till it suddenly
    kicks free the body, hideously mangled.   87

Those spheres," and he looked up into the heavens,
    "will not revolve for long before my words,
    which I have left obscure, will be made clear.   90

Now I must leave you. I have lost much time,
    walking along with you at your own pace,
    and time is precious to us in this realm."   93

As sometimes from a troop riding to war
    a horseman at a gallop will rush out
    to win the honor of attacking first—   96

so he strode faster leaving me to go
    my way, accompanied by those two shades
    who were such mighty marshals of the world.   99

When he had raced so far ahead of us
    my eyes could follow him no better than
    my mind could understand what his words meant,   102

I took my eyes from him—and, suddenly,
    there in the road in front of me, appeared
    another tree with verdant, laden boughs.   105

Beneath the tree I saw shades, arms outstretched,
    crying out something up into the leaves,
    like greedy children begging foolishly   108

to someone who will not answer their plea
    but who, instead, tempting them all the more,
    holds in full view the things they cannot reach.   111

At last, the souls gave up and went away.
    Then we drew close to that imposing tree,
    which was impervious to prayers and tears.   114

"Pass on. Do not come closer. Higher up,
    there is a tree which gave its fruit to Eve,
    and this plant is an offshoot of its root."   117

Thus spoke a voice from somewhere in the leaves.
    So we moved on, Virgil, Statius, and I,
    close to each other as we hugged the cliff.   120

"Recall," the voice went on, "those wicked ones,
    born of a cloud who, in their drunkenness,
    fought double-breast to breast with Theseus.   123

Recall those Hebrews drinking at their ease,
    whom Gideon, then, refused to take along
    as comrades down the hills to Midian."   126

So, walking close to one side of the road,
    we listened to accounts of Gluttony
    and learned the wages that these sinners earned.   129

Then, walking freely on the open way,
    each of us silent, deeply lost in thought,
    we had gone more than a full thousand steps,   132

when, suddenly, a voice called out: "You there,
    you three alone, what occupies your mind?"
    I gave a start like some shy beast in panic.   135

I raised my head to see who just now spoke;
    and never in a furnace was there seen
    metal or glass so radiantly red   138

as was the being who said to me: "If you
    are looking for the way to climb, turn here:
    here is the path for those who search for peace."   141

Though blinded by the brilliance of his look,
    I turned around and groped behind my guides,
    letting the words just heard direct my feet.   144

Soft as the early morning breeze of May,
    which heralds dawn, rich with the grass and flowers,
    spreading in waves their breathing fragrances,   147

I felt a breeze strike soft upon my brow:
    I felt a wing caress it, I am sure,
    I sensed the sweetness of ambrosia.   150

I heard the words: "Blessed are those in whom
    grace shines so copiously that love of food
    does not arouse excessive appetite,   153

but lets them hunger after righteousness."

8. *He is climbing at a slower pace:* The "he" is, of course, Statius. It should be clear that the narrative break of the first two tercets of this canto does not indicate an interruption of the conversation between Forese and the Pilgrim, who had just pointed out Statius ("the other spirit standing over there") to his companion. The Pilgrim must have had the feeling that if the newly released Statius had been alone and not talking with Virgil, he would have been moving upward more quickly.

10. *Piccarda:* The sister of Forese Donati, whom Dante later meets in Paradise (*Par.* III, 34–123). According to early commentators, Piccarda was forced by her brother Corso (whom Dante places in Hell) to leave the nunnery where she had taken vows and to marry, for political reasons, a Florentine named Rossellino della Tosa. Shortly after the marriage, she fell ill and died.

15. *on High Olympus:* That is, Heaven.

16. *No reason why:* Forese appears to be a bit overscrupulous in reaching his conclusion, since on none of the terraces is it forbidden for a shade to reveal the names of his companions.

19. *Bonagiunta:* Bonagiunta Orbicciani of Lucca, son of Perfetto di Orbicciano, was a poet, many of whose verses survive, as well as an orator of some repute. He was born around 1220, and we find him still writing well into the last quarter of the century. His poetry tends to be facile, and he was accused by a contemporary poet of being a slavish imitator of the Notary, Giacomo da Lentino; in the *De vulg. eloqu.* I, XIII, Dante criticizes him for the "municipal language." According to Lana, Bonagiunta was acquainted with Dante's poetry and addressed a few of his poems to him. Benvenuto comments that Bonagiunta had a great fondness for drinking wine. He died in 1297. For the text of all of Bonagiunta's poetry with English translations, see Miller's critical edition.

21. *that face:* Simon de Brie of Tours, who served as Pope Martin IV from 1281 to 1285. He was made a cardinal in 1261 by Urban VI and was elected pope at Viterbo through the influence of Charles of Anjou, six months after the death of Nicholas III. As pope he destroyed the possibility of uniting

the Eastern and Western churches by excommunicating the Greek emperor, Michael VIII Palaeologus, at the urging of Charles. He also appointed as cardinal Benedetto Caetani, Dante's hated enemy, who later became pope as Boniface VIII. Martin IV died in 1285, from eating, it is said, an excess of eels from Lake Bolsena, stewed in wine.

29. *Ubaldino della Pila:* Ubaldino degli Ubaldini della Pila was a great feaster and entertainer, who devoted much care to the preparation of meals. His brother, Cardinal Ottaviano degli Ubaldini, roasts in Hell with Farinata and other Epicureans (*Inf.* X, 120). Another brother, Ugolino d'Azzo, is spoken of with great respect in *Purg.* XIV, 105. The Archbishop Ruggieri, whose scalp we see being gnawed by Count Ugolino in Hell (*Inf.* XXXIII, 14), was his son. Ubaldino died in 1291.

29. *Boniface:* Bonifazio de' Fieschi of Genova, archbishop of Ravenna from 1274 to 1294, was very wealthy and served as an arbitrator and ambassador, bringing about a reconciliation between Alfonso III of Aragon and Philip the Fair, and negotiating the release of Charles II of Naples. He died February 1, 1295.

30. *who with his crook led multitudes to graze:* The irony here is manifest: instead of feeding his Christian flock with the evangelical word, Boniface feeds the greed of the hungry flock of courtiers who crowd around him.

31. *Milord Marchese:* He was a member of the Argogliosi family of Forlì and podestà of Faenza in 1296. A great wine drinker, when told that people thought he did nothing but drink, he replied that they should instead think of him as being always thirsty.

37. *Gentucca:* Though nothing regarding this lady of Lucca is known with certainty, she was probably one who befriended Dante during his exile. The earliest commentators, however, take the word *gentucca* to be a pejorative form of *gente*, i.e. "low people." Buti seems to have been the first commentator to supply the modern interpretation. See Levi.

45. *my city, which all men revile:* The city of Lucca had the reputation of being a hotbed of political corruption (cf. *Inf.* XXI, 41–42).

51. *"Ladies who have intelligence of Love"*: This is the opening verse of the first *canzone* of the *Vita nuova*. The poem marks a turning point in Dante's love for Beatrice and in his conception of love in general. With this *canzone* Dante turns from a tentatively erotic and thoroughly selfish love to discover the beauty of loving unselfishly, purely (see Musa [1973], pp. 137–74).

52–54. *I am one who, when Love*: This is a description of Dante's new poetic method: he follows the dictates of love, of the selfless, nonerotic love of which he learned in the *Vita nuova*, and of love as the desire for the highest good (love as explained at length is the *Purgatory* by Virgil in Cantos XVII–XVIII). And furthermore, we must remember that our poet's absolute, unqualified subjection to love is ultimately subjection to that "Love which moves the sun and other stars" (*Par.* XXXIII, 145). And indeed, Dante, as the poet of the *Divine Comedy*, certainly demonstrates the fact that his inspiration has come from this "Love," that he is writing in accord with the divine purpose and the highest good.

55. *the knot*: The "knot" that kept Guittone, Giacomo, and Bonagiunta from attaining to the "sweet new style" of Dante, from following his method of deriving inspiration from "Love," must have been precisely their narrow and self-centered conception of love. Furthermore, we must remember that Bonagiunta is here in Purgatory "loosing the knot" of Gluttony—atoning for the sin of Gluttony; and Gluttony conceived in the larger sense, as the vice of utter self-centeredness and greediness, is exactly what kept him from realizing a higher conception of love (see note to 60).

56. *Guittone*: Guittone d'Arezzo, born ca. 1230 at Santa Firmina, seems to have been responsible for establishing the Sicilian mode of poetry in Tuscany, though he often outdoes his predecessors in employing difficult technical devices in his poems. In or around 1266 Guittone underwent a religious conversion and left his wife and family to join the order of the Frati Gaudenti, where he devoted himself to religion and the writing of religious poetry. For a further reference to Guittone, suggesting Dante's lack of appreciation of his poetry, see *Purg.* XXVI, 124. For the complete edition of his poems, see Egidi; for a discussion of his poetry and his circle of poets, see Malagoli and Musa (1965).

56. *the Notary:* Giacomo da Lentino (or Lentini), a judge at the court of Frederick II, was the major figure of the Sicilian school of poetry that flourished during the first half of the thirteenth century and that established the poetry of courtly love in Italy. Although little information regarding Giacomo exists, it is possible that he studied law at Bologna and later lived in Tuscany. Giacomo is credited with being the probable inventor of the sonnet. In the *De. vulg. eloqu.* I, xii, 8, Dante cites, without naming the author, the first verse of Giacomo's *canzone* "Madonna, dir vi voglio" as an example of polished style. For the critical edition of his poetry with English translations, see Popolizio.

57. *the sweet new style I hear:* In these words Bonagiunta is obviously referring to the words just spoken by the Pilgrim and still ringing in his ears: "I am one who. . . ." Bonagiunta is speaking literally of "the knot" that held Guittone and the Notary and him back from the words that Dante has just uttered, from the "sweet new style *I hear.*" That his words have been taken to refer to the difficulty that held the three of them back from writing poetry in a way suggested by the Pilgrim is only natural; even so, this way of writing poetry can apply, as the context clearly shows, only to the poetry of Dante.

Just why modern critics should adopt Bonagiunta's phrase "sweet new style" to use as a label (*dolce stil nuovo*) for a certain school of Florentine poets, where there is no indication that Bonagiunta had in mind anyone but Dante, is to be explained, perhaps, by their treatment of the next tercet, which contains, in the original, the words *vostre penne.* I take the *penne* to refer not to "pens" (the common interpretation) but to "wings"; what is more important, I interpret the *vostre* as an honorific plural (= *tue penne*): not "yours and others" but "yours" alone. Everyone else apparently has interpreted the *vostre* as a true plural—which is to assume that a group of poets is involved. Supposedly, then, Bonagiunta would have gone on from a reference to the poetry of Dante alone to a wider reference including a group of poets with whom Dante could easily be associated. And the plurality of *vostre*, with its reference to a group, would have been read back into Bonagiunta's earlier phrase "the sweet new style"—with total neglect, of course, of "[that] I hear." And the image offered by the interpretation *penne,* "pens," is ludicrous: a few pens (held in invisible hands?)

writing and moving forward behind the being who is dictating to them, and who must either be moving in reverse or else has his back turned on them as he dictates and moves ahead. (See Musa [1966], pp. 361–67, and [1974], pp. 111–28).

58. *your wings*: Dante's poetic process, like his journey, is now presented in terms of winged flight, inspired by love.

60. *This, certainly, could not be said of ours*: Dante the Poet was unfettered by the "knot" that held Bonagiunta back—the sin of Gluttony, in the larger, poetic sense of this sin. For what greater contrast to the "winged flight behind Love" can be found than indulgence in Gluttony? Movement forward, upward, away from the things of this earth, as opposed to the act of filling oneself, making oneself heavy with the things of this earth. Gluttony is a taking into oneself, for oneself, a glorification of self. The "winged flight" is an escape from self into Love—a falling up into Love. And that Love and Gluttony represent not only two opposed attitudes but two opposed movements is brought out clearly at the beginning of the preceding canto: we remember the *Labia mea*—sung by all the Gluttons—the lips that they had used for taking into themselves they now use in uttering, in sending forth, praise of God.

64. *As birds that winter down along the Nile*: A continuation of the flight imagery.

82. *The guiltiest of them all*: Corso Donati, brother of Forese. He was the leader of the Black faction in Florence and persuaded Boniface VIII to send Charles of Valois to Florence. Later, Corso attempted to gain supreme authority over Florence but was checked by the Blacks, who condemned him to death and killed him during his effort to escape.

83. *dragged to his death at a beast's tail*: Dante, for poetic reasons, here gives a rather exaggerated, apocalyptic account of Corso's death. What appears literally to have happened (see Villani VII, 43) is that Corso, having been captured and taken to Florence, threw himself from his horse and was speared in the throat by one of his captors.

89. *my words*: That is, the words just uttered, describing the forthcoming death of "the guiltiest of them all," whom Forese has failed to name. Corso Donati dies on October 6, 1308. The

obscurity of Forese's prophetic words will be referred to again in verse 102.

91. *I have lost much time*: A reiteration of one of the ever-present themes of the *Purgatory*.

115. *Higher up*: In the Earthly Paradise is the tree of the knowledge of good and evil, and this tree, here on the Terrace of Gluttony, is an offshoot of it.

121. *those wicked ones*: The centaurs, half man, half horse ("double-breast," 123), said to be the offspring of Ixion, king of the Lapithae, and Nephele, a cloud-woman, hence Dante's allusion "born of a cloud" (122). The incident referred to in this passage is the wedding feast of Pirithous and Hippodamia, where the centaurs, disgracefully drunk, attempted to carry off the bride and various other women. They were thereupon slain in great numbers by Theseus and the Lapithae.

125. *Gideon*: In the campaign of the Jews against the Midianites, Gideon was instructed by the Lord to observe how his ten thousand men, when they arrived thirsty at a river, drank. Rejecting those who abandoned caution and put their faces to the water, Gideon led three hundred more prudent soldiers to victory.

127. *walking close to one side of the road*: The travellers must keep close to that side of the road where the cliff rises in order to get around the tree without risking falling off the edge.

133–135. *when, suddenly, a voice called out*: The Pilgrim, Virgil, and Statius are "deeply lost in [the] thought" (131) of something (and we are never told precisely what that something is). The voice that calls out is that of the angel rebuking the three of them for such deep concentration, and we are reminded of the voice of Cato in Canto II, rebuking the newly arrived souls at the foot of the mountain for allowing themselves to concentrate on Casella's song instead of their journey to God. And verse 135, "I gave a start like some shy beast in panic," recalls the frightened pigeons who fly off in panic as a result of Casella's song (*Purg.* II, 124–29). Here too, perhaps, these three travellers have their minds fixed too deeply on poetry and not enough on their true mission. Ever since Statius joined Virgil and his ward in Canto XXI, there has been much talk of poetry and poets, the culmination of which takes place at the close of Canto XXVI, where the great Provençal poet Arnaut Daniel speaks to the Pilgrim in Provençal.

136. *I raised my head to see who just now spoke*: The startled Pilgrim looks up to see the fiery radiance of the angel of Temperance.

145. *Soft as the early morning breeze of May*: In contrast to the blinding brilliance of the angel's aspect is the gentleness with which he strokes the Pilgrim's brow with one wing: the air stirred by this gentle movement is soft and fragrant as the early morning breeze of May.

151–54. *I heard the words: "Blessed are those"*: These verses are a lengthy paraphrase of the beatitude of Temperance (see note to *Purg*. XXII, 5). The concluding verse of this canto (154) reads in the Italian: "esuriendo sempre quanto è guisto," which can have a double meaning: hungering only in due measure (that is, temperance in eating), or hungering after righteousness, as the beatitude itself says.

CANTO XXV

As THEY CLIMB, the Pilgrim asks how the Gluttonous could be so lean, since they are shades and have no need of food. After a short, metaphorical introduction to the problem, Virgil calls upon Statius, who delivers a lengthy discourse on the relationship of the soul to the body, touching on the generation of the body, on the soul breathed into the embryo by the Creator, and finally on the nature and formation of the diaphanous body. When he has finished, the three have arrived at the seventh and last terrace, where they discover a wall of flame that shoots out and up from the inner bank of the cliff, forcing them to walk at the extreme outer edge of the ledge. From within the flames, the Pilgrim hears the hymn *Summae Deus clementiae*, and he sees the spirits of the Lustful. After singing the hymn through, they recite together an exemplum of the chastity of the Virgin Mary. Softly they begin the hymn again and conclude with another exemplum: the tenacious virginity of the goddess Diana. After the third singing of the hymn, shouts of praise are heard for the wives and husbands who observe the laws of virtuous wedlock.

Now was the time to climb without delay,
    for Taurus held the sun's meridian,
    and night had left its own to Scorpio.   3

Even as a man spurred by necessity
    can never be deterred no matter what,
    but goes straight on his way until the end,   6

so did we make our entrance through the gap
    and, separated by that narrow space,
    in single file, we started climbing stairs.   9

And as a little stork that longs to fly
    will lift a wing, then, still not bold enough
    to leave the nest, will let it drop again—   12

just so was I: my longing to inquire,
    first bold, then weak; all I did was attempt
    to speak, and then I quickly changed my mind.   15

My gentle father, though our pace was swift,
    encouraged me to talk: "Release your bow
    of speech, I see it drawn right to the tip."   18

Then, moved by confidence, I spoke to him,
    asking: "How could they have become so lean
    since, anyway, they have no need for food?"   21

"If you recall how Meleager burned
    as simultaneously the brand burned through,
    this should not be too hard to understand.   24

Or think how, when you stand before a glass
    at every move you make your image moves.
    Does this not make things clearer than they were?   27

But now to set your anxious mind at ease,
    we have here Statius: I shall call on him
    to be the doctor for your open wound."   30

"If, in your presence, I explain to him,"
    Statius replied, "God's view of things, it is
    because I can deny no wish of yours."   33

Then he began: "Son, let your mind take in
    and ponder carefully these words of mine,
    they will explain the 'how' that troubles you.   36

The perfect blood—the blood that's never drunk
    by thirsty veins (like food left on the table
    still unconsumed) but is preserved entire—   39

acquires, within the heart, formative powers
    to build the members of the human shape
    (as does the blood that serves to nourish them),   42

then, purified again, flows down into
    the part best left unmentioned; thence, it sprays
    in nature's vessel on another's blood,   45

and there the two bloods blend. Each is designed
    to play a passive or an active role,
    due to its perfect place of origin;   48

this joined to that begins to work on it:
    first it clots, then it quickens what it made
    compact to serve as working matter now.   51

The active force, having become a soul
    (like a plant's soul, except that this has reached
    its goal—the active force has just begun),   54

reaches the stage, then, of a jellyfish:
    it moves and feels. Then organs start to form
    for faculties of which it is the seed.   57

It keeps on swelling, spreading out, my son,
    this force that comes from the begetter's heart,
    where nature plans for all the body's parts.   60

But how, from animal, this thing becomes
    a child, you cannot see yet—and this point
    has led astray a mind wiser than yours,   63

for in his teaching he would separate
    possible intellect from soul, because
    he found no organ for that faculty.   66

Open your heart to what I now reveal:
    when the articulation of the brain
    has been perfected in the embryo,   69

then the First Mover turns to it, with joy
    over such art in Nature, and He breathes
    a spirit into it, new, and with power   72

to assimilate what it finds active there,
    so that one single soul is formed complete,
    that lives and feels and contemplates itself.   75

(And if you find what I have said is strange,
    consider the sun's heat that turns to wine
    when it joins forces with the juice that flows.)   78

Then, when Lachesis has run out of flax,
    the soul is freed of flesh and takes with it,
    in essence, both the human and divine;   81

its lower faculties no longer thrive,
    but memory, intelligence, and will
    are active and far keener than before.   84

By its own weight it falls, immediately,
    marvelously, on one or the other shore,
    and there it learns its course for the first time.   87

Then, once the soul is there, contained in space,
    the informing power radiates around
    to reshape what the body had before.   90

And as the air, after a heavy rain,
    adorns itself with different, fragile hues
    born of the outer rays relfected there,   93

just so, the air enveloping the soul
    where it has fallen must assume the form
    imprinted on it by the soul's own powers;   96

as flame inevitably goes with fire,
    following it wherever it may shift,
    so the new form accompanies the soul.   99

Since air around it makes it visible,
    it's called a 'shade'; and out of air it forms
    organs for every sense, including sight.   102

And we can speak, we shades, and we can laugh,
    and we can shed those tears and breathe those sighs
    which you may well have heard here on the mount.   105

The shade takes on the form of our desire,
    it changes with the feelings we may have:
    this, then, is what amazed you earlier."   108

We had, by now, arrived at the last round
    and, having made our usual right turn,
    our minds became absorbed by something else: 111

there, from the inner bank, flames flashed out straight,
    while, from the ledge, a blast of air shot up,
    bending them back, leaving a narrow path   114

along the edge where we were forced to walk
    in single file; and I was terrified —
    there was the fire, and *here* I could fall off!   117

"In such a place as this," my leader said,
    "be sure to keep your eyes straight on the course,
    for one could slip here easily and fall."   120

Summae Deus clementiae, I heard then,
    sung in the very heart of the great heat;
    this made me want to look there all the more.   123

And I saw spirits walking in the flames;
  I watched them, but I also watched my steps,
  caught between fear and curiosity.   *126*

When they had sung that hymn through to the end,
  they cried out loudly: *Virum non cognosco*,
  then, softly, they began the hymn again.   *129*

When it was finished, they cried out, "Diana
  kept to the woods and chased out Helice,
  whose blood had felt the poison lust of Venus."   *132*

Then came the hymn again; then came their shouts
  praising those married pairs who had been chaste,
  as virtue and the marriage laws require.   *135*

And this I think, they do continuously
  as long as they must burn within the fire:
  the cure of flames, the diet of the hymns —   *138*

with these the last of all their wounds is healed.

NOTES

2. *Taurus held the sun's meridian:* Moore (1887, p. 108) explains: "The Sun being now rather backward in Aries, the time when Taurus is on the Meridian of Noon, and the opposite sign of Scorpio on that of midnight as here described, would be generally understood to be about 2:00 P.M., though, as each constellation covers many degrees of space, the indication is only an approximate one." With the reference to Scorpio we are reminded that it is 2:00 A.M. in Jerusalem.

19–27

Virgil's initial response to the Pilgrim's question follows a standard scholastic procedure: the "explanatio per argumenta exemplorum," or explanation from analogy. But the connection between the emaciated state of the Gluttonous and the fate of Meleager or the situation of a man contemplating his image in a mirror is not immediately clear to the reader.

Virgil, in answering his ward's question (19–21), draws upon classical mythology (Meleager) and natural philosophy or science (the image in the mirror). Later on in the canto (88–100), Statius will describe the relationship of soul to aerial body in terms of rays and reflection, and it is to this that Virgil's two tercets (22–27) look ahead, while, at the same time, they establish the categories of separation and imitation, which are essential to Statius's explanation of the soul and its aerial body. We learn that while there is no visible bond between soul and body in the Afterlife, the aerial body imitates the movements of the soul. The hunger in the soul (as in the case of the Gluttonous) is projected onto or mirrored by the air around the soul. The two metaphors used by Virgil, then, are stressing the relationship between the soul and its aerial body: the "brand" (23), while separate from Meleager's body (= to the soul), is consumed with his body (= aerial body); the reflected image in the mirror (25), while separate from its source, imitates every movement of its source.

20. *How could they have become so lean:* Dante has been eager to ask this question ever since he first set foot on the Terrace of the Gluttonous (*Purg.* XXIII) and saw the thin, hungry shades there. His hesitation on the one hand and his nearly overwhelming desire to ask on the other, are clearly expressed in this canto through the tender image of the little stork (10–15), and the more vigorous image, supplied by Virgil, of the bow drawn back all the way to the iron tip of the arrow (17–18).

22. *Meleager:* Ovid (*Metam.* VIII, 445–632) tells the story of Meleager, whose fate it was to live only as long as a piece of wood burning on his mother's hearth remained unconsumed. Upon learning this, his mother, Althaea, took the wood from the fire, extinguished it, and hid it. Years later, Meleager fell in love with Atalanta, killed the Calydonian boar for her, and presented her with the skin. However, his mother's brothers, the sons of Thestius, stole it from her, and Meleager killed them. To avenge her brothers' death, Althaea threw the piece of wood back into the fire, and, as it was consumed, Meleager expired.

29. *We have here Statius:* Virgil's desire to let Statius answer the Pilgrim's question here is not entirely out of respect and deference to him: Statius's explanation, inspired at the beginning by Aristotelian physiology, will touch one important point of specifically Christian doctrine, namely the "breathing in" of the soul by God (70–72). Hence it is fitting that the lesson be delivered by the Christian Statius, since it will, at least in part, exceed the knowledge and understanding of Virgil.

36. *the 'how' that troubles you:* What troubles the Pilgrim is the extreme emaciation of the Gluttons. To explain how this could be, Statius offers a threefold discussion of body and soul. First, the creation and immediate development of the embryo (37–60); then, the development and creation of the soul (61–78); finally, the formation after death of an aerial body by the same "formative virtue" that produced the embryo (79–108). Obviously it can only be in the final stage that Statius will have a chance to explain away the Pilgrim's perplexity. The first of the three sections is based on Aristotle, the second conforms with Christian doctrine, and the third is an invention of Dante the Poet.

37–45

According to Nardi (1960, pp. 46–49), Dante is following Aristotle's idea, as amplified particularly by Avicenna, of blood turning into sperm. Dante, however, begins at a later stage in the development of the blood: he does not consider, as his predecessors had, the transformation of food into blood. According to Avicenna, four digestions took place: the first in the stomach and belly; the second in the liver, where the chyle begins to be transformed into blood; the third in the veins, where this imperfect blood is purified of its superfluities and converted into perfect blood; what is known as the fourth digestion takes place in the "single members" that it serves to nourish. The best part of this perfect blood goes to nourish the heart and brain, but some of the blood that goes to the heart is not consumed, and undergoes two more transformations: it receives a "formative virtue" (its creative power) and then is purified into sperm.

37–38. *the blood that's never drunk / by thirsty veins:* These words have led some scholars, who base themselves on Dante alone, to believe that the blood destined to become sperm does not enter into circulation through the veins. This is surely false according to Avicenna's scheme, nor need we assume that Dante is stating something different. He simply says that the blood destined to become sperm is not drunk up by the veins in spite of their thirst: it is not consumed, but remains intact, "like food left on the table unconsumed."

42. *(as does the blood that serves to nourish them):* All blood has formative powers of a sort. The "perfect blood" (that is, the

best part of this blood) has the power of creating the members of the human body in the embryo; the rest of the blood helps preserve the form of the already-created members by nourishing them.

43. *then, purified again:* Here we have to do with the transformation of blood into sperm. Dante seems to believe that this transformation takes place, like the one, previously mentioned, in which the blood acquires its formative powers, before the blood descends to the genital region. According to Avicenna, however, the descent takes place before the final transformation is achieved.

46. *and there the two bloods blend:* The "there" is, of course, the woman's uterus. Conception takes place when the perfect and active male blood (sperm) goes to work on the passive female blood, causing it to coagulate and then quickening it to life (50–51).

48. *its perfect place of origin:* According to Avicenna, the heart is hardly the place of origin of the blood that becomes sperm, but then Dante, as we have seen, omits reference to the "four digestions." See note to 37–45.

52. *The active force, having become a soul:* As the embryo develops, it passes through a "plant stage," where it exhibits the characteristics of vegetable life, i.e., it grows and feeds; its faculties are those of the vegetative soul. It then continues to develop and reaches an "animal stage" (like a jellyfish), where it becomes capable of rudimentary motion and sensation: its faculties are those of the sensitive soul.

61–78

After describing the development of the vegetative soul and the sensitive soul as the last stages of a purely physical process, Statius turns to the creation of the intellective soul (or the "possible intellect"). When the articulation of the brain, which serves as the organ of the two lesser souls, has been completed, God, happy over Nature's art, breathes a spirit into the brain. This spirit assimilates "what it finds active there"— that is, it absorbs into itself the two lower faculties, forming one unit "that lives [vegetative] and feels [sensitive] and contemplates itself [intellective]." And that the spirit of God can supposedly fuse with a concrete object is shown by the simile of the sun's heat, which fuses with the sap in the grape (76–78).

According to Statius, every individual possesses this three-fold soul; Averroës, however, allowed the individual to possess only the first two "layers" of this soul; as for the intellective faculty or possible intellect, since he could find no organ for it in the human body, this was to him a universal transcendent intellect that the individual could have recourse to but could never actually possess. And this possibility of participation is withdrawn from him at death; thus, Averroës is denying the immortality of the soul, a hypothesis obviously at odds with Christian doctrine.

63. *a mind wiser than yours:* The wiser mind that erred was that of Averroës, a Spanish Moor and commentator of Aristotle.

79. *Lachesis:* Lachesis, the second of the three fates, spins the thread of life. She "runs out of flax" at the moment of death.

81. *both the human and divine:* The soul freed of its body still contains both the human (vegetative and sensitive) faculties and the divine (the intellective soul). Statius goes on to say that the former faculties no longer thrive (in the original they are declared to be "mute"), but the latter, by the absence of the body, is more acute than ever.

The interim that Statius posits between the loss of the natural body and the acquisition of the aerial body (an interim surely brief) is not a part of Christian doctrine, as the creation of an aerial body is not a part of it. For the theologians, the soul after death must remain without a body until the Judgment Day, when it will receive the post-Resurrectional body.

85. *By its own weight it falls:* At death the soul inevitably falls either on the shore of the Acheron, if it is damned, or, if it is saved, on the shore of the Tiber, to await transportation to Purgatory.

88–108. *Then, once the soul is there . . . :* The formative power that once created and organized the members of the body in the flesh now goes to work on the air surrounding each soul and generates a visible aerial body, or shade. This body has all the sense organs; it is also able to reflect the feelings of the soul; hence the shades can speak, laugh, and weep; hence, too,

Statius seems to be saying (106–108), the desire of the Gluttons for the fruit can be reflected in their emaciated bodies.

The aerial body, as has been said (see note to 36), is an invention of Dante; it was obviously necessitated by the demands of his poetic fiction, particularly the problems of representation involved. The Pilgrim, the reader, must see and hear Virgil; they must see and hear Francesca and Ulysses and *tutti quanti;* they must be able to observe the punishments of the Damned and Penitent.

109. *We had, by now, arrived at the last round:* The travellers have arrived on the Seventh Terrace, where the sin of Lust is purged.

120. *for one could slip here easily and fall:* Though Virgil's words to the Pilgrim are meant to apply first of all to the physical dangers offered by the Seventh Terrace, where one must make his way between the flames and the precipice, they can be interpreted symbolically: Lust is the easiest sin to fall into, and the flames are always close at hand.

121. *Summae Deus clementiae:* "God of Supreme Clemency." This is the hymn of the Lustful, now known as *Summae Parens clementiae* (see Moore [1899], pp. 260–61), which asks God to banish Lust and every sinful instinct from their hearts, and to cleanse them with His healing fire. In the liturgy the hymn was traditionally sung at Matins on Saturday. This prayer may remind us of the compline hymn *Te lucis ante,* sung in the Valley of the Princes (see note to *Purg.* VIII, 13).

128. *they cried out loudly: "virum non cognosco":* This is the first example of the virtue of Chastity: "I know no man," taken, as always, from the life of the Virgin Mary. The incident referred to is the Annunciation: when Mary was told by the angel Gabriel that she would conceive and bear a son, she answered, "How shall this be, since I know not a man?" (cf. Luke 1:34).

130–31. *Diana / . . . Helice:* The second example of Chastity is taken from classical myth. To preserve her virginity, Diana took refuge in the woods as a huntress. When one of her attendants, the nymph Helice (daughter of Lycaon, king of Arcadia), fell prey to the "poison of Venus" and was seduced by Jove, Diana dismissed her. Helice gave birth to Arcas but was later transformed into a she-bear by Jove's wife, Juno. Jove then placed her in the sky as the constellation Ursa Major.

CANTO XXVI

ONE OF THE souls in the flames asks the Pilgrim, whose
body has attracted a good deal of attention, to stop and speak,
but as he is about to do so, they are interrupted by another
group of souls rushing from the opposite direction. The members of the two groups greet each other quickly and then, before separating, shout out exempla of Lust. One group cites
Sodom and Gomorrah, and the other, the shameful lust of
Pasiphaë for the bull. When the commotion has died down, the
Pilgrim sets forth the purpose of his journey, and the same soul
who had questioned him earlier speaks again. He explains that
the souls who had rushed on and off so hurriedly are the
Sodomites, and thus they cry "Sodom" in self-reproach. The
others are those whose sins have been heterosexual (or hermaphroditic, as Dante puts it), but since they have not acted
like human beings, they cry out, to their shame, the animal lust
of Pasiphaë. After these clarifications, the speaker identifies
himself as Guido Guinizelli, and the Pilgrim demonstrates a
profound affection for the Bolognese poet. But Guido protests
that there is a far greater poet among them, and yields his place
to Arnaut Daniel. Arnaut is the only (non-Italian) figure in the
Divine Comedy to speak in his native tongue, Provençal.

While we were walking at the ledge's edge
　　in single file—my good guide telling me
　　from time to time: "I warn you now, take heed!"—　　　3

the sun shone on my shoulder from the right,
　　and now, the azure of the western sky
　　was slowly turning pale beneath its rays;　　　6

my shadow made the flames a deeper red,
　　and even this slight evidence, I saw,
　　caused many souls to wonder as they passed.　　　9

And this was the occasion for those souls
　　to speculate about me. I heard said:
　　"He seems to have a body of real flesh!"　　　12

Then some of them toward me began to strain,
  coming as close to me as they could come,
  most careful not to step out of the fire.   15

"O you who walk behind the other two,
  surely, as sign of your deep reverence,
  stop, speak to me whom thirst and fire burn.   18

I'm not the only one—all of us here
  are thirsty for your words, much thirstier
  than Ethiopes or Indians for cool drink.   21

Tell us, how is it possible for you
  to block the sun as if you were a wall,
  as if you had escaped the net of death?"   24

So said a voice to me. I would have tried
  already to explain, if something else
  unusual had not just caught my eye: 27

straight down the middle of the blazing road
  facing this group, another band of souls
  was on its way. I stopped to stare, amazed,   30

for I saw shades on either side make haste
  to kiss each other without lingering,
  and each with this brief greeting satisfied.   33

The ants in their black ranks do this: they rush
  to nose each other, as if to inquire
  which way to go or how their luck has been.   36

As soon as friendly greetings are exchanged,
  before taking the first step to depart,
  each one tries to outshout the other's cry;   39

the group that just arrived: "Sodom, Gomorrah!"
  The rest: "Pasiphaë enters the cow
  so that the bull may rush to mount her lust!"   42

Imagine cranes forming two flocks: one flies
  off toward the Riphean heights, one toward the sands,
  one to escape the frost, and one the sun—   45

so, here, two groups went their opposing ways,
  and all, in tears, took up once more their chants,
  with cries that fit each of their penances.   48

Then those same shades who had first questioned me
  drew close to me as they had done before,
  intent on listening, their faces glowed.   51

And I, who twice now knew their eager wish,
  began: "O souls assured of entering
  beatitude whenever it may be,   54

I did not leave my body, green or ripe,
  below on earth: I have it with me here;
  it is real flesh, complete with blood and bones.   57

I climb to cure my blindness, for above
  a lady has won grace for me, that I
  may bear my mortal burden through your world.   60

But please—so may what you desire most
  be quickly yours, and Heaven's greatest sphere
  shelter you in its loving spaciousness—   63

tell me, who are you? Who are those that run
  away behind us in the other group?
  I shall record your answers in my book."   66

No less dumbfounded than a mountaineer,
  who, speechless, gapes at everything he sees,
  when, rude and rustic, he comes down to town,   69

were all those shades there judging from their looks;
  but when they had recovered from surprise
  (which in a noble heart lasts but a while),   72

the same soul who had earlier questioned me
  began: "Blessed are you, who from our shores
  can ship experience back for a better death!   75

The shades that do not move with us were marked
  by that same sin for which Caesar as he
  passed in triumph heard himself called a 'Queen';   78

and that is why you heard 'Sodom!' cried out
  in self-reproach, as they ran off from us;
  they use their shame to intensify the flames.   81

And ours was an hermaphroditic sin,
  but since we did not act like human beings,
  yielding instead, like animals, to lust,   84

CANTO XXVI / 281

when we pass by the other group, we shout
   to our own shame the shameful name of her
   who bestialized herself in beast-shaped wood.   87

Now you know what our guilt is. Should you want
   to know our names, I do not know them all,
   and if I did, there still would not be time.   90

As for my name, I can fulfill your wish:
   I am Guido Guinizelli—here so soon,
   for I repented long before I died."   93

As King Lycurgus raged with grief, two sons
   discovered their lost mother and rejoiced—
   I felt the same (though more restrained) to hear   96

that spirit name himself—father of me
   and father of my betters, all who wrote
   a sweet and graceful poetry of love.   99

I heard no more, I did not speak, I walked
   deep in my thoughts, my eyes fixed on his shade;
   the flames kept me from coming close to him.   102

At last my eyes were satisfied. And then
   I spoke, convincing him of my deep wish
   to serve him in whatever way I could.   105

He answered me: "What I just heard you say
   has made a deep impression on my mind,
   which even Lethe cannot wash away.   108

But if what you have told me is the truth,
   now tell me what it is that makes you show
   in words and looks this love you have for me?"   111

And I to him: "Those graceful poems of yours,
   which, for as long as our tongue serves for verse,
   will render precious even the ink you used."   114

"My brother, I can show you now," he said
   (he pointed to a spirit up ahead),
   "a better craftsman of his mother tongue.   117

Poets of love, writers of tales in prose—
   better than all of them he was! They're fools
   who think him of Limoges a greater poet!   120

They judge by reputation, not by truth,
    their minds made up before they know the rules
    of reason and the principles of art.   *123*

Guittone was judged this way in the past;
    many praised him and him alone—though, now,
    most men have been won over to the truth.   *126*

But now, if that high privilege be yours
    of climbing to the cloister, there where Christ
    is Abbot of the holy college, then,   *129*

please say a *Paternoster* for me there—
    at least the part appropriate for us,
    who are by now delivered from all evil."   *132*

Then, to make room for someone else, perhaps,
    he disappeared into the depths of fire
    the way fish seeking deeper waters fade.   *135*

I moved up toward the shade just pointed out,
    and told him my desire had prepared
    a gracious place of welcome for his name.   *138*

He readily and graciously replied:
    "Tan m'abellis vostre cortes deman,
    Qu'ieu no me puesc ni voill a vos cobrire.   *141*

Ieu sui Arnaut, que plor e vau cantan;
    consiros vei la passada folor,
    e vei jausen lo joi qu'esper, denan.   *144*

Ara vos prec, per aquella valor
    que vos guida al som de l'escalina,
    sovenha vos a temps de ma dolor!"   *147*

Then in the purifying flames he hid.

NOTES

4. *the sun shone on my shoulder from the right:* The travellers
have not been long on the Seventh Terrace and already it
would seem that the time must be between four and five
o'clock in the afternoon. It was precisely two o'clock when they
left the Sixth Terrace (see *Purg.* XXV, 1–3).

13. *Then some of them toward me began to strain:* The Pilgrim is walking alongside the flame, between the flame and the precipice, moving in the same direction as the passing shades. In order for them to join him, they would have to step out of the flame; what they do is to move as close to the burning edge as possible—what they will not allow themselves to do is to pass beyond the sacred edge of their self-maintained penance.

25. *So said a voice to me:* The voice, as we learn later (92), is that of Guido Guinizelli.

28–48

This passage describes the movements of the two groups of penitents. The groups move in opposite directions; at first this movement brings them together, then it separates them. In the first case, space seems to be constricted; the reader is invited to concentrate his gaze on the minimal: on the small movements of tiny ants. Then, space expands: the movement is the sweep of great wings, and we must extend our gaze to take in the extremes of north and south. Dante has given special force to this second image by inventing an impossible phenomenon (see note to 43).

29. *facing this group, another band of souls:* The group that moves in a direction contrary to the first group and the three travellers is that of the Lustful who practiced homosexuality. This sin will be suggested in verse 40 and will be made explicit by Guinizelli in verses 76–81. This is the only instance in the *Purgatory* of two groups moving in opposite directions. That the one group moves in the opposite direction is surely suggestive of the irregularity of their sin.

32. *to kiss each other:* The shades kiss each other briefly, in accordance with the apostolic admonition of Paul: "Greet one another with a holy kiss" (Rom. 16:16).

40. *the group that just arrived: "Sodom, Gomorrah!":* These words cried out by the newly arrived group are shouted in self-reproach. The city of Sodom gave its name to the sin of sodomy. For clear evidence that homosexuality was a common practice among the inhabitants of this city, see Gen. 19:1–28.

41. *The rest: "Pasiphaë enters the cow":* Pasiphaë was the wife of King Minos of Crete, to whom Poseidon sent a black bull to

be offered up as a sacrifice. Minos put it in his herd and Poseidon, out of revenge, caused Pasiphaë to lust after the bull. She had Daedalus, the craftsman, make a wooden structure in the shape of a cow, which was covered with a cowhide. Pasiphaë entered the cow and was possessed by the bull. The result of this union was the birth of Minotaur, a creature half bull, half human (see *Inf.* XII, 12–18). Dante could have taken the story from Ovid, *Metam.* VII, 131–37; *Ars amat.* I, 289–326, or from Virgil, *Aen.* VI, 24–26, 447; *Eclog.* VI, 45–60.

Curiously enough, the story of Pasiphaë is offered as an example of natural lust, as opposed to the unnatural lust of those who shout "Sodom and Gomorrah," yet Pasiphaë's intercourse with the bull would surely seem to be a form of sodomy. But the only form of unnatural lust considered by Guinizelli is that of homosexuality; just how he could consider Pasiphaë's act to represent natural lust is suggested in his belated explanation of the kind of lust practiced by him and those of his group: it was heterosexual, but instead of acting like human beings, they acted like animals, and so they shout the name of her "who bestialized herself in beast-shaped wood" (87). Thus, Pasiphaë's act is seen first of all as the most extreme case imaginable of human lust become bestial.

43. *Imagine cranes forming two flocks:* The flight of two separate flocks of cranes in opposite directions is, of course, an impossibility. No birds would migrate both north and south in the same season. There is only one other canto in the *Divine Comedy* in which the simile of cranes is used, and we are certainly meant to have it in mind at this point in the journey: the canto of the Lustful in Hell (*Inf. V,* 46–47).

59. *a lady has won grace for me:* To most scholars the lady in question is Beatrice; some, however, believe the Virgin Mary is involved.

62. *Heaven's greatest sphere:* The Empyrean, the place from which Beatrice descended to Limbo in order to help her lover.

67. *No less dumbfounded than a mountaineer:* The amazement of the group addressed by the Pilgrim is caused not by his last words to them but by his account in verses 55–60 of the heavenly grace he has received. It is interesting that these sophisticated souls, among whom are numbered two famous poets, and who are characterized as "being of noble heart" in

verse 72, should be likened, in their amazement, to a rude, rustic, speechless, gaping mountaineer. Yet that is how they appear in the context of comparison with the Pilgrim, who has received special grace.

73. *the same soul who had earlier questioned me:* Again Dante chooses to withhold from us the name of Guinizelli.

78. *called a 'Queen':* Because of his supposed relationship with Nicomedes, king of Bithynia, Caesar at one of his triumphs was hailed as "Regina" by some of his men. Suetonius, in his life of Caesar (*De vita Caesarum* I, xl, ix), writes at length of the notoriety that this sexual relationship achieved and of the reactions provoked in the people. But Dante's authority was probably Uguccione da Pisa in his *Magnae derivationes*. See Toynbee (1902), pp. 97–114.

82. *hermaphroditic:* Heterosexual, male with female.

86. *the shameful name of her:* The name of Pasiphaë (see note to 41).

92. *Guido Guinizelli:* Few undisputed facts concerning Guinizelli's life exist, though it is generally believed he died before November 1276. Guinizelli was at first an admirer of the ornate and rhetorical Guittone d'Arezzo, whom he calls "father" in one of his sonnets (as the Pilgrim calls him here), but later he criticized him and went on to head a school of Bolognese poets and become the forerunner of the so-called *dolce stil novo.* He was also in poetic correspondence with Bonagiunta da Lucca, who attacks him in one of his poems for "altering the manner of pleasant love poetry" with "obscure discourses." On the poetry of Guinizelli, see Montanari and Biondolillo. For the text of the poems, see Contini (1960, pp. 450–85, 893–98) and, concerning Guinizelli's most famous *canzone* ("Al cor gentil rempaira sempre amore"), see Torraca (1933–34) and Muscetta.

94–95. *two sons / discovered their lost mother:* Hypsipyle, wife of Jason, to whom she had borne two sons, was captured by pirates and sold to Lycurgus, king of Nemea, who appointed her nurse of his infant son. While in her charge, the baby was bitten fatally by a snake. Lycurgus, in his grief and wrath, ordered her death. As she was being led to execution, her two long-lost sons appeared, recognized their mother, rushed to embrace her in spite of the danger offered by her armed captors, and succeeded in having her freed.

96. *I felt the same (though more restrained)*: The Pilgrim does not brave the danger of the flame by rushing to embrace Guinizelli, in spite of his great joy at their unexpected meeting. The Pilgrim's fear of the flames is, understandably, very real (see verse 102 and note his reactions in the next canto).

108. *which even Lethe cannot wash away:* This is the traditional river of oblivion, which we are soon to see at the summit of the mountain of Purgatory.

112. *Those graceful poems of yours*: The possessive pronoun used in the Italian is not the singular *tuoi* but the plural *vostri*—evidently the honorific plural, reflecting the Pilgrim's respect for Guinizelli. The Pilgrim has met many distinguished souls so far in his journey, but up till now he has used the honorific plural only three times: first, with his close friend Guido Cavalcanti's father (*Inf.* X, 63); second, with his old teacher Brunetto Latini (*Inf.* XV, 30); third, with Pope Adrian V (*Purg.* XIX, 131).

117. *a better craftsman of his mother tongue*: The Provençal poet Arnaut Daniel, who flourished between 1180 and ca. 1210. He belonged to a noble family of Riberac in Périgord (the modern department of Dordogne), may have been a personal friend of Bertran de Born, and spent much of his time at the court of Richard Coeur de Lion. He is credited with the invention of the sestina, which Dante adopted, and he wrote in the obscure style of the *trobar clus*. He is also the author of some of the most pornographic poetry in Provençal literature (see Jernigan). For the critical edition of Daniel's poetry, see Toja.
Incidentally, the possessive pronoun ("*his* mother tongue") does not appear in verse 117 of the Italian text; we find *la lingua materna*. Accordingly, the opinion has been expressed that here Guinizelli is speaking not of the Provençal language but of the vernacular in general, and thus would be proclaiming Arnaut Daniel to be superior also to poets writing in other languages. But even if we interpret "*his* mother tongue," Guinizelli would be making the same claim of absolute superiority (if *lingua materna* is taken generically): Arnaut writ-

ing in his mother tongue (Provençal) is better than X, Y, or Z writing in their mother tongues (French, Spanish, Italian). Guinizelli has already confessed himself to be inferior to Arnaut; he would also be putting Dante on the same level with himself.

118. *Poets of love, writers of tales in prose*: In my translation I have altered the original text in a way that may have changed its meaning. Dante's words taken literally are, "love verses and tales in prose, / all of them he surpasses." These lines (in which a poet is represented as superior to poetry!) once inspired the idea among scholars that Arnaut Daniel had also written prose tales—an idea largely abandoned today, and rightly so, if one considers the concentrated, terse style of Arnaut's poetry. But these lines could still mean that Dante himself believed that Arnaut had written also in prose; and why should he believe this unless he had read or heard about examples of Arnaut's prose? There is a third possibility. Dante could simply have meant that Arnaut was the best vernacular writer of his time, his *opera* surpassing that of all others, whether they wrote poetry or prose or both. In spite of Dante's perplexing last-minute reference to prose, I have decided to adopt this last interpretation.

120. *him of Limoges*: Guiraut de Bornellh (1175–1220) was another famous Provençal poet, with a far simpler style than Arnaut Daniel's. He was called by his contemporaries "master of the Troubadours." Dante cites him (*De vulg. eloqu.* II, ii, 9), along with Arnaut Daniel and Bertran de Born, as one of three characteristic Provençal poets. His poetry is presented by Dante as that of "rectitude," in contrast to the martial poetry of the second and the love poetry of the first. See the critical edition of Kolsen (1935) and the excellent anthology of de Riquer.

124. *Guittone was judged this way*: For Guittone d'Arrezzo, see note to *Purg.* XXIV, 56.

131. *the part appropriate for us*: The part of the Lord's prayer not appropriate for the Penitents is obviously the plea "Lead us not into temptation but deliver us from evil." The reader will remember that in *Purg.* XI, when the Proud quote this prayer, they comment on this verse as being irrelevant to them (22–24).

133. *Then, to make room for someone else, perhaps*: Guinizelli, who has been on stage since verse 16, now retreats farther into the flame.

138. *a gracious place of welcome for his name*: Note the *préciosité* of the Pilgrim's words addressed to Arnaut Daniel, the master of *préciosité*.

140–147

"Your elegant request so pleases me,
   I could not possibly conceal my name.   *141*

I am Arnaut, singing now through my tears,
   regretfully recalling my past follies,
   and joyfully anticipating joy.   *144*

I beg you, in the name of that great power
   guiding you to the summit of the stairs:
   remember, in good time, my suffering here."   *147*

Since Arnaut Daniel is the only (non-Italian) character allowed to speak in his native language, I have left this Provençal passage untranslated in the text. Arnaut Daniel was the chief exponent of the *trobar clus* or hermetic style in poetry, and it is interesting that he is allowed to speak here in a very simple forthright manner, whereas the brief question addressed to him by the Pilgrim (137–38) is as elaborately contrived as anything in Arnaut's poetry—and is appreciated by Arnaut.

144. *e vei jausen lo joi qu'esper*: The manuscript tradition allows for *lo jorn* ("the day") instead of *lo joi*. Some editors consider this reading aesthetically superior, since it avoids repetition of the same idea, which would not be expected from such an elegant stylist as Arnaut. But the poets of Old Provençal love songs delighted in exploiting the repercussions of a key motif, as expressed by the same word-family.

CANTO XXVII

THE SUN IS near setting when the poets leave the souls of the Lustful and encounter the angel of Chastity, singing the beatitude "Blessed are the Pure of Heart." The angel tells them that they can go no farther without passing through the flames, but, numbed with fear, the Pilgrim hesitates for a long time. Finally Virgil prevails upon him and they make the crossing through the excruciating heat. As they emerge on the other side, they hear the invitation "Come O ye blessed of my Father," and an angel exhorts them to climb as long as there is still daylight. But soon the sun sets and the poets are overcome by sleep. Toward morning the Pilgrim dreams of Leah and Rachel, who represent the active and contemplative lives respectively. When he awakes, he is refreshed and eager and races up the remaining steps. In the last few lines Virgil describes the moral development achieved by the Pilgrim—such that he no longer needs his guidance. These are the last words that Virgil will speak in the poem.

It was the hour the sun's first rays shine down
   upon the land where its Creator shed
   his own life's blood, the hour the Ebro flows   *3*

beneath high Scales, and Ganges' waters boil
   in noonday heat: so day was fading, then,
   when God's angel of joy appeared to us.   *6*

Upon the bank beyond the fire's reach
   he stood, singing *Beati mundo corde*!
   The living beauty of his voice rang clear.   *9*

Then: "Holy souls, no farther can you go
   without first suffering fire. So, enter now,
   and be not deaf to what is sung beyond,"   *12*

he said to us as we came up to him.
   I, when I heard these words, felt like a man
   who is about to be entombed alive.   *15*

Gripping my hands together, I leaned forward
and, staring at the fire, I recalled
what human bodies look like burned to death.   18

Both of my friendly guides turned toward me then,
and Virgil said to me: "O my dear son,
there may be pain here, but there is no death.   21

Remember all your memories! If I
took care of you when we rode Geryon,
shall I do less when we are nearer God?   24

Believe me when I say that if you spent
a thousand years within the fire's heart,
it would not singe a single hair of yours;   27

and if you still cannot believe my words,
approach the fire and test it for yourself
on your own robe: just touch it with the hem.   30

It's time, high time, to put away your fears;
turn towards me, come, and enter without fear!"
But I stood there, immobile—and ashamed.   33

He said, somewhat annoyed to see me fixed
and stubborn there, "Now, don't you see, my son:
only this wall keeps you from Beatrice."   36

As Pyramus, about to die, heard Thisbe
utter her name, he raised his eyes and saw
her there, the day mulberries turned blood red—   39

just so, my stubbornness melted away:
hearing the name which blooms eternally
within my mind, I turned to my wise guide.   42

He shook his head and smiled, as at a child
won over by an apple, as he said:
"Well, then, what are we doing on this side?"   45

And, entering the flames ahead of me,
he asked of Statius, who, for some time now
had walked between us two, that he come last.   48

Once in the fire, I would have gladly jumped
into the depths of boiling glass to find
relief from that intensity of heat.   51

My loving father tried to comfort me,
  talking of Beatrice as we moved:
  "Already I can see her eyes, it seems!"   54

From somewhere else there came to us a voice,
  singing to guide us; listening to this,
  we emerged at last where the ascent begins.   57

Venite, benedicti Patris mei,
  came pouring from a radiance so bright,
  I was compelled to turn away my eyes.   60

Then, the voice said: "The sun is setting now
  and night is near; do not lose time, make haste
  before the west has given up its light."   63

The passageway cut straight up through the rock,
  at such an angle that my body blocked
  the sun's last rays that fell upon my back.   66

We had not climbed up many steps when I
  and my two guides knew that the sun had set
  because my shadow had just disappeared.   69

Before the colors of the vast expanse
  of the horizon melted into one,
  and Night was in possession of the sky,   72

each of us chose a step to make his bed:
  the nature of the mountain took from us
  as much the power as the desire to climb.   75

Like goats first fast and frisky on the mount,
  before they stop their play to crop the grass,
  then settling down in ruminating calm,   78

quiet in the shade, free from the burning sun,
  watched by the shepherd leaning on his staff,
  protecting their repose; or yet again,   81

a herdsman who beds down beneath the sky,
  watching beside his peaceful flock all night,
  lest they be scattered by some beast of prey—   84

so were the three of us there on the stair:
  I was the goat, and they the shepherds, all
  shut in by walls of stone, this side and that.   87

Beyond that height little was visible,
  but through that little I could see the stars,
  larger, brighter than they appear to us.   90

While meditating, staring up at them,
  sleep overcame me—sleep, which often brings
  the knowledge of events before the fact.   93

At just about the hour when Cytherea,
  who always seems to burn with love's own flames,
  first sent her eastern rays down on the mount,   96

I dreamed I saw a young and lovely girl
  walking within a meadow picking flowers;
  and, as she moved along, she sang these words: 99

"If anyone should want to know my name,
  I am called Leah. And I spend all my time
  weaving garlands of flowers with my fair hands,   102

to please me when I stand before my mirror;
  my sister Rachel sits all the day long
  before her own and never moves away.   105

She loves to contemplate her lovely eyes;
  I love to use my hands to adorn myself:
  her joy is in reflection, mine in act."   108

And now, before the splendor of the dawn
  (more welcomed by the homebound pilgrim now,
  the closer he awakes to home each day),   111

night's shadows disappeared on every side;
  my sleep fled with them: I rose to my feet,
  for my great teachers were already up.   114

"That precious fruit which all men eagerly
  go searching for on many different boughs
  will give, today, peace to your hungry soul."   117

These were the words that Virgil spoke to me,
  and never was a more auspicious gift.
  received, or given, with more joyfulness.   120

Growing desire, desire to be up there,
  was rising in me: with every step I took
  I felt my wings were growing for the flight.   123

CANTO XXVII / 293

Once the stairs, swiftly climbed, were all behind
and we were standing on the topmost step,
Virgil addressed me, fixing his eyes on mine: 126

"You now have seen, my son, the temporal
and the eternal fire, you've reached the place
where my discernment now has reached its end.   129

I led you here with skill and intellect;
from here on, let your pleasure be your guide:
the narrow ways, the steep, are far below.   132

Behold the sun shining upon your brow,
behold the tender grass, the flowers, the trees,
which, here, the earth produces of itself.   135

Until those lovely eyes rejoicing come,
which, tearful, once urged me to come to you,
you may sit here, or wander, as you please.   138

Expect no longer words or signs from me.
Now is your will upright, wholesome and free,
and not to heed its pleasure would be wrong: 141

I crown and miter you lord of yourself!"

NOTES

1–6. *It was the hour*: The canto opens with a periphrastic
description of the times both at Purgatory and at the east, west,
and center of the inhabited world. It is six o'clock in the morning at Jerusalem, midnight at Spain (where the Ebro River is
located), noon at India (through which the Ganges flows), and
six o'clock in the evening at Purgatory. By indicating the time
at three other major points on the earth's circumference, and
by naming Jerusalem as the place where the Creator of the sun
shed his blood, the poet sets the whole action of the canto, in
which the Pilgrim's purgation is achieved, against the universal
background of Christ's redeeming death.

After this canto there will be no further references in the
Comedy to the rising and setting of the sun; the concluding six
cantos of the *Purgatory* will narrate the events of Wednesday
morning in the Earthly Paradise. Here on the mountain, it is
just before dusk on Tuesday; night will fall and Wednesday's

dawn will come, and the sunlight will be bright before the canto ends.

8. *Beati mundo corde*: These words begin the last beatitude (Matt. 5:8), "Blessed are the pure of heart, for they shall see God." They are spoken by the angel just beyond the purifying flames through which all souls on the way to Paradise must pass.

10. *no farther can you go*: The wall of fire of which the angel speaks is at once the punishment of the Terrace of Lust and the barrier through which everybody must pass before seeing God, whether guilty of Lust or not. It was these purifying flames that the Pilgrim foresaw, perhaps, in his first dream.

The tradition of a wall of flame guarding Eden dates from the earliest Christian interpretations of the cherubim with fiery sword in hand, set by God at the edge of the Earthly Paradise to prevent access to the Tree of Life (Gen. 3:22–24).

14–15. *like a man / who is about to be entombed alive*: Terror-stricken, the Pilgrim sees the passage through the flames as death; it does not occur to him that this "death" is a Baptism of Fire, a dying that will restore him to a new life of perfect freedom.

22. *Remember all your memories:* Virgil tries to dispel the Pilgrim's paralyzing fear of the flames by recalling a similar situation when they were in Hell (*Inf.* XVII). At that point, the only means available to descend the great distance down to the Malebolge was to ride the untrustworthy monster of Fraud, Geryon; this venture ended successfully. But here again, as on other occasions when new trials confront him, the Pilgrim is unable to make use of his experience and cowers in terror like a child.

35. *Now, don't you see, my son:* Virgil reasons with the Pilgrim as one coaxes a stubborn child. Here, as a last resort, Virgil abandons all attempts at logical persuasion and points forward to Beatrice, the source of revelation to which he is leading the Pilgrim, but which he himself does not comprehend. In the last analysis, what leads the Pilgrim to pass through the wall of fire is not a sense of duty, and not reason, but love.

37. *As Pyramus, about to die, heard Thisbe:* Pyramus and Thisbe dwelled in adjoining houses in Babylon. They fell in

love, but, as their parents refused to sanction their union, they were forced to communicate through a hole in the wall. On one occasion, they arranged a tryst at the tomb of Ninius. While Thisbe, who arrived first, was waiting for Pyramus, she saw a lion that had just gored an ox, and she ran off in fright. In her haste to get away, she dropped her veil, which the lion mangled with its bloody paws. Pyramus, arriving soon after, saw only the bloody veil, and assumed that Thisbe had been killed. In despair, he stabbed himself, and the white berries of a nearby mulberry bush became red with his blood. At this point Thisbe returned to the tomb, and seeing her lover near death, she called to him, naming herself. He recognized her and died. Then Thisbe, after offering a prayer that mulberries should henceforth be red as a memorial to their love, killed herself. Ovid relates the story of the lovers in the *Metamorphoses* (IV, 142–46).

Both the Pilgrim and Pyramus are on the verge of dying. The pagan hero is for a moment brought back to life by the name of his beloved. The Christian hero is fortified, by the mention of his beloved's name, to confront the death that will bring life. In Ovid's tale the mulberry bush is an eternal monument to love; in Dante's poem it is an emblem of the soul's transformation from a state of resistance to one of cooperation with grace.

43–45. *He shook his head and smiled, as at a child:* Why the teasing tone of this tercet? And how can Dante, with his reference to "an apple," treat in such a trifling way the promise of a meeting between the Pilgrim and Beatrice? (See note to 115.)

55–58. *there came to us a voice:* The ninth angel of the mountain sings from the other side of the flames, leading the three poets on to Eden, whose guardian he is. His words are those of Jesus (Matt. 25:34) to the Elect on the Last Day: "Venite, benedicti Patris mei possidete paratum vobis regnum a constitutione mundi" ("Come ye blessed of my father and enter into the kingdom which has been prepared for you since the foundation of the world"). Although Dante uses only the first four words of the Latin phrase, the reading is certainly meant to go as far, at least, as the words "possidete paratum vobis regnum," for it is precisely what the Pilgrim is about to do: enter into that kingdom prepared for every saved soul.

No mention is made at this point of the removal of the last *P* from the Pilgrim's brow. One must assume that if the angel does not do so now, it has already been burned away in the wall's purifying fire.

70. *Before the colors:* Just before nightfall, the three travellers, who have just passed through fire and begun climbing the mountain again, have a fleeting glimpse of vast geographical perspectives—a foretaste of the revelation that is shortly to begin unfolding and that will be the final theme of the poem.

75. *as much the power as the desire to climb:* This is a reminder of Sordello's words (VII, 53–57) describing the Law of the Mountain: after sunset no further upward movement is allowed. The effect of the law is to take away the power to climb, but this, in turn, would weaken the desire.

76. *Like goats first fast and frisky:* The goats who gamboled on the mountaintop at noon and are now at rest correspond in a number of ways to the Pilgrim. Like him, they are associated with the sin of the Seventh Terrace: the adjectives that describe them suggest lasciviousness. The mention of the "burning sun" recalls the flames of the fire that purifies Lust. The goats, after their feast of grass, are chewing their cud; the Pilgrim found food for thought in his experience, which he is now "ruminating" as he waits for sleep.

80. *the shepherd leaning on his staff:* The figure of the shepherd leaning on his staff will be followed immediately by the herdsman lying on the ground; obviously, only the second figure corresponds to the situation in the narrative: the Pilgrim's guardians are lying on the steps. According to Torraca, quoted by Singleton (p. 657), Dante has realized the discrepancy involved in the description of the shepherd and chosen to replace it with that of the herdsman who, like Virgil and Statius, is recumbent. But Dante has not "replaced" one figure with another: he has added the second to the first. Only the herdsman serves as the base of a simile ("a herdsman who . . ."); the shepherd represents a marginal detail within the description of the goats ("Like goats, first fast . . ."). It is, then, the recumbent shepherd that Dante puts into particular relief.

Since Virgil was one of the greatest representatives of the genre of pastoral poetry in Latin literature, it seems most fitting that the writer who portrayed poets as shepherds in his *Eclogues* should appear here as a shepherd or herdsman.

92–93. *sleep . . . the knowledge of events before the fact:* This strongly suggests that the dream (the third and final dream on the mountain of Purgatory) is a prophetic one.

94. *the hour when Cytherea:* This is the hour just before dawn. The Pilgrim, ruminating, falls asleep; then comes the briefest and least ambiguous of the Pilgrim's three dreams. It is introduced by a comparatively short periphrastic indication of the hour, which, even though it alludes to pagan mythology, has none of the disquieting sensuality and violence that marked the introduction to the first dream in *Purg.* IX.

97. *a young and lovely girl:* The woman of this dream appears in exactly the same way as Matelda will in the next canto—singing and gathering flowers in a lovely landscape.

100–108. *. . . I am called Leah:* The story of Leah and Rachel, the two daughters of Laban, is found in the Old Testament (Gen. 29:10–31). Leah was Jacob's first wife, Rachel his second; Leah was fertile, Rachel sterile, but Rachel had beautiful, clear eyes, and Leah, troubled vision. The fathers of the church took the two women as symbols of the active and the contemplative life, respectively.

Whereas the Siren's song in the second dream (*Purg.* XIX, 19–24: "I am the sweet Siren, I am . . .") told how the ancient witch leads men astray by giving total satisfaction to their sensual desires, the song of Leah (101: "I am called Leah") tells of the two states in which the Christian in this life may find genuine satisfaction: action, here represented by the task of gathering and weaving flowers, and contemplation, represented by concentrated gazing into the Mirror of Truth.

According to Leah's words, she too, from time to time, looks into her mirror to admire the results of her handiwork and perhaps her lovely hands. But her sister never moves from her mirror, gazing into her own eyes. As Dante says in the *Convivio* (IV, ii, 18): "the philosophizing soul not only contemplates the Truth, but also contemplates its own contemplation and the beauty thereof."

Leah prefigures Matelda, who, like her, will soon appear singing and gathering flowers in a lovely landscape. Matelda will be the Pilgrim's guide through Eden. She represents the happiness that men can attain here on earth by love of one's neighbor and by virtuous behavior. Rachel prefigures Beatrice, who will appear to the Pilgrim in Eden. She represents divine revelation, which leads men to the love of God and the unending joy of the Beatific Vision. The landscape of the dream foreshadows the Earthly Paradise, which we are about to enter.

110. *welcomed by the homebound pilgrim:* Our Pilgrim, too, is homebound, since Eden is the home of the human race.

113. *my sleep fled with them:* The Pilgrim woke from his other dreams well after dawn, troubled and frightened, his sleep destroyed by his dream. Here he wakes naturally, and at peace with himself, at the moment when night's shadows disappear and light is about to fill the skies. The physical light corresponds to the spiritual light that will burst upon him when he meets Beatrice.

115. *That precious fruit:* The fruit that grows on many different branches is, of course, the ideal happiness that mankind seeks in various ways (see Boethius, *Consol. philos.* III, 2). Here Virgil is referring specifically to the Pilgrim's meeting with Beatrice, which will take place this very day.

Incidentally, the word that I have translated "fruit" is in the original *pome,* "apple." Perhaps we have an explanation for the *pome,* "apple," used earlier in this canto (45) to refer precisely to Virgil's promise of the meeting in question.

123. *I felt my wings were growing for the flight:* The Pilgrim is almost ready for the unimpeded flight to God, which is the main action of the *Paradise,* but he will first spend some time in Eden, where he will attain the pristine purity of Adam before the Fall.

127–28. *the temporal / and the eternal fire:* The temporal fire is the fire of Purgatory: the purifying punishments of the mountain, including the wall of fire on the Seventh Terrace, which will disappear on the Judgment Day. The eternal fire is, of course, the fire of Hell,

142. *I crown and miter you lord of yourself:* In the most solemn terms, Virgil gives his benediction to the Pilgrim, whose development has reached the point where his lesser faculties are subject to his reason, so that he may henceforth follow his desires without peril. It is the stage that will lead directly to the gift of Sanctifying Grace, which he will receive upon the appearance of Beatrice.

CANTO XXVIII

THE PILGRIM WANDERS in the heavenly forest until his path is blocked by a stream. On the other side of the stream he sees a lady singing and gathering flowers. At the Pilgrim's request, she approaches him, and, smiling from the opposite bank, tells him that this forest is the Earthly Paradise, the Garden of Eden, whence sprang the human race. She explains that the constantly moving gentle breeze is due to the earth's rotation, and she discusses the dissemination of plant life from the garden, carried on the moving air to all the lands of the earth. She further speaks of the two inexhaustible streams of the garden, Lethe and Eunoë, of which the former washes away all memory of sin and the latter restores the memory of good deeds. This lady, who, as yet, has not been named, concludes by telling the Pilgrim that the poets who sang of the Golden Age and of Parnassus perhaps had this place in mind.

Now eager to explore on every side
   the heavenly forest thick with living green,
   which made the bright new morning light more soft,   *3*

without delay I left the bank behind
   and slowly made my way across the plain,
   whose soil gave its own fragrance to the air.   *6*

My forehead felt the stirring of sweet air,
   whose flowing rhythm always stayed the same,
   and struck no harder than the gentlest breeze;   *9*

and, in the constant, moving air, each branch
   with trembling leaves was bending to one side
   toward where the holy mount first casts its shade;   *12*

they did not curve so sharply toward the ground
   that little birds among the topmost leaves
   could not continue practicing their art: *15*

they welcomed in full-throated joyful sound
   the day's beginning to their leafy boughs
   whose soughing sound accompanied their song—   *18*

that sound we hear passed on from branch to branch,
   in the pine forest on the shore of Chiassi
   when Aeolus sets free Sirocco winds.   21

By now, although my steps were slow, I found
   myself so deep within the ancient wood
   I could not see the place where I came in;   24

then suddenly, I saw blocking my way
   a stream whose little waves kept pushing back,
   leftwards, the grass that grew along its bank.   27

The clearest of all waters on our earth
   would seem to have, somehow, a cloudy tinge
   compared to this flowing transparency—   30

transparent though it flows dark, very dark
   beneath an everlasting shade, which will
   never admit a ray of sun or moon.   33

I had to stop, but with my eyes I crossed
   beyond the rivulet to contemplate
   the many-colored splendors of the boughs,   36

and there appeared—as sometimes will appear
   an unexpected sight so marvelous,
   all other thoughts are driven from the mind—   39

a solitary lady wandering there,
   and she was singing as she gathered flowers
   from the abundance painted on her path.   42

"Oh, lovely lady, glowing with the warmth
   and strength of Love's own rays—if I may trust
   your look, which should bear witness of the heart—   45

be kind enough," I said to her, "to come
   a little nearer to the river's bank,
   that I may understand the words you sing.   48

You bring to mind what Proserpine was like,
   and where she was, that day her mother lost her,
   and she, in her turn, lost eternal Spring."   51

Just as a lady in the dance will turn,
   keeping her feet together on the ground,
   and one before the other hardly moves,   54

so she, among the red and yellow flowers,
    turned round toward me, her virgin modesty
    enjoining her to look with downcast eyes,   57

and, satisfying my desire, she started
    moving toward me and, with the melody,
    there came to me the sweetness of the words.   60

When she had come to where the tender grass
    is barely touched by ripples from that stream,
    she graciously did raise her eyes to mine.   63

The eyes of Venus surely were not lit
    so radiantly that day her loving son
    quite innocently pierced her with his dart.   66

Smiling, she stood there on the other bank,
    arranging in her hands the many colors
    that grew from no seeds planted on that height.   69

The stream kept us only three feet apart,
    but Hellespont, where it was crossed by Xerxes
    (whose fate should be a lesson to the proud),   72

hurling its waves from Sestos to Abydos,
    was hated by Leander less than I
    hated this one: it would not open up!   75

"This place is new to each of you," she said,
    "it could be that you find yourself amazed,
    perplexed to see me smiling in this place   78

once chosen as the cradle of mankind;
    but let the *Delectasti me* shed light
    and clear away the mist that clouds your minds.   81

And you who are in front and spoke to me,
    if there is something more you want to know,
    I came prepared to tell you what you wish."   84

"The flowing water and the woodland sounds
    seem to be inconsistent," I began,
    "with what I have been told about the mount."   87

She said, "I shall explain the logical
    necessity of what perplexes you,
    and thus remove what has obscured your mind.   90

That Highest Good, Himself pleasing Himself,
  made Adam good, to do good, then gave
  this place as earnest of eternal peace.   93

Because he sinned, he could not stay here long;
  because he sinned, he changed his childlike mirth,
  his playful joy, for anguish and for toil.   96

In order that the storms that form below
  (caused by the vapors from the earth and sea
  as they are drawn upwards to solar heat)   99

should not disturb the garden's peacefulness,
  this mount was made to rise so high toward Heaven
  that past the gate no storm is possible.   102

Now, since the air is moving constantly,
  moving as primal revolution moves
  (unless its circulation is disturbed),   105

here on the mountain's height, completely free
  in the encircling air, this movement strikes
  and makes the dense leaves of the forest sing;   108

and every smitten plant begins to make
  the pure air pregnant with its special power,
  which, then, the whirling scatters everywhere;   111

all lands elsewhere conceive and bring to flower
  the different plants endowed with different powers,
  according to the climate and the soil.   114

If they knew down on earth what you know now,
  no one would be surprised to see a plant
  start growing where no seed was sown before.   117

And know, the holy land you stand on now
  is rich in every species and brings forth
  fruit that no man has ever plucked on earth.   120

The water here does not spring from a source
  that needs to be restored by changing mists,
  like streams on earth that lose, then gain, their force: 123

it issues from a spring of constant flow,
  immutable, which, by the will of God,
  regains what it pours forth on either side.   126

CANTO XXVIII / 303

The water here on this side flows with power
    to erase sin's memory; and on that side
    the memory of good deeds is restored;   *129*

it is called Lethe here, Eunoë there
    beyond, and if one does not first drink here,
    he will not come to know its powers there—   *132*

the sweet taste of its waters has no peer.
    And even though your thirst may now be quenched
    by what you know already of this place,   *135*

I offer you a corollary gift:
    I think you will not cherish my words less
    if you learn more than I first promised you.   *138*

Perhaps those poets of long ago who sang
    the Age of Gold, its pristine happiness,
    were dreaming on Parnassus of this place.   *141*

The root of mankind's tree was guiltless here;
    here, in an endless Spring, was every fruit,
    such is the nectar praised by all these poets."   *144*

As she said this, I quickly turned around
    to my two poets: I saw, still lingering,
    the smile her final words brought to their lips.   *147*

Then I turned back to face her loveliness.

NOTES

1–21

    According to Carroll (p. 373), Ruskin in his *Modern Painters* has said that these lines represent "the sweetest passage of wood description which exists in literature." Already in Canto VII, when treating of the Valley of the Princes, I compared their habitat, with its elaborately contrived artificial beauty, with the Earthly Paradise, whose charm consists of its natural beauty. Here for the first time birds appear onstage, no longer caged in similes as in the many previous descriptions of bird images. But while there is nothing artificial in the makeup of this landscape, there is something stylized: e.g., the wind blowing always in the same direction. Here, as will be seen, we have a touch of the supernatural.

There is another important difference between the description of the Valley of the Princes and that of the garden where the Pilgrim is: the former is presented merely as a habitat, as a background for those who dwell there; we are told not that the grass is green and the flowers beautiful but that a group of souls are sitting, singing, on the green grass among the beautiful flowers. But this garden or forest is presented as a creation in itself.

1. *Now eager to explore on every side*: Encouraged by Virgil's optimistic words of dismissal, the Pilgrim, full of enthusiasm and curiosity, begins his exploration of the new height they have just reached, whose beauty Virgil had briefly mentioned in his final words to the Pilgrim. At first he makes his way slowly, slowly (verse 4: *lento, lento* in Italian). Often in the past Virgil had upbraided him precisely for his curiosity and his slowness, but now the Pilgrim has been assured that henceforth he can do no wrong.

20. *in the pine forest on the shore of Chiassi*: In Dante's time Chiassi was the harbor of Ravenna, which today is several miles inland since the sea has long since withdrawn. The pine forest retained many of the beautiful features mentioned here until the present century.

21. *when Aeolus sets free Sirocco winds*: Aeolus, king of the winds, kept them confined in a vast, hidden cave. The Sirocco is a warm, moist wind that blows on southern Europe from North Africa.

26. *a stream*: This stream, the Pilgrim will be told later (130), is the river Lethe, whose function it is to wash away the memory of sin. In classical mythology Lethe was a river of Hades from which the souls of the dead drank forgetfulness of their first existence.

40. *a solitary lady wandering there*: This is Matelda, though her name is mentioned, and then quite casually, only in the closing canto (XXXIII, 119). Because she is given a name, much controversy has arisen over the various attempts to identify her with an historical figure. Moore (1903, p. 213) has classified several theories: (1) the Countess Matelda of Canossa, (2) some Matelda from Germany, (3) some friend or associate of the young Beatrice. Though it is difficult to see why this figure was given a name, still I believe that it is pointless to attempt to identify her with an historical person.

As to what this lady is supposed to represent, to symbolize, a number of aspects of her personality and of her function in the garden will be revealed in the next few cantos—aspects that have given rise to considerable debate. But all critics seem to agree: she must represent, among other things, the active life, as she is clearly reminiscent of the Leah of the Pilgrim's final dream in the preceding canto. It may be noted, however, that in one point she differs in an important way from Leah: the flowers she is gathering are not exploited to enhance her charms.

Verses 40–42, with their simple description of what could be a commonplace situation, are preceded by and followed by a suggestion of the extraordinary. Before Matelda is presented—in fact, before we know that a lady is involved—we are told to expect something marvelous, a sight that holds the observer spellbound: Matelda is preceded by her own miraculousness. She can never be understood if this quality of hers is forgotten. Verses 43–45, representing the Pilgrim's immediate, spontaneous, joyful reaction to what he sees in this lady explains the miraculous effect of her appearance; she radiates the very essence of love. Later on it will be revealed just what it is that Matelda loves so intensely.

49. *Proserpine*: Proserpine was the daughter of Jupiter and Ceres. While gathering flowers in a meadow, she was carried off by Pluto to the netherworld, where she was made queen. At the urging of Ceres, Mercury was sent to fetch her back, but she had already eaten a quarter of a fateful pomegranate and so was constrained to return to the netherworld for one-fourth of the year. Proserpine thus represents the vegetative cycle, remaining on earth during spring, summer, and autumn, but returning to the land of the dead during winter (see Ovid, *Metam*. V, 385–408).

51. *and she, in her turn, lost eternal Spring*: The word "eternal" is not found in the original, but simply *primavera*, "Spring." Most scholars, however, basing themselves on Ovid, who speaks of the "eternal Spring" that reigned in the grotto where Proserpine was picking flowers, interpret Dante's *primavera* as *primavera eterna*. It is eternal Spring that reigns in the Earthly Paradise and that Adam lost. It is easy to see some parallel between the myth of Proserpine and the Fall (see Brown).

64. *Venus*: When Venus stooped over to kiss her son Cupid, she was accidentally scratched on the breast by one of his ar-

rows and thereupon fell in love with the beautiful god Adonis (see Ovid, *Metam*. X, 525–32).

69. *that grew from no seeds planted on that height:* Later (109–20) the extraordinary richness of the soil in the Earthly Paradise will be discussed.

70. *The stream kept us only three feet apart:* The Pilgrim could easily have stepped across this narrow stream to be with Matelda, but he does not do so. He wants the waters to open up for him as the Red Sea at God's will opened up for the Israelites, and because this does not happen he *hates* the river (74). The word *hate* indicates the intensity of his desire to be walking with Matelda, but he must feel a mysterious barrier separating them: only if he were encouraged by a miracle would he dare attempt to cross that barrier.

It has been suggested that the "three feet" that separate the Pilgrim from Matelda symbolize the three stages that lead to the sacrament of Confession: *contritio cordis, confessio oris, satisfactio operis*. But only after his soul-searching talk with Beatrice and after he has drunk of the river Lethe will he have completed these stages—to find himself on the same side of the river with Matelda.

71. *Xerxes:* The son of Darius, Xerxes was the Persian king who, setting out from Sardis with a great army, crossed the Hellespont in 465 B.C. on a bridge of ships and invaded Greece. Despite his army, however, Xerxes was defeated and his navy was dispersed at the battle of Salamis, whereby he was forced to retreat.

74. *Leander:* Leander, a young man of Abydos, fell in love with the priestess Hero, who lived at Sestos across the Hellespont. Since the difference of their social positions made marriage impossible, the two met secretly at night, when Leander would swim across the channel guided by a light in Hero's tower. One night the light went out, and Leander became lost, was carried away by the current, and drowned. Later Hero found the body on the shore and threw herself into the water.

80. *but let the* Delectasti me *shed light:* Matelda is referring to the ninety-first psalm, and surely the lines she has in mind are: "Thou didst delight me, Lord, in Thy work / and in the works of Thy hands, I will rejoice. / How praiseworthy are Thy works, O Lord." Thus, Matelda is explaining her smile as due to

her joy over the beauties of the Earthly Paradise; her unselfish delight (see note to 40) in its beautiful flowers has twice been referred to. And the love that the Pilgrim felt radiating from her the moment he saw her face must be love for the Creator of the beauty of the universe. See Singleton (1958) pp. 206–207.

88. *I shall explain*: Here Matelda begins her speech to the three poets, which comes to an end in verse 144. What she explains is the nature of the Earthly Paradise: first, its spiritual significance: "earnest of eternal peace" (93); then the physical conditions that characterize it as a place.

102. *past the gate no storm is possible*: Matelda is in the midst of clearing up the second point that perplexed the Pilgrim since it seemed to contradict Statius. The breeze that produced the "woodland sounds" he mentioned (85) has nothing to do with the conditions of the earthly atmosphere, where the force of a wind as well as its direction may vary. In the Earthly Paradise the light wind is constant and blows always in the same direction, from east to west, the direction taken by the spheres of the heavens; it is determined by the *Primum Mobile*, that is, directly by God.

121. *The water here*: Matelda is now answering the first part of the Pilgrim's question: how can there be a river here if, according to Statius, rain never falls?

128. *to erase sin's memory*: It would be natural to infer from Matelda's words that Lethe has the power to destroy completely and forever the memory of one's sinful deeds. This, however, cannot be the case, as the Pilgrim will learn in Paradise, where he meets a number of souls who refer to their sins; in fact, Cunizza speaks almost happily of the truths she learned from her sin of Lust (*Par.* IX, 3). Perhaps it could be said that the memory of sin is lost on the emotional plane (no longer remembered as an experience) but not on the intellectual. And, then, how could souls be truly grateful to God for their salvation if they were to forget their sins?

130. *it is called Lethe here, Eunoë there*: The word "Lethe" comes from the Greek word for "oblivion" (see note to 26); "Eunoë" derives from the Greek for "well minded" (see Toynbee, 1902, p. 104). The waters of the first miraculous stream "erase sin's memory" (128), while those of the second restore "the memory of good deeds"(129).

CANTO XXIX

WHEN THE LADY has finished speaking, she sings and begins to walk upstream, the Pilgrim keeping pace with her on
the opposite bank. They have not gone far when the lady stops
and instructs the Pilgrim to be attentive. A burst of incandescence lights up the air, and the Pilgrim sees the approach of the
heavenly pageant. It is led by seven golden candlesticks, which
emit a stream of multicolored light that extends over the procession that follows them. Next come twenty-four elders, two
by two, and behind them, four creatures. Within a square determined by the positions of these four, comes a chariot drawn
by a griffin. To the right of the chariot are three ladies, one red,
one white, and one green; to the left are four ladies clad in
purple. Behind them come two aged men, then four more men
of humble aspect, and finally one old man alone. When the
chariot has reached a point directly opposite the Pilgrim, a
thunderclap resounds, bringing the entire procession to a sudden halt.

Then, like a lady moved by love, she sang
    (her revelations now come to an end):
    Beati quorum tecta sunt peccata!   3

And like those nymphs that used to stroll alone
    through shaded woodlands, one seeking the sun,
    another trying to avoid its light,   6

so she began to walk along the bank,
    moving upstream, and I kept pace with her,
    matching on my side her small, graceful steps.   9

Not a hundred steps between us had we gone,
    when the two river banks curved perfectly
    parallel—and I faced the east again;   12

when we had gone a little farther on,
    the lady stopped and, turning to me, said:
    "My brother, look and listen." Suddenly,   15

a burst of incandescence cut the air,
    with one quick flash it lit up all the woods—
    at first I thought it was a lightning flash.   18

But lightning goes as quickly as it comes;
    what I saw stayed, its radiance increased.
    "What can this be?" I thought, and as I did,   *21*

a gentle melody was drifting through
    the luminous atmosphere. Then righteous zeal
    made me curse the presumptuousness of Eve: *24*

to think that, while all earth and Heaven obeyed
    His will, a single woman, newly made,
    would dare strip off the veil imposed by Him!   *27*

Had she remained submissive to His will,
    I could on these ineffable delights
    have feasted sooner and for much more time.   *30*

As I was moving in a blissful trance
    among these first fruits of eternal joy,
    yearning for still more happiness to come,   *33*

the air, beneath green boughs, became transformed
    before our eyes into a blazing light,
    and the sweet sound had now become a chant.   *36*

Most holy Virgins, if because of you
    hunger or cold or vigils I endured,
    allow me now to ask for my reward: *39*

let Helicon pour forth its streams for me,
    and let Urania help me with her choir
    to put in verse things difficult to grasp.   *42*

A little farther on, I saw what seemed
    to be seven trees of gold—a false effect
    caused by the distance separating us;   *45*

but when I had come close enough to them
    that distance could no longer hide detail,
    and what had tricked my senses now was clear,   *48*

that power which feeds the process of our thought
    identified the shapes as candlesticks
    and heard the word *Hosanna* in the chant.   *51*

Above the splendid gold—a brilliant light,
    brighter than moonlight in a cloudless sky
    at midnight shining in her bright mid-month!   *54*

Full of bewilderment, I turned around
    to my good Virgil. His answer was a glance
    charged with no less amazement than I felt.   57

Then I turned back to gaze at those high things
    moving toward us as though they did not move—
    more slowly than a modest, newmade bride.   60

The lady cried: "Why are you so intent
    on looking only at those living lights?
    Have you no wish to see what comes behind?"   63

Then I saw people following the glow,
    as if they were attendants; all were clothed
    in garments supernaturally white.   66

The waters on my left received the light,
    and when I looked into this shining glass,
    my left side was reflected clearly there.   69

When I had reached the point along my bank
    where only water separated us,
    I stopped to watch the scene more carefully: 72

I saw the slender flames as they advanced,
    leaving the air behind them color-streaked—
    so many streaming pennants overhead!   75

And thus the sky became a painted flow
    of seven bands of light, all the same shades
    as Delia's cincture or Apollo's bow.   78

These bands extended farther back than eyes
    could see and, all together, I would say,
    they measured, side by side, a good ten strides.   81

And under that magnificence of Heaven
    came four-and-twenty elders, two by two,
    all of them wearing crowns of fleur-de-lis.   84

They sang as they moved on: "*Benedicta* thou
    of all of Adam's daughters, blessed be
    thy beauty throughout all eternity!"   87

When once the group of God's elect had passed
    (the flowers and the tender grass that grew
    along the other bank once more in view),   90

as groups of stars will replace other stars
  high in the heavens, following them there came
  four creatures wearing crowns of forest green.   93

Each had six wings with feathers that were all
  covered with eyes; were Argus still alive,
  his eyes would be exactly like all those.   96

Reader, I cannot spend more verses now
  describing them, for I have other needs
  constraining me—here I must spare my words;   99

but you can read Ezekiel's account:
  he saw them once approaching from the north
  borne on the wind, moving in cloud and fire,   102

and as he pictured them, so were they here,
  except that, in the matter of their wings,
  Saint John agrees with me and not with him.   105

The four of them were corners for a space
  filled by a triumphal two-wheeled chariot
  drawn by a griffin, harnessed to its neck.   108

He kept both wings raised high, and each one flanked
  the mid-banner between the three and three:
  so perfectly that neither one was cut.   111

His wings rose higher than my sight could rise;
  the parts of him that were a bird were gold
  and all the rest was white, with deep red marks.   114

An Africanus or Augustus never
  had such a splendid chariot from their Rome;
  indeed, that of the Sun could not compare—   117

that of the Sun which strayed and was destroyed
  at the devout petition of the Earth,
  when Jove in his mysterious way was just.   120

There were three ladies circling in a dance
  near the right wheel, and one was red, so red
  she hardly would be visible in fire;   123

the second looked as if her flesh and bones
  were fashioned out of emerald; the third
  had all the whiteness of new-fallen snow;   126

at times the white one led the dance, at times,
   the red, and from the song the red one sang
   the others took the tempo of their dance.   *129*

Beside the left wheel, dancing festively,
   were four more ladies—dressed in purple robes
   and led by one with three eyes in her head.   *132*

Behind the dancing figures, three and four,
   there came two aged men, differently dressed,
   but similar in bearing, staid and grave.   *135*

One wore the garments of a follower
   of great Hippocrates, whom Nature made
   to heal those creatures that she loved the most;   *138*

the other seemed to be his counterpart:
   he bore a sword, so sharp, gleaming so bright,
   that I, though on the other bank, felt fear.   *141*

Then I saw coming four of humble mien,
   and, last of all, an old man, by himself,
   who moved in his own dream, his face inspired.   *144*

And these last seven, just like the group up front,
   were clad in white, except the wreaths that crowned
   their heads were not entwined with lily blooms,   *147*

but roses and other flowers that are red.
   Had I been farther off, I would have sworn
   a crown of flames encircled every head.   *150*

And when the chariot was opposite me,
   thunder was heard! The exalted creatures, then,
   as though forbidden to move on, stopped short,   *153*

as did the flaming ensigns at the front.

NOTES

3. *Beati quorum tècta sunt peccata:* Matelda is quoting an abbreviated version of Psalm 32:1: "Beati quorum remissae sunt iniquitates, et quorum tecta sunt peccata" ("Happy are they whose faults are taken away, whose sins are covered.") This abbreviation is due, no doubt, to the fact that Matelda is now

thinking particularly of the ritual of the river Lethe, which should "cover" the Pilgrim's sins in his memory.

4. *And like those nymphs:* It is curious that the solitary lady Matelda is compared to a group of nymphs skipping in or out of the shade. This group, which has contrary interests, must be intended to throw some light on Matelda's mood or temperament. But the parallel is not too clear.

15. *look and listen:* These words serve to introduce the procession. The allegory of the Earthly Paradise is not introduced by an Address to the Reader (cf. *Inf.* IX and *Purg.* VIII). Here the approach is direct as well as dramatic.

16. *a burst of incandescence:* The Pilgrim not only sees a burst of light but hears a gentle melody (23). The light must come from the seven candlesticks that he will see later (50). The melody comes from the singers in the procession, as yet unseen, whose words he will come to recognize as "Hosanna" (51).

26. *a single woman:* I have translated the *femmina sola* of the Italian to emphasize the contrast between this single figure and the worldwide havoc she wrought. It has been suggested, however, that the *sola* puts into relief Eve's responsibility: she does not have the excuse of having received evil counsel from another human being.

29–30. *I could . . . / have feasted:* It may strike the reader as strange that the Pilgrim, in imagining what would have been, had Eve remained obedient, thinks in terms not of the welfare of the human race but of his own pleasure. Of course, it could be said that the Pilgrim represents mankind.

37. *Most holy Virgins:* Dante the Poet is invoking the pagan Muses (here Christianized by the use of the term "holy Virgins"), imploring their aid because of the great difficulty of the task that he will begin to perform in verse 43: the description of the procession seen by his Pilgrim. To the reader who strives to follow this description, the Poet's need for help should be understandable.

40. *Helicon:* The mountain range of Boetia, sacred to Apollo and the Muses, where Aganippe and Hippocrene, the fountains of the Muses, were located.

41. *Urania:* The Muse of Astronomy and, hence, of heavenly things. Compare Dante's earlier invocation of Calliope, the Muse of Epic Poetry, at the beginning of the *Purgatory* (I, 9–12).

43–150

In this section the procession begins to come into view. The first elements are seven golden candlesticks, their flames burning brightly, which the Pilgrim had first mistaken for seven trees of gold. They are followed (and they can actually be followed since they are in movement) by twenty-four elders wearing crowns of fleur-de-lis. Then come four "creatures" with six wings, wearing crowns of green; they form a frame enclosing a splendid chariot drawn by a griffin. To the right of the chariot are three ladies dancing in a circle; to the left, also dancing, are four others. Last of all come seven men: two, then four, then one alone. To the members of this company will be added, as they continue to move forward, a group of one hundred angels, and finally, Beatrice herself. The cortège as described up to this point is best taken to symbolize the history of Christianity, including its roots as contained in the Old Testament. Later events will suggest the growth of the church up to the time of Dante.

The symbolic significance of this company is as follows:

The seven candlesticks represent the seven gifts of the Holy Spirit: Wisdom, Understanding, Counsel, Might, Knowledge, Piety, and Fear of the Lord.

The twenty-four elders stand for the books of the Old Testament, as counted by Saint Jerome.

The four creatures symbolize the four Gospels; four beasts with six wings are to be found in the Apocalypse of St. John and had been long accepted as representing the four evangelists.

The chariot represents the church. Literally, the griffin is a mythical beast who is part eagle and part lion. Here, his dual nature is symbolic of the two natures of Christ, who was both human and divine.

The three ladies dancing to the right of the chariot are the theological virtues: Faith, Hope, and Charity; the four to the left, the cardinal virtues: Prudence, Justice, Fortitude, and Temperance.

The seven men who follow the chariot are the rest of the books of the New Testament. The first is the Book of Acts,

written by "the beloved Physician Luke," the second, the Epistles of St. Paul, who was often pictured with a sword in hand.
The four of humble mien are the minor Epistles, those of Peter, John, James, and Jude. The last figure represents the
Apocalypse of St. John.

49. *that power which feeds the process of our thought:* This is
the power of discernment. It is the subject of the verb "heard"
in verse 51.

50. *identified the shapes as candlesticks:* According to some
critics, what the Pilgrim saw was not seven candlesticks but a
candelabrum with seven branches.

57. *no less amazement than I felt:* The erstwhile pupil turns to
his erstwhile teacher, but Virgil has reached the point he mentioned at the end of Canto XXVII and can no longer satisfy the
Pilgrim's ignorance.

59. *moving toward us as though they did not move:* Only now
does the Pilgrim realize that the candlesticks have been slowly
moving toward him, proceeding on their own momentum.

61. *Why are you so intent:* Matelda, knowing what is behind
the candlesticks, is a little impatient with the Pilgrim for con-
centrating his attention on the first things to appear. But the
brilliant description of the sky lit up by the candles' flames
(52–54) would seem to justify the Pilgrim's fascination.
Moreover, he has just perceived, surely to his amazement, that
the golden objects are moving.

78. *as Delia's cincture or Apollo's bow:* Delia is Diana (born on
the isle of Delos), and her cincture is the lunar halo. Apollo's
bow is the rainbow.

81. *they measured, side by side, a good ten strides:* That ten is a
perfect number in Christian numerology is reason enough for
Dante to have chosen this figure in his measurement. Some,
however, have preferred to particularize, finding here a symbol
of the Ten Commandments.

84. *crowns of fleur-de-lis:* The garlands of the elders represent
the lily of purity, which accords with the supernatural whiteness of their garments (66).

85. *"Benedicta* thou": It is to the Virgin that this blessing is offered, and it is most significant that it is uttered by the representatives of the Old Testament—a witness to the prophetic nature of those Scriptures. See Luke 1:28.

88. *When once the group of God's elect had passed*: This group representing the books of the Old Testament will be followed by the four creatures representing the four Gospels. There is considerable space intervening between the two groups, this spatial break corresponding to the temporal break between the Old and the New Testaments.

95. *Argus*: The son of Arestor (according to one account), who had a hundred eyes. Jove fell in love with Io; Juno, jealous of her husband, turned Io into a cow and summoned Argus to keep an eye on her. In retaliation, Jove summoned Mercury, who descended to earth and, having lulled Argus to sleep, cut off his head. Juno fixed Argus's eyes in the tail of the peacock, her favorite bird. See Ovid, *Metam.* I, 622–723.

97. *I cannot spend more verses now*: If Dante is so eager to go on with his description, the reader may wonder why he delays as he does for three tercets (97–105). He had no need to justify his procedure (97–99), and the following two tercets give us no new information about the four creatures. Perhaps, since the creatures of St. John had always been identified with the cherubim of Ezekiel, Dante is simply taking the opportunity to stress the homogeneity of the Old and New Testaments, a theme most essential to this canto and symbolized in the composition of the procession.

105. *Saint John agrees with me and not with him*: The four six-winged beasts of the Apocalypse of St. John have been identified with the four four-winged cherubim in Ezekiel. As for the "agreement" between Dante and St. John's account in Revelations, everyone takes it for granted that only the number of wings is involved, and this is probably all that concerns the poet at this point. But his words are inaccurate: the four creatures in the procession have their six wings covered with eyes, and there is no suggestion of this feature with St. John. A similar lack of precision occurs in verse 103: we are given to understand that, apart from their wings, the creatures seen by the Pilgrim look the same as those that appeared to Ezekiel. But the cherubim of Ezekiel had four faces each. If this were true

of the creatures in the procession, surely Dante would have said so.

113–14. *the parts of him that were a bird were gold:* That the "bird" parts of the griffin which represent his divine nature, should be of incorruptible gold is understandable; less obvious is the choice of white mixed with red for the "lion" part, which signifies his human nature. Sayers offers three possibilities: "White and red are the colors which Dante assigns to the Old and New Testaments respectively; so that here again he emphasizes the meeting of the two Dispensations in the Incarnation. They are also the colors of righteousness and love. But they are most especially the colors of the Sacrament itself—the Flesh and the Blood, the bread and the wine" (p. 305). By saying that Dante assigns the colors of red and white to the Old and New Testaments respectively, Sayers is evidently thinking of the white garlands of the twenty-four elders (83) and the red garlands of the final group of seven (145–48).

115. *Africanus*: Scipio the Younger (Publius Cornelius Scipio Aemilianus Africanus Numantinus), the son of Scipio Africanus the Elder, who defeated Hannibal, was born ca. 185 B.C. and died 129 B.C. He was honored with a triumph at Rome following his conquest of Carthage.

Augustus: He was the first Roman emperor (63 B.C.–A.D. 14). His real name was Gaius Octavius (see *Purg.* VII, 6); Augustus was a title of veneration conferred upon him by the people and senate of Rome.

118. *that of the Sun which strayed*: The reference is to Phaëton's tragic attempt to drive the chariot of the sun, referred to earlier in *Purg.* IV, 71–72, and in *Inf.* XVII, 107. Apollo allowed his son Phaëton, at the latter's insistence, to guide the horses. Phaëton, however, was too weak and lost control; the chariot went off course, scorching the sky and nearly setting the earth on fire. Jupiter, however, intervened in answer to the earth's prayer and struck Phaëton down with a thunderbolt. In his epistle to the Italian cardinals (*Epist.* VIII), Dante accuses them of being modern-day Phaëtons who are negligent in guiding the church.

122. *and one was red, so red*: Of the three colors represented by the three ladies, red is the sign of Charity, green of Hope, and white of Faith. There is surely a hierarchical distinction

intended in the fact that Hope, unlike the other two, does not lead the dance (127–29).

130–31. *Beside the left wheel*: The left side is a lesser position than the right—which is to give more importance to the ladies dancing near the right wheel (121), representing the three theological virtues, than to these four ladies "dancing festively" to the left, who represent the four moral or cardinal virtues: Prudence, Temperance, Justice and Fortitude. These natural virtues are essential to the happiness or blessedness of this life, for they are the ones that govern or regulate human conduct. And because they are the basis of imperial authority, without which there can be no Earthly Paradise, these four ladies are dressed in purple, the color of Empire.

Since the basic ingredient of purple is red, this color, then, can also been seen as symbolic of love. Landino states: "He presents these dressed in purple to denote charity and the fervour of love, without which no one can have these virtues." According to Aquinas (*Summa theol*. I-II, q. 65, a. 2, 3; II-II, q. 23, a. 7), the moral virtues cannot exist without charity when "a supernatural last end" is the goal. For such a goal, charity is essential. For further discussion, see Moore (1903), pp. 184–86.

132. *led by one with three eyes in her head*: The leading lady among the four cardinal virtues is Prudence, whose function is to apply the restraints of reason to all aspects of our earthly life. Her three eyes indicate her ability to see the past, present, and future. Prudence, according to Dante (*Conv*. IV, xxvii, 5), means "a good memory of things formerly seen, and good knowledge of things present, and good foresight of things to come."

136. *One wore the garments*: The reference is to Luke, the physician of the soul, and author of Acts (see Col. 4:14, where he is described as "the beloved physician"). Hippocrates, the most famous doctor of the ancients, is placed by Dante among the souls in Limbo (*Inf*. IV, 143).

139. *the other:* The old man with the sharp, gleaming sword represents the various Epistles of St. Paul. Paul himself was often artistically represented with a sword, which symbolized the word of God, the word of his Epistles.

142. *four of humble mien:* These represent the minor Epistles of James, Peter, John, and Jude.

144. *who moved in his own dream, his face inspired:* This line is a reminder of John's vision, his dream, which inspired him to write Revelations—a book so different from the others of the New Testament that it is most fitting that this figure be presented as moving alone.

145–46. *And these last seven, just like the group up front:* The figures representing the New Testament are dressed in garments the same color as those representing the Old Testament because of the overall homogeneity of the two divisions of the Bible. But the wreaths the former wear are not white but red—the color of the first of the three theological virtues: Charity. See Singleton (1973), p. 725.

152. *thunder was heard!:* The main action of the journey stops with this peal of supernatural thunder, and the procession of revealed truth comes to a dramatic halt before the Pilgrim's eyes. The thunder announces the beginning of a process of clarification of things seen, the unveiling of Revelation.

CANTO XXX

As the procession comes to a halt, the twenty-four elders turn to face the chariot. One of them sings, "Come, O bride, from Lebanon." One hundred singing angels appear in the sky overhead; they fill the air with a rain of flowers. Through the flowers, Beatrice appears. The Pilgrim turns to Virgil to confess his overpowering emotions, only to find that Virgil has disappeared! Beatrice speaks sternly to Dante, calling him by name and reprimanding him for having wasted his God-given talents, wandering from the path that leads to Truth. So hopeless, in fact, was his case, to such depths did he sink, that the journey to see the souls of the Damned in Hell was the only way left of setting him back on the road to salvation.

When the Septentrion of the First Heaven
   (which never sets nor rises nor has known
   any cloud other than the veil of sin),   3

which showed to everyone his duty there
   (just as our lower constellation guides
   the helmsman on his way to port on earth),   6

stopped short, that group of prophets of the truth
   who were between the griffin and those lights
   turned to the car as to their source of peace;   9

then, one of them, as sent from Heaven, sang
   Veni, sponsa, de Libano, three times,
   and all the other voices followed his.   12

As at the Final Summons all the blest
   will rise out of their graves, ready to raise
   new-bodied voices singing 'Hallelujah!'   15

just so rose up above the heavenly cart
   a hundred spirits *ad vocem tanti senis,*
   eternal heralds, ministers of God,   18

all shouting: *Benedictus qui venis!* then,
   tossing a rain of flowers in the air,
   Manibus, O, date lilia plenis!   21

Sometimes, as day approaches, I have seen
   all of the eastern sky a glow of rose,
   the rest of heaven beautifully clear,   24

the sun's face rising in a misty veil
   of tempering vapors that allow the eye
   to look straight at it for a longer time: 27

even so, within a nebula of flowers
   that flowed upward from angels' hands and then
   poured down, covering all the chariot,   30

appeared a lady—over her white veil
   an olive crown and, under her green cloak,
   her gown, the color of eternal flame.   33

And instantly—though many years had passed
   since last I stood trembling before her eyes,
   captured by adoration, stunned by awe—   36

my soul, that could not see her perfectly,
   still felt, succumbing to her mystery
   and power, the strength of its enduring love.   39

No sooner were my eyes struck by the force
   of the high, piercing virtue I had known
   before I quit my boyhood years, than I   42

turned to the left—with all the confidence
   that makes a child run to its mother's arms,
   when he is frightened or needs comforting—   45

to say to Virgil: "Not one drop of blood
   is left inside my veins that does not throb:
   I recognize signs of the ancient flame."   48

But Virgil was not there. We found ourselves
   without Virgil, sweet father, Virgil to whom
   for my salvation I gave up my soul.   51

All the delights around me, which were lost
   by our first mother, could not keep my cheeks,
   once washed with dew, from being stained with tears.   54

"Dante, though Virgil leaves you, do not weep,
   not yet, that is, for you shall have to weep
   from yet another wound. Do not weep yet."   57

322 / CANTO XXX

Just as an admiral, from bow or stern,
　　watches his men at work on other ships,
　　encouraging their earnest labors—so,   60

rising above the chariot's left rail
　　(when I turned round, hearing my name called out,
　　which of necessity I here record),   63

I saw the lady who had first appeared
　　beneath the angelic festival of flowers
　　gazing upon me from beyond the stream.   66

Although the veil that flowed down from her head,
　　fixed by the crown made of Minerva's leaves,
　　still kept me from a perfect view of her,   69

I sensed the regal sternness of her face,
　　as she continued in the tone of one
　　who saves the sharpest words until the end: 72

"Yes, look at me! Yes, I am Beatrice!
　　So, you at last have deigned to climb the mount?
　　You learned at last that here lies human bliss?"   75

I lowered my head and looked down at the stream,
　　but, filled with shame at my reflection there,
　　I quickly fixed my eyes upon the grass.   78

I was the guilty child facing his mother,
　　abject before her harshness: harsh, indeed,
　　is unripe pity not yet merciful.   81

As she stopped speaking, all the angels rushed
　　into the psalm *In te, Domine, speravi,*
　　but did not sing beyond *pedes meos.*   84

As snow upon the spine of Italy,
　　frozen among the living rafters there,
　　blown and packed hard by wintry northeast winds,   87

will then dissolve, dripping into itself,
ꞏ　when, from the land that knows no noonday shade,
　　there comes a wind like flame melting down wax;   90

so tears and sighs were frozen hard in me,
　　until I heard the song of those attuned
　　forever to the music of the spheres;   93

but when I sensed in their sweet notes the pity
    they felt for me (it was as if they said:
    "Lady, why do you shame him so?"), the bonds   *96*

of ice packed tight around my heart dissolved,
    becoming breath and water: from my breast,
    through mouth and eyes, anguish came pouring forth.   *99*

Still on the same side of the chariot
    she stood immobile; then she turned her words
    to that compassionate array of beings: *102*

"With your eyes fixed on the eternal day,
    darkness of night or sleep cannot conceal
    from you a single act performed on earth;   *105*

and though I speak to you, my purpose is
    to make the one who weeps on that far bank
    perceive the truth and match his guilt with grief.   *108*

Not only through the working of the spheres,
    which brings each seed to its appropriate end
    according as the stars keep company,   *111*

but also through the bounty of God's grace,
    raining from vapors born so high above
    they cannot be discerned by human sight,   *114*

was this man so endowed, potentially,
    in early youth—had he allowed his gifts
    to bloom, he would have reaped abundantly.   *117*

But the more vigorous and rich the soil,
    the wilder and the weedier it grows
    when left untilled, its bad seeds flourishing.   *120*

There was a time my countenance sufficed,
    as I let him look into my young eyes
    for guidance on the straight path to his goal;   *123*

but when I passed into my second age
    and changed my life for Life, that man you see
    strayed after others and abandoned me;   *126*

when I had risen from the flesh to spirit,
    become more beautiful, more virtuous,
    he found less pleasure in me, loved me less,   *129*

and wandered from the path that leads to truth,
    pursuing simulacra of the good,
    which promise more than they can ever give.   *132*

I prayed that inspiration come to him
    through dreams and other means: in vain I tried
    to call him back, so little did he care.   *135*

To such depths did he sink that, finally,
    there was no other way to save his soul
    except to have him see the Damned in Hell.   *138*

That this might be, I visited the Dead,
    and offered my petition and my tears
    to him who until now has been his guide.   *141*

The highest laws of God would be annulled
    if he crossed Lethe, drinking its sweet flow,
    without having to pay at least some scot   *144*

of penitence poured forth in guilty tears."

NOTES

1. *When the Septentrion of the First Heaven:* The constellation
sometimes called Septentrion is probably the Little Dipper
(Ursa Minor), which contains seven stars, including the North
Star. Thus, the "Septentrion of the First Heaven" (the Empyrean) must be the seven blazing candlesticks that direct the
procession.

11. *Veni, sponsa, de Libano:* "Come, bride, from Lebanon" is
taken from the Song of Songs (Cant. 4:8), where the bride is
interpreted as the soul wedded to Christ. Here the song has to
do with the advent of Beatrice, one of whose allegorical meanings is Sapientia, or the wisdom of God.

17. *ad vocem tanti senis:* "At the voice of so great an elder."

19. *Benedictus qui venis:* "Blessed are Thou that comest" is a
slightly modified version of Matt. 21:9, *Benedictus qui venit,*
"Blessed is He who cometh." Note that while Dante felt free to
shift from the third to the second person in quoting this line,
he left intact *Benedictus,* with its masculine form. In this way the
word, though applied to Beatrice, who is about to appear, re-
tains its original reference to Christ.

21. *Manibus, O, date lilia plenis:* "O give us lilies with full hands." This quotation from the *Aeneid:* (VI, 883) is surely intended as high tribute to Virgil, the Pilgrim's guide, since his words are placed on the same level as verses from the Bible. If Virgil has not yet disappeared from the scene, as he will have done by verse 49, this passage may be taken as a most gracious farewell to the great Roman poet.

31–33. *appeared a lady:* The lady is Beatrice, and the colors she wears are those of the three theological virtues: Faith, Hope, and Charity.

35. *since last I stood trembling before her eyes:* A number of times we are told in the *Vita nuova* of the spell that Beatrice would cast on the young, enamored Dante, who was always unnerved by her presence and would often faint.

48. *I recognize signs of the ancient flame:* As we come closer to the final disappearance of Virgil from the poem, Dante, as a farewell gesture to his mentor, again reminds his reader of a verse of Virgil's: *Adgnosco veteris vestigia flammae* (*Aen.* IV, 23). The words are spoken by Dido of her passion for Aeneas, which she had thought no longer existed. And with this verse Virgil is gone from the poem.

54. *once washed with dew*: In the opening canto of the *Purgatory*, Virgil, at the suggestion of Cato, had washed his ward's cheeks with dew to cleanse them from any traces of the mists of Hell. This was an act symbolizing purgation (see *Purg.* I, 124–29).

55. *Dante, though Virgil leaves you*: This is the first time that the Pilgrim hears his own name during his journey. Most critics believe that Beatrice is naming him to his shame. It has been suggested, however, that the naming of the Pilgrim has a lofty, solemn significance suggesting a second baptism. Given the context that follows, such an interpretation does not seem likely.

57. *from yet another wound*: The "wound" will be that caused by the harsh words of Beatrice.

58. *Just as an admiral*: Earlier the masculine form *Benedictus* had been applied to Beatrice; here she is compared to a male figure. Porena points out that in the simile "Beatrice—admiral"

there is only one detail in common: a person whose upper body is seen rising above some kind of railing.

61. *above the chariot's left rail*: Beatrice is not in the center of the chariot but on the side nearest the Pilgrim.

63. *which of necessity I here record*: At first glance these words would merely seem to be Dante's apology for recording his own name in what he has written: it was made necessary by his concern for truth, accuracy, and precision in his narrative. But he means more than this. When the poet records his own name in verse 55 by having Beatrice call him in stern fashion— "Dante"—he is telling his reader at this point to shift his perspective: Dante the Pilgrim, until now Everyman, must here be seen as the individual who represents only himself at this point, as he is about to answer to a number of personal charges and make a very personal and painful confession to his lover.

73. *Yes, look at me! Yes, I am Beatrice!*: After having named the young Dante, Beatrice names herself, and surely in the same cutting tone. She is saying, as it were, "Yes, I am that Beatrice that you abandoned; you have still to know what I, Beatrice, represent!"

What I have translated as "look at me!" is in the original *guardaci ben*, in which I have taken the *ci* to mean "here." It could, of course, represent the first person plural, being the plural of majesty. In that case, the rest of the line, *ben son . . . Beatrice*, must be changed to *ben sem*. To me the mixture of sarcasm with the plural of majesty is hardly appropriate.

74. *So, you at last have deigned to climb the mount?*: These sarcastic words of Beatrice are not meant to be taken literally. She is reproaching the Pilgrim for his slowness in learning what constitutes true human bliss.

83–84. *In te, Domine, speravi*: The angels are singing the first part of the thirty-first psalm, which begins, "In The, O lord, have I put my trust." They continue through verse 8 (*pedes meos*), "Thou hast set my feet in a spacious place"— which is precisely the place where the Pilgrim is standing at this moment.

85–99

In this canto the range and intensity of the Pilgrim's emotions are put into relief to a degree unparalleled in the *Divine Comedy*. The most poignant stage is surely that when the Pilgrim bursts into tears. To describe this occasion, the poet devotes five tercets to a simile that likens the contrast between his feelings at that moment and those just preceding to the contrast between the climates of northern Europe and Africa.

85–86. *As snow upon the spine of Italy*: This is a reference to the Appenines. The "living rafters" are the pine trees.

89. *the land that knows no noonday shade*: Equatorial Africa, where the sun is often directly overhead, sending its rays straight down so that objects cast no shadow.

106. *and though I speak to you*: The reader may wonder why Beatrice expresses her grievances to the angels instead of addressing the Pilgrim directly. Perhaps her doing so would more effectively check their over-ready pity. Then, too, the distraught state of the Pilgrim would make such a direct address inappropriate.

126. *strayed after others and abandoned me*: So far Beatrice has spoken only of the excellence of the Pilgrim's natural gifts, suggesting simply that he had not put them to the best use. Now she becomes slightly more specific: after her death he became unfaithful to her. The only example recorded in the *Vita nuova* of unfaithfulness on Dante's part is his brief infatuation with the Lady at the Window, by whose compassion he allowed himself to be too easily consoled (*Vita nuova*, XXXV), but having had a vision of the child Beatrice when he first saw her (XXXIX), he repents deeply and vows to write a book in which he will speak of Beatrice as no other woman had been spoken of before (XLII). It is hardly conceivable that Beatrice is here reproaching the Pilgrim for an action for which the Pilgrim has sincerely repented. Rather, she is attacking him for the weaknesses of which he has not yet fully repented. Perhaps the pronoun *altrui* (which I translate as "others") should be taken not as a reference to a human individual (or individuals) but as a personification of the deceptive images of good that he was tempted to follow. After all, the individual Beatrice is presenting herself here to the Pilgrim primarily as a symbol of certain virtues and forces; particularly, perhaps, she represents Revelation.

136. *To such depths did he sink*: As she approaches the end of her address, Beatrice makes it clear that she believes that the

young Dante had reached a stage of utter degeneration. But she still refuses to state explicitly the nature of his sin. She accuses her lover of none of the Seven Deadly Sins; she mentions only his confusion after her death, which induced him to lower his standards. Beatrice's words are a demonstration of a general truth, of which her lover offers the perfect exemplum. "Imagine," she is saying, "a young man endowed by God with unique gifts and privileged to have as guide one who represents the goal of the Supreme Good. But he loses this guidance and abandons this goal. His must become not only a worthless life but a destructive one: destructive of the gifts with which he had been endowed." This abuse of his talent can lead only to degradation.

We have seen the range of emotions experienced by the Pilgrim in this canto: his grief over the loss of Virgil, his fascination by the beauty and power of Beatrice once she reveals herself, the bittersweet surge of adoration for a beloved being he has lost, his shame and timidity, the writhings of an inarticulate contrition, and, finally, the relief, induced by the angels' pity, which takes the form of a torrent of anguished tears. It is this individual—whose feelings, caused by the exceptional circumstances in which he finds himself, have been presented so vividly—that Beatrice addresses in such impersonal terms. Beatrice can be stern in her judgment because she is engaged in a demonstration of a supreme truth; she is interested in Dante not as a suffering individual but as a means to an end: his past conduct is evidence that proves the truth of her words. Or if, at the very end, she reveals her awareness of the Pilgrim's suffering, she also reveals her satisfaction over his punishment, which means that he has not been allowed to break "the highest laws of God." There is no room for a note of pity in her peroration.

CANTO XXXI

BEATRICE CONTINUES TO upbraid Dante, who, nearly incapable of speech, weeping and sighing, finally confesses his guilt; then, overcome by remorse, he faints. Upon regaining consciousness he discovers that Matelda has drawn him into the stream of Lethe up to his neck. She carries him across and dips his head beneath the surface that he might drink of the waters. Then she leads him, now pure, into the dance of the four lovely maidens who flank Beatrice's chariot. They bring him in turn to Beatrice, and as he stares into her eyes, he sees the reflection of the griffin, manifested now in its one nature, now in the other. Finally the other three attendant ladies induce Beatrice to unveil her mouth to her "faithful one."

"You, standing there, beyond the sacred stream,"
  she cried, not pausing in her eloquence
  and turning now the sword point of her words   3

toward me, who had already felt its blade,
  "speak now, is this not true? Speak! You must seal
  with your confession this grave charge I make!"   6

I stood before her paralyzed, confused;
  I moved my lips, my throat striving to speak,
  but not a single breath of speech escaped.   9

She hardly paused: "What are you thinking of?
  Answer me, now! Your bitter memories
  have not as yet been purged within this stream."   12

My fear and deep chagrin, between them, forced
  out of my mouth a miserable "yes" —
  only by ears with eyes could it be heard.   15

A crossbow, drawn with too much tension, snaps,
  bowstring and bow together, and the shaft
  will strike the target with diminished force;   18

so I was shattered by the intensity
  of my emotions: tears and sighs burst forth,
  as I released my voice about to fail.   21

She: "In your journey of desire for me,
    leading you toward that Good beyond which naught
    exists to which a man's heart may aspire,   24

what pitfalls did you find, what chains stretched out
    across your path, that you felt you were forced
    to abandon every hope of going on?   27

And what appealed to you, what did you find
    so promising in all those other things
    that made you feel obliged to spend your time   30

in courting them?" I heaved a bitter sigh,
    and barely found the voice to answer her;
    my lips, with difficulty, shaped the words.   33

Weeping, I said: "Those things with their false joys,
    offered me by the world, led me astray
    when I no longer saw your countenance."   36

And she: "Had you kept silent or denied
    what you have just confessed, your guilt would still
    be clear to the great Judge who knows all things.   39

But when the condemnation of his sin
    bursts from the sinner's lips, here in our Court,
    the grindstone is turned back against the blade.   42

Still, so that you may truly feel the shame
    of all your sins—so that, another time,
    you will be stronger when the Sirens sing—   45

master your feelings, listen to my words,
    and you shall learn just how my buried flesh
    was meant to guide you in another way.   48

You never saw in Nature or in Art
    a beauty like the beauty of my form,
    which clothed me once and now is turned to dust;   51

and if that perfect beauty disappeared
    when I departed from the world, how could
    another mortal object lure your love?   54

When you first felt deception's arrow sting,
    you should have rushed to rise and follow me,
    as soon as I lost my deceptive flesh.   57

No pretty girl or any other brief
    attraction should have weighed down your wings,
    and left you waiting for another blow.   60

The fledgling waits a second time, a third,
    but not the full-fledged bird: before his eyes
    in vain the net is spread, the arrow shot."   63

As children scolded into silence stand
    ashamed, with head bowed staring at the ground,
    acknowledging their fault and penitent—   66

so I stood there. Then she: "If listening
    can cause you so much grief, now raise your beard
    and look at me and suffer greater grief."   69

With less resistance is the sturdy oak
    uprooted by the winds of storms at home
    in Europe or by those that Iarbas blows,   72

than my soul offered to her curt command
    that I look up at her: she called my face
    my "beard"! I felt the venom in her words.   75

And when I raised my head, I did not look
    at her, but at those first-created ones:
    they had already ceased their rain of flowers.   78

Then when I turned my unsure eyes once more,
    I saw that Beatrice faced the beast
    who in two natures is one single being.   81

Though she was veiled and on the other shore,
    lovelier now, she seemed, than when alive
    on earth, when she was loveliest of all.   84

I felt the stabbing pain of my remorse:
    what I had loved the most of all the things
    that were not she, I hated now the most.   87

The recognition of my guilt so stunned
    my heart, I fainted. What happened then is known
    only to her who was the cause of it.   90

When I revived, that lady I first saw
    strolling alone was now bent over me,
    saying: "Hold on to me, hold tight." She had   93

led me into the stream up to my neck;
  now drawing me along she glided light,
  and with a shuttle's ease, across the stream.   96

Before I reached the sacred bank I heard
  Asperges me — so sweetly sung, my mind
  cannot recall, far less my words retell.   99

The lovely lady, opening her arms,
  embraced my head and dipped it in the stream
  just deep enough to let me drink of it.   102

She took me from those waters, cleansed, and led
  me to the dance of the four lovely ones,
  who raised their arms to join hands over me.   105

"Here we are nymphs and in the heavens, stars;
  before Beatrice came into the world
  we were ordained her handmaids. It is for us   108

to lead you to her eyes. The other three,
  who see more deeply, will instruct your sight,
  as you bathe in her gaze of joyful light,"   111

they sang to me; then they accompanied me
  up to the griffin's breast, while Beatrice
  now faced us from the center of the cart.   114

"Look deeply, look with all your sight," they said,
  "for now you stand before those emeralds
  from which Love once shot loving darts at you."   117

A thousand yearning flames of my desire
  held my eyes fixed upon those brilliant eyes
  that held the griffin fixed within their range.   120

Like sunlight in a mirror, shining back,
  I saw the twofold creature in her eyes,
  reflecting its two natures, separately.   123

Imagine, reader, how amazed I was
  to see the creature standing there unchanged,
  yet, in its image, changing constantly,   126

And while my soul, delighted and amazed,
  was tasting of that food which satisfies
  and, at the same time, makes one hungrier,   129

the other three, revealing in their mien
    their more exalted rank, came dancing forth
    accompanied by angelic melody.   *132*

"Turn, Beatrice, turn your sacred eyes,"
    they sang, "and look upon your faithful one
    who came so very far to look at you!   *135*

Of your own grace grant us this grace: unveil
    your mouth for him, allow him to behold
    that second beauty which you hide from him."   *138*

O splendor of the eternal living light!
    Who, having drunk at the Parnassian well,
    or become pale within that mountain's shade,   *141*

could find with all of his poetic gifts
    those words that might describe the way you looked,
    with that harmonious heaven your only veil,   *144*

when you unveiled yourself to me at last?

NOTES

1. *"You, standing there, beyond the sacred stream:* Beatrice, who
had been patient with the angels (XXX, 103–46), changes her
tone when she addresses Dante. Perhaps because he stands on
the opposite bank of Lethe ("beyond the sacred stream"), and
so, as we will see, is still fully conscious of his sins, Beatrice
takes this opportunity to indict him mercilessly and to demand
a confession. We are reminded of the Beatrice of the *Vita
nuova,* not an allegorical figure but a woman whose love has
been betrayed. Hence, she confronts Dante, the lover, on a
personal level.

That Lethe here is called "sacred stream" reminds us that we
are witnessing a sacramental act of penance in this confrontation and in the Pilgrim's subsequent confession, forgiveness,
and absolution.

3. *turning now the sword point of her words:* Recalling from
the previous canto the metaphor of the wound, "you shall have
to weep from yet another wound" (XXX, 56–57), the poet
now envisions Beatrice's words as a sword. When she listed the
Pilgrim's transgressions, her accusations were indirect: she was

literally addressing the angels. The Pilgrim was "wounded" only with the "blade." Now, addressing him directly, she has turned the "sword point" on him.

7. *I stood before her:* Like the young lover-protagonist of the *Vita nuova,* the Pilgrim is "paralyzed, confused," and appears incapable of completing the necessary steps in the act of penance. (Cf. note to XXVIII, 70.) We know that he has taken the first step *(contritio cordis),* that he is truly sorry for his sins, for his "anguish came pouring forth" (XXX, 99) almost immediately upon seeing Beatrice. But he must also "confess" his sins *(confessio oris)* in order to be forgiven.

10. *"What are you thinking of?":* This question, along with the next two verses, emphasizes Beatrice's continued sternness in the face of the confused Pilgrim. Once before on the journey Dante stood with his head bowed, unable to speak. It was in the circle of the Lustful, Circle Two of Hell, right after he had heard Francesca's eloquent story of her fated love for Paolo, and at that point it was Virgil who asked, "What are you thinking of?" *(Inf.* V, 111). The contrasting mood is important here: Francesca's romantic tale was deceptive; in telling it she used her eloquence wrongly, and the Pilgrim's response was inappropriate. Here, the Pilgrim faces the righteous eloquence of a woman whose love he has wronged.

12. *within this stream:* As we will soon see, the waters of Lethe wash away the memory of sin (on the emotional plane—see note to XXVIII, 128).

14. *a miserable "yes":* Dante, not as Everyman, but rather like the young lover-protagonist of the *Vita nuova,* begins his confession with the weak sound of one word: "yes." His actual confession occupies one tercet: verses 34–36.

16–21. *A crossbow, drawn with too much tension, snaps:* Here the poet has chosen to visualize the Pilgrim's progression from *contritio cordis* to *confessio oris* as a crossbow and string snapping under too much tension. This image is essentially one of "breaking" and so recalls the "melting" or "breaking up" of the snow in the preceding canto (XXX, 85–90) and anticipates the image of the "uprooted" tree later in this canto (70–72). "Breaking" is the literal meaning of *"contritio"* (cf. Thomas Aquinas, *Summa theol.* III, suppl. of 1a. 1, resp.: "Now he that persists in his own judgment, he is called metaphorically rigid and hard even as what in material things is called hard is that which does not yield to the touch: wherefore anyone is said to be broken when he is torn from his own judgment"). When he actually does confess, the Pilgrim's words are barely audible, said with a "voice about to fail" (21). Thus his words correspond to the "shaft" that strikes its target "with diminished force" (18). See Singleton (1973), p. 759.

23. *that Good:* God.

36. *your countenance:* The Italian reads "vostro viso." Dante will always use the honorific plural *vostro* when addressing his lady Beatrice, though she continues to address him with the familiar *tu* form.

41. *here in our Court:* This is a reference to both the heavenly court, where Beatrice and the angels dwell in the presence of God, and the divine tribunal, before which every man will one day be judged.

42. *the grindstone is turned back against the blade:* Again we have the image of the sword wound (cf. **XXXI**, 3–4 and **XXX**, 56–57). Here the grindstone symbolizes mercy as it is "turned back against" or used to blunt the blade of the sword of justice. In the heavenly court, when a sinner openly confesses, God's justice is tempered with mercy. In earthly courts, confession often has very different results.

45. *the Sirens:* Beatrice refers here to those attractions of the world which give false pleasure and recalls that Siren who appears to the Pilgrim in his second dream on the mountain (**XIX**, 19–24), the same one who turned Ulysses from his true course.

46. *listen to my words:* The Italian reads, "pon giù il seme del pianger, ed ascolta" ("put down the seeds of crying and listen"). Now that the Pilgrim has cried properly, he may stop and listen. The injunction is, of course, to listen not to the Sirens, to the lures of false goods, but to the words of Beatrice, bearing the eloquence of Heaven.

55. *When you first felt deception's arrow sting:* The argument here is that Dante should have realized from Beatrice's death that all mortal joys must be deceptive, because transitory, and

therefore unsatisfying. His response should have been to follow Beatrice, no longer mortal, to the source of permanent and true joy in Heaven.

58. *No pretty girl:* The Italian text reads *pargoletta;* the diminutive suffix stresses youth and connects the pretty girl with the young, inexperienced "fledgling" *(augelletto)* of verse 61. Taken together, they begin the emphasis on the immaturity of vision that Dante had displayed after the death of Beatrice. The Pilgrim will soon be even more painfully reminded of his immaturity, when Beatrice refers sarcastically to his beard (75).

The "pretty girl" also refers back to Beatrice's charge that soon after her death, Dante "strayed after others" (XXX, 126). Some scholars have read Dante's attraction to the "pretty girl" as a brief moral lapse, a yielding to the "false pleasure of present things." Others prefer an allegorical interpretation: Dante's lapse was an intellectual one; he was for a time after Beatrice's death attracted to Philosophy, neglecting the Divine Revelation that Beatrice represented.

61. *The fledgling waits a second time, a third:* In the Italian *augelletto,* the diminutive suffix emphasizes the youthfulness and lack of experience of the fledgling. Beatrice's association of Dante's misguided affections with the faults of a young bird may for the moment seem to be a softening of tone on her part. It is not, however, as verse 68 will make clear.

68. *now raise your beard:* Dante is no longer a child, and Beatrice's reference to his beard here is sarcastic. Her intention is to remind him that, even though he has acted as a foolish child and has been chastised as one, he is in fact an adult.

72. *Iarbas:* The south wind. Iarbas or Hearbus was king of the Gaetulias in Libya, North Africa, and an unsuccessful suitor of Dido. (See Virgil *Aen.* IV, 36, 196, 326). The image of the sturdy oak uprooted by the wind continues the image of contrition as "breaking up" (cf. note to 16–21).

75. *I felt the venom in her words:* The painful reference to his beard (68) brings home to the Pilgrim the sarcasm that has been implicit all along in Beatrice's treating him as a naughty child.

76. *And when I raised my head:* While Dante has been standing shamefaced, "with head bowed staring at the ground" (65),

the scene around him has changed significantly. When he finally responds to Beatrice's command to look up, he still does not have the courage to look directly at her and so fixes his gaze instead on the angels. His first inkling of the changed scene comes when he notices that they have stopped showering flowers. The "rain of flowers" had earlier been associated with a veil (XXX, 31–33), one of two that stand between Dante and the face of his beloved Beatrice. Now that the Pilgrim has freely confessed his sins, the first of those veils is removed. The change of scene and the removal of the first veil signify the new perspective that the repentant Pilgrim has achieved.

80–81. *I saw that Beatrice faced the beast:* Beatrice had been standing motionless on the chariot, behind its left rail (XXX, 61), facing the Pilgrim, who stood on the other side of the stream. Even while addressing the angels, Beatrice had not changed her position (XXX, 100–102). Now, still on the chariot, she has turned and is facing the back of the griffin, the beast "who in two natures is one single being." Here those "two natures" are symbolic of the two natures of Christ: divine and human (cf. note to XXIX, 113–14).

83. *lovelier now, she seemed, than when alive:* Now that she is gazing on the griffin, Beatrice has taken on a beauty that far surpasses even her great beauty "when alive on earth." When she was alive, Dante tells us in the *Vita nuova,* Beatrice was not only a woman but one of the most beautiful angels of Heaven. This mixture of divine and human beauty in Beatrice continues the symbolism of the dual nature of Christ. Just as the young Dante of the *Vita nuova* was not able to comprehend fully the human and divine role of Beatrice, so here, at this point in the action at the top of the mountain of Purgatory, the poet still does not see perfectly his beloved lady through her veil.

89. *I fainted:* Fully aware at last of the extent of his guilt and the full import of his sins, the Pilgrim faints, unable to endure such complete recognition of his errors. Earlier (XXX, 76–78) the Pilgrim was so ashamed that he could not bear to see his own reflection in the water at his feet.

Close to the beginning of his journey the Pilgrim twice fainted (*Inf.* III and V) when he was overwhelmed by emotion. Dante the Poet uses all three of these faints as devices of transition or scene shifting, moving the Pilgrim, unaware, from one geographical location to awaken in another.

The Pilgrim awakens from his faint to find himself being drawn by Matelda across Lethe, the river of oblivion. He is submerged up to his neck. Matelda, for her part, is walking on the surface of the water with the Pilgrim clinging to her. Is she perhaps walking backwards, bent over the body she is drawing and holding his head as he clings to her legs? In any case, before they reach the far bank, where Beatrice is waiting, Matelda opens her arms, allowing the Pilgrim's head momentarily to be submerged in Lethe's cleansing waters.

91. *that lady I first saw:* Matelda. Although she was introduced as early as Canto XXVIII (40), Dante has not yet named her and will not until the closing canto (XXXIII, 119). Matelda seems to be assigned the task of administering the waters of Lethe and Eunoë to all those souls who reach the Earthly Paradise. That she does not perform the task only for the Pilgrim will be demonstrated in *Purg.* XXXIII, 134–35, when she invites Statius, too, to drink from the waters of Eunoë.

95–96. *now drawing me along:* Matelda's walking on the water cannot help but remind us of Christ's similar miracle. She is here a *figura Christi,* cleansing man of his sins. She draws the Pilgrim "with a shuttle's ease," i.e., as easily as a shuttle passes back and forth, lightly and rapidly, in the process of weaving cloth.

98. *Asperges me:* "Cleanse me of sin," from Psalm 51:7 (Vulg. 50:9): "Cleanse me of sin with hyssop, that I may be purified; wash me, and I shall be whiter than snow." The *Asperges* is sung at the beginning of the Mass, when the priest sprinkles the people with holy water. Here, presumably, it is sung by the angels on the far bank. These lines are part of a longer prayer of repentance, in which David asks the Lord for mercy and forgiveness of his sins. Here they signify the completion of the Pilgrim's personal confession, for his immersion now washes off the final stains of the sins he has confessed to Beatrice.

101–102. *dipped it in the stream / . . . to let me drink of it:* The act of drinking the water of Lethe, it should be noted, is different from being immersed in the river. Immersion cleanses the Pilgrim's soul of the guilt remaining from the sins he confessed to Beatrice; it is the last step of his personal confession. His drinking from the waters of Lethe (the "river of oblivion") is part of the ritual that every soul that reaches the summit must perform; it takes away the emotional memory of sin just as drinking of the waters of Eunoë, which the Pilgrim and Statius will do later on (**XXXIII**, 133–35), restores the memory of all good deeds.

103–105. *She took me from those waters, cleansed and led:* The word "cleansed" stresses the spiritual purifying powers of this "sacred river." Matelda now leads the Pilgrim to Beatrice's handmaids, the four cardinal virtues (Prudence, Justice, Fortitude, Temperance), who are dancing at the left wheel of the chariot. There he stands at the center of their dance while the four join hands, as though forming a crown, over his head. Each handmaid in this way signifies her infusing of the Pilgrim with her own special virtue, thus protecting him from its opposite vice.

106–14. *"Here we are nymphs and in the heavens, stars":* The handmaids are referring to their position as four stars in the sky above the south pole. They are the stars the Pilgrim noticed at the very beginning of his journey up the mount, but which the Poet did not elaborate on at the time (*Purg.* I, 23–24): it was merely noted that they were seen by Adam and Eve from Eden and had been seen by no one else since then. In song they tell the Pilgrim that they will lead him to stand in front of the griffin, where he will see Beatrice—who is now standing at the front of the chariot and is turned toward the left, though her eyes remain fixed on the two-natured beast. They will later be joined by the other three handmaids, the three theological virtues, who have been dancing at the chariot's right wheel, and who will soon move toward the front to join Beatrice. The Pilgrim faces the front ("the breast") of the griffin which is drawing the chariot, and sees Beatrice standing on the chariot, toward the front, gazing at the griffin from behind. We are being prepared by this stance for the new role Beatrice is about to assume: that of Sapientia or Wisdom.

116. *now you stand before those emeralds:* Beatrice's eyes are green, symbolizing Hope. Here we are presented with a clear indication of Beatrice's two interconnected roles in the poem. The Pilgrim is reminded first of the Beatrice of the *Vita nuova* ("a thousand yearning flames of my desire," 118), the woman

whose love should have sufficed to teach him to aspire to the Ultimate Good. But when he actually does look into Beatrice's eyes (119), the Pilgrim sees the image of the griffin. One of Beatrice's other roles, then, is that of Revelation. The mystery of Christ's dual nature is still beyond the Pilgrim's understanding, and so, allegorically, he is as yet unable to gaze directly at the griffin, the symbol of those two natures. But he can begin to comprehend through Beatrice's (Revelation's) green eyes.

122. *I saw the twofold creature in her eyes:* The Pilgrim encounters in Beatrice's eyes, as in a mirror, the mystery of Christ's dual nature. The words of Paul (I Cor. 13:12) come to mind: *Videmus nunc per speculum in aenigmate,* "We see now through a mirror in an obscure way."

Just as Christ is both God and man in one, and at the same time, so he is represented by the griffin, which is part eagle and part lion. The Pilgrim can "see" the two natures of the beast imaged in Beatrice's eyes (123), but he cannot comprehend their oneness; hence the natures are visible to him only alternately ("separately," 123) and not simultaneously. He can only marvel at the mysteriousness of oneness by describing an image that changes natures (from eagle to lion and back again) while the creature itself remains unchanged (125–27).

128–29. *that food which satisfies:* Dante is paraphrasing the words of Sapientia in Ecclus. 24:21: "They that eat me shall yet be hungry, and they that drink me shall yet be thirsty." The food that makes one hungrier is the Truth that comes through Revelation (Beatrice) and that points always to something higher, to Christ himself.

134. *"and look upon your faithful one":* Now that his wanderings from the path Beatrice first set for him in the *Vita nuova* have been forgiven, the Pilgrim can truly be called Beatrice's "faithful one." In Canto II of the *Inferno* (97–99) the Pilgrim was also called "faithful," indicating that even then, beneath his wanderings, there had always been an unconscious faithfulness that had been guiding his steps back to his beloved Beatrice.

136. *unveil:* The action of unveiling further indicates Beatrice's symbolic role as Revelation.

138. *that second beauty:* Beatrice's smile, i.e., salvation. The first beauty was that of her emerald eyes, the "ancient flame" of

hope and the means by which wisdom and truth were demonstrated. With Beatrice's smile comes the unveiled or inner light of wisdom: the promise of salvation for all mankind.

141. *or become pale within that mountain's shade:* Dante is referring to those who, like himself, labor tirelessly at mastering the art of poetry. Even the best of poets would have difficulty describing the unveiled beauty of Beatrice.

144. *with that harmonious heaven your only veil:* Heaven here refers to the seven streamers of light from the seven golden candlesticks. These streamers, symbolizing the seven gifts of the Spirit of the Lord, were first described by the Pilgrim as "seven bands of light" (XXIX, 77). Now, however, with the unveiling of Beatrice, the Pilgrim sees the harmony of the seven gifts, which together form a "heaven" that overshadows the entire procession in general and Beatrice in particular. Such "harmony" is again an indication of the Pilgrim's growing ability to glimpse briefly the larger design of God.

CANTO XXXII

FOR THE FIRST time in ten years, Dante the Pilgrim stares into the face of Beatrice. Looking away, he is left temporarily blinded, and when he recovers his sight, it is to discover that the pageant is now moving off. He and Statius, along with the lovely lady, follow the procession, which stops in front of a tree, where Beatrice descends. This is the tree of the knowledge of good and evil, but it is stripped bare of leaf and fruit. The griffin takes the pole of the chariot he has been pulling and attaches it to the tree, which immediately bursts into bloom. As the company begins to chant an unidentifiable hymn, the Pilgrim falls asleep. He is awakened by the lovely lady to find that the pageant has departed and that Beatrice, with her seven handmaidens, is left alone, seated beneath the tree. She directs the Pilgrim to fix his eyes on the chariot. As he watches, an eagle swoops down through the tree, tearing off the newborn leaves, and strikes the chariot with full force. Then a fox leaps up into the cart but is driven off by Beatrice. Again the eagle comes, but this time it perches on the chariot and sheds some of its golden feathers there. Suddenly the ground beneath the chariot opens, and a dragon drives its tail up through the floor of the cart. Withdrawing its stinger, it takes a portion of the floor with it. What is left of the chariot now grows a rich cover of feathers and then sprouts seven heads. Seated now upon the chariot is an ungirt whore, who flirts lasciviously with a giant standing nearby. When the whore turns her lustful eyes toward the Pilgrim, the giant beats her and drags the chariot off into the woods.

I fixed my eyes on her; they were intent
  on quenching their ten years of thirst at last—
  I was bereft of every other sense.   3

My eyes, walled in by barriers of high
  indifference, were drawn to her holy smile—
  they were entranced by her familiar spell.   6

But, suddenly, my gaze was forced away
  to where those goddesses stood at my left.
  "He should not look so hard!" I heard them say.   9

I was like one who had just strained his eyes
    by looking straight into the sun too long;
    indeed, I was left blinded for a while.   12

When I had grown accustomed to dim light—
    dim light, I mean, compared to that effulgence
    from which I had been forced to turn away—   15

the glorious host, I saw, had wheeled about
    on its right flank and now was moving back,
    facing the seven torches and the sun.   18

When squadrons under shields start to retreat,
    it is the front-line troops, bearing their colors,
    who turn before the others can begin—   21

just so, those soldiers who were in the front
    of the blest host had all marched past our post
    before the chariot had turned its pole.   24

The ladies took their place beside the wheels:
    the griffin moved, pulling his sacred charge,
    without a single feather being ruffled.   27

Statius and I, along with the fair maid
    who had towed me across the stream, now moved
    behind the wheel which made the smaller arc.   30

As we walked through that high wood, empty now
    because of her who listened to the snake,
    our steps kept time to strains of heavenly notes.   33

We had already walked perhaps three times
    the distance any arrow shot full strength
    could reach, when Beatrice left the cart.   36

I heard them all murmuring Adam's name;
    and then they formed a circle 'round a tree
    whose every branch was stripped of leaf and fruit.   39

A tree like this in India's wooded lands
    would seem a very miracle of height:
    the more it rose, the wider spread its boughs.   42

"Blessed art thou, Griffin. Thy sacred beak
    tears not a shred of this tree's savory bark,
    which makes the belly writhe in deadly pain!"   45

These words were sung by all the others there
around the tree. And the two-natured beast:
"Thus is preserved the seed of righteousness."   48

Then, turning to the pole which he had pulled,
he brought it up against the widowed tree,
returning to it what it once brought forth.   51

Just as the trees on earth in early spring—
when the strong rays fall, mingled with the light
that glows behind the heaven of the Fish—   54

begin to swell, burst into bloom, renew
the color that was theirs, before the sun
hitches his steeds beneath some other stars,   57

just so, that tree whose boughs had been so bare,
renewed itself, and bloomed with color not quite
roselike but brighter than a violet.   60

I did not recognize the hymn that group
began to sing—it is not sung on earth,
and then, I did not listen to the end.   63

Could I describe how those insistent eyes
were lulled to sleep by the sad tale of Syrinx—
the eyes that paid so dear for their long watch—   66

as painter painting from his model, I
would try to show you how I fell asleep.
But let whoever can paint sleep, paint sleep!   69

So, I shall tell you only how I woke:
a splendor rent the veil of sleep, a voice
was calling me: "What are you doing? Rise!"   72

When they were led to see that apple tree
whose blossoms give the fruit that angels crave,
providing an eternal marriage-feast,   75

Peter and John and James were overpowered
by sleep, and then brought back to consciousness
by that same word that broke a deeper sleep;   78

they saw their company had been reduced,
for Moses and Elijah were not there;
they saw their Master's robe changed back again.   81

Just so, I woke to see, bent over me,
   the sympathetic lady who, before,
   had been my guide along the riverbank.   84

Fearful, I cried: "Oh, where is Beatrice?"
   The lady said: "See, she is sitting there
   on the tree's roots beneath the newborn leaves;   87

behold the company surrounding her.
   The rest go with the griffin up to Heaven
   to sweeter music and to deeper strains."   90

I do not know if she said more than this,
   for now I was allowed to see again
   the one who reigned completely in my mind.   93

She sat there on the bare earth, left alone
   to guard the chariot that I had seen
   bound to the tree by the two-natured beast.   96

The circle of the seven nymphs now formed
   a cloister for the lady; in their hands
   they held those lights no wind on earth could quench.   99

"A short time you shall dwell outside the walls;
   then you, with me, shall live eternally,
   citizen of that Rome where Christ is Roman.   102

Now, for the good of sinners in your world,
   observe the chariot well, and what you see,
   put into writing, when you have returned."   105

Thus Beatrice. I obediently,
   devoutly, at the feet of her commands,
   gave mind and eye to satisfying her.   108

No bolt of lightning flashing through dense cloud,
   shot from the farthest region of the sky,
   has ever struck with such velocity   111

as moved the bird of Jove who then swooped down
   and through the tree, tearing off newborn leaves,
   rending the bark, destroying all the blooms;   114

with his full force he struck the chariot,
   which staggered like a ship caught in a storm,
   careened by waves, tilting starboard and port.   117

Into the cradle of the glorious car
    I saw a fox leap up, so lean it seemed
    the food it fed on had no nourishment.   *120*

My lady made it turn and run away,
    as fast as its weak skin and bones could go,
    accusing it of foul abominations.   *123*

Once more the eagle swooped down through the tree:
    this time into the framework of the car,
    to shed some of its golden feathers there;   *126*

like sorrow pouring from a grieving heart
    a voice from Heaven was heard: "My little ship,
    O what ill-fated cargo you must bear!"   *129*

And then I saw the ground between the wheels
    opening up: a dragon issued forth,
    driving its tail up through the chariot;   *132*

then, as a wasp withdraws its sting, that thing
    drew back its poison tail, tearing away
    part of the floor—gloating, it wandered off;   *135*

the rest, like fertile soil left for thick weeds
    to thrive on, grew a rich cover of plumes
    granted with good intentions, it would seem,   *138*

and all the chariot, with both its wheels
    and pole as well, was overgrown with them
    in less time than it takes to heave a sigh.   *141*

Thus changed, the holy shrine began to sprout
    heads from all parts: three on the chariot's pole
    and one from each of its four corners grew.   *144*

The three were horned like oxen, but the four
    had but one horn upon each of their heads.
    No one has ever seen a monster like it!   *147*

Seated thereon, securely, like a fort
    high on a hill, I saw an ungirt whore
    casting bold, sluttish glances all around.   *150*

Acting as if someone might take her from him,
    a giant, I saw, standing there by her side;
    from time to time the two of them would kiss.   *153*

But when she turned her roving, lustful eyes
  on me, her lover in a fit of rage
  beat her ferociously from head to foot.   *156*

Then, furious with jealousy, the giant
  ripped loose the monster, dragging it away
  far off into the woods, until the trees   *159*

blocked from my sight the whore and that strange beast.

NOTES

2. *their ten years of thirst*: According to the *Vita nuova* (XXIX, 1), Beatrice died in 1290. Since the fictional date of the journey through Purgatory is 1300, the Pilgrim has encountered Beatrice after ten years' separation.

4–6. *My eyes, walled in by barriers*: Dante continues to have in mind the Beatrice of the *Vita nuova*. The Pilgrim fixes his attention on her without distraction, for the "barriers of high indifference," which failed him before when he was "led astray" by "false joys" (*Purg.* XXXI, 34–35), are now firmly in place. He is drawn now in a new and purer way to the "familiar spell," the smile of the woman he loves.

9. *"He should not look so hard"*: With this admonition of the "goddesses" (the three theological virtues), we are reminded that Beatrice has a second role, that of Revelation. When the Pilgrim fixed his gaze on Beatrice's familiar smile, he unwittingly looked too hard at the unveiled mysteries of Revelation. The virtues are reminding him that his vision is not yet adequate for the bright light of eternal truth.

16. *the glorious host, I saw, had wheeled about*: The Pilgrim's attention and ours are returned to the procession. Having come out of the east as far as the bank of the stream, the procession now wheels around and, led by the candles, retreats to the east, toward the morning sun. The procession is compared to an army turning "under shields." (Note the stress on military terms to make us see the "glorious host" as a "squadron, as troops bearing their colors," soldiers marching.) Dante is in this way preparing us for the coming pageant (109–60), in which we will see the chariot transformed to represent symbolically the history of the Church Militant.

24. *had turned its pole*: The pole (*primo legno* or "first wood" in Italian) represents Christ's cross.

27. *without a single feather being ruffled*: Christ (the griffin) guides his church (the chariot) without confusion, in a divinely ordered motion. His divine nature (his "eagle" part) is no way disturbed.

30. *behind the wheel which made the smaller arc*: Since the procession has turned to the right, it is the right wheel that makes the smaller arc in turning. Dante, Statius, and the "fair lady" are now accompanying the three theological virtues on the right hand side of the chariot.

It should be remembered that Statius has been on the scene all along, even though he has not been mentioned since the disappearance of Virgil (XXVIII, 146). It is interesting to note that in the thirteen cantos in which Statius is present, he plays an active role in only three.

36. . . . *when Beatrice left the cart*: This movement or change in Beatrice's position indicates a change in her symbolic role. Here, Beatrice's dramatic descent from the chariot signals the beginning of the pageant or masque of the Church Militant— the church struggling with the forces of evil in history.

37–42

The name "Adam" and the tree "stripped of leaf and fruit" focus our attention on the Garden of Eden and the tree of the knowledge of good and evil (Gen. 2:15–17)—the very beginning of the history of mankind's struggle with evil and injustice. The lofty tree is stripped bare as a result of Adam's sin, the consequences of which have been borne by mankind ever since. This tree will remain the central allegorical symbol throughout the canto (see notes to 40 and 43).

40. *A tree like this*: Towering so high, this tree represents the Holy Roman Empire, the foundation of the highest earthly law. Towering trees were used in Scripture as symbols of great empires (the empires of Assyria and Babylon were so symbolized in Ezek. 31 and Dan. 4), and in his *Georgics* (II, 122–24) Virgil had noted the fame of India's high trees. Here Dante's comparison to "India's wooded lands" emphasizes the superiority of the Christian empire.

The peculiar shape of the tree, whose branches expand as

they go upwards, reminds us of its offshoot on the Terrace of the Gluttons (*Purg.* XXII, 130, and XXIV, 106): an inverted pine so shaped that it was impossible for the yearning souls to climb. The tree's shape reminds us here of God's original interdict to Adam, "Thou shalt not," and reminds us, too, of His justice. Shortly (XXXIII, 64–72), Beatrice will explain to the Pilgrim the moral significance of this tree's height and shape.

43. *"Blessed art thou, Griffin"*: The griffin is being praised because, unlike Adam, he submits obediently to God's divine plan. Likewise, during his lifetime, Christ submitted to the jurisdiction of the Roman Empire, commanding his followers to "Render to Caesar that which is Caesar's" (Matt. XXII, 21), and accepting his own death sentence from Pontius Pilate, the representative of the empire. Dante may have been suggesting in the griffin's reply (48) that divine justice is best preserved when the church refrains from usurping the prerogatives of the empire.

48. *"Thus is preserved the seed of righteousness"*: The words are spoken by the griffin; it is the only time the creature speaks. The "seed of righteousness" firmly identifies the tree as the allegorical representation of Justice, the Justice of God, which includes in its design the justice of human institutions ("empire") as well. "Thus" refers backward to Christ's obedient submission to God's just design (cf. Rom. 5:19: "For just as by the disobedience of the one man the many were constituted sinful, so also by the obedience of the one the many will be constituted just"). Kaske sees the griffin's words as the first in a series of images that celebrate figuratively the regeneration of mankind through the atonement of Christ and the joyous tidings of Christianity that resulted from it.

49–51. *Then, turning to the pole*: Drawing the chariot (the church) with him, the griffin attaches its pole (his cross) to the "widowed tree" (divine justice). On one level Dante is no doubt recalling the popular legend that Christ's cross was formed from the wood of the tree of the knowledge of good and evil. The story is recorded in the *Aurea Legenda* c. XVIII (see Moore [1903], 219–20).

Seth is said to have planted an offshoot from the Tree of Knowledge on Adam's grave. By the time of Solomon it had grown to a very large tree. This he cut down, and employed either for one of his palaces or as a bridge to cross a pool. The Queen of Sheba, to whom it was miraculously revealed that the Saviour of the world should one day hang upon this wood, refused to set foot on it, and warned Solomon of the revelation she had received. Solomon, hoping to avert such an evil prophecy, . . . caused the beam to be buried at a great depth in the earth. At the spot was afterwards dug the Pool of Bethesda whose healing properties were due to the presence of the wood. Shortly before the Passion, the wood came to the surface and was employed to form the Cross.

The pole of the chariot, representing the cross (cf. note to 24), is reunited with the Tree of Knowledge, thus joining the instrument of the Fall with the instrument of Redemption.

On another level, since the tree is also symbolic of divine justice, "widowed" now because of mankind's fallen state, the griffin's act of attaching the chariot to the tree by means of the pole would signify the reconciliation of humanity with divine justice through the workings of Christ and his church.

53–54. *the light / that glows behind the heaven of the Fish*: the light of the sun shining through Aries, the constellation that follows Pisces ("the Fish").

56–57. *before the sun / hitches his steeds:* The sun is seen as Apollo, the charioteer, hitching his steeds to Taurus, the next constellation to appear in the sky after Aries—that is to say: "before the month has passed."

59–60. *not quite / roselike, but brighter than a violet*: Purple is the color between red and violet. Purple could signify the passion and death of Christ; hence, it is his sacrificial blood that infuses the tree with its color. The four cardinal virtues of the procession also wear purple, signifying their accessibility to mankind after the shedding of Christ's blood. Without these virtues no righteous government is possible.

63. *I did not listen to the end*: The Pilgrim falls asleep before the hymn is over. Perhaps lulled to sleep by the beauty of the heavenly song, the Pilgrim's tranquility and peace symbolize the condition of all mankind. We live in the happiness of spiritual peace now because Christ's sacrifice has reconciled us with God.

64. *Could I describe how those insistent eyes*: The hundred eyes of Argus, Juno's gamekeeper, commanded by her to keep watch over Io, Juno's rival for the love of Jupiter. Argus failed in his task, for Jupiter sent Mercury to lull Argus to sleep with

the tale of Syrinx and Pan. Argus paid dearly (66) for this one lack of vigilance: once asleep, he was beheaded by Mercury.

71. *a splendor rent the veil of sleep*: A mysterious radiance, which Dante never explains, penetrates the Pilgrim's sleep, and he wakens to hear the words of "the sympathetic lady" (83) bidding him arise. Though unexplained, the sudden brightness prepares the reader for a change of scene, and, as is so often the case with changes in these last cantos, the new scene will involve Beatrice in a changed role (cf. note to 85–99).

72. *"What are you doing? Rise!"*: These are the words of "the sympathetic lady" (83), who has not as yet been identified as Matelda. Similar words were used by Christ at the Transfiguration (cf. Matt. 17:7). See note to 73–84.

73–84

Dante compares the Pilgrim's awakening to that of Peter, James, and John on Mount Tabor after the Transfiguration of Christ. Unable to sustain the vision of Christ in all his glory conversing with Moses and Elisha, or to listen to the words of God the Father speaking to them through a cloud, the three apostles covered their eyes and fell trembling to the ground. Not until Jesus spoke to them and touched them were the apostles able to rise. By then the transfiguration vision had ended: Moses and Elisha had gone and Christ's raiment had changed back again.

Just so, the Pilgrim, rising at the words of the lovely lady bending over him, finds that the procession scene had been transformed. The griffin (Christ) and the processional host have returned to Heaven, leaving Beatrice and the seven nymphs (the three theological virtues and the four cardinal virtues) to guard the chariot (the church).

74. *whose blossoms give the fruit that angels crave*: The "apple tree" (73) is Christ (Apoc. 18:14). When in full bloom it represents Christ's promise to mankind that what will follow is the fruit of eternal bliss, enjoyed now by the angels living in perpetual union with Christ in Heaven.

78. *by that same word that broke a deeper sleep*: "Arise" was the word with which Christ called Lazarus back from death, a "deeper sleep" (cf. Luke 7:14–15).

81. *they saw their Master's robe changed back again:* Christ's robe became snow-white during the Transfiguration (cf. Matt. 17:3) but had returned to its former color when the apostles rose to see that the vision had ended. The Italian word for "robe," *stola,* also means "aspect" and could imply a change not only in Christ's garments but also in his nature, i.e., from full divine glory to his dual God/man nature.

85–99

Frightened upon awakening, the Pilgrim calls after Beatrice. She is sitting on the roots of the tree, beneath its "new-born leaves," guarding the chariot now that Christ and his host have ascended to Heaven. Allegorically, this new position signifies a new role for Beatrice. The scene has shifted: the tree no longer indicates only Eden; transformed by its attachment to the chariot, it signifies the world of the young ("newborn," 87) Christian church in the time directly following Christ's Ascension. Beatrice, surrounded by the seven virtues, represents created Wisdom, that *Sapientia creata* which remained on earth among men after the Ascension of Christ in order to protect the fledgling church.

93. *the one who reigned completely in my mind:* Once again the Pilgrim's attention is fixed solely on Beatrice, as it was at the opening of this canto.

94–96. *She sat there on the bare earth, left alone:* Beatrice is like the church in its primitive stage before the corruption of the papal court. She sits under the new foliage of the Roman Empire.

97–99. *The circle of the seven nymphs:* The seven nymphs, or seven virtues, are holding the seven torches that were originally at the head of the procession. They are "those lights no wind on earth could quench" (99); i.e., they cannot be extinguished by earthly forces. That the torches, which originally moved in the procession under their own power, are now in the hands of the nymphs signifies the close relationship between the spirit of Christ and the seven virtues now that Christ no longer dwells physically on earth.

100–102. *A short time you shall dwell outside the walls:* The prophetic words, along with the injunction that follows them (103–105), are Beatrice's. The city "where Christ is Roman" is, of course, the heavenly city (cf. Augustine's famous *City of God*). To dwell for "a short time" outside its walls is to live on earth or, in terms of Augustine, to dwell in the earthly city, whose citizens are composed of both the righteous and the sinners. Dante, when he returns for "a short time" to the earthly city ("short" only in comparison to eternity in Heaven), must then report (for the benefit of earth's sinful citizens) what he is now about to see.

107. *at the feet of her commands:* In this figure, the Pilgrim's will is bent in humility to the will of Beatrice.

109–60

Dante begins, as commanded, to report the pageant being enacted before him. The pageant is composed of a series of seven tableaux, all but the last of which Dante describes in two tercets each. As a whole, the pageant depicts chronologically the church's mission on earth from the time of Christ's Ascension to the year 1300, the fictional date of the *Divine Comedy*. Each of the seven tableaux (which will be treated in separate notes) is a symbolic vision of one of the successive catastophes that befell the church during that time span.

109–17. *No bolt of lightning:* The first catasurophe (112–17) is introduced by a meteorological image. The "farthest region of the sky" is the sphere of fire; hence lightning emanating from that region would be especially powerful and swift. The tableau signifies the persecutions of the early church under the Roman emperors from Nero (A.D. 54–68) to Diocletian (A.D. 284–305). The "bird of Jove" is the eagle, the standard of the empire, here acting as a bird of prey, "tearing," "rending," and "destroying." Dante compares the assaulted chariot, the church, to "a ship caught in a storm." The ship is a traditional symbol of the church (cf. Dante's reference to Peter's ship in *Par.* XI, 119–20).

118–23. *Into the cradle:* The second tableau represents the internal heresies that threatened the early church, particularly the heresy of Gnosticism. The mischief caused from within the church by heretics (as opposed to open assaults from the outside, as in the case of the persecutions), is aptly symbolized here in the fox, traditionally known as a cunning deceiver, which leaps into the "cradle" of the car. Dante follows Ezekiel in choosing the fox as a symbol for heretics: "Thy prophets are like the foxes in the deserts" (Ezek. 13:4). (Cf. also *Inf.* XXVII, 75.) That the animal is "all skin and bones" signifies that heretics never partake of the nourishing food of true doctrine.

The fox is put to flight by Beatrice, here representing the wisdom left by Christ to protect his church from such assaults. Her accusations may be likened to those of the early church fathers, who rose to the defense of traditional church doctrine and disproved the claims of the heretics.

124–29. *Once more the eagle swooped down:* The third catastrophe, again initiated by action of the eagle, is a tableau representing the church's acquisition of temporal wealth and power through what came to be renowned as the "Donation of Constantine," the alleged gift of the Western Empire to the papacy, the "ill-fated cargo" of verse 129.

The eagle here proves to be more harmful working from within, in friendship with the church, than it was as an enemy attacking from without. Its "golden plumes" shed on the chariot begin the process by which the church becomes overgrown with plumes (140), or encumbered with the possessions appropriate for a worldly empire but incongruous and unnatural to the church of Christ. The "voice from Heaven" is that of St. Peter, the first captain of the "little ship," the church.

130–35. *And then I saw the ground:* The meaning of the fourth catastrophe is less certain. The dragon is a traditional representation of Satan (cf. Rev. 12:9), here issuing up from below to rend the floor of the chariot (i.e., the foundation of the church). Historically, the tableau probably represents one of the schisms that divided the early church, perhaps Mohammedanism, which rose to threaten her in the seventh century. That Dante considered Mohammed a schismatic is attested by his having placed him in the ninth *bolgia* of the Eighth Circle of Hell: the *bolgia* of the Schismatics (see *Inf.* XXVIII).

At the end of this tableau, the dragon (Satan) withdraws his tail and wanders away from the chariot (135). In Italian, he is said to wander off *"vago, vago,"* the meaning of which is unclear. The sense here seems to be that there is something sinister in the dragon's simply wandering away from the chariot once he has attacked and damaged it—that, just as he goes off unpredictably, he may return at any time from any direction.

136–41. *the rest, like fertile soil:* The tableau of the fifth catastrophe shows the church's further acquisitions of temporal wealth and power. The imagery is the same as that of the third tableau: the chariot is unnaturally covered with plumes. Dante may be referring specifically to the Donations of Pepin (A.D. 755) and Charlemagne (A.D. 775), which relatively quickly ("in less time than it takes to heave a sigh," 141) increased the church's land holdings and transformed her into a powerful medieval state. Such a devastating transformation might not in Dante's estimation have been the intention of the donors (138), but they nonetheless originated a process that continued into Dante's own time, making the church progressively less recognizable as the institution left behind by Christ when he ascended into Heaven.

142–47. *Thus changed, the holy shrine:* The devastating transformation of the chariot of the church continues through the sixth tableau. The imagery, as in the fourth tableau, is apocalyptic, referring to the beast of Revelations with seven heads and ten horns. The seven heads that the chariot sprouts immediately remind us of the seven ladies (the virtues) standing guard at Beatrice's side, and so may represent their antitheses: the Seven Deadly Sins. If so, those with two horns ("horned like oxen," 145) might be Pride, Envy, and Anger, which are sins of the spirit, sins against both God and neighbor. Those with a single horn—Avarice, Sloth, Gluttony, and Lust—are sins of the flesh only and do not necessarily harm one's neighbor.

If Dante meant this tableau to represent a specific historical catastrophe and not the general degeneration of the church's moral leadership throughout the Middle Ages, then a possible historical event might be the appointment by the pope (ca. A.D. 1000) of seven electors who were thenceforward to select the Holy Roman Emperor. In *De Monarchia* (iii, 16) Dante expressly denounced the intrusion by the pope on hereditary rule as an unnatural intrusion upon the role of God as the empire's sole elector. It is possible that Dante saw this incident as further historical evidence of the church's inappropriately exerting temporal power.

148–59. *Seated thereon:* The seventh catastrophe brings us to the period of history close to Dante's own time. In this tableau the seat on the chariot once occupied by Beatrice is now taken over by "an ungirt whore" (149). The whore represents the corrupted papacy, which had been prostituting itself by forming lucrative alliances with the kings of France. The jealous "giant" (152) is most probably Philip the Fair (Philip III, 1285–1314) of France, and his kissing the whore "from time to time" (153) represents the mutual interests of king and pope served by their temporal alliances. Again, the imagery is apocalyptic.

The relationship between the whore and the giant abruptly changes, however, in the second two tercets devoted to the tableau. As has been noted, each of the preceding tableaux was described in two tercets; the seventh is described in four. It is possible that the abrupt change moves us into an eighth tableau depicting a further catastrophe involving Philip's relations with the papacy. In any case, when the whore (at this point representing Pope Boniface VIII) casts her eyes on the Pilgrim, she is beaten by the jealous giant, who then removes both whore and transformed cart "far off into the woods" (159).

Dante undoubtedly has in mind here the siege ordered by Philip on September 7, 1303, against the papal palace, during which the aging Boniface was captured and humiliated by Philip's men. Boniface died some weeks later. His successor, Clement V, allowed the papal seat to be moved in 1305 from Rome to Avignon in France, where future popes would be more easily subject to Philip's will.

The Pilgrim has been merely a spectator up to this point, but in verses 154–55 we are told that it is because the whore turns her eyes on him that she was beaten. The exact significance of the Pilgrim's participation here is uncertain. He may represent Everyman or every Christian, as he often does in the *Divine Comedy*. In that case, Dante may be saying that when the popes attempted to resume their pastoral role by turning their attention where it should have been, on their Christian flock, their temporal alliances prevented them from doing so. Or the Pilgrim may represent more specifically the Italian people, in which case the popes' turning their attention to Italy would have incurred the jealous anger of their French allies.

160. *blocked from my sight:* With the seventh catastrophe (the removal of the papacy to Avignon in 1305), we have moved into prophetic or future time, with respect to the fictional date of the journey (1300). Thus the Pilgrim is unable to see the further activities of the whore, the jealous giant, and the cart-turned-monster.

This canto, with its 160 verses, is the longest one in the poem.

CANTO XXXIII

THE SEVEN LADIES sing, weeping over the sorrowful fate of the chariot, and Beatrice grieves. But soon they set off, the seven in front of Beatrice, and the Pilgrim, Matelda, and Statius behind her. As they walk, Beatrice, in a very obscurely worded prophecy, predicts the eventual deliverance of the church and commands the Pilgrim to note her words and to repeat them exactly when he writes, in order to teach the living. The Pilgrim asks her why her words fly so high above his power to understand, and she answers that it is to teach him the difference between divine and earthly ways. They come to the source from which the two rivers of Lethe and Eunoë spring, and Matelda, on Beatrice's orders, leads the Pilgrim to drink of the restoring waters of Eunoë. The Poet protests that he would describe this inestimable pleasure at length, but that he has already filled the pages allotted for the second canticle. And so he says only that he came away from that holy water refreshed, eager to rise, and ready for the stars.

Deus venerunt gentes, sang the nymphs
   chanting in tears the dulcet psalmody,
   their voicès alternating, three, then four,   *3*

and Beatrice listened to their song,
   sighing and sorrowful—hardly more grief
   showed in the face of Mary at the cross.   *6*

But when among those virgins silence reigned,
   yielding to her response, she stood up then
   and glowing like a flame, announced to them: *9*

"*Modicum et non videbitis me;*
   et iterum, sisters so dear to me,
   modicum et vos videbitis me."   *12*

Then, having placed the seven in front of her,
   she had us move behind with just a nod
   to me and to the lady and the poet.   *15*

So she moved forward, and she had not gone
   ten steps into the wood when, suddenly,
   she turned to fix her eyes on mine, and said,   *18*

looking at me serenely: "Make more haste,
so that, if I should wish to speak with you,
you would be close enough to hear my words." 21

I did as I was told. Once I was close,
she said: "Why, brother, do you hesitate
to question me, now that you are with me?" 24

Like those who feel a paralyzing awe
when in the presence of superiors
and scarcely can find breath enough to speak— 27

I, too, could utter, indistinctly though,
the words: "My lady, you know all my needs,
and how to satisfy them perfectly." 30

Then she to me: "It is my wish that you
from now on free yourself from fear and shame,
and cease to speak like someone in a dream. 33

Know that the vessel which the serpent broke
was, and is not. Let him who bears the blame
learn that God's vengeance has no fear of sops. 36

The eagle that shed feathers on the car
that would become a monster, then a prey,
will not remain forever without heirs; 39

I tell you this because I clearly see
those stars, already near, that will bring in
a time- -its advent nothing can prevent— 42

in which five hundred, ten, and five shall be
God's emissary, born to kill the giant
and the usurping whore with whom he sins. 45

Perhaps my prophecy with its dark words,
obscure as those of Themis or the Sphinx,
has not convinced you but confused your mind; 48

but soon events themselves shall be the Naiads
that will untie this riddle's complex knot—
with no destruction of the sheep or grain. 51

Note well my words: what I have said to you,
you will repeat, as you teach those who live
that life which is merely a race to death. 54

And when you write, be sure that you describe
  the sad condition of the tree you saw
  despoiled, not once but twice, here on this spot.   57

Whoever robs this tree or breaks its limbs
  sins against God, blasphemes in deeds, for He
  created it to serve His Holy Self.   60

Because God's first soul tasted of this tree,
  more than five thousand years in pain he yearned
  for Him Who paid the penalty Himself.   63

Your mind's asleep if you do not perceive
  the special reason for the tree's great height
  and why it grows inverted toward the top.   66

If your vain thoughts had not been to your mind
  waters of Elsa, and your joy in them
  a Pyramus to your mulberry, then   69

from the tree's two strange attributes alone,
  you would have recognized its moral sense,
  and seen God's justice in the interdict.   72

But since I see your mind has turned to stone
  and, like a stone, is dark and, being dark,
  cannot endure the clear light of my words,   75

it is my wish you carry back with you
  if not my words themselves, at least some trace,
  as pilgrims bring their staves back wreathed with palm." 78

And I to her: "As wax stamped by the seal
  will never lose the outline of the print,
  so, your seal is imprinted on my mind.   81

But your desired words, why do they fly
  so high above my mind? The more I try
  to follow them, the more they soar from sight."   84

She said: "Why do they? So that you may come
  truly to know that school which you have followed,
  and see how well its doctrine follows mine—   87

also, that you may see that mankind's ways
  are just as far away from those divine
  as earth is from the highest spinning sphere."   90

To that I answered: "I cannot recall
ever having estranged myself from you:
I have no guilty conscience on that score."   93

"You say that you do not remember it?"
smiling, she said. "But, surely, you recall
drinking of Lethe's waters just today;   96

and even as fire can be inferred from smoke,
your lack of memory is patent proof
that your estrangement from me was a sin.   99

But from now on, I promise you, my words
will be as plain as they will have to be
for your uneducated mind to grasp."   102

And blazing brighter, moving slower now,
the sun was riding its meridian ring,
whose point in space depends upon the viewer,   105

when—just as someone who escorts a group
stops short if something very strange appears
in front of him—those seven ladies stopped   108

as they approached the margin of a shade,
pale as a mountain's shadow on cool streams
flowing beneath green foliage and dark boughs.   111

Ahead of them I saw spring from one source
what might have been the Tigris and Euphrates!
Then, like close friends, they slowly drew apart.   114

"O light, O glory of the human race,
what is this water pouring from one source,
and then dividing self from self?" I asked.   117

She answered: "Ask Matelda to explain."
And then the lovely lady spoke, as though
she felt she had to free herself from blame: 120

"I have already made this clear to him,
this and much more; and Lethe, I am sure,
could not have washed away the memory."   123

Then Beatrice: "A more important thing,
perhaps, weighs on his mind, depriving him
of memory and clouding his mind's eye.   126

But here before us is the stream Eunoë:
    now, lead him there and, as it is your wont,
    revive his weakened powers in its flow."

129

Then, gracious as she was, without demur,
    submitting her own will to another's will,
    once this was made apparent by a sign,

132

the lovely lady took me by the hand,
    and said to Statius as she moved ahead
    with queenly modesty: "And you come too."

135

Reader, if I had space to write more words,
    I'd sing, at least in part, of that sweet draught
    which never could have satisfied my thirst;

138

but now I have completed every page
    planned for my poem's second canticle —
    I am checked by the bridle of my art!

141

From those holiest waters I returned
    to her reborn, a tree renewed, in bloom
    with newborn foliage, immaculate,

144

eager to rise, now ready for the stars.

NOTES

1. *Deus venerunt gentes*: Saddened by the tableau depicting the captivity of the church, the seven virtues begin to sing Psalm 78[79], a lamentation for the destruction of the temple of Jerusalem, which begins: "O God, the nations have come into your inheritance; / they have defiled your holy temple, they have laid / Jerusalem in ruins."

3. *their voices alternating, three, then four*: The psalm is being sung antiphonally: the three theological virtues and the four cardinal virtues sing alternate verses.

10–12. *Modicum et non*: During the mournful psalm, Beatrice is said to resemble Mary looking at her Son on the cross (5–6). When the psalm ends, however, Beatrice changes and speaks the words of Christ to his disciples concerning his own departure and return: "A little while and you shall not see me; and again, a little while and you shall see me because I go to the Father . . ." (John 16:16). Christ and his church, Beatrice reassures all, will someday return triumphant.

13–15. *Then, having placed the seven in front of her*: A new procession is formed by Beatrice's mere nod. The seven virtues, still holding torches as in the previous canto (XXXII, 98–99), precede Beatrice, who here and now represents Sapientia or Wisdom and is herself filling the spot occupied by the chariot in the original procession. Beatrice is followed by the Pilgrim, Statius ("the poet," who has been in silent attendance all along), and Matelda.

17. *ten steps*: It is Dante's custom to employ numbers symbolically, and many commentators have proposed symbolic meanings for the number ten here. None of the interpretations is particularly satisfying, however, and since it is not actually ten steps that Beatrice takes, but rather some unspecified number fewer than ten ("and she had not gone ten steps," 16–17), it is quite possible that Dante meant us simply to understand "ten steps" as several steps.

19–21. *"Make more haste"*: Beatrice is in complete control here, but her role is now more the gentle than the stern mother. The change in Beatrice's tone and glance from the severe to the serene reflects the change in the Pilgrim's state. Having confessed and been forgiven, he no longer deserves Beatrice's righteous anger.

31. *"It is my wish"*: Beatrice is preparing Dante to cross the second river, Eunoë. Just as all memory of his sins was washed away by the Pilgrim's drinking Lethe's waters in *Purg.* XXXI, 102, so the memory of his good deeds and their strength will be restored when he drinks the waters of the Eunoë. Until then, however, the Pilgrim must strive to put aside his fears and shame.

34–35. *the vessel which the serpent broke / was, and is not*: Here, with the beginning of Beatrice's explanation to Dante of the allegorical meaning of the pageant, we return to the apocalyptic atmosphere. Her words echo those of the angel in Revelations as he explains the mystery of the woman on the scarlet beast: "The beast that thou sawest was, and is not" (Apoc. 17:8).

35. *Let him who bears the blame*: A collective reference to Pope Clement and Philip the Fair.

36. *learn that God's vengeance has no fear of sops*: The Italian reads "che vendetta di Dio non teme suppe." The precise meaning of the word *suppe* is not clear. Early commentators mentioned customs, prevalent in Dante's time and before, according to which vengeance for a crime could be expiated if the criminal ate a ritual meal of atonement (a *sop* of bread and wine) over the grave of his victim. If the murderer could accomplish this feat, he would then be free of the vengeance of his victim's family. For a summary of the earlier commentators, see Chimenz (p. 611).

37–39. *The eagle that shed feathers*: The eagle is the Roman Empire. Dante considered Frederick II as the last true heir of the Caesars. Since his death in 1250 the empire has lived in expectation of a strong leader capable of restoring order and tranquility.

43. *five hundred, ten, and five*: Beatrice is prophesying the coming of such an heir to the Caesars: "God's emissary" (44) to Italy. Exactly whom Beatrice had in mind is a question that continues to puzzle readers of the poem. As he was in the *Veltro* prophecy spoken by Virgil at the beginning of the poem (see *Inf.* I, 101–105), Dante is being purposely vague here. Grandgent points out (p. 612) that the practice of equating numbers with the letters of a name is an ancient one, found, for example, in the Hebrew Kabbala, or in Lucian's *Alexander or the False Prophet*, or in Rev. 13:18. It was a practice very much in vogue in thirteenth- and fourteenth-century Europe and comes up elsewhere in Dante's writing (cf. *Vita nuova*, XXX). One guess at an identity for the emissary is based on transforming 515 into the Roman numerals DXV and reversing the last two letters, which gives DVX or dux (leader, a temporal monarch). This code word is then associated with the great emperor and leader Henry VII. The positive tone of Beatrice's presentation in 40–42, "I clearly see . . . its advent nothing can prevent," indicates, perhaps, that Dante was confident of the success of Henry VII's expedition to Italy in 1310. Henry died in 1313. For a summary of the many solutions proposed for this problem, see Mazzamuto's article in the *Enciclopedia dantesca*.

47. *Themis or the Sphinx*: Both Themis and the Sphinx are

associated in classical mythology with "dark words" and obscure riddles. Themis, the daughter of Gaea (Earth) and Uranus (Heaven) and second wife of Zeus, was a prophetic deity, purportedly Apollo's predecessor at Delphi. When consulted by Deucalion and Pyrrha concerning the repopulating of earth after the deluge, Themis told them to cast their mother's bones behind them. Her meaning was that they were to cast stones behind their backs (See Ovid, *Metam.* I, 379–94).

The Sphinx (a monster possessing the head of an innocent girl and the body of a fierce beast) was an oracle of Themis's, who sat on a rock outside the city of Thebes. To every Theban who passed by, she posed the same riddle: "What walks on four legs in the morning, on two at noon, and on three at night?" Those who failed to solve the riddle were slain. Oedipus, the ill-fated king of Thebes, solved the riddle: Man in his infancy crawls on all fours, in his maturity walks erect, and in old age is supported by a staff. Enraged at having the correct answer, the Sphinx threw herself down from the rock and was killed. Themis later avenged the death of her oracle by dispatching a monster to ravage the Thebans' fields and flocks (See Ovid, *Metam.* VII, 762–65).

49–51. *The Naiads . . . no destruction of the sheep or grain*: Dante erroneously attributes the solving of the riddle of the Sphinx to the Naiads, or water nymphs, having gotten his information from a faulty text of Ovid's *Metamorphoses* (VII, 757), in which the word "Naiades" was substituted for "Laiades" (= Oedipus, the son of Laius).

Beatrice is saying here that her prophecy (or riddle), unlike that of the Sphinx, will be solved with no destruction, with no ravaging of the Thebans' fields and flocks.

54. *that life which is merely a race to death*: St. Augustine (*De civ. Dei* XIII, 10) says the same thing: "ut omnino nihil sit aliud tempus vitae huius, quam cursus ad mortem."

56–57. *the tree you saw / despoiled, not once but twice*: The Pilgrim saw the tree in the Earthly Paradise despoiled first by Adam (as verses 61–63 indicate) and then by the vicissitudes of *Purg.* XXXII, 109–60, especially the episode when the giant (Philip the Fair) detaches the chariot from the tree. (When the chariot was attached to the tree, it had burst into bloom [XXXII, 50–60].)

62. *more than five thousand years in pain he yearned*: Dante (using a round number) adopts the chronology of Eusebius, which puts the birth of Christ at 5200 years and his death on the cross 5232 years after the Creation. The "pain" refers to the 930 years of Adam's life on earth after his exile from the Earthly Paradise; the fact that "he yearned" refers to the 4302 years Adam spent in Limbo waiting for Christ to descend and release him (*Inf.* IV, 52–55). According to these figures, the Crucifixion took place in the year 5232.

65–66. *the special reason for the tree's great height*: The height of the tree is the might of the empire, and the reason it "grows inverted toward the top" is to indicate God's wish for the inviolability of the empire (see *Purg.* XXII, 133–135, and XXXII, 40–42).

68. *waters of Elsa*: The Elsa is a river that flows into the Arno between Florence and Pisa; at certain locations (especially near Colle) it had the property of "petrifying" objects immersed and left in its waters.

69. *Pyramus*: For the story of Pyramus, Thisbe, and the mulberry tree, see the note to *Purg.* XXVII, 37–39. Beatrice is saying that because the Pilgrim's "vain thoughts" (67) have hardened his intellect (68), and because the pleasure he derived from them has left some stain of sin on his mind (it has darkened it as the blood of Pyramus once stained the white mulberry a dark red), he does not understand the significance of the tree: why God prohibited Adam from eating of the tree (70–72).

85–87. *She said: "Why do they?"*: Beatrice is explaining to the Pilgrim why her words are so difficult to grasp; that is, she is answering the question he asked in the preceding tercet (82–84). In this way he will see just how inferior to her "doctrine" (87)—and let us keep in mind that Beatrice is speaking here in her role of Sapientia or Wisdom—were his philosophical studies ("that school which you have followed," 86), based primarily on Aristotle and expounded by Dante in his *Convivio*.

90. *the highest spinning sphere*: This is the outermost of the nine revolving heavens, the *Primum Mobile*.

103–105. *And blazing brighter, moving slower now*: It is now noon in Purgatory, and at noontime the sun appears to be moving slower. The meridian, unlike the equator, which is a fixed line, shifts from one place to another, according to the longitude of the place in which the viewer is situated. Midday, according to St. Bonaventure, is the noblest hour of the day, the hour in which Christ ascended to Heaven. This is the last reference to time measured by the sun in the *Comedy*.

113. *the Tigris and Euphrates*: These two rivers of southwest Asia rise in Turkey, join in Iraq, and flow into the Persian Gulf. They are the last two of the four rivers mentioned in Genesis (2:14) as watering the Earthly Paradise. Dante's information that these two rivers spring from the same source may have come from Boethius (*Consol. philos.* V, i, 3–4).

115. *"O light, O glory of the human race"*: The Pilgrim addresses Beatrice in her allegorical role of Wisdom.

118. *"Ask Matelda to explain"*: At last the "lovely lady" who brought the Pilgrim across the river to Beatrice is named, and in a very casual way indeed—as if she were one of Beatrice's best friends (see Singleton, p. 823).

124. *Then Beatrice: "A more important thing"*: She is probably alluding to her reproach of the Pilgrim or, perhaps, to the meaning of the procession that has passed.

127. *the stream Eunoë*: See note to *Purg.* XXVIII, 130.

128. *as it is your wont*: This phrase makes clear Matelda's role at the top of the mountain of Purgatory: we must assume that the "lovely lady" performs this service for all souls who pass through the garden; in fact, she says to Statius in verse 135: "And you come too." Beatrice, on the other hand, will come just once to the top of the mount, as she did in this case, to judge her lover (as Christ will come once at the Final Judgment to judge all mankind). Beatrice's advent, then, is an allegory, a dumbshow for the sake of one man, Dante, the Pilgrim, while Matelda's appearance and action is a reality for every saved soul on its way to Paradise.

129. *revive his weakened powers*: By drinking of the waters of Eunoë, the memory of good deeds done in the past is restored (see *Purg.* XXVIII, 129–31). And it is Matelda (the active life) who performs this office.

134. *Statius*: This is the last reference to Statius in the poem. We must assume that once he has tasted of Eunoë he will, like every purged soul ready to leave Purgatory, rise directly to his predestined seat in the Empyrean.

136–41. *Reader, if I had space*: If it were not for the following tercet and concluding verse (142–45), the *Purgatory* would, indeed, come to a pedantic ending here, in Dante's final Address to the Reader, where the Poet implies a preestablished plan for the structure of his poem.

142–45. *From those holiest waters . . . now ready for the stars*: The Pilgrim describes his condition after drinking (or being submersed in) the waters of Eunoë and returning to Beatrice in terms of rebirth, new life, resurrection, purity, and freedom to rise—the major motifs of the opening canto of the *Purgatory*. Returning to Beatrice from Eunoë represents the fulfillment of Cato's instructions at the foot of the mountain (*Purg.* I, 94–105). As at the end of the *Inferno*, the Pilgrim finds himself at the foot of a mountain that is not unlike that mountain he found he could not climb in Canto I (or the opening) of the *Inferno*. Now, at the end of the *Purgatory*, it is as though for a brief moment the Pilgrim were again at the base of this island, where rushes grow in soft sand, again ready for ascent.

As do the other two canticles of the *Divine Comedy*, the *Purgatory* ends with the word *stelle* ("stars"), stressing the upward movement toward God, the goal and motivating force of the entire poem.

REFERENCES

*All classical Greek and Latin texts cited are those of
the Loeb Classical Library unless otherwise stated.*

Alighieri, Dante. *La Commedia secondo l'antica vulgata.* Edited by
Giorgio Petrocchi. Vol. I: Introduzione; Vol. III: *Purgatorio.* Milan,
1966, 1967.
———. *Le opere di Dante: Testo critico della Società Dantesca Italiana.* 2d
ed. Florence, 1960.
Andreas Capellanus. *De amore.* Edited by E. Trojel. Copenhagen,
1892.
———. *The Art of Courtly Love.* Translated by John Jay Parry. New
York, 1941.
Aquinas, Thomas. *Opera omnia.* Parma, 1852–73. Photolithographic
reimpression, with Introduction by Vernon J. Bourke, New York,
1948–50.
———. *On the Truth of the Catholic Faith, Summa contra Gentiles.* Gar-
den City, N.Y., 1955–57.
———. *Summa theologica.* Translated by Fathers of the English
Dominican Province. 3 vols. New York, 1947–48.
Anonimo fiorentino. *Commento alla Divina Commedia d'anonimo fioren-
tino del secolo XIV.* Edited by Pietro Fanfani. Vol. II. Bologna, 1868.
Aristotle. "Antiqua Translatio." In Thomas Aquinas, *Opera omnia.*
———. *Nicomachean Ethics.* In Thomas Aquinas, *Commentary on the
Nicomachean Ethics,* translated by C. I. Litzinger, O.P. 2 vols.
Chicago, 1964.
Auerbach, Eric. "Dante's Addresses to the Reader." *Romance Philology*
VII (1954): 268–78.
Augustine. *The City of God. Books VIII–XVI.* Translated by Gerald G.
Walsh, S.J., and Grace Monahan, O.S.U. *Books XVII–XXII.* Trans-
lated by Gerald G. Walsh, S.J., and Danield J. Honan. New York,
1952, 1954.
———. *St. Augustine's Confessions.* Translated by William Watts
(1631), preface by W. H. D. Rouse. Vol. I. LCL, 1912.
Austin, H. D. "Dante Notes." *MLN* XXXVII (1922): 36–39.

Averroës. *Commentarium magnum in Aristotelis De anima libros.* Edited by F. Stuart Crawford. Cambridge, Mass., 1953.

Baldassaro, Lawrence. "Structure and Movement in *Purgatorio* X." *Lingua e stile* X (1975): 261–74.

Barbi, Michele. "Ancora della tenzone di Dante con Forese." *Studi danteschi* XVI (1932): 69–103.

———. "Tenzone con Forese Donati." In *Rime della Vita nuova e della giovinezza,* edited by M. Barbi and F. Maggini, pp. 275–373. Florence, 1956.

Benvenuto da Imola. *Comentum super Dantis Aldigherij Comoediam.* Edited by Giacomo Filippo Lacaita. Vols. III, IV. Florence, 1887.

Bernard of Clairvaux. *Sermones de tempore.* In Migne, ed., *Patrologiae cursus,* CLXXXIII.

Biondalillo, Francesco. "La poesia di Guido Guinizelli." *Archivum Romanicum* 21 (1937): 327–35.

Boccaccio, Giovanni. *Il Decameron.* Edited by Charles S. Singleton. 2 vols. Bari, 1955.

Boethius. *The Theological Tractates; The Consolation of Philosophy.* Edited and translated by H. F. Stewart and E. K. Rand. Cambridge, Mass., 1962.

Boni, Marco. *Sordello: Le poesie. Nuova edizione critica con studio introduttivo, traduzioni, note, e glossario.* Biblioteca degli "studi mediolatini e volgari." Bologna, 1954.

Bowra, Cecil M. "Dante and Sordello." *Comparative Literature* 5 (1953): 1–15.

Britt, Matthew, ed. *The hymns of the Breviary and Missal.* New York, 1955.

Brown, Emerson, Jr. "Proserpina, Matelda, and the Pilgrim." *Dante Studies* LXXXIX (1971): 33–48.

Buti, Francesco da. *Commento di Francesco da Buti sopra la Divina Comedia di Dante Allighieri.* Edited by Crescentino Giannini. Vol. II. Pisa, 1860.

Carroll, John S. *Prisoners of Hope.* London, 1971.

Cassell, Anthony. "'Mostrando con le poppe il petto' (*Purg.* XXIII, 102)." Dante Studies XCVI (1978): 75–81.

Chimenz, Siro A. *La Divina Commedia di Dante Alighieri.* Turin, 1968.

Ciardi, John. *The Purgatorio.* New York, 1961.

Contini, Gianfranco, ed. *Poeti del Duecento.* 2 vols. Milan, 1960.

———. *Rime.* Turin, 1965.

Cook, Mabel P. "Indigo legno." *PMLA* XVIII (1903): 356–62.

Davidsohn, Robert. *Firenze ai tempi di Dante.* Translated from the German by Eugenio Duprè Theseider. Florence, 1929.

Egidi, Francesco. *Le rime di Guittone d'Arezzo.* Bari, 1940.

Enciclopedia dantesca. Edited by Umberto Bosco. 5 vols. Rome, 1970.

Fiero, Gloria K. "Dante's Ledge of Pride: Literary Pictorialism and the Visual Arts." *Journal of European Studies* V (1975): 1–17.

Fiore di filosofi e di molti savi attribuito a Brunetto Latini. Edited by Antonio Cappelli. Bologna, 1865.

Foster, K., and Boyde, P. *Dante's Lyric Poetry.* 2 vols. Oxford, 1967.

Freccero, John. "Casella's Song." *Dante Studies* XCI (1973): 73–80.

Grandgent, Charles H., ed. *La Divina Commedia.* Revised by Charles S. Singleton. Cambridge, Mass., 1972.

Gregory I. *Moralium libri, sive Expositio in librum b. Iob.* In Migne, ed., *Patrologiae cursus,* LXXV–LXXVI.

Heilbronn, Denise. "Dante's Valley of the Princes." *Dante Studies* XC (1972): 43–58.

———. "The Prophetic Role of Statius in Dante's *Purgatory.*" *Dante Studies* XCV (1977): 53–67.

Hill, Thomas D. "Dante's Palm: *Purgatorio* XXII: 130–135." *MLN* 82 (no. 1, 1967): 103–105.

Hollander, Robert. "*Purgatorio* II: Cato's Rebuke and Dante's *Scoglio.*" *Italica* LII (1975): 348–63.

Isidore of Seville. *Etymologiarum sive Originum libri XX.* Edited by W. M. Lindsay. Vol. II. Oxford, 1911.

Jernigan, Charles. "The Song of Nail and Uncle: Arnaut Daniel's Sestina *Lo ferm voler q'el cor m'intra.*" *Studies in Philology* 71 (1974): 127–51.

John the Deacon. *Sancti Gregorii Magni vita.* In Migne, ed., *Patrologiae cursus,* LXXV.

Kantorowicz, Ernst H. "Dante's 'Two Suns.'" *University of California Publications in Semitic Philology* XI (1951): 217–31.

Kaske, R. E. "'Sì si conserva il seme d'ogne guisto' (*Purg.* XXXII, 48)." *Dante Studies* LXXXIX (1971): 49–54.

Kleinhenz, Christopher. "Food for Thought: *Purgatorio* XXII, 146–147." *Dante Studies* XCV (1977): 69–79.

Kolsen, Adolf. *Sämtliche Lieder des Trobadors Giraut de Bornelh, mit Übersetzung Kommentar, und Glossar.* 2 vols. Halle, 1910, 1935.

Lana, Jacopo della. *Comedia di Dante degli Allagherii col commento di Jacopo della Lana bolognese.* Edited by Luciano Scarabelli. Vol. II. Bologna, 1866.

Landino, Cristoforo. *Dante con l'espositioni di Christoforo Landino et d'Alessandro Vellutello. Sopra la sua Comedia dell'Inferno, del Purgatorio, e del Paradiso.* Venice, 1596.

Levi, Ezio. *Piccarda e Gentucca: Studi e ricerche dantesche.* Bologna, 1921.

Lisini, A. *La Pia Dantesca.* Siena, 1939.

Maggini, F. Review of Francesco Filippini, *Il Marco Lombardo dantesco,* 1924. *Studi danteschi* X (1925): 146–47.

Malagoli, Luigi. *Motivi e forme dello stile del duecento,* pp. 201–31. Pisa, 1960.

Migne, J. P., ed. *Patrologiae cursus completus: Series Latina.* Paris, 1844–64 (with later printings).

Miller, Kenneth W. "A Critical Edition of the Poetry of Bonagiunta Orbicciani da Lucca." Ph.D. dissertation, Indiana University, 1973.

Momigliano, Attilio, ed. *La Divina Commedia di Dante Alighieri.* Vol. II: *Purgatorio.* Florence, 1956.

Montanari, Fausto. "La poesia di Guinizelli come esperimento di cultura." *Giornale storico della letteratura italiana* 104 (1934): 241–53.

Moore, Edward. *The Time References in the Divina Commedia.* London, 1887.

————. *Studies in Dante. First Series: Scripture and Classical Authors in Dante.* Oxford, 1896 (reprinted 1969). *Second Series: Miscellaneous Essays,* 1899 (reprinted 1968). *Third Series: Miscellaneous,* 1903 (reprinted 1968).

Musa, Mark. *The Poetry of Panuccio del Bagno,* pp. 219–35. Bloomington, Ind., 1965.

————. "Le ali di Dante (e il dolce stil novo): *Purg.* XXIV." *Convivium* 34 (1966): 361–67.

————. "Advent at the Gates." *Papers of the Midwest Modern Language Association* No. 1 (1969): 85–93.

————. *Dante's Inferno.* Bloomington, Ind., 1971.

————. *Vita nuova.* Bloomington, Ind., 1973.

————. *Advent at the Gates: Dante's Comedy.* Bloomington, Ind., 1974.

————. "The Sensual Pilgrim." *Dante Studies* (1982).

Muscetta, Carlo. "Al cor gentil . . ." *Leonardo* XII (1941): 145–52.

Nardi, Bruno. *Lectura Dantis: Il canto XV del Purgatorio.* Rome, 1953.

————. *Studi di filosofia medievale.* Rome, 1960.

Orosius. *Historiarum adversum paganos libri VII.* Edited by Karl Zangemeister. Leipzig, 1889.

————. *Seven Books of History against the Pagans: The Apology of Paulus Orosius.* Translated by Irving Woodworth Raymond. New York, 1936.

Orr, M. A. *Dante and the Early Astronomers.* Rev. ed. London, 1956.

L'Ottimo Commento della Divina Commedia. Edited by Alessandro Torri. Vol. II. Pisa, 1828.

Pietro di Dante. *Super Dantis ipsius genitoris Comoediam commentarium.* Edited by Vincenzio Nannucci. Florence, 1845.

Popolizio, Stephen. "A Critical Edition of the Poetry of Giacomo da Lentino." Ph.D. dissertation, Indiana University, 1975.

Poletto, Giacomo. *La Divina Commedia di Dante Alighieri.* Rome, 1905.

Porena, Manfredi. *La Divina Commedia di Dante Alighieri.* Vol. II: *Purgatorio.* Bologna, 1964.

Rajna, Pio. "'Ugo Ciappetta' nella *Divina Commedia ('Purgatorio,'* canto XX)." *Studi danteschi* XXXVII (1960): 5–20.

Riquer, Martin de. *Los Trovadores: Historia literaria y textos.* 3 vols. Barcelona, 1975.

Sanesi, Ireneo. "Sapìa." *Studi danteschi* VI (1923): 99–111.

Sapegno, Natalino, ed. *La Divina Commedia.* Milan, 1957.

Sayers, Dorothy, trans. *The Comedy of Dante Alighieri, Cantica II, Purgatory.* Harmondsworth, Middlesex, 1955.

Shoaf, R. A. "'Aura sacra fames' and the Age of Gold (*Purg. XXII,* 40–41 and 148–150)." *Dante Studies* XCVI (1978): 195–99.

Singleton, Charles S. *Dante Studies 2: Journey to Beatrice.* Cambridge, Mass., 1958.

———, trans. *The Divine Comedy.* Vol. II: *Purgatorio,* pt. 2: *Commentary.* Princeton, N.J., 1973.

Spitzer, Leo. *Romanische Literaturstudien,* pp. 574–95. Tübingen, 1959.

The Temple Classics. A Translation of the Latin Works of Dante Alighieri. London, 1940.

Toja, Gianluigi. *Arnaut Daniel: Canzoni. Edizione critica.* Florence, 1960.

Torraca, Francesco. *Nuovi studi danteschi nel VI centenario della morte di Dante.* Naples, 1921.

———. "La canzone *Al cor gentil ripara sempre amore."* *Atti dell R. Accademia di Archeologia, Letteratura e Belle Arti di Napoli.* Vol. 13 (1933–34): 43–66.

———, ed. *La Divina Commedia.* 12th ed. Vol. II: *Purgatorio.* Rome, 1952.

Toynbee, Paget. *Dante Studies and Researches.* London, 1902.

———. *A Dictionary of Proper Names and Notable Matters in the Works of Dante.* Revised by C. S. Singleton. Oxford, 1968.

Valerius Maximus. *Factorum et dictorum memorabilium libri novem.* Edited by Karl Halm. Leipzig, 1865.

Vasari, Giorgio. *Le opere di Giorgio Vasari: Le vite de' più eccellenti pittori scultori ed architettori scritte da Giorgio Vasari pittore arettino.* Edited by Gaetano Milanesi. Vol. I. Florence, 1906.

Villani, Giovanni. *Cronica di Giovanni Villani.* Edited by Gherardi Dragomanni. 4 vols. Florence, 1844–45.

Zaccagnini, Guido. "Personaggi danteschi." *Giornale dantesco* XXVI (1923): 8–14.